Economic Development
in Local Government

Economic Development in Local Government

A Handbook for Public Officials and Citizens

Edited by ROGER L. KEMP

McFarland & Company, Inc., Publishers
Jefferson, North Carolina, and London

British Library Cataloguing-in-Publication data are available

Library of Congress Cataloguing-in-Publication Data

Economic development in local government : a handbook for public
officials and citizens / edited by Roger L. Kemp.
   p. cm.
   Includes index.
   ISBN 0-7864-0095-1 (lib. bdg. : 50# alk paper) ∞
   1. Industrial promotion—United States. 2. Local government—
United States. 3. Community development—United States.
4. Economic development. I. Kemp, Roger L.
HC110.I53E25 1995
338.973'009173'2—dc20   95-800
                                          CIP

Manufactured in the United States of America

McFarland & Company, Inc., Publishers
 Box 611, Jefferson, North Carolina 28640

To my mother,
for many reasons

Acknowledgments

Grateful acknowledgment is made to the following organizations and publishers for granting permission to reprint the articles contained in this volume: Alabama League of Municipalities; American Economic Development Council; American Planning Association; American Society for Public Administration; The Atlantic Monthly Co.; Communication Channels, Inc.; Congressional Quarterly, Inc.; Government Finance Officers Association; International City/County Management Association; Lawyers Title Insurance Corporation; League of California Cities; League of Minnesota Cities; Missouri Municipal League; National Academy of Sciences; National Association of Housing & Redevelopment Officials; National Association of Towns and Townships; National Civic League; National Council for Urban Economic Development; National Economic Development & Law Center; National League of Cities; New Jersey State League of Municipalities; The Privatization Council; Real Estate Research Corporation; Texas Municipal League; U.S. Chamber of Commerce; Urban Land Institute; Western Governmental Research Association; World Future Society.

Contents

ix

VI : THE FUTURE

Preface

The role of public officials in local governments has traditionally been to let private enterprises compete in the marketplace with few restrictions and little interference. The primary example of this has been the one-company town, where economic activity and employment is based on the success of a single company. As early as the post–World War II years public officials, even in these cities, recognized the importance of diversifying their local economy. This was especially true as America's industrial base changed after the war. Although economic diversification was the goal, few formal municipal structures, processes, or incentives existed to achieve this end.

The use of economic development incentives received national media focus and public attention with the passage of the Urban Development Action Grant (UDAG) legislation, approved by Congress and implemented under the Carter Administration in 1977. Since this time, economic development practices have evolved from a loose assortment of a limited number of inducements to the use of many diverse, yet highly focused, incentives. They deal with all facets of a development. Nowadays they frequently include, but are not limited to, land subsidies, low interest financing, flexible zoning laws, infrastructure improvements, the use of public land for private purposes, and the facilitated processing of development applications through local planning and building department bureaucracies.

It has historically been the role of higher levels of government—at the state and federal levels—to regulate business in order to protect free trade, guard against monopolies, and ensure proper professional and trade standards through licensing in order to safeguard the public against unscrupulous practices. Also, from time to time, state and federal tax laws are amended to provide investment tax credits that serve to stimulate economic growth at the local level.

Cities have typically extracted taxes from, and charged user fees to, private sector development applicants. Local taxes include those rates levied for real and personal property, business licenses, utilities, and for the sale of goods and services. User fees include charges for services rendered such as planning, building, and engineering permits, as well as on-site inspection services to ensure compliance with state and municipal codes in these areas. It should be

1

noted that taxes are levied for revenue-generation purposes only, while user fees are assessed for the actual cost of services rendered during the course of construction, including issuance of the final certificate of occupancy. While taxes are raised only occasionally, user fees are typically adjusted on a more frequent basis to reflect the actual cost of doing business.

Because of this, the relationship between cities and the business community over the years has usually been somewhat adversarial. When public officials at the local level propose new or increased taxes or fees, they are almost always vigorously opposed by pro-business elements in the community such as chambers of commerce, merchants groups, and professional and trade associations. Also, applications for new developments, as well as the expansion of existing companies, were frequently met with opposition from local boards and commissions. In recent years, however, because of the difficult economic times, fewer grants from higher levels of government, the public's aversion to increased taxation, and the so-called "property taxpayers' revolt," locally elected officials have come to realize the economic benefits of having commercial and industrial projects within their political boundaries.

The direct and indirect economic benefits of private development to a community may be substantial—especially for larger projects. The increased amount of taxes and user fees generated, as well as the number of jobs created during these times of high unemployment and even higher underemployment, have served to strengthen the political philosophy of using economic development incentives as a tool to generate additional revenues and balance local budgets without having to resort to either increased taxation or undesirable service reductions. These development inducements vary greatly from city to city, and frequently involve the formation of positive partnerships with the private sector. This evolving pro-business political philosophy has led to a host of new incentives designed to attract private development, primarily commercial and industrial, to communities throughout the nation.

The use of economic rewards as a development tool has evolved primarily over the past few decades and are typically applied in a piecemeal and incremental fashion by public officials from community to community, depending upon those unique inducements that have evolved in individual cities. While state and federal laws may limit the type of incentives that can be provided, the need exists to codify the existing information concerning generally acceptable local economic development incentives that public officials have made available to stimulate private sector investment in their respective communities. They may change as state and federal laws are amended, usually based on the economic conditions of the time.

This book has been developed over the past several years with the goal of bringing together existing information relative to the economic development structures, practices, and incentives that are commonly used in cities throughout America. For ease of reference, this volume has been divided into six sections as follows—Introduction, The Structure, The Process, The Incentives, The Application, and The Future. The longest section sets forth actual case studies dealing with the application of successful economic development incentives that are being used by public officials in many communities to attract private sector investment.

The municipalities examined in this volume represent a broad mix of cities that includes a representative sampling relative to size, location, population, geography, economic condition, and type of governance. The various economic development incentives used in these communities can be applied by public officials with equal success in other local governmental settings, regardless of their unique characteristics. This volume represents a first-time effort to codify the various types of economic development structures, processes, and incentives, as well as how they are actually applied by public officials to stimulate their government's local economy.

The final section, The Future, offers insight into how this newly evolving field of economic development is shaping the future of America's cities. This new economic climate has served to facilitate a positive relationship between the public and private sectors at the community level. More importantly, public officials in local governments increasingly recognize the importance of the jobs and revenues generated by new businesses, and the impact that new development has on the local economy. Not only does economic development expand and improve upon the existing local economic base, it also facilitates its diversification and the ability of a city to withstand the impact of future economic uncertainties.

Over the past few decades the relationship between municipal public officials and private sector representatives—corporate executives, chambers of commerce, merchant groups, and professional and trade associations—has shown a drastic change from an adversarial position to one of favoring the formation of positive and mutually advantageous economic partnerships. This new era of cooperation between the public and private sectors at the municipal level has spawned a new positive relationship that is surely in the best interest of both sectors, as well as taxpayers in general, and future generations of Americans.

The goal of this volume is to illustrate this trend and to make existing information available to public officials, both elected and appointed, as well as business persons, merchants, and citizens in general, relative to the value of forming reasonable and prudent economic development partnerships between the public and private sectors for the benefit of the entire community.

ROGER L. KEMP
Meriden, Connecticut
January 1995

I : Introduction

Chapter 1

Raising Revenues Without Increasing Taxes

ROGER L. KEMP

Government Cycles

Government organizations, like their business counterparts, have different life cycles. The phases that an organization goes through during its life generally fall into four categories—growth, stability, retrenchment, and revitalization. Different political and management strategies are needed to set the course and guide an organization properly through these different phases. Strategy is concerned with defining purpose and developing goals and plans to chart an organization's future direction and growth.

The history of local governments in America can be divided into these same phases. These cycles, and their financial and operational variations, have had an impact on local governments just as they have private sector organizations. During this century, these phases have been chronicled in four distinct periods. During the growth phase of local government, services were generally expanded, and new programs were added in response to citizen demands. During the stabilization phase, the level of services was fairly constant, and citizens made few requests for more services. Minor adjustments to services were made, but limited revenues checked the overall growth of government.

The retrenchment phase forced public officials to consider such issues as which services to reduce, which to maintain, and where to expand needed services at the expense of less desirable programs. These changes were brought about by citizen mandates sources, and a political philosophy of fiscal conservatism. Against this background, a new cycle of self-renewal, or revitalization, is taking place in local governments across America. This new strategy is based upon the premise of raising revenues without increasing taxes, and relies on the philosophy of offering economic development incentives to the private sector.

Public officials in local governments throughout the nation are now focusing their attention and efforts on strategies and incentives to stimulate economic development. Through economic development, local governments have been able to get a "new lease on life" financially by expanding revenues from existing sources, such as sales taxes, property taxes, business licenses, utility taxes, and related revenues, without creating new taxes or increasing existing taxes.

Virtually dozens of incentives are now being offered by public officials to achieve financial stability without increasing taxes. Many of these incentives are new and innovative. All have been created and fostered by a political philosophy emphasizing fiscal responsibility for their government's financial destiny. The emphasis on economic development also places a decreasing reliance on grants from higher levels of government. Some of these emerging economic development incentives are highlighted below.

Economic Development Incentives

Political philosophy. The underlying political philosophy of elected officials frequently recognizes the need to stimulate economic development. A political philosophy of self-reliancy, recognizing the need to expand a city's tax base and create jobs, sets the political background against which all economic development activities occur.

Political climate. The climate created by a local government's political philosophy may serve to entice development. Elected officials favoring economic development, or specific types of projects, may make their intentions known through a number of different methods. News travels fast about the availability of economic incentives to the private sector.

Positive staff relations. The ability of a government's staff to work with the development community can create a healthy business atmosphere. The time spent by the staff explaining the rules, trying to work with property owners, and negotiating within predetermined guidelines fosters a positive relationship with the private sector.

One-stop permit process. Many local governments have implemented a one-stop permit process to facilitate the processing of development applications. Rather than make applicants go to several locations to obtain permits, they are issued at one central location. This saves the private sector both time and money when seeking approval of development plans.

Business assistance programs. Because of the increasing number of economic incentives offered by local governments, this type of program makes information about all incentives available at a single location. Existing staff members are educated as to all programs and resources. This information is made available to both existing and new businesses.

Enterprise zones. A new phrase which merely refers to an area targeted by local government officials for development. They are typically blighted areas, ones where jobs are needed or increased revenues are desired to finance public services. Economic incentives may be offered in specific areas, subject to approval of the elected officials.

Development standards. Local government officials have the power to alter many development standards, such as parking, lot coverage, setbacks, and landscaping, to name a few. Requirements may be waived, or lowered, depending upon the type of development and the agreement negotiated. These changes usually require the approval of elected officials.

Business retention programs. These programs are designed to monitor the economic climate of important businesses and industries in a community. Staff members make contact with failing enterprises, offering financial and technical assistance as appropriate. This helps maintain a healthy business climate where jobs and revenues are important.

Small business development. Sometimes referred to as "incubator" programs, both the public and private sectors are creating developments that offer amenities to attract and foster the growth of small businesses. These amenities include low-cost rental rates, small office spaces, and shared secretarial services.

Low-cost financing. Various forms of low-interest financing are available to the private sector. These programs typically save the developer a few percentage points below market lending rates. The project is usually the security for the loan, and the payments are normally made by the property owner.

Zone changes. Local elected officials may approve an upgrade to the zoning applicable to a site, thereby permitting a higher land use. Frequently, single-family residential zoning may be upgraded to multiple-residential, industrial, or commercial, depending upon the location of the site and the type of development desired by the community.

Mixed land uses. Zoning within particular areas is usually standardized to protect property values and to separate different land uses. A trend is developing to permit commercial uses in residential developments, and vice versa, in order to generate additional revenues and jobs. Mixed land uses have been more popular in central city areas.

Density bonuses. Many local governments are offering increased dwelling unit densities in selected areas. The number of residential units permitted can be increased, thereby enhancing the value of the development. Greater building densities can make a community more attractive to the development community.

Tax rebates. Local governments may provide tax rebates as a development incentive. Rebates typically involve property taxes, sales taxes, business taxes, utility taxes, and so forth. The amount returned, and the duration of the rebate, are subject to negotiation and usually based on the economic benefits generated by the project.

Redevelopment project areas. Redevelopment projects are formed in blighted areas targeted for economic revitalization. The property tax base is frozen upon formation. As development occurs the increased property taxes, called tax increments, are spent in the project area to attract more businesses.

Tax increment financing. In redevelopment project areas, the additional property taxes (i.e., tax increments) received after the base year can be spent in several ways. They can be used, with appropriate approvals, to finance on-site and off-site improvements, provide land subsidies, and for the acquisition of property for private development.

Off-site improvements. Local revenues, including tax increment funds, are most frequently used to finance off-site improvements such as curbs, gutters, sidewalks, storm drains, sewers, streets, street lights, and similar types of projects. An agency's financial participation, which is subject to negotiation, tends to increase based on the desirability of the project.

On-site improvements. Although not as frequent, tax increment revenues can be used to finance on-site improvements on projects in redevelopment areas. Surface parking lots and multistory parking structures are the most common types of improvements. An agency's financial participation, ownership rights, and maintenance responsibilities are subject to negotiation.

Land subsidies. In redevelopment areas, tax increment funds may be used to purchase land for private development. This cannot be done outside of legally designated redevelopment areas. The extent of an agency's subsidy, which may be as high as 100 percent, is subject to prior agreement. Desirable industries, generating jobs and revenues, frequently request such subsidies.

Economic development corporations. Local governments, frequently together with business groups, have formed this type of nonprofit organization. Their purpose is to offer low-interest financing and economic development assistance to the private sector. Several smaller agencies, which may have limited funds and staff expertise, commonly bank together to form such corporations.

Knowledge of available resources. Other public and private agencies may offer forms of economic development assistance. A knowledge of these resources, which may be available from higher levels of government, chambers of commerce, colleges and universities, and economic development corporations, may be used to foster the expansion of existing businesses as well as to help attract new development.

The Future

Some local governments are in the growth phase of their life cycle, primarily in suburban areas where an expanding tax base can support new services. Others have reached a state of stability, where there is a match between available financial resources and citizen expectations concerning service levels. Many, however, are coping with fewer tax dollars and greater demands for services.

For these local governments, a strategy of self-renewal and revitalization is necessary for economic survival. Since it is difficult, if not impossible, to raise taxes, economic development provides the most politically acceptable vehicle to improve a local government's financial health.

Many new and innovative techniques are emerging to stimulate economic development. All require some form of partnership with the private sector. The number and types of incentives are still evolving and are limited only by the imagination and creativity of public officials. The only limitations that exist are the parameters established by existing state and federal laws. Since local governments have their own unique political cultures and the decisions of public officials are subject to scrutiny by the electorate, the economic development strategy and incentives selected must be tailored to fit the needs of the community. Public officials in areas with a great need for additional jobs and revenues must consider aggressive economic development strategies.

The bottom line is that public officials, both elected and appointed, must assume responsibility for their government's long-term financial health. The political philosophy adopted will provide the background against which all economic development activities occur. The resulting political climate will determine both the type and number of incentives provided to the private sector. Economic development incentives that stress creativity and innovation, such as those described above, will continue to be developed in the future. It is only through practices such as these that services can be maintained and the public's confidence in their government can be restored. Public officials in local government throughout the nation have and will continue to meet this challenge.

Chapter 2

Local Roles and Responsibilities

RICHARD STARR

The future substance and, in many cases, continued existence of community and economic development programs will be decided in the very near future. While many officials believe the issues will be decided in Washington (or at the statehouse), in fact, the fate of these programs will be determined at the municipal level. It is not clear whether recent successes in economic and neighborhood development efforts will be enough to save these programs. This is unfortunate, since the need and capacity to perform have never been greater. There is, however, a method of performing a long overdue assessment of current programs with the goal of assuring the continuation of those programs that make sense.

Program Evolution

Community and economic development programs have evolved out of the "New Frontier" and "Great Society" eras of the 1960s. This evolution and its implications are often unappreciated by many current practitioners. The predecessor programs (that is, urban renewal, poverty, and model cities programs), contributed a variety of features to the current block grant approach that quite possibly have hampered program effectiveness or at least the ability to respond to changing conditions. While compliance with federally mandated requirements (housing priorities, citizen involvement, neighborhood designation) was laudable in intent, and made sense when the federal government was local government's financial partner, municipalities should reexamine these procedures now that their partner is withdrawing from the relationship.

There are a few carry-over features of the present federally sponsored programs that should be examined in light of the current administration's thrust toward expanded flexibility and diminished resources.

Reprinted with permission from *Journal of Housing,* Vol. 39, No. 4, July/August, 1982. Published by the National Association of Housing and Redevelopment Officials, Washington, D.C.

1. *Neighborhood designation.* From the early urban renewal days, there has been a need to designate the area to be aided. This approach, which appears to be continued under the urban enterprise zone concept, may tend to focus scarce resources in areas with the greatest need, but with the least potential for attracting private investment or solving problems.
2. *Program goals.* From the "workable program" through today's block grant submissions, federal programs have encouraged federally conceived and often unrealistic goal statements. This concept has misdirected many local programs and made it extremely difficult to conduct program evaluations. For example, federally encouraged housing goals that ignore population decline, market conditions and, most importantly, diminished federal support programs result in a "no win" situation for local officials.
3. *Citizen participation.* Another carry-over from the 1960s is the concept of citizen participation in program policy and design. Even in situations where the citizen representatives are actually elected, it seems highly unlikely that they will have the expertise and objectivity to deal with diminishing program resources.

There are numerous other examples of how urban programs are ill-prepared to deal with the issues of the 1980s. The capacity to leverage diminishing resources, build off strengths, and maximize federal funds has yet to be developed in many local programs. On the other hand, and a more positive note, the expertise and sophistication of local urban policymakers has been increasing. There is a growing appreciation of how best to use resources and how to conduct public-private urban projects. There is an expanded realization that downtown revitalization, industrial retention or attraction, and neighborhood revitalization will take imaginative programs involving local government assistance and private expertise.

Thus, community and economic development programs enter the 1980s burdened by some obsolete policies and diminishing resources, but with an increasing understanding and appreciation of how to achieve results. Given the obvious urban problems and needs, it is imperative that effective community development programs survive the impending federal retreat.

Perhaps the first step for local government is an objective evaluation of its current urban programs. Program goals, designated neighborhoods and active projects should be reexamined in light of federal policy changes and current local economic conditions. Are local housing goals valid in light of federal financial cutbacks? Can local governments attract private resources to the areas selected? Does job retention or creation deserve a higher priority? Can local officials better leverage block grant funds?

It is possible, but unlikely, that reassessing community and economic programs will result in the continuation of current programs. What is more apt to happen in most cities is that the evaluation will result in programs that are more effective and more suited to current conditions, resources and opportunities.

Perhaps the most important finding of any program evaluation would be that there are a large number of critical urban issues that are not going to be addressed if current community development programs die. The need for cities to have a professional staff dealing with economic, housing, and neighborhood issues has never been more apparent. The new skills and public/private successes need to be increased if cities are to prosper. A municipal agency is needed to maintain the urban data base, identify development opportunities in older neighborhoods, orchestrate public-private development, and provide seed money for urban and job retention projects.

There is a necessary community and economic development function to be conducted in most American cities and it will not occur if current programs go the way of urban renewal, the poverty program and model cities. However, the local agency role must be more than just distributing federal dollars, or the agency will die if that money disappears. The new flexibility that accompanies the rapidly diminishing resources provides local administrators with one last chance to assure the survival of their programs. The key issues include reassessing current programs, developing new concepts and financial resources, and gaining support through demonstrated successes.

Program Evaluation

Perhaps the most important step for community and economic development officials to take is an immediate, objective evaluation of their current situations and programs. This evaluation should answer the following questions: What are the critical urban and economic issues that presently affect the municipality? What can be done to alleviate or minimize problems with current and anticipated resources? Which opportunities or constraints deserve the focus of limited resources in the immediate future? How can public resources best be leveraged with the private sector?

As a general procedure, the reevaluation should incorporate two factions of the community: the citizen organization that designed the current programs and goals, and representatives of broader municipal leadership. The leadership group should include elected officials, downtown and chamber of commerce members, lenders, major employers and representatives of community-wide organizations. In most cities, these two groups will represent a new coalition and could be named as a mayor's task force to examine and make recommendations on the local community development process. With as much objectivity and as little fault-finding as possible, this task force should perform a two-stage evaluation.

Stage 1 should include an objective evaluation of current program goals, activities and results. This process must include an honest attempt to recognize the economic, political, and legislative factors that have impacted the evolution of all community and economic development programs. Because so many conditions have changed in recent years, the focus of any evaluation should be on that which is actually being accomplished as opposed to why a particular course of action was originally selected.

Stage 2 requires an objective assessment of the municipality's current economic situation, with an emphasis on the opportunity areas that may exist. The experience of the Urban Development Action Grant program demonstrates that it is far easier to leverage public dollars and attract private investment to projects with market potential than to those designed to overcome economic and social problems. The primary opportunity that exists in most every municipality is the potential to maximize existing community development resources. Federal funds are being reduced, but so is the amount of regulation and red tape. In today's money market, block grant funds, loaned to private developers at reduced or no interest rates, can be a tremendous catalyst to private investment. Vacant or under-utilized urban land offers local officials another valuable resource and an opportunity to work with developers on innovative projects. Sale/lease-back arrangements involving municipal property offer still another opportunity to leverage public tax benefits.

The result of the two-stage evaluation should be a more realistic program to deal with traditional community and economic development issues and quite possibly some new approaches more suited for the current national urban policy. Revised approaches could include focusing housing programs on neighborhoods where limited public funds can be maximized or attract the greatest amount of private investment. Neighborhood improvement projects should give priority to areas that will agree to underwrite a portion of the cost or accept a lien that eventually will repay to the city some of the appreciation generated by the public investment.

Some of the current public works aspects of community and economic development programs might be more intelligently financed as part of a municipal bond effort. This approach would free block grant funds for a municipal action grant program (that is, low-interest loans to help local businesses expand), with a pay-back being used to offset all or part of the bond program. In any event, there are undoubtedly many ways that some existing programs could be improved if they are objectively evaluated by someone other than those directly benefiting from the current process.

While almost all community and economic development efforts would benefit from objective evaluation and adjustment to current conditions, this will not assure the long-term survival of the programs. To continue the programs, city staffs will need to expand their roles, find new resources to replace lost federal dollars, and begin to implement innovative financing mechanisms. The expanded role is necessary so that locally sponsored programs become a permanent part of local goverment activities and so that municipal programs are not entirely dependent on federal funding. Community and economic development must be viewed by elected officials and local citizens as a necessary service.

The most immediate "new" funding source should be a more effective use of remaining community development block grant funds. In most cities, the objective evaluation of existing programs will result in identifying some block grant funds that now are not being effectively employed. An obvious example would include maintaining current levels of effort while using fewer community development dollars and making up the difference through increased leveraging and private participation. This would be accomplished by identifying new sources of funds by tapping corporate, lender, or property owner resources.

Although every city will have to devise its own approach, expanded flexibility in community development funding will facilitate leveraging, particularly opportunities to revolve funds. Consideration should be given to a local action grant program where community development funds are a catalyst for local projects.

Given today's money market, most community development programs should have little difficulty in identifying development projects that would result in employment and tax base expansion. The guaranteed repayment of these community development loans could be used to offset future grant reductions or to repay bonds that have financed other projects.

Additional tax revenues—"new" money—could be generated by using some of the community/economic development resources and tools to attract private development to vacant land. All cities have this very important resource that can be tapped. Real Estate Research Corporation completed a national study for the Department of Housing and Urban Development entitled "Urban Infill." The project evaluated the development potential of vacant land that, for a wide variety of reasons, exists in every urban area. This land is usually fully serviced, surrounded by development but, for some legal, financial, physical, or marketing reason, is undeveloped.

While the RERC research assignment focused on a wide range of local actions that could be employed to attract infill development, two aspects of the project should be of interest to local development officials. The first is that much of the vacant or under-utilized property in many cities is owned by public or semi-public entities. Land assets can be found on the books of tax, highway, park, school, public housing, urban renewal and various other city departments. Changing demographics have left most urban school districts with considerable excess property and, if private institutions are included, the potential resource is even more impressive. When cities inherited a renewal authority or transit company, an often overlooked asset was the real estate that came with the function.

A second, more important aspect is that the public entity involved usually does not have the necessary skills (or possibly the interest) in utilizing its excess property assets. A legitimate objective of the community or economic development department should be to encourage the maximum development of vacant or underutilized urban property. These land assets offer an opportunity for new development and the creation of jobs and tax resources. In addition, this concept offers community development officials an opportunity to work with sister agencies, use their skills and resources, and to share with them in the rewards. An aggressive community development agency should be able to (1) work with public officials (mayor and council) to identify excess public and semi-public vacant or under-utilized land resources; (2) obtain excess public real estate through donation, option, or purchase at fair market value if necessary; (3) improve the value of the acquired real estate through assemblage, capital improvements, zoning, or financial development assistance; and (4) achieve the desired development of the property through the sale, lease or joint venture approach that replenishes any community development funds expended in the process and, in most cases, results in a net profit for the agency.

Perhaps the most important criterion for survival in a less federally dominated environment will be that of successful projects. While many previous project activities have had federal agency and local political appeal, they have existed only as long as the federal funds continued to flow. If local programs can accomplish hard community and economic development objectives, cities can get local private long-term support.

There is, and will continue to be, a legitimate community and economic development function for local government. Each city will have to decide how it will carry out this activity and which department will perform these functions. City assets such as staff, land, dollars, taxes, improvements, and controls should be viewed as potential public investments. The local development entities that get a return on their investments, adapt to new conditions, and produce will survive and, indeed, may even prosper in the 1980s.

Chapter 3

The Need for
Community Self-Evaluation

AL GOBAR

The key to a successful economic development program is to generate early winners, while keeping an eye on clear, quantifiable long-term goals. But, many economic development efforts have reflected effort more than achievement and style more than substance. Such programs suffer from a lack of clearly defined goals, strategies to achieve these goals, and implementation processes which build on existing resources to achieve the most effective outcome.

Crucial to an action plan for community development is the simple Biblical admonition, "Know thyself." Here's a story to illustrate how important this is: A highly placed policymaker in one California county with an enviable record of economic growth was concerned about the county's job base being composed primarily of "hamburger flippers," when, in fact, the county has more manufacturing jobs per thousand jobs than any other area in Southern California. An economic development strategy based on the erroneous assumption that the area's population was composed of fast food service personnel would have been fruitless.

Therefore, a precondition to an efficient and successful economic development effort is an audit and evaluation of current conditions and the establishment of very specific goals.

The initial self-study process should define a specific reason for an economic development effort that is carefully and objectively articulated. In an oversimplified form, the problem can be reduced to the following simple queries:

1. Why do we want economic growth?
2. What resources do we have that other communities do not have that would be especially appealing to specific engines of economic growth?
3. Would these elements of potential economic growth contribute to the basic reasons we want to expand the local economy in the first place?

Reprinted with permission from *Western City*, Vol. LXIX, No. 8, August, 1993. Published by the League of California Cities, Sacramento, California.

4. Who are these elements, how do we reach them, and what is our most appealing message?

Economic development goals should be quantified in specific terms such as a target increase in property tax base per capita population, a defined increase in sales tax revenue, increases in local employment opportunities, and removal or mitigation of community limitations.

The first step in this process is a community appraisal of a wide range of objective measures of the community's advantages and limitations. For instance, many communities have consumer support bases well in excess of the level of retail sales activity within their boundaries. That means residents are shopping elsewhere, and their communities are losing retail sales tax revenues, *ad valorem* property tax revenues, and business license revenues to surrounding communities. More successful exploitation of existing and future consumer support increases city revenues from local taxes and provides a source of local jobs.

The City of Apple Valley's retail sector, for example, captures only about 40 percent of the retail expenditure potential of the community, but the scale of the town's population would permit a maximum effective capture rate of approximately 80 percent. Achieving this level of efficiency in the retail sector would double sales tax collections, create more local jobs, and enhance *ad valorem* taxes and business license revenues.

Similarly Tustin and Fountain Valley identified underexploited retail opportunities not only in their own cities' populations but the surrounding population, resulting in a substantial increase in sales tax revenues from the development of such new retail facilities as the Tustin Marketplace, the Price Club, etc.

Another important element is understanding where local employed residents actually work. Antelope Valley's economy, for example, is largely supported by commuters to jobs located in the more urban portions of Los Angeles County. The city loses the *ad valorem* tax base associated with work places and long commutes impose a burden on local residents.

Availability of land is also an important factor. Evanston, Illinois, for example, is bounded by other cities and Lake Michigan. So there is no land available for expansion. As a result, the city's economic development strategy involved reuse of previously developed land to achieve the city's specific economic goals of enhanced property tax base, expansion of local government opportunities based on the skills of local residents, and higher convenience for the people of Evanston.

Public service facilities and infrastructure capacity also represent a community advantage in some instances but a limitation in others. Adelanto has capitalized on abundant land by installing infrastructure to accommodate industrial development, giving the city a significant competitive advantage over communities without adequate and similarly priced inventories of immediately developable industrial land. Irwindale is another example of a community in which economic development has been facilitated by the installation of infrastructure.

Communities that provide an attractive residential environment attract high-energy decision-makers who like to live close to their jobs, which generates more local business, increases tax revenues and raises the level of local job opportunities.

Specific elements to be considered in this category include general neighborhood characteristics including household income profiles, educational levels of local residents, and other factors. Executives work hard and play hard, so recreational opportunities are important to such movers and shakers. They also are concerned about the availability of superior schools and a broad-based cultural program, including churches, Lions, Kiwanis, etc.

Such executive amenities have been important to Orange County as a whole, which has a higher ratio of manufacturing employment per 1,000 jobs than any other part of Southern California as well as a higher ratio of employment to population than any other part of California—despite the area's high housing prices and traffic congestion. Its success in attracting manufacturing jobs can be traced to one factor: Corporate executives like to live there. They don't like to commute, and manufacturing jobs grew in this area because decision-makers were attracted to the community as a place to live. This resource is not typically identified in the establishment of a data base for long-range economic development plans.

The Temecula-Murrietta area experienced a mini-boom in industrial development in large measure because of the area's ability to market itself to upper-income, enterpreneurial households as a place to live and eventually to establish businesses. Irvine is another example, as is Newport Beach.

A user-friendly, cooperative local political climate—while difficult to quantify—is another advantage associated with economic growth. A commercial developer we know, whose entitlement process in one California city has now endured for more than four years, has stated that he would "never, ever attempt to develop another project in that city." Executive "flight" is especially problematic when a nearby city is not only passive with regard to new and desirable development, but also active in providing subsidies through sales tax rebates or other techniques which have become increasingly common.

Effective economic development also takes advantage of the city's natural resources. Big Bear Lake—home to two major ski resorts and one of the few major recreation lakes in Southern California—enjoys a substantial advantage in generating economic growth. Modesto experienced a boom in the mid–1980s by promoting its central location to attract distribution and warehouse facilities to serve much of urban California. Ontario has capitalized on the confluence of four major freeways and the existence of a major airport by spurring massive development of distribution facilities.

Barstow, Lake Elsinore, and the unincorporated Imperial Valley community of Cabazon have capitalized on their locations adjacent to major freeways but removed from urban areas to support the development of factory outlet centers. The Oxnard–Port Hueneme area has benefited from its proximity to port facilities by encouraging distribution activities.

Many of the limitations to economic development are simply the flip-side of the advantages described above. Limited infrastructure or lack of available land implies a redevelopment strategy as distinct from an economic development strategy. Inadequate availability of low-cost housing either within the community or nearby has an indirect, adverse effect on the availability of a suitable labor force. Remote locations with no nearby, easily accessible market imply a strategy aimed at generating businesses which produce products and services with a high value-to-weight ratio to overcome this limitation. Lack of executive housing has also been a contributing factor to the slow economic development of some areas which otherwise have substantial advantages and resources.

Many of the elements described here can be defined objectively and with sufficient accuracy to facilitate decision making on the basis of relatively inexpensive research methodologies. Some of these are as follows:

• Standard retail site analysis techniques are useful in defining underpopulated consumer markets which represent an immediate potential for economic development. The process models retail sales expected within the community in light of its structure, population base, surrounding area population base, etc., in relationship to sales tax patterns and the existing inventory of retail facilities. Retail development in Fountain Valley, for example, was inhibited by the city's proximity to two regional shopping centers and a major auto plaza. Almost by default, the most effective retail development except for some minor fine-tuning was the attraction of a major "big box" retailer. Through a focused effort. Fountain Valley was able to attract a Price Club which, in turn, stimulated an influx of other hyper-efficient retailers. National City had the potential to support regional shopping center facilities. Community support surrounding Murrietta was more than adequate to justify consideration of a conventional regional shopping center there. The High Desert region of San Bernardino County has an inadequate number of new car dealerships in relationship to its market, so targeting such high ticket retailers could be a productive strategy there.

• The 1990 Census data provides a rich source of information from which to define the study area's affluence, its labor force characteristics, commute patterns, employment by industry, and a variety of other elements related to skills, education, and age. This information provides the data base that is a prerequisite to effective economic development. The socio-demographic analysis potential inherent in the data is also useful in evaluating the compatibility of the community with high-income, executive-type residents.

• Analysis of published data regarding land sales, prices, etc., is a reasonable method for identifying the limitations and advantages of a community's land and infrastructure resources.

Evaluation

An audit of local community resources and limitations can be compared with other communities or with averages for the larger area in which it is located. These comparisons define the special advantages and limitations of the local community against potentially competitive local economies. A simple financial analysis of city revenues and costs in the context of a peer group of cities is another useful indicator in defining limitations, resources, and the political climate. Cities with a high per capita cost of development services in relationship to historical development levels typically are communities in which development is difficult. A simple history of building permit activity at the city level as compared with peer group cities in similar locations is also often a useful diagnostic tool.

The results of the audit process can be integrated with input from local community leaders to define and prioritize specific goals of an economic development effort. Examples of goals that can be defined by this process are:

Expanding the community's retail section. This captures sales tax dollars escaping the community by attracting specific types of retailers for which there is a viable market opportunity. The experiences of Tustin, Fountain Valley, National City, and Evanston illustrate this example.

Attracting industrial employers. This achieves a better job-to-population balance and minimizes long commutes for local residents. Adelanto has made substantial progress through a program of infrastructure development specifically oriented to industrial users, a process preceded by the establishment of a strong and financially efficient redevelopment agency. Identification of local residents working in the finance sector in Antelope Valley contributed to the attraction of a major national financial printing organization.

Increasing the areas' value-to-weight ratios in products and services. The thinking of many planners involved in community development continues to focus on the outmoded, over-estimation of the economic value of local manufacturing jobs. Although they are a source of job-to-population balance, they are not the solution for all communities. Manufacturing jobs provide little in the way of fiscal benefit to the communities in which they are located, and frequently, the cost of securing a manufacturing job (dictated by the large number of communities competing for these jobs) exceeds their value to the community not only in a quantitative sense but probably also on a subjective basis.

The process of defining resources and limitations would, for example, highlight the limitations of some communities that are located at some distance from major markets. Ideal export industries for such communities would include the types of products that are "shipped" electronically and services and specialized goods which exhibit a high value-to-weight relationship, etc. Credit card processing organizations, for example, have selected such remote locations as the Dakotas, Phoenix and Las Vegas, based on those areas' tax structures and labor force availability because their product is essentially information.

Conceiving a practical implementation program is a relatively simple matter once the community's advantages, limitations, and goals are defined. The most effective implementation programs are highly focused. The process also should result in specific goal prioritization and implementation processes that build on one another. The achievement of an early goal provides a platform for the achievement of more difficult goals ahead through focused marketing efforts targeted at industries that have a special affinity for the specific attributes of the community.

The entire process should be reviewed on at least a five-year cycle, if not more frequently, to measure progress toward achieving specific goals, to provide a basis for reevaluating the practicality of achieving certain goals, and to redefine the goals in light of the achievement of intermediate goals. This regular review and updating is not often a part of a long-range economic development strategy.

Pre-conditions for an efficient and successful economic development effort include the following:

Goals should be specific and carefully articulated. Such goals could include a target increase in property tax base per capita population, specified increases in sales tax capture, defined ratios of local jobs to local labor force, and defined new development by type—70 percent residential, 22 percent commercial, 8 percent industrial, etc.

An effective development plan also includes an objective definition of the community's resources and limitations.

The next step is a realistic appraisal of how available resources can be mobilized to exploit special opportunities defined by the pattern of resources and limitations. One community with which we are familiar, for example, has a strongly established medical industry economic base which can be built upon to attract retirees and to fill in gaps in the representation of specific types of medical service capability.

Another has ample excess capacity in resort facilities during the third quarter of each year, which would accommodate an increase in visitor population. A small investment in new facilities would contribute to the overall economic efficiency of the facilities themselves as well as the entire community.

Another community, located on the western edge of a population base, is not now served by adequate retail facilities, causing this hinterland population to pass through the community to other, more established retail sectors located to the west of the city in question. Targeting retail business would improve the city's economy.

A commuter city's population base includes a substantial number of residents employed in the finance sector who travel long distances to work. That implies the city has a skilled available labor force which could help attract backroom financial service activities.

Too often communities engage in promotional activities without having a clear-cut definition of their message or their specific target audience, let alone of the appropriate media to reach this target. This means that a valuable community resource for economic development is an objective, comprehensive, and continuously updated data base available to all agencies and private sector elements interested in promoting the local community. Once that information has been gathered and evaluated, then a community can begin to effectively market itself to the business sector.

Chapter 4

The Difference Between Economic Developers and Planners

Timothy W. Gubala

Introduction

The average citizen would think that the purposes and goals of local government for comprehensive planning and economic development are synonymous. In practice, the reverse often seems true. Economic developers complain that planners hold up site plan reviews of industrial projects over trivial matters such as requiring the planting of shrubs for landscaping or screening of dumpsters. Planners charge that economic developers circumvent the adopted comprehensive plan, encouraging growth and traffic congestion in areas not envisioned for development. The argument goes on; the lines are drawn and internal department conflicts occur in local government buildings and courthouses across the country.

Planners and economic developers have roles that are in conflict due to basic differences in attitude, perspective and approach to business that perpetuates conflictual relations with each other.

But the picture is not hopeless. There are opportunities for team building that allow both professions to achieve their goals and work together. Out of the conflicts come problem solving techniques that will benefit the community.

Whose Vision of the Community?

A community's Comprehensive or Master Plan sets forth the long range goals and objectives for land use, transportation, housing and public facilities. This plan is prepared either by a planner employed by the local government,

Reprinted with permission from *Economic Development Review*, Vol. 10, No. 2, Summer, 1992. Published by the American Economic Development Council, Rosemont, Ill. All rights reserved.

a regional planning agency or private consultants. The public reviews the plan during citizen workshops or public hearings. A series of maps and printed reports is prepared that describes the future community. Recommendations for implementation and action are referenced and are given priorities.

The plan may be considered current but most likely, it was prepared more than five years ago. A 1990 Virginia publication showed that 73 of 135 (55%) cities and counties had plans that were adopted before 1985.[1] The community's adopted vision lags behind the actual pressures for additional industrial land, roads and public water and sewer improvements.

The adopted plan reflects the attitudes of the community. Public services boundaries may be officially delineated by means of an urban service boundary. Beyond this line, urban activities are discouraged. Economic development areas are depicted by commercial or industrial designations.

To the economic developer, the plan may be a document conceived in the past and out of date with the reality of what the prospect wants.

The local government economic developer has a mission of attracting new business and industry. He may be involved in identifying and developing separate industrial sites as well as parks. All sites identified for industrial use may not be shown on the comprehensive plan. Planners regard this as illogical and irresponsible.

Economic developers see it as a normal procedure to create an inventory of sites and begin the long term process for rezoning, extending utilities or improving access.

The issue is whom, specifically which professional, should make the determination about the designation of land for industrial use. Is this a selfish "turf fight" or a serious question that requires an answer in communities?

What does light industrial mean? If the Comprehensive Plan is the fabric of a community's future, then the zoning ordinance is the structure. Every economic developer wants an inventory of industrial zoned land. Or do we? A study of zoning for cities and counties in Virginia in 1990 showed that 125 of 136 localities (81%) have a zoning ordinance adopted or revised before 1985.[2] Zoning definitions, standards and requirements reflect the era of the 1950s with "light" and "heavy" industrial districts. Automobile graveyards and petroleum storage are allowed alongside laboratories and electronic assembly facilities. Since most zoning ordinances follow a Euclidean Standard (i.e., each zoning district includes uses allowed in the lesser intense district, such as commercial uses allowed in industrial), a variety of uses may be permitted in the most intense industrial district. Unwanted land uses need to be stated somewhere in the zoning ordinance, and preferably restricted in any zoning district adjacent to a residential area.

When the economic developer brings forward an industrial prospect such as a robotics manufacturer, a thermoplastics company or a maker of ceramic chip capacitors, the planner looks through the schedule of permitted uses in the industrial zoning district to determine if the particular use is permitted. He/she may make an interpretation that would allow these uses to go into one or more industrial districts. He/she may determine that a zoning amendment is needed to allow the use or he/she may refer to a quasi-judicial body such as a Board of Zoning Appeals to make an interpretation. The economic developer would hope that a favorable interpretation could be made to allow these uses rather than face an extended time period for public hearings, review and a determination on a zoning amendment. If the latter occurs, the prospects will be seeking a community that has zoning in place or flexible interpretation procedures.

Planners and economic developers are aware of the Office of Management and Budget guidelines known as the Standard Industrial Classification (SIC) Manual.[3] The entire field of economic activity is included and divided into groups and divisions by means of a numerical designation of two, three and four digit numbers.

The system is more detailed and inclusive than the district uses of the typical zoning ordinance. Economic developers routinely refer to the SIC Manual in targeting and identifying prospects. Planners find the SIC Manual less useful than the economic developer because impact measures such as noise, separation of hazardous waste and traffic cannot be assigned by SIC numerical designations. At best, planners use the SIC Manual as a reference while economic developers may use it more as a "Bible."

Process vs. Product. Planning is a process and not an end in itself. It is continuous, ongoing and dynamic. Concepts such as inventory and analysis, goal setting, and the development of alternatives are indicative of the planning process. The object of preparing a plan and having it adopted is not as important as the process whereby the community is involved and accepts the plan. Once a planning process is established, it is used continuously to review and comment on planning-related issues facing a community, such as a zoning ordinance revision, a controversial rezoning or a capital improvement plan. Planners will use a successful process as a model to review economic development proposals even if economic developers do not agree that this is the best method.

Economic developers are product-oriented. They seek to close the deal, locate the prospect and get going on the next project. Activity is sales-driven. Dollars of new investment, jobs created and acres developed are some of the measures by which economic developers evaluate their success. If there is any emphasis on process for economic developers, it is short-range and aimed at achieving a goal that will improve the product that the local community has to offer.

Product development is a goal that encompasses site development, image enhancement and identification and improvement of the community's quality of life. Local economic developers find themselves viewing the community in a broader sense, focusing on areas that need improvement to make them into assets. In doing so, they cross over into areas traditionally viewed as being in the realm of planning, such as determining priorities for capital improvement projects. The goal of product development comes into conflict with the planning process because of timing and plan compliance issues.

Specificity vs. Flexibility. Daily, planners rely on comprehensive (or master) plans and ordinances to assist them in performing their job. Tasks such as reviewing site plans for building permits and evaluating concept plans for rezonings cause planners to apply standards and policies outlined in ordinances and plans. This review process creates conflict between economic developers and planners. An individual business, flushed with the publicity of a recently announced building expansion or location decision, often faces the realities of its decisions as the company enters the development review process. "Bureaucracy" is the mildest term used to describe the procedures that a business must go through to comply with local government codes, ordinances, and standards. In order to obtain a building permit, applicants must first show "on paper" — on the site plan — provisions for parking (including handicapped spaces), landscaping, screening of dumpsters, location and area of all signs and truck loading/unloading spaces. Innocuous enough, but the interpretation of the regulations by individual planners is as varied as night and day; economic developers each have "horror stories" about planners applying specific regulations to a business location and threatening to withhold the issuance of a Building Permit or Certificate of Occupancy until these regulations are met.

Economic developers want the widest latitude in interpretation of ordinances and standards. The Comprehensive Plan of the community which shows "long range recommendations for the general development of the jurisdiction"[4] is used to back up zoning ordinance decisions for specific parcels of land. In some jurisdictions, the Comprehensive Plan has become a document "formed in concrete" and is considered inflexible to proposals for change. The plan must be amended by a rezoning applicant. The general document then becomes specific and the focus of planning dwells on the site rather than the community as a whole.

It is becoming commonplace to regard a community planner as that professional who applies ordinances and codes to development proposals. Planners risk becoming so site-specific that they lose their vision of the community. They become truly engrossed in the "shrubs and trees" of a site plan rather than the larger community as a whole.

Incentives. As part of the effort to sell the community, local economic developers continually seek out incentives for businesses to relocate, expand or enlarge their local capital investment. These may take the form of tax abatements, free land, rent-free clauses for industrial buildings or connections to public water and sewer. These may supplement state incentives for industrial training, construction of highway improvements or additional tax abatement and financing programs.

Incentives are committed up front and evolve as a part of the confidential location process. When they become public, these incentives may conflict with existing master plans and capital improvement budgets. An industrial location may cause water and sewer lines to be extended to a site that is not envisioned for growth within the time frame of the plan or capital improvement budget. This would affect the growth potential of adjacent properties resulting in a conflict between the planners and the master plan, on the one hand, and economic developers and prospect location on the other.

Sometimes commitments for a change in a zoning district, a variance for the height of an accessory use or a promise of an "expedited" building permit are made to a prospect. This infuriates the planner who believes that the process of planning has been violated. The community has no input, no influence on the project, if economic developers make promises ahead of time. Expediting a building permit may be done, but planning staff feel pressured and may more closely scrutinize plans to be certain that everything strictly conforms with codes.

Opportunities for Team Building

With the range of potential roles in conflict between planners and economic developers, it is a wonder that businesses ever locate in a community. The impetus for ending conflicts may come from the public disclosure of internal conflicts from a dissatisfied business owner or from a self-imposed truce. In any case, the economic developer can provide for leadership and take the initial steps to resolve conflicts with planners. There is an opportunity for joint resolution of conflicts and problems between the professionals that will provide opportunities for team building.

The economic development strategy. Economic development planning occurs separately from the Comprehensive/Master Plan process. Many communities today have developed and adopted a strategic plan for economic development. This is the "process by which an organization envisions the future and develops the necessary procedures and operations to achieve that future."[5] (Note that strategic planning is process-oriented.) Further, strategic planning for economic development is the process by which an area's resources are allocated and used in accordance with an overall program designed to maintain, diversify and or expand the economic base of the community.[6]

Given the background of planning in a community, there is an opportunity to develop a strategic plan for economic development that supports the adopted Comprehensive Plan. Consultants and businesses evaluating a community routinely ask for a copy of the Comprehensive/Master Plan and

Ordinances. Making a copy of an adopted Economic Development Strategy available as well, demonstrates the community's commitment to economic development.

The ideal team-building scenario would have the economic developer prepare an Economic Development Strategy that references and or complements the adopted community Master Plan. The planner and the economic developer can work together to prepare a document that serves their joint needs and, since the documents will most likely have been adopted at different times, the Strategy may serve as an interim document that points out proposed or recommended changes in the Plan, making it more supportive of local economic development issues.

A Strategic Plan is implemented by means of an annual work plan or action plan that sets forth specific tasks to be accomplished in economic development. Since this action plan may directly conflict with an adopted Comprehensive/Master Plan that is out of date, close coordination with the planner is critical for achieving positive results.

Involvement. Planners pride themselves on their ability to involve various segments of the community in the planning process. The traditional public hearing has become the final formal step before an elected governing body adopts a new Comprehensive Plan. Most of the negotiations, compromise and input occur months before at the staff level, in committee meetings and during community workshops with the citizens. This is the time frame during which economic developers should be involved. Opportunities to change plans, ordinances and standards exist while they are still draft proposals. Later, the adoption and approval process becomes more formalized and opportunities for change become less likely.

The economic developer must rely upon contacts in the business community to assist in influencing the drafting of ordinance proposals. For instance, in communities where separate study committees are used, a proposed sign ordinance should seek outdoor advertising representatives to review the draft. Comprehensive/Master Plan updates may be presented to the local Chamber of Commerce as part of the adoption process. A zoning ordinance revision that affects commercial and industrial uses may be improved by having commercial realtors comment on the draft before its adoption.

Since planning is a public process, the economic developer has a responsibility to ask questions about the changes being proposed and how he/she and the business community can be involved. Local government planners see the entire community as their clientele but do not know how to involve the business community as a specific interest group. Getting the business community involved in the public planning process is both a challenge and opportunity for the local economic developer.

On being an ombudsman. Economic developers recognize that up to 80% of the new jobs in a community are created by existing business. This job creation is not a spontaneous process; it requires conscientious efforts and commitments from community leadership. The role best suited for the local economic developer is that of "ombudsman."[7]

There are difficulties with site development plan approvals, building permits, business licenses, rezonings, variances, utility connections, assessments and taxes and public safety that cause business to be in conflict with local government. The economic developer must learn to cut through the "red tape," to expedite plans and permits and solve problems for business.

Where business expansions are handled in a professional manner by local government, the positive relationship contributes to the business being satisfied with the community. If businesses have a poor opinion of local government, the word travels and the community is labeled as anti-business. That counters efforts by the economic developer to attract out-of-area prospects.

Local economic developers can "take care of business" by becoming problem solvers. They establish an existing industry program firmly seeking out the issues and concerns that business has with local government regulations. Rather than complain about the planners, the economic developer works to understand the codes and ordinances, the standards required and the procedures by which development occurs in the community. He/she builds rapport with the regulatory agencies of local government. Then the economic developer can assist a project by understanding the problem, explaining the procedure to resolve it and or describing the alternatives. He/she will be recognized in the business community as someone who is a problem solver, and in the long run, becomes recognized as the person to handle opportunities.

Public-private partnerships. The ultimate opportunity for team building between economic developers and planners is the formation of a public-private partnership. This concept involves the design of a joint project between the local government and the private sector. A good example is a site development project that involves the extension of public water and sewer and the construction of a new access road to a privately owned industrial site to attract a new company.

The planner and the economic developer must work together to accomplish the project. When both are committed and have ownership in the project, the team concept is strengthened. Public-private partnerships enable the planner, as a public official, to understand the calculated benefits and payback from incentives offered by the developer and apply his/her knowledge of economic impact analysis techniques. By working together, the impact measures and public benefits can be determined and the project supported.

Through his/her contacts with the planners, the local economic developer can gain access to the arena of grants. Even though federal grant programs have decreased, the states have taken over grant administration. Economic developers can apply for the limited grant funds and programs available to support projects that aid product development. For instance, in Virginia, funds for site planning and development are available from the State Community Development Block Grant program.

The economic developer should understand the grant process, the role and support that the planner can lend, and the relationship of these grants to the overall community Comprehensive Plan.

Conclusion

Local Government planners and economic developers need not exist as separate office entities. Although conflicts will occur, they must learn to overcome differences and work together to solve problems.

The two professional groups can work together to develop a vision of the community that includes both the long range elements of the Comprehensive or Master Plan and the short range action agenda set forth in the Economic Development Strategy. The two documents can complement each other and present the community in a positive and progressive manner to both prospects and existing businesses.

Regulatory reform can be accomplished with less conflict if the planners and economic developers can openly share observations, concepts and ideas that support the community vision established in the Plan and Economic Development Strategy. Definitions of zoning, descriptions of industrial uses and standards for site plan review can be updated and amended together. An approach of openness and joint problem-solving will more quickly resolve a zoning question than one of conflict and confrontation.

Being an "ombudsman" means that the economic developer becomes a vocal and visible contact within local government for the business community. He/she can use his/her internal contacts to obtain information, route requests for services and resolve issues before they become problems. By working within the governmental structure, the economic developer can be a positive force affecting the success of the community's economic development program. The economic developer can find the balance between economic opportunities and regulation of development.

Economic developers are aware of the financing gaps faced by businesses as they seek private financing for building expansions, new construction and purchases of capital equipment. Planners' skills in obtaining grants and loans can be of benefit to the developer who is preparing an application package for state funds or providing supporting documentation for a company's application for financing from a lender. The justifications, impacts and benefits of economic development can be shown by economic developers through public-private partnerships.

The issues of economic development provide opportunities for team building between the two professions. Through the team concept, the goal of improving the community can be achieved. From the different perspectives of the economic developer and planner, the team can achieve the vision of the community.

NOTES

1. "Directory of Local Planning in Virginia 1990," Planning Assistance Office, Department of Housing and Community Development, Richmond, Virginia, 1990.

2. Ibid.

3. *Standard Industrial Classification Manual.* Executive Office of the President, Office of Management and Budget, US Government Printing Office, Washington, DC, 1987.

4. "Local Planning Legislation," Office of Local Development Programs, Department of Housing and Community Development. Reprint from the Code of Virginia of 1950 and 1986 Cumulative Supplement, The Michie Company, Charlottesville, Virginia, 1986.

5. Goodstein, Leonard D., et al. "Applied Strategic Planning: A New Model for Organizational Growth and Vitality." *Strategic Planning: Selected Readings* (San Diego: University Associates, 1986), p. 2.

6. Kolzow, David R., "Strategic Planning for Economic Development," American Economic Development Council, Rosemont, Illinois, 1988.

7. A Swedish word for a government official or representative who investigates complaints, reports, findings and helps achieve an equitable settlement.

II : The Structure

Chapter 5

Setting Up Shop for Economic Development

RUTH KNACK
JAMES J. BELLUS
PATRICIA ADELL

Introduction

Deciding what form an economic development organization should take — a hot issue right now — is a relatively new problem. Economic development used to be primarily the province of the local chamber of commerce, perhaps with some facts and figures supplied by a small economic development office within the municipal planning office. In the late 1950s, federally funded urban renewal offices took the lead in organizing development projects, which, throughout the next two decades, were almost exclusively real estate projects.

The connection between development and jobs strengthened some during the Model Cities era of the late 1960s, but the work of retaining and attracting the big industrial job producers was more often a state than a local responsibility. In the mid–1960s, the advent of the U.S. Economic Development Administration spurred the creation of economic development committees, and the Community Services Administration began to fund neighborhood development corporations. Other nonprofit corporations were formed to take advantage of Small Business Administration programs. Downtown business interests formed their own development corporations.

Philadelphia may have been the first city to establish a nonprofit corporation concerned with the economic development of the entire city, and a lot of places are looking to it as a model now. Today, some 50 citywide economic development corporations are listed in the directory published by the National Council for Urban Economic Development. Some of these groups evolved from

Reprinted with permission from *Planning*, Vol. 49, No. 9, October, 1983. Published by the American Planning Association, 1313 E. 60th St., Chicago, IL 60637.

Model Cities agencies. The Dayton City-Wide Development Corporation is an example. Others are creations of a local chamber of commerce or, like the Philadelphia Industrial Development Corporation, of the chamber and the city government. Some concentrate on financing and land development for industry, as PIDC did in the beginning. Later, it broadened its focus to include financial assistance for commercial enterprises—an emphasis of many of the newer corporations as well.

Some of the corporations have an extremely close relationship with the city government (the Baltimore Economic Development Corporation, BEDCO, for one). Others are governed by boards completely composed of private sector representatives. A mixture may be more typical. For example, a new economic development commission in the small city of Aurora, Illinois, is sponsored equally by the city and the chamber of commerce. The salary of the single staff member is shared by both, with office space provided by the chamber. The nine-member board is appointed by the mayor, four from a list provided by the chamber of commerce, and five from a list drawn up by the city.

Although all the quasi-public corporations pride themselves on their no-strings approach to development, evidently this stance is not enough to allay private-sector frustration entirely. Recently, some 25 big corporations in Philadelphia each agreed to chip in $50,000 a year to support a new, completely private, economic development corporation, the Greater Philadelphia First Corporation. According to a planner in the Delaware Valley Regional Planning Commission, the new group grew out of the dissatisfaction of those who felt that economic development groups in the metropolitan area were working at cross purposes and that private contributions were not being invested according to a clearly defined strategic plan. The new corporation, which is directed by Ralph Widner, will fund specific projects in response to proposals by civic organizations and quasi-public agencies. Its board includes a representative of PIDC.

Staying put. At the opposite end of the spectrum from the private groups are those economic development departments that determine to remain an integral part of city government. The model in this case is Portland, Oregon, which in 1973 merged five bureaus and commissions into one umbrella agency, the Office of Planning and Development (which has since been disbanded). Other examples are St. Louis, which recently reorganized its planning department to include economic development, and Oakland, California, which in 1979 merged its community development and employment and training offices into a super-agency—the Office of Economic Development and Employment.

In the view of Alan Gregerman, research director of the National Council for Urban Economic Development (CUED) in Washington, both options—the strengthened city department and the quasi-public corporation—have their own strengths and limitations. "The form that works best in a particular city," he suggests, "is a function of many factors, including community size, economic circumstances, local development objectives, and the level of commitment of public and private sectors to economic improvement. In big cities, he adds, "it's reasonable to have a number of different economic development organizations—as long as they communicate and complement each other."

Gregerman believes the public approach works well in cities where the local government has given a high priority to economic development and the private sector is already actively involved—as it is in St. Paul. In contrast, he says, a quasi-public corporation may be more effective in communities where economic development is only one of many priorities competing for scarce public dollars, or where the private sector is uneasy about working directly with local government. (To put it more frankly, in a city where clout rules, a corporation, which can often bypass the city council, may get more done.)

Increasingly, Gregerman notes, communities are choosing the quasi-public route. He sees no reason to change, however, if an effective economic development department is already in place. In short, if it isn't broken, don't fix it.

The organizational issue came to a head in Chicago, where a business-sector advisory group, Chicago United, pointing to Philadelphia as a model, was pushing for the creation of a strong, new quasi-public entity. However, Robert Mier, who was appointed economic development commissioner by Mayor Harold Washington, expressed opposition to the idea of putting too much power in the hands of a private body. Mier, a planner, was the director of the Center for Urban Economic Development at the University of Illinois at Chicago. His confirmation by the city council, it should be noted, is [at the time of writing] by no means a sure thing in the city's politically turbulent atmosphere. Some business leaders have expressed fears that his interests are too slanted toward the neighborhoods, to the neglect of downtown.

"The major question," says Mier, "is the degree to which economic development gets privatized. The city must retain responsibility for policy making, and it must remain accountable for its use of public resources."

New direction. Mier does believe, however, that there is a place for an implementation organization "to take on things when the market fails." He has proposed, in fact, that the city create a new industrial development corporation—an idea that Mayor Washington made part of his platform. But Mier would make the new body responsible to the economic development commission rather than remaining independent, as Chicago United would prefer.

Rather than strengthening the private side, Mier wants to beef up the city's economic development planning—pulling development and employment training together in one agency along the lines of Oakland or San

Antonio, both of which he often refers to as models. "In the past," he says, "economic development in American cities meant real estate development. I think we seduced ourselves into thinking that if we could solve the land problem, we could solve the economic development problem. What we ended up with is economic development in cities that were good at real estate development. What's needed now is to put jobs back at the center."

St. Paul: We Kept It in City Government

In St. Paul, we believe that economic development can best be accomplished by an agency that is an integral part of city government. Our proof is a track record that compares favorably to that of any private or nonprofit development agency.

In the early 1970s, the situation was different. Efforts by local government to spur development in the depressed inner city were hampered by in-fighting among agencies, lack of political leadership, and an inefficient government structure. Development functions were split among three agencies, the Housing and Redevelopment Authority, and the offices of planning and community development. None of the three had the authority or the wherewithal to deal with the problems caused by a stagnating local economy. (With a population of 270,000, St. Paul is the smaller, and somewhat more industrial, of the Twin cities. The Minneapolis–St. Paul metropolitan area has a million residents.)

Immediately after his 1976 election, Mayor George Latimer began to push the creation of an umbrella agency that would merge the city's economic development functions. A year later, the Department of Planning and Economic Development was formed. PED operates with five divisions: community development, housing, business redevelopment, downtown development, and planning.

In the six years since then, PED has been widely recognized for its development successes, starting with a downtown project, the $100 million Town Square office-retail complex. Through PED's efforts, St. Paul ranks fourth in the nation in overall volume of Urban Development Action Grants (UDAGs) received, with $50.8 million awarded for 15 grants. In 1981 the city ranked first in the total amount of revitalization grants and loans to small businesses. In five years, we have provided $111 million to small businesses and helped create or retain over 3,000 jobs.

During this time, PED has shepherded through numerous other commercial development projects, hospital expansions, and neighborhood office developments. A major source of funds is the city's tax-exempt revenue bond program, which also has netted $218 million for new housing development since 1977. In addition, PED has financed the rehabilitation of more than

6,800 housing units in low-income neighborhoods and aided commercial development with such projects as the Selby Avenue business revitalization program. This year, using community development block grants and city tax funds, PED established a $2.25 million self-help fund, the Neighborhood Partnership Program, to which neighborhood groups can apply for development projects.

We're responsible. We think this kind of activity can take place only when city departments are working cooperatively and when they are fully aware of the city's total economic, housing, commercial, and recreation needs. A private or quasi-public development agency is less likely to be responsive to public sentiment and to the opinions of major decision makers than we are. One reason is that city government staff members have easier access to their mayors and city councils. They have the advantage of working closely with other city departments and they are more involved with the citizen participation process. A city agency has a vested interest in following the development goals established by the city's comprehensive plan. Because citizens are involved, development does not take place in isolation.

There are drawbacks, of course. Bureaucracy can be a problem, and public disclosure requirements can cause delays. But corporations have their own bureaucracies, and they also suffer from the human inadequacies that cause delays in any type of organization. Nonprofit development agencies have their own hierarchies of staffers who must sign off on various decisions. They, too, are accountable to boards and community groups.

Whenever possible, we try to refine our procedures to speed up development. For example, we recently received permission from the city council to place options on property without holding a public hearing—allowing us to enter into negotiations with potential developers without setting off a speculative flurry. Final acquisition of a site does require public review, but by then the details are unlikely to change.

An often-heard complaint is that government has too little expertise to handle complicated development financing. The key here is for government development agencies to hire people who are motivated, inquisitive, creative, and flexible, and who can relate both to the needs of the public and the goals of the private developer—just as a private or nonprofit entity would have to do. These people can and do exist in government. But they must be sought out; trained in real estate, financing, and tax law; and given sufficient staff support to make the best use of their talents.

PED inherited a staff of 300 when its three predecessor agencies were merged. Since then, it has grown much leaner—today's staff is about half that number—as a result both of city budget reductions and a conscious effort to operate more efficiently. One reason that the department can operate with a small staff is that it works cooperatively with other agencies. A major project currently, for instance, is Energy Park, a $250 million venture of PED and the

St. Paul Port Authority. The project will include an "energy technology center," primarily to house small, energy-related businesses and to be managed by the Control Data Corporation. With the aid of a $50 million revenue bond issue, PED is financing and coordinating the construction of 950 housing units on the site. In addition, the city secured two UDAGs to provide the necessary infrastructure.

A total approach. In sum, we feel that by combining housing and commercial financing, planning, zoning, and small business programs in one agency, PED is able to take a total development approach to any area of the city. For example, in Lowertown, the historically significant warehouse district east of the downtown core, PED, working with the foundation-backed Lowertown Redevelopment Corporation, is providing revenue bond financing, UDAGs, and technical assistance for a variety of renewal projects. At the same time, it is working with the artists who are being priced out of the area's lofts — providing one group with a Neighborhood Partnership Program grant to buy a warehouse and convert it into cooperative housing and work space.

It is interesting to note how closely our activities parallel those of quasi-public organizations. Technically, we also have the ability to handle industrial development, although in St. Paul that activity has been left to the port authority. Of course, not all governments are set up to get maximum performance from a public development agency. For them, a private, or a quasi-public, development corporation may be the best bet. However, when a city has good political leadership and key staff members have the foresight and acumen to understand the value of good, city-controlled development, then a public development agency should be the choice.

Philadelphia: We Set Up a Separate Corporation

Twenty-six years ago, the Greater Philadelphia Chamber of Commerce and the city itself jointly established a nonprofit corporation, the Philadelphia Industrial Development Corporation, to find ways of creating and retaining jobs, and of improving the city's tax base. PIDC's initial strategy was to help finance industrial enterprises and to develop and market city-owned industrial land. It has since expanded its focus to include financing and marketing assistance to commercial interests, and it has become recognized as one of the nation's most successful economic development agencies. Since 1960, it has settled 1,758 projects with a capital investment of over $1.5 billion; over 175,000 jobs have been created and retained as a result.

We think its success is due in large measure to the fact that the corporation is a collaborative effort of the public and private sectors.

For one thing, its structure is more effective and flexible than the alternative — an economic development department that is an integral part of city government. PIDC's policies are set by a 32-member board, composed of representatives from the public and private sectors. The city itself has seven ex officio seats. A third of the board changes every year and is selected by a nominating committee. A 17-member executive committee meets biweekly; the full board meets quarterly. We have found that the public-private board composition has encouraged the public sector to adopt development policies favorable to business expansion and retention. Even more important, the formal organization provides a platform for public-private interaction.

More freedom. Moreover, our implementation powers are significantly less restrained by the legal strictures of the city charter than a city department's would be. Thus, PIDC, through its subsidiaries, can acquire, develop, sell, and lease land; provide financing through tax-exempt bonds and mortgages; act as a conduit for direct loans from private lending institutions; and put together a variety of financial packages. We have enough flexibility in managing and investing our financial resources to meet the needs of new and growing businesses — avoiding most of the red tape often associated with public-sector bureaucracies. Because project-by-project citizen review is usually not required, we can act much faster than a public agency, although, of course, we are governed by the lending and development policies approved by the public sector and our own board. As a quasi-public entity, we have an easier time gaining the trust of private business than our public counterparts, and we are not as directly affected by political changes.

We can provide a wide range of development assistance — from selling and improving land through our land banking program, to marketing and negotiating the sale or lease of publicly owned properties. As a corporation, we have the flexibility to negotiate the sale of property directly, or to open the sale to bids by qualified developers. Whereas the public sector often is required to accept the lowest bid, we can select a developer who demonstrates financial capability, high-quality design, and experience. Finally, our implementation capabilities are enhanced by a variety of subsidiaries and affiliates, including the Philadelphia Authority for Industrial Development (PAID), a state-authorized, tax-emempt mortgage program; and the PIDC Financing Corporation (PIDC-FC) and the PIDC Local Development Corporation (PIDC-LDC), mechanisms for low-interest, second-mortgage financing.

Our involvement in the 34-acre waterfront redevelopment area known as Penn's Landing is one example of how we work. PIDC is responsible for marketing and developing the landfill site for offices and housing. That means selecting developers and working with the U.S. Army Corps of Engineers and other nonlocal agencies to get the necessary transportation links and to line up environmental permits.

One-stop shop. In effect, we have created a one-stop shop for companies interested in coming into the city or expanding their current operations. As a quasi-public corporation, we've been able to integrate implementation powers with the responsibilities of research, planning, and marketing, and even acting as ombudsman — for instance, by pushing for building code enforcement and more police protection for a company fearful about expanding in a rough neighborhood.

We can also respond quickly in an area where timing is crucial. Manufacturing firms cannot afford to hold off on production and expansion plans while an agency requests various public approvals. We can put together a tailormade loan package, using a combination of local and state funds. In turn, this financing can be used to leverage private mortgage and loan money. The revolving fund used to write down the cost of land sold through our land bank was capitalized with community development block grant money, and the block grants are a mainstay of the second-mortgage loan program, a special, inner-city loan program, and a technology program for start-up firms.

The public-private structure maximizes the powers of both sides. Since the municipal debt ceiling is not affected by debts created by the corporation, the city is protected from financial risk. At the same time, the corporation can draw upon the city's power of eminent domain and its zoning and taxing powers.

Part of the reason that we can do all these things is that we can recruit and hire competent and experienced people without the restrictions of the city's civil service system. Since the beginning, we have offered salaries that are competitive with the private sector — an important incentive in attracting high-caliber staff members. Over the years, we've grown from a tiny staff of three to our present complement of 42 professionals with a yearly budget of over $2 million.

Our legal status as a tax-exempt entity alllows us to accept donations from corporations and business groups. On the public side, we have covered some of our administrative expenses through the Economic Development Administration's 302(a) planning funds. In addition, we've received some state and city grants and at various times have contracted with the city, through our subsidiary, the PIDC Development Management Corporation, to perform specific services. PIDC also can generate its own funds through loan settlement, processing, and application fees.

We think the quasi-public corporation, with its legal flexibility and combination of public and private resources, offers the broadest range of powers and the strongest opportunity for coordination between the public and private sectors. Although independent to some degree, it also recognizes its responsibility to both sides — to the private sector in creating a favorable business climate and to the public sector in creating job opportunities and improving the city's tax base.

Chapter 6

Community-Based Development Organizations

HERBERT J. RUBIN

Community-based development organizations (CBDOs) are nonprofit, housing and commercial developers who do "the difficult job of providing service and leadership in communities that need help and that other agencies cannot or will not serve" (Vidal, 1992, p. 111). Within neighborhoods that the mainstream economy has neglected, CBDOs build homes, offices, and commercial centers, manage apartments, and create jobs. For the dispossessed, CBDOs provide a stake in society through home ownership; for the welfare poor, they open the possibility of employment; for impoverished neighborhoods, CBDOs provide a focus for planning and local control. The accomplishments of CBDOs reduce the sense of disempowerment and failure felt by those trapped in poor communities (Rubin, 1992, 1993).

In partnership with local governments, CBDOs have accomplished much. Yet, CBDO directors feel that the public sector has hesitated in fully committing to the nonprofits. Public administrators face regulatory and bureaucratic constraints that restrict their support of nonprofits. Further, public administrators are concerned about the limited administrative capacity of many nonprofits and the documented failures in the past. CBDO directors, in turn, argue that regulatory and bureaucratic constraints can be changed through the political process and that the limited administrative capacity of CBDOs would improve if the public sector provided more of the operating expenses of community developers.[1]

Directors of CBDOs suggest that those in the public sector do not understand the CBDO perspective toward community development and fear that public officials have difficulty comprehending what it means for an organization to be simultaneously nonprofit, community based, and a developer. As developers CBDOs build homes and businesses, but as community-based non-

Reprinted with permission from *Public Administration Review*, Vol. 53, No. 5, September/October, 1993. Published by the American Society for Public Administration, Washington, D.C.

profits (and recipients of grant funds) their work is guided by community residents and, in part, is intended to empower the poor. As developers of physical properties, they perform very much like for-profit builders; as organizations responsive to community needs, they behave more like nonprofit service providers. To those in the public sector, CBDOs seem to act both as a nonprofit fish and a commerical fowl, a confusing combination.

Partnering Between CBDOs and Local Government

With local government support, community-based development organizations have shown they can produce. They have constructed shopping centers in burnt out areas of inner cities, established quality housing in place of slums, enabled the poor to own homes, helped start up minority-owned companies with small loans, and sponsored job development programs for minorities and abused women (Peirce and Steinbach, 1987, 1990; Kelly et al., 1988). Physical output has been impressive. For example, CBDOs "have produced almost 320,000 units of housing in total for very poor people, including close to 87,000 in the past three years . . . [and] almost 90,000 permanent jobs were created or retained in the past five years" (NCCED, 1991, p. 2).

For success in these projects, local government support is vital. Of the 1,160 CBDOs responding to a study, 413 reported receiving support from local government, in addition to pass-through money from the Community Development Block Grants (NCCED, 1991). Some local governments provide the core administrative expenses that enable CBDOs to maintain themselves while planning development projects. In several cities, CBDOs receive public funding as the delegated representatives of city governments in programs to retain jobs, repair store facades, and facilitate neighborhood fix-up. For instance, under Mayor Washington, Chicago's economic development office funded neighborhood organizations to help keep industries in their communities. More than a hundred CBDOs obtained their core financing through such programs (Clavel and Wiewell, 1991).

Supportive administrators have played catalytic roles in community projects by using city or CDBG funds to take the least-secure position on a mortgage for a CBDO-sponsored housing or commercial development project. By assuming the financial risk, government encourages conventional financiers to participate (Dreier, 1989; Suchman et al., 1990). Government has also supported CBDOs indirectly by focusing portions of the city capital budget on neighborhood needs. Local government funding is especially useful and appropriate when it picks up the added costs of development caused by its location in a declining neighborhood. It costs more to refurbish a building adjacent to an abandoned environmental hazard; likewise, it is more expensive to build in a neighborhood where construction materials might be stolen by those needing money for a drug purchase.

Government support extends beyond financial aid. For example, local officials have provided administrative waivers of building and inspection fees and have donated buildings to CBDOs from those obtained by government because of tax liens. Supportive officials have joined with CBDOs in building inspection programs that pressure slumlords to sell their property for rehabilitation by community groups. Cities help fund training for CBDOs. Cincinnati, for instance, has a line item in its development budget that provides community-based developers with training and expertise.

Some public administrators offer strategic and tactical support to CBDOs. In one city, a progressive administrator described how he worked with community groups to pressure the banks to set aside funding for neighborhood development. While negotiating with the banks on a set-aside for poor neighborhoods, this administrator informed community activists which of the banks were recalcitrant and suggested those that might be responsive to direct action campaigns carried out by the community groups.

Tensions in the Partnership

Although cooperation is often successful, tension can develop between city officials and community developers, a tension aggravated through mutual misunderstanding. Public officials comment on the ephemeral nature of many community groups, and delicately refer to scandals in neighborhood expenditure of public funds. They worry about the capacity of CBDOs to produce to scale.

Community developers, on the other hand, sometimes feel they are treated by the cities as second-rate citizens. The head of a successful, large-scale producer of housing described her feelings that city officials often show "disregard or disrespect for [CBDOs]. . . . It is incredible like feeling that [CBDOs] are not worth all the time and effort." She argued that "a for-profit person does not have to go through the months of work that we put in to prove to them that we were a professional, viable organization." CBDO directors complained about the extensive paperwork and long delays involved in obtaining public money, especially pass-through federal grants. Others questioned the paternalism involved when cities placed large sums into community redevelopment while insisting that CBDOs follow city planning procedures. In a city where that was occurring, a director of a successful neighborhood-based CBDO pondered whether "you can encourage the development of a bottom up system from the top?"

The perspectives of both government officials and CBDO directors are based on their experiences. CBDO directors can legitimately argue that they are not getting enough money to stabilize and develop the administrative capacity cities would want them to have. Although large numbers of CBDOs report receipt of city money, the total amounts are small, especially in comparison to city development budgets (NCCED, 1991; Vidal, 1992). In comparison to conventional economic development programs, public support of community-based work is limited. A national survey of low-income housing concludes that it is doubtful if cities "are providing the assistance necessary for [CBDOs] to operate effectively" (Goetz, 1992, p. 421). Moreover, support is disproportionately concentrated in a limited number of cities in which public officials already recognize the need to work with the communities (Vidal, 1992, p. 15). Even in cities reputedly most supportive of the neighborhood movement, CBDOs were, at best, relatively invisible to governmental agencies involved in the development business (Vidal, 1992, p. 95). For instance, despite an announced tilt toward the neighborhoods, community groups in Cleveland receive only a small percentage of that city's development funds (Schorr, 1991).

Government officials, in turn, face the realities of past failures of the community movement and fear new funds might also be misspent. They remember the scandals of the Model Cities era in which some community-based agencies did little to alleviate problems of the poor. City officials are aware of stalled production among CBDOs. Two of the organizations I am studying have each worked for over half a decade on projects that have received city money and have yet to break ground. While the downturn in the economy can be blamed, from the city's perspective, little has been accomplished, while much support has been provided.

On a daily basis, administrators who support the community movement witness the contention between CBDOs, and shudder as racial and social class schisms become evident. In recent meetings in one city, CBDOs fought with one another and the city in trying to word the Community Housing Assistance Strategy[2] in ways that favored the particular needs of their neighborhoods while depriving other neighborhoods of city money.

Even when they work to help CBDOs, public administrators still confront limitations created by state and federal regulations. For example, federal community-development block grant regulations are so cumbersome that both officials and CBDOs alike fear using such funds in innovative programs, especially those creating revolving loans. In both Wisconsin and Ohio, public administrators were limited in their involvement in housing projects as housing was not considered by the state constitutions as a public purpose.[3]

In projects in which CBDOs, for-profit investors, and the public sector partner, city officials are caught in a bind. For the CBDO, it is of no great import whether the city or a for-profit partner provides the equity share in a community project, so long as adequate funds are available. The city contribution allows the project to work by providing the for-profit participants a comfort zone for their investments. However, to extend the impact of its limited development funds, the city tries to encourage the maximum investment from for-profit participants. A senior public official described the resulting bargaining over how much public money and how much private money will be invested: "So it is like you are playing a game of financing chicken, you know, where we will give you money if they will give you money. They will give you money if we give you money." The delays created by these negotiations may create resentment and anger by those in the community movement at the apparent dalliance by the public sector.

Toward an Understanding of Community-Based Development Organizations

Directors of community-based development organizations must renew the trust of public administrators who have been disappointed by community groups in the past. Once trust has been earned through the completion of successful projects, those in the community-based movement then can work to educate public officials to understand their ethos toward community renewal. Three areas of dialogue are needed.

First, CBDOs do not define themselves primarily as a delivery system for a public service. Rather, they see themselves as activist, community promoters in which the physical project is a tool for community empowerment and capacity building. Their mission of holistic change is accomplished by linking social welfare or training programs with physical construction. Many CBDO projects are both fish and fowl.

Second, CBDOs feel that the mind-set of public administrators toward nonprofits has been shaped by the service-delivery nonprofits—agencies engaged in counselling, aiding the abused and the abandoned, providing specific job-training skills, and other similar endeavors.[4] At times, CBDO successes are visible and countable—number of houses built, for instance. These outcomes are similar to those of service-delivery nonprofits whose accomplishments are measured by the number of clients served. But CBDOs are a markedly different form of nonprofit. They are nonprofits that own and manage property and invest capital and whose clients are often a community, not individuals.

Third, to further complicate the picture, the service provided by many CBDOs is to facilitate the efforts of others who deliver the actual product. CBDOs encourage meetings between local entrepreneurs and building owners that create jobs within the community. CBDOs are asked to verify the bonafides of one business person to another. They place start-up businesses in contact with pro-bono law firms and affordable accountants. On one occasion witnessed, the CBDO, through its neighborhood contacts, was able to reassure a local housing investor that a fire in an adjacent building was an accidental occurrence and not part of an arson scam. Such actions are hard to document and to show as "products" to funders in the public sector.

Acting as mediator and facilitator while providing unfunded services to community members—advice on how to pay for a mortgage, referrals to family service agencies, small loans for appliance replacement, backup support for community anti-crime campaigns—places the CBDO on the financial edge. CBDOs try to support their administrative costs and fund these services to the poor through developer fees received from physical development projects. To the public sector, these fees appear as "profits." To the CBDO, they are the way the organization stays alive between projects and the means to handle the unanticipated problems of community members. The very projects in which CBDOs engage almost necessitate the provision of a social service. An apartment building for abused women, for instance, may require a social worker to counsel the tenants.

CBDOs use physical development as a tool toward empowerment, and advocate for community change. They do not fall cleanly into the existing roles that city officials work with, for-profit developers, or not-for-profit service providers. Moreover, CBDOs as advocates for community empowerment, suggest to some city officials the bumbling, perhaps corrupt, community organizations of the past. Because city officials have no positive and accurate preexisting role for the CBDO, their directors must present their case to those in the public sector. What follows is such a discussion.

The Ideology of Holistic Empowerment

To CBDO leaders, physical development is a tool, the means, toward accomplishing the broader end of economic empowerment and economic transformation for the poor. To aid the CBDOs in these efforts, those in the public sector must first understand the holistic vision for the community held by CBDOs in which physical and social consequences of projects overlap and the equity consequences of development are as important as its profitability.

To remain solvent, CBDOs need to break even in their work, but unlike for-profit companies, CBDOs try to ensure that at least some of the benefits redound to the poor and support a broader community renewal. A CBDO will refurbish an abandoned convent or school to house the elderly poor in the neighborhood who no longer can afford or are able to maintain fully independent living. It might be cheaper to move people away but far less equitable. In addition, maintaining the building preserves a community symbol.

CBDOs encourage community members to share in the self-esteem that occurs as a neighborhood that others have abandoned takes on a new life. In north Chicago, a CBDO converted an abandoned supermarket to a "Mercado," a shared market for small-scale community merchants. In Grand Rapids, a community organization helped transform a derelict block into a minority-owned shopping mall that returned to the community stores that had abandoned it. In south Chicago, the community-development organization refurbished an eyesore building into an art incubator, housing artists whose work reflects local ethnic and cultural pride.

Doing holistic programs involves linking together service and training programs with physical construction projects. In programs found in several cities, the poor are placed in an ownership position in rehabilitated homes through a lease-purchase arrangement. The CBDO buys and refurbishes the home and rents it at affordable rates (made possible by public subsidies) to the working poor. Part of the rent is treated as a down payment and the poor accumulate assets. Meanwhile families who have never owned a home receive ownership training — in making repairs, funding a reserve fund, and making a mortgage payment. The financing is established so that within a few years, title can be passed to the renter and empowerment occurs as community members gain economic and social control. Ownership gives the poor a stake and a willingness to fight back, as a CBDO director argued, "If you own your own house, you are empowered."

Ownership empowers not only those within the community, but also the community-based development organization itself. Having equity on which to borrow allows the community-based organization to take the initiative, create a project, and then persuade others to join in; a reversal of top-down paternalism. The need to follow the changing fashion of granting agencies is reduced, enhancing the capacity for community-directed change.

The combination of goals in holistic development can complicate projects, especially as the goals of material ownership and empowerment of the poor merge. The development of the Mercado in north Chicago incorporated a conscious effort to demonstrate to community members their power, but that effort made the project more difficult. The CBDO director described how it was done:

> Community people have been involved.... We now have a group that includes both businesses, representatives from other [community] groups and churches, some of our tenants, some of our poor people. We have tenants on our board to help make sure that the board doesn't take control away from that steering committee.... This Mercado committee ... is going to select the contractor. [The goal was to] put the knowledge and experience in the hands [of poor people], and make decisions.... The whole approach is community controlled development and empowerment through development.

Another approach to empowerment is to assure that those in the neighborhood, rather than outsiders, benefit from the consequences of the projects. In explaining the motivation for undertaking a $2 million building in an economically marginal community, a CBDO director said:

> a lot of stuff is all owned by people from outside.... There are eight bars ... all with, we call them shirts, people who are professionals.... They are all owned by people from outside. And, employees are family or people from the ...

suburbs . . . all the cash those eight bars generate, none of it ever changes hands in the community even once. It leaves at 2 and it is gone. We are going to put businesses on the first floor, then do a restaurant, nightclub, and have small businesses . . . and maintain ownership [in the community].

The CBDO owns, designs, runs, and manages a project itself and then spins-off ownership to those in the community as part of a holistic social agenda.

Community empowerment can be a source of contention with city administrators. An inexperienced community board may not inspire trust in their judgments. Boards composed of minority group members can evoke negative stereotypes among city officials, even though the board members are highly trained professionals. One director in an African-American community reflected that because his CBDO board was all Black,[5]

the city . . . would demand things of me that had nothing to do with the proficiency of the project. They even went so far as to suggest that I put some Caucasians on my board of directors, [they said] "you need to expand your board." I said, "what do you mean expand your board?" "You know, so you have got a more diverse representation on your board." Now I got school teachers, I got business owners, I got directors of alternative education programs. I got an accountant. You know, all of them African-American. But . . . [a]ll he saw was a bunch of black folk down there and "you need to expand your board." So I said, "what do you mean expand my board?" [the city official responded] "Well, you know it is perceived as being a very closed corporation and you know a lot of people won't trust that situation, the way it is, so if you expanded it, you know, a little more expertise, and what not." "So you're talking, put some white people on my board?" "Well that would help, you know, that would help." I gave him their $50,000 back.

From the perspective of CBDO directors, public administrators show distrust of neighborhood people. They put more faith in people from the business community, and are more comfortable when business people tell those in poor communities what is needed. Such a model is problematic to CBDOs, not only because of the top-down decision making, which is disempowering, but also because the business people that city officials trust may be the same ones who have already disinvested from the community. As a Caucasian CBDO director in a small city put it,

the mayor had a mayor's housing forum. Good folks, well-intentioned people. But the people who run the whole damn thing are the same people who discriminated against inner-city neighborhoods, community leaders, bank presidents. They don't give a s____ about one of these neighborhoods.

Holistic development represents a different approach to development than cities generally use, but for precisely that reason, it can bring jobs, shops, and housing to neighborhoods that have been abandoned by traditional investors. City officials need to realize that they cannot use top-down tools in these circumstances, as they have already failed. The newer tools are community directed, and require a different set of techniques to evaluate competence and the likelihood of success.

Spanning the Developmental Gap

To accomplish their ideological agenda of economic empowerment for those in need, the CBDO must bring together resources from government, charities, and private investors. With their knowledge of neighborhood problems and capabilities and access to outside resources, CBDOs can customize projects for specific neighborhoods and attempt new approaches to community problems. An astute CBDO and neighborhood association director observed:

> I think that is the great value of [CBDOs], you can conceive of an idea and test it. And, the whole world doesn't fall apart if it doesn't succeed because it is a small enough activity that you can adjust it the next time . . . and, I don't think cities or government understand or appreciate that. That they want to do something that applies everywhere all at once and that is the only way, it has to be a comprehensive program. You don't have to make a comprehensive program cause one shoe doesn't fit every foot.

Many cities do understand the value of such tailored projects for distressed neighborhoods, but lack the staff and detailed knowledge of the neighborhoods to create appropriate, targeted projects. Supportive public administrators seek out constructive partnerships with community groups to capitalize on the CBDO's ability to both get outside funding and design projects of appropriate, neighborhood scale.

CBDOs sometimes manage loan funds for micro-enterprises. Such funds provide a few hundred to ten thousand dollars to community businesses, sums too small for the city or banks to bother with, but precisely the amounts needed to handle start-up or cash flow problems of neighborhood businesses. This ability to target programs to the smaller beneficiaries also occurs in employment training and job retention efforts. A CBDO can focus on the employment needs of manufacturers too small for the attention of public agencies. Cities can support such activities financially, without the impossible commitment of staff time for supporting numerous small businesses.

Community-based development organizations bridge the gap between city-wide development goals and those within neighborhoods. In Cleveland, a coalition of community groups was established to prevent industrial flight from a working class neighborhood. The coalition convinced the city to oppose a mall that would have displaced many small industries that employed community members. A board member of the coalition explained,

> the City of Cleveland was approached by [downtown developers] who targeted a piece of land to be the first indoor shopping mall . . . we would lose 450 jobs

and very highly paid unionized jobs ... we had to convince the city that the choice was not just rejecting a mall, but making a commitment to the industry that was there and saying "this is not a good trade off." ... The City of Cleveland, when they were approached, had no idea of what was going on in that industry ... the manufacturers don't trust the city. [The manufacturers] will not share that type of [financial] information with them directly, where they will share it with us, because they know that we can be trusted.

Community-based development organizations span the gap between large governmental programs and specific needs within their communities.

In addition, they can do something else that governmental agencies find it difficult to do, and that is to combine physical development with social programs in a single project. Government agencies are normally specialized and find it difficult to manage projects that involve multiple agencies with different ideologies, clients, and methods of operations.

CBDO projects combine physical development and social improvement recognizing that within the neighborhoods of the poor, the two are inseparable. People need housing, but cannot be expected to pay the rent unless they have the jobs. Owners will not repair homes when drug-trade is rampant, and small shopping malls provide a base for increased community integration. As a community developer reflected when "you get it down to the community level that is where people will force it to be integrated. Because, their lives are integrated."

When local government partners with a CBDO in restoring a community mall, or supporting a small business, the CBDO, through its knowledge about community members and its permanence within the neighborhood, can assure that community people are hired and trained for the specific needs of local businesses. In a case in which such a project was carried out, the community developer of the $2 million building observed, "We've got an agreement with the construction trades who are going to provide journeymen as trainers [for community workers].... The focus is going to be training people and then moving them into apprenticeships and then skilled training."

Both government and CBDOs together and separately can build homes and house the dispossessed. By themselves, or through linkages with community service agencies, CBDOs introduce social service programs to housing programs. The CBDO maintains the trust with community members that allows it to provide the training in family budgeting and home maintenance that poor people require to make the transition from renter to owner. Organizers working for a CBDO have helped tenants form a tenant's organization to empower the tenants and encourage them to assert control over unruly elements that could damage the property. CBDOs have joined with neighborhood-based anticrime programs to root out the drug trade that discourages community reinvestment. Joining social concerns with physical redevelopment makes projects successful and gives the community more hope.

CBDOs can initiate such projects. In one city, a CBDO that had gained credibility with public officials through its previous successes in housing and industrial park development, moved to span the gap in community needs. It combined employment training and a gap in social services in the community with physical development by establishing home-based daycare for the children of the working poor. A foundation provided the CBDO the wherewithal to plan the scheme. The CBDO, with city funds, refurbished derelict homes up to the standards required for home daycare. Teenagers from the community were employed on the housing construction to obtain job experience. Meanwhile, with the support of public welfare officials, women on AFDC received instruction as daycare providers. The daycare would be provided primarily for community members in the newly refurbished homes that they would own. Government support allowed the daycare providers to continue AFDC benefits while starting up their businesses. A gap is spanned by the CBDO between social needs, community objectives, and government programs.

Being the Smallest Guy on the Block

The perception of public officials that community-based development organizations lack administrative capacity is generally correct. Surveys show that CBDOs are administratively fragile, can only fund small staffs, and operate on a marginally adequate administrative budget (Vidal, 1992). Although a handful of CBDOs have a stable income stream from a successful apartment or commercial complex and others are fortunate enough to receive a subsidy from religious organizations, most live from hand-to-mouth, dependent on small grants for their core expenses and hoping to eke out a small surplus from housing or commercial development projects. Community-based development organizations must meet overhead expenses and find subsidies for the social costs associated with their development programs. Foundations provide some of this money, but the lion's share is obtained through governmental sources, especially CDBG funds.

For organizations working with the poorest people, organizations whose need for a social subsidy is greatest, the withdrawal of public funds can lead to the death of a CBDO. After a minor financial scandal, one CBDO temporarily lost its local government support, yet, retained its moral and legal responsibility for hundreds of affordable apartments:

> Oh, it's been hell! The past three years, it's been pure hell, believe me! Because we were 65% dependent upon the City for funding, then all of a sudden the City voted . . . to withdraw all funding. Just like that [made a "shoo" sound]! It's like having a welfare check and all of a sudden 65% of it's gone.
> And they still expected me to run this organization and provide housing for

poor and low-income. So, we have not had any City funding. We have been living just by rents. A lot of bills have been unpaid. I went without salary, any kind of money at all for nine months.

Just recently, [name] Bank, [I was] trying to borrow there. And, the banker says to me "Well, we understand you've had your problems in the past. It's only been a couple of years. Why don't you continue to operate for another couple of years and come back and see us in a couple of years. Let's see you build your track record back again." Well, two years from now we'll be out of business. You know, I need financial help now.

To avoid such frightening losses, CBDOs may try to build their own economic base from earned equity in projects or charging management fees. A second approach is to work as members of coalitions to pressure government to set up steady funding sources for CBDOs. Both efforts can be misunderstood by local administrators and complicate the government-nonprofit relationship.

Is a Nonprofit Allowed to Make Money?

Each of a handful of larger, nationally known community-based development organizations has sufficient equity so they can, if necessary, invest their own funds, or borrow on their equity. Other organizations seek this freedom by making a small profit on a development project. CBDO directors, however, indicate that city administrators are puzzled by the idea of a nonprofit increasing its own equity reserve from a development fee on a project to help the poor. In a more extreme case, the CBDO director argued:

> The city has its kind of little ideas about how much developers ought to get and how much overhead, how much the nonprofits ought to get. And, for the most part they think the nonprofits ought not to get very much. And for the most part we are starving because of that idea.

That organization was economically marginal and resentful of the situation. But a similar feeling was expressed by a stable organization, whose director claimed the stability in part was due to not taking losses on projects "[CBDOs] cannot work for free and we are not going to work for free. . . . You have to pay your people."

To city officials, restricting what a CBDO can take out of a project might be a responsible way of stretching community development funds. To many of the community developers, however, not allowing a CBDO to pull ahead on a project indicates a lack of respect for the nonprofit in comparison to the commercial developer (Rubin, 1992).

In an effort to keep alive, CBDOs take on far more neighborhood tasks than thin administrative resources permit. While negotiating on multimillion dollar housing or commercial development projects, to pay for their fixed costs, CBDOs have to divert their small staffs to run paint-up fix-up programs, or store-facade rehabilitation efforts. These bread-and-butter programs are useful for the neighborhoods and necessary to keep the CBDO alive, but doing them distracts effort from the broader, holistic projects that can lead to community empowerment.

Coalition Building

To stay alive, CBDOs become political advocates for a public agenda that refocuses city efforts on the neighborhoods and provides core funding for community-based development. As Lipsky and Smith (1990, p. 645) point out "nonprofit agencies routinely tried to affect contract requirements or state regulations governing their programs" yet, feared public retribution. To bypass that fear and increase their political power, CBDOs band together and form coalitions to pressure for change in the laws and regulations that make community-based development difficult. For instance, the CBDO trade association, the NCCED, is involved in a major lobbying effort for federal legislation to provide administrative support for community-based economic development organizations.

Once coalitions are formed, they work aggressively to influence public policies in favor of locally based development. The CBDO coalition in Cincinnati was set up in response to the slowness of the city's payments to community groups. One of its first accomplishments was pressuring the city to form a department of neighborhoods, separating community development from the more dominant downtown interests. In Chicago, coalitions convinced city administrators to apply to their neighborhoods laws that had been passed to benefit Chicago's downtown. A tax reactivation program initiated through coalition actions in Cook County enable CBDOs to obtain deteriorating properties on which slumlords were refusing to pay taxes. CANDO, a coalition of community business-development groups in Chicago, pressured the city to adopt the CDFLOAT program that allows community groups to borrow against city CDBG funds that have not yet been expended. Getting this innovation accepted required a pressure campaign in which CANDO acquire data from HUD on Chicago's woefully slow use of CDBG funds and threatened to embarrass public officials with disclosure. A similar tactic was used by a housing coalition that produced a data book showing both the need for inner city housing and the city's lack of responsiveness to this need.

Coalition actions can create a tense environment between supportive city officials and community groups because community groups are biting the hands that feed them. Coalitions are formed because relationships with the local governments are not working well enough, but forming activist coalitions risks making relationships worse.

Conclusions and Implications

With increased understanding between those in the public sector and the community movement, the public-nonprofit partnerships can be strengthened. But why should those in the public sector want to work to bridge the gap and work more intensely with CBDO? Community developers require extensive nurturance, are not fully sympathetic to the regulatory constraints faced by government, and demand large amounts of time for what appear to be modest results.

One reason for support is that CBDOs work in the poor neighborhoods whose redevelopment is not only fair on social grounds, but may be necessary for the survival of the city as a whole. The neighborhoods in which CBDOs work are those from which the private sector has withdrawn and "private entrepreneurs have exhibited relatively little willingness over the past two decades to invest their capital in such communities" (Stephenson, 1991, p. 111). CBDOs provide a viable and customized approach to economic development and job creation in poor communities. And, they do so by promoting many of the broader values of the society—self help, entrepreneurial spirit, home ownership, and other icons of present day America.

There are also programmatic reasons for supporting the movement. The multibillion dollar HOME program, the most recent incarnation of a federal program for low-income housing, requires that at least 15 percent of its money be spent by qualified not-for-profits (Center for Community Change, 1992). Later amendments to the legislation encourage money to be spent to support the operating costs of community-based housing organizations (Development Times, 1992, p. 1).

Cities can partner with CBDOs in ways that encourage neighborhood input into development planning. The city, however, should not insist on standardization of programs within these partnerships (Lipsky and Smith, 1990), as standardization undermines the strength of neighborhood focused, community-based development movement. What might work in the more stable south side of Chicago would fail in the transitional west side. It is not isolated homes that are being built, but homes in distinct neighborhoods with markedly different configurations of social and economic problems.

Such projects need a public subsidy to make up for social costs: they are often built in neighborhoods in which construction is more expensive because of crime or environmental contamination. Furthermore, they are owned by people who have no experience in property maintenance and need be taught.

In part, this social subsidy can be paid if public adminsitrators fund the core operating expenses of credible CBDOs. That way, the time of CBDO directors can be spent in packaging projects, not merely in struggling to keep the organization alive. A social partnership enables CBDOs to develop their capacity to undo the damage of business flight and racial animosity that plague poor communities.

Meaningful partnerships can be accomplished by the creation of city-wide organizations in which city officials, CBDO activists, and funders meet as equals and share with one another their different language and developmental ethos. Or the public sector can employ as developmental administrators those who both understand and are sympathetic to the community movement, as it did in Cleveland by hiring Chris Warren, former CBDO director, later head of a city-wide CBDO network, now the development director for the city. To bring about effective partnering means, as the National Conference of State Legislatures argued, "local organizations cannot continue to be considered agencies that just mobilize public resources. Rather, they must be viewed as able concerns that will manage the entire development process" (National Conference of State Legislatures, 1991, p. v).

Most important, *governmental officials should learn that the partnership with CBDOs involves a process and not just a project.* CBDOs use physical development as a lever for community economic empowerment, to encourage reconstruction in areas that others have abandoned. The particular projects, whether building affordable housing, working with women to extend home-industries to the marketplace, or creating the psychological uplift of a new supermarket in an abandoned lot, differ from place to place and from time to time. To CBDOs, development is a bricks and mortar process, but development is also an ongoing process of building toward economic empowerment and community capacity.

Community-based development organizations are neither effervescent advocacy organizations nor passive, delivery systems for government programs. They understand the importance of fiscal responsibility, and balance it with response to social need. They are willing to experiment with economic projects that others fear to try and are proudest when they become the catalysts for community improvement. They are physical developers that live and die on the economic success of their projects. CBDOs are exposed to the vagaries of the market place; but they gain their sense of direction by maintaining their roots in communities of the poor. Small is beautiful, not for any abstract reason, but because only a small organization can find the gaps between social and physical needs and respond to the many demands in communities of the poor.

Community-based development organizations span the development and advocacy models (Rubin and Rubin, 1992) by fighting for the wherewithal to provide community members with economic empowerment. Their strength is in demonstrating the capacity of poor communities to create organizations that can succeed. Government has often been willing to accept CBDOs as delivery systems for services and products, but less often been willing to accept their role as system transformers. The former is easy to measure—homes built, facades improved—and constitutes no threat to the status quo. But community building is far more important. The real impact of CBDOs lies not in the number of housing units produced, but in the community's sense of pride and collective achievement, in the renewal of a sense of possibility. Development organizations with a firm community base are the wedge for entry into the communities of the deprived. Regenerating these communities physically and socially is a goal worth working toward.

The community-based development movement requires an empathetic city administration that recognizes that the movement requires nurturance not dominance. Public administrators should be willing to help CBDOs because their experimentation provides one hope for the renewal of the inner city. Government can help achieve these goals by listening carefully to the voices of those involved in the field.

NOTES

1. For example, local officials point out that federal housing funds under HOME could not be used to pay for administrative expenses of community-development agencies. Revisions in the Housing and Community Development Act of 1992 that resulted from lobbying by nonprofit housing agencies and advocates, now allow up to 5 percent of the HOME funds to be used for CBDO operating support.

2. A planning document required by the Department of Housing and Urban Development (HUD) before housing support is provided under the HOME program.

3. A state-wide referendum initiated by the nonprofit sector eliminated this restriction in Ohio.

4. CBDO directors reinforce this image. Like other nonprofits, CBDOs and local administrators contend over the degree of detailed contract monitoring and uniformity in service provision (Lipsky and Smith, 1990, p. 626). Additionally, CBDOs, like direct service providers, want to be selective in their choice of clientele whereas government is more interested in providing broader service (Lipsky and Smith, 1990, p. 635).

5. I have no way of judging the truth of the director's assertions. His group was successful and the projects a visible boost to the community. Yet, he felt awkward in his continuing negotiations with the city, an awkwardness he claimed grew out of the politics of race.

REFERENCES

Center for Community Change, 1992. *The HOME Program: A Brief Guide for Community Organizations.* Washington, D.C.: Center for Community Change.

Clavel, Pierre and Wim Wiewell, eds., 1991. *Harold Washington and the Neighborhoods: Progressive City Government in Chicago, 1983–1987.* New Brunswick, NJ: Rutgers University Press.

Dreier, Peter, 1989. "Economic Growth and Economic Justice in Boston: Populist Housing and Job Policies." In Gregory D. Squires, ed., *Unequal Partnership: The Political Economy of Urban Redevelopment in Postwar America.* New Brunswick, NJ: Rutgers University Press, pp. 35–38.

Emerson, Robert M., ed., 1983. *Contemporary Field Research: A Collection of Readings.* Prospect Heights, IL: Waveland.

Goetz, Edward G., 1992. "Local Government Support for Nonprofit Housing: A Survey of U.S. Cities." *Urban Affairs Quarterly,* vol. 27 (March), pp. 420–435.

Kelly, Christine K., Donald C. Kelly, and Edward Marciniak, 1988. *Non-profits with Hard Hats: Building Affordable Housing.* Washington, DC: National Center for Urban Ethnic Affairs.

"Key changes to HOME will benefit CDCS." 1992. *Development Times,* vol. 1 (5), p. 1.

Lipsky, Michael and Steven Smith, 1990. "Nonprofit Organizations, Government and the Welfare State." *Social Science Quarterly,* vol. 104, pp. 625–648.

National Conference of State Legislatures, 1991. *Breaking New Ground: Community-based Development Organizations.* Denver: National Conference of State Legislatures.

National Congress for Community Economic Development (NCCED), 1991. *Changing the Odds: The Achievements of Community-based Development Corporations.* Washington, D.C.: National Congress for Community Economic Development.

Peirce, Neil R., and Carol F. Steinbach, 1987. *Corrective Capitalism: The Rise of America's Community Development Corporations.* New York: Ford Foundation.

_____, 1990. *Enterprising Communities: Community-based Development in America.* Washington, D.C.: Council for Community Based Development.

Rubin, Herbert J., 1983. *Applied Social Research.* Columbus, OH: Merrill.

_____, 1993. "Community Empowerment Within an Alternative Economy." In Dennis Peck and John Murphy, eds., *Open Institutions: The Hope for Democracy.* New York: Praeger, pp. 99–121.

_____, 1992. "Renewing Hope in the Inner City: Conversations with Community Based Development Practitioners." Paper presented at the 22d Annual Meeting of the Urban Affairs Association. Cleveland, April/May.

Rubin, Herbert J. and Irene S. Rubin, 1992. *Community Organizing and Development,* 2d ed. Columbus, OH: MacMillan (Merrill).

Schorr, Alvin L., ed., 1991. *Cleveland Development: A Dissenting View.* Cleveland: David XPress.

Spradley, James P., 1979. *The Ethnographic Interview.* New York: Holt.

Stephenson, Max O., 1991. "Whither the Public-Private Partnership: A Critical Overview." *Urban Affairs Quarterly,* vol. 27, pp. 109–127.

Suchman, Diane R., D. Scott Middleton, and Susan Giles, 1990. *Public/Private Housing Partnerships.* Washington, DC: Urban Land Institute.

Vidal, Avis C., 1992. *Rebuilding Communities: A National Study of Urban Community Development Corporations.* New York: Community Development Research Center, Graduate School of Management and Urban Policy, New School for Social Research.

Chapter 7

Business Improvement Districts

ED HENNING

Cities throughout California are rediscovering one of the most viable methods of financing business district programs, activities and improvements; namely, Business Improvement Districts or "BIDS" as they are often dubbed. From El Centro to Crescent City there is considerable interest in this unique assessment mechanism which can fund an exciting array of activities ranging from farmer's markets, art festivals and street fairs to beautification projects such as banners, holiday decorations and landscape planters, to urgently needed services such as added security or maintenance. Once considered synonymous with downtowns, BIDs are now being considered in the funding of varied programs and improvements for auto rows, tourist and entertainment centers and citywide marketing and promotions. In a time of dwindling resources, BIDs remain one of the most valuable and effective finance tools available.

BIDs have been in use for nearly three decades in California with an estimated 150 BIDs in place and dozens more being formed or contemplated. A BID can be defined as a type of assessment district in which business owners are assessed a mandatory fee by the local government agency (city or county) to fund predetermined business-related activities and improvements which will benefit the assessed businesses. By pooling private business resources, BIDs are able collectively to pay for activities which would not be possible on an individual basis.

BIDs have many inherent advantages when compared to other funding alternatives.

- BIDs are, technically speaking, relatively simple to establish. Very few local documents are required—a resolution, an ordinance and an agreement.
- BIDs are one of the most flexible funding tools available in that they can, by

Reprinted with permission from *Western City*, Vol. LXIX, No. 8, August, 1993. Published by the League of California Cities, Sacramento, California.

law, fund a vast array of activities, programs and improvements ranging from business promotions to parking to maintenance.

- BIDs can be easier "to sell" than other forms of assessments and taxes in that they are structured on an annually renewable, "pay as you go" basis without incurring long-term debt.
- BIDs require minimal government involvement and typically allow for a large degree of programmatic and administrative control by those paying the assessments.
- BIDs are usually associated with very visible and tangible program elements which, in turn, can produce very colorful and exciting business enhancing results.

The Importance of BIDs in the 90s

In light of ongoing state economic woes, cities and redevelopment agencies are experiencing depleted project and operation budgets which historically funded business district-related services and activities. Programs are being eliminated, projects are being shelved, and levels of service are being reduced.

Coupled with this, the stalled economy is creating much tougher competition among downtowns, malls, off-price centers and giant warehouse retailers. Today there is a much greater need to market goods and services aggressively and create physical environments and services comparable to the competition. Business districts everywhere must work harder and smarter just to capture their proportionate marketplace share.

In addition, with an increased awareness of social issues such as crime (swindlers, armed robberies, carjackings, civil unrest) and environmental concerns (littering, recycling, graffiti, landscaping), there is a greater perceived need by the public for supplemental downtown security and maintenance services.

Business districts are now finding that to survive and coexist in the myriad of competition, they cannot rely solely on the discretionary government funding or normal tax-supported programs and services. Business owners need to pool resources to fund independently, at least in part, vital activities, services and improvements. BIDs are a logical solution.

BID Legislation

BIDs in California date back to 1965 when AB 103, the "Parking and Business Improvement Area Law" was approved. The purpose of this law was to allow California cities to establish assessment districts on behalf of business owners to fund business district promotions, improvements and activities. This

---

BID TIDBITS

Average BID size .... 250 businesses
Average BID assessment range .... $150–$300/year
Average BID budget $60,000
Largest BID .... Downtown Stockton
                                         (1047 businesses)
Smallest BID .... Huntington Beach
                                         Auto Dealers (10)
Northernmost BID .... Crescent City
Southernmost BID .... Chula Vista
City with the most BIDs .... San Diego (11)

Source: California Downtown Association Sample Survey

---

legislation was initiated by various "volunteer" downtown associations in search of a more stable funding source which would allow downtowns to compete more effectively with their counterpart mall and shopping center marketing associations.

Under the leadership of the California Downtown Association, a statewide professional organization representing over 100 downtowns, the law was rewritten in 1978 as AB 1693 and again in 1989 as SB 1424; first to convert BIDs from a "tax district" to a "benefit assessment district" and the second time to reinforce the benefit assessment relationship. While BIDs have faced numerous judicial challenges over the years, the courts have upheld the legality and appropriateness of the basic benefit assessment concept each time. The current BID enabling law appears as Section 36500 of the California Streets and Highway Code.

Establishing a BID

A BID is typically initiated by local business owners desirous of promoting their business area and making certain area-wide improvements. Interested business owners can request or petition their city to establish a BID on their behalf. The business owners can work either through an existing business district organization, if applicable, or as a new independent committee. The committee should have a city representative for continuity and may choose to retain an outside consultant to assist with the development of an annual program, annual budget, boundaries, benefit zones and an assessment formula. The committee should attempt to gain support of the BID concept from as many affected business owners as possible. This can be done through mailers and/or informal workshops prior to beginning formal hearings at the City Council level.

The adoption process begins with approval of a resolution of intention by the city council. A copy of the BID proposal and resolution is sent to all affected businesses. Two public hearings are conducted by the city council. While the highest percentage of BID support is desired, the city council may approve the BID establishment by ordinance following the public hearings, provided written protests are not received from business owners who will represent 50 percent or more of the total assessments to be collected. Thus, while not mandatory, it is desirable going into the public hearing to have support of the BID concept from business owners who represent a majority of the proposed BID assessments.

Once the BID is in place, benefit assessments are levied and collected by the city, usually on an annual basis and often in conjunction with the collection of business license taxes, although they cannot be commingled. Assessments collected are typically remitted to a third party nonprofit entity such as a chamber of commerce or a merchants association. A two-party agreement is developed which stipulates the responsibilities of each, the city and the nonprofit. While a nominal administrative fee is sometimes retained by the city to offset collection costs, these expenses are often absorbed by the city as a matching service contribution to the BID.

BID Mechanics

BID boundaries are scribed around a geographic area which includes all businesses expected to derive benefit from the activities and improvements to be funded by the assessments. Within the overall boundaries, subareas or zones may be established which reflect varying conditions, settings or land-use patterns which, in turn, could affect the level of benefit derived by respective businesses.

The BID assessment formula typically incorporates three factors which affect the amount of assessment to be paid: type, size and location. A sample formula may classify businesses into three types: retail, service/restaurant, and professional/all other. This will vary from one BID to another depending on the specific programs and improvements to be funded and the projected level of benefit to be derived by the various business types.

Business size may be determined by any number of parameters such as number of employees, length of business frontage, business square footage or gross business sales. While gross sales was at one time the most common factor used, it tends to be problematic due to confidentiality rules related to disclosure of private business sales and income data. Number of employees is the most common factor used today due to its ease of computing and reporting.

The BID formula can be further augmented by business location or benefit zone placement.

Under the original 1965 BID law (AB 103), assessments were exclusively computed as multipliers or surcharges on business license fees. While this was a simple concept for calculating assessments, over time, it presented several problems. Some cities did not require business licenses, and it was unclear how they could impose a surcharge in the form of a BID. Also, certain businesses such as banks, savings and loans and insurance sales offices are precluded by state law from paying local taxes, which a business license fee is, but a BID assessment is not. This created confusion and inconsistencies from city to city.

Finally, following the enactment of Proposition 13 in 1978, the approval process for establishing a new tax became quite different from that required for a benefit assessment; i.e., two-thirds voter approval required for a new tax versus a "51 percent majority protest" for an assessment. State BID law was then modified in 1978 and again in 1989 to stipulate that a BID fee is a benefit assessment and not a tax. Formulas which continue to associate BID fees with city business license fees (taxes) can lead to numerous complications and challenges. Most BIDs established today use an assessment formula completely independent of city business license tax rates. Many cities using older formulas have amended and updated their BID formulas, eliminating affiliations with business license rates.

BID assessments are unique in that they are levied directly on business owners within a prescribed area rather than on property owners as is done in all other assessment districts. BID assessments are levied on businesses on the basis of relative benefit from the improvements and activities to be funded and defined in the state law as follows:

"Improvements" means the acquisition, construction, installation, or maintenance of any tangible property with an estimated useful life of five years or more including, but not limited to, parking facilities, benches, trash receptacles, street lighting, decorations, parks, or fountains.

"Activities" means, but is not limited to, all of the following:

1. Promotion of public events which benefit businesses in the area and which take place on or in public places within the area.
2. Furnishing of music in any public place in the area.
3. Activities which benefit businesses located and operating in the area.

Sample BID Programs and Activities

BID-funded organizations are associated with some of the more creative and successful business district activities around the state. Examples include the internationally acclaimed Thursday Night Farmer's Market and BBQ in San

Luis Obispo; American Graffiti Weekend in Modesto; Summer Arts and Crafts Street Festival in Whittier; Art & Wine Harvest Festival in Napa; Heritage Days in Pleasanton and the Tomato Festival in Fairfield. Eligible BID activities and improvements would include:

PROMOTION PROGRAMS
• Promotions/special events
• Holiday programs/promotions
• Farmers markets
• Street fairs/Parades
• 5/10 K runs/Bike races

PUBLIC RELATIONS/
MARKETING PROGRAMS
• Business retention/attraction programs
• Restaurant guide/Shopping directory
• Linkage with hotel/tourist/convention bureaus

MEMBER SERVICES/PROGRAMS
• New business orientation/welcome
• Business development
• Display/merchandise seminars
• Property owners forum
• Professional members forum

• Communications (newsletter, directory, etc.)
• Office w/professional staff

PUBLIC IMPROVEMENT/
BEAUTIFICATION PROJECTS
• Trees/landscaping/flowers
• Street furniture/decorative lighting
• Street/sidewalk/crosswalk improvements
• Parking expansion/upgrading
• Banners/flags/public art
• Holiday decorations/displays/lighting/music

PUBLIC SERVICES
• Streetscape/parking area maintenance
• Centralized trash pickup
• Common awning/window cleaning
• Police "foot patrol"/private security guards
• Graffiti removal
• Transit/shuttle bus systems

A sampling of some specific BID applications are as follows:

Grass Valley—Nevada County Waiters Race. Waiters and waitresses from local eateries compete for a cash prize and the title of "best waiter in Nevada County." They begin by uncorking a bottle of wine and pouring it into two wine glasses and then race up Mill Street in Historic Grass Valley balancing the tray laden with the wine bottle and two full wine glasses. The first to finish with all items still standing wins the heat. Elimination heats are run for a final championship race. This event is tied in with showing of Draft Horses and a three-hour "hot deals" sales promotion.

Bakersfield—Turkey Bowling Tournament. In conjunction with a Thanksgiving promotion, a turkey bowling tournament was held. Full two-liter soda bottles were the pins; frozen turkeys were the "bowls." Rules identical to regulation bowling were followed. Gutter balls were considered "fowl bowls." Some inexperienced participants had to "wing it" while veteran players seemed to "have a leg up" on the competition. Prizes awarded included Thanksgiving turkeys as well as other food prizes.

Los Gatos — Passport to Holiday Shopping. The passport program offered customers the chance to win various prizes including a grand prize European vacation for two. A validation stamp and ink pad were the primary tools used by Los Gatos merchants to invite customers into their business establishments during November and December. Window posters indicated participating merchants. Every "passport" form validated by a merchant was entered into the drawing at the end of the promotion.

Whittier — Farmers Market. Due to overwhelming success, this effort recently has been expanded to a second day. Held each Tuesday evening and Friday morning, the market features many food items not found in local supermarkets. Rare items include mini-watermelons, Chinese garlic, a hybrid apple variety crossing an Empire with a Northern Cross, sweet miniature corn and cranberry beans. Patrons walk in the sun and talk directly to the person who grows the produce.

Santa Ana — Fiestas Patrias De Independencia. This is the biggest annual downtown celebration in observance of the independence of six Latin American countries from which many of Santa Ana's residents emigrated. This three-day event features 100 + booths for local merchants, nonprofits and many of the government center offices. The Golden City Grand Prix Bicycle Race and Parade is held during the Fiesta.

Davis — Downtown Business Directory. A very colorful and informative downtown directory was developed featuring a categorical listing of all downtown merchants and services as well as a downtown map showing streets, points of interest and public parking locations. A companion directory featuring all professional businesses was also developed.

San Luis Obispo — Window Display Contest. In conjunction with the spring La Fiesta event, Cal Poly fashion merchandising students developed a promotional strategy, store layouts, window displays, merchandising plans, and print and broadcast ads for participating downtown merchants. The merchants provided a budget and all display materials and props. The promotion gave students hands-on real-world design experience and provided merchants with the opportunity to tap into creative local talent. Results were judged by the Downtown Beautification Committee with prizes awarded to the winning designers. Merchants "win," too, by garnering valuable publicity.

Pasadena (South Lake Avenue) — Streetscape Improvements. The South Lake Avenue Business Association funded the installation of numerous supplemental theme streetscape elements including park benches, trash receptacles, bike racks, entry monument signs, news rack enclosures, tree well covers, median island landscaping and street trees. Maintenance of many of these elements was also funded.

Huntington Beach — Auto Dealers Freeway Sign. The Huntington Beach Auto Dealers Association with the assistance of the city funded the installation of a large freeway-oriented reader board/identification sign at the entrance to the "Boulevard of Cars." The city advanced the funds while ten auto dealers pay monthly BID fees into a trust fund which will cover city costs not recouped from projected increased auto sales tax revenue as a result of the sign installation. Additional BID funds pay for auto dealer promotions and advertising.

Buena Park — Entertainment Corridor Improvements. The city and various entertainment-related businesses in this unique corridor adjacent to Knotts Berry Farm are exploring the use of a BID to fund landscape and streetscape improvements, ongoing maintenance, a freeway-oriented reader board sign advertising the "Entertainment Corridor" and related marketing activities.

Huntington Park — Supplemental Security and Maintenance. The city and the Chamber of Commerce are considering the use of a BID to fund additional downtown security and maintenance services in what is considered one of the most successful Hispanic shopping districts in Southern California. The area was affected by the L.A. riots, and the proposed supplemental services are intended to reinforce the area's viability and attractiveness.

Rosemead — Citywide Marketing and Promotions. The city and the Chamber of Commerce are considering the use of a BID to fund citywide business marketing activities which can no longer be funded by volunteer Chamber dues and fundraisers. A primary thrust of the program will be targeted to city residents in a "Shop Rosemead First" campaign. A directory of locally available goods and services is proposed.

The Future of BIDs

Business Improvement Districts have been a major force in the resurgence and revitalization of California's historic downtowns over the past three decades. BIDs have proven to be invaluable in both troubled and prosperous times. The concept that all benefiting business owners pay a fair share to pool their resources, rather than depending on a few benevolent volunteers, continues to make sense today and well into the future.

While BIDs have typically been associated with promotional type activities in downtown business areas, a departure from this traditional application is occurring. BIDs are being established along declining nonhistoric commercial boulevards. They are also being considered more for citywide applications to fund general economic development and regional marketing activities. Also, BIDs are being applied to specialized business groups with specialized common needs such as "auto rows," entertainment attractions, and tourist-related businesses. There is also greater demand to fund supplemental public services such as security and maintenance. Interest is also being shown to establish BIDs in areas being rebuilt following natural disasters as well as civil unrest. The popularity of BIDs can be attributed to their versatility and simplicity.

Challenges lie ahead for all assessment districts as approval procedures face scrutiny in the wake of a deluge of new and increased special district fees, assessments and taxes over the past few years. All Californians are leery of additional fees and property taxes. As a result, some BIDs are facing stiff opposition during the formation stages and again during the annual renewal period. In spite of these challenges, BID formations are at an all-time high as new and unique BID applications are being considered for a variety of business-related activities and improvements. The business of Business Improvement Districts appears indeed to have a very bright future.

Chapter 8

Downtown Managers

LAWRENCE O. HOUSTOUN, JR.

More than 30 men and women from throughout the state participated in a meeting devoted to the subject of downtown management, following the Downtown New Jersey conference in Newark last December. From this start, the statewide nonprofit corporation devoted to improving the state's business districts hopes to develop a cadre of skilled professionals who can assist one another as they improve the centers of their individual communities.

Downtown management is a concept applied throughout the United States to districts as large as Manhattan's vast Grand Central area and as small as Salem, New Jersey's business center. According to Downtown New Jersey:

Downtown management is the system applied locally to maintain and enhance the economic vitality of business districts of any size. At minimum, a system requires a manager, a policy body, an assured annual source of funds and one or more year-round services or activities that benefit commercial centers.

While a downtown manager may be full- or part-time, he or she is the most essential component in a system. For decades, community volunteers have struggled with these civic chores in addition to their main business or other responsibilities. The product is more often frustration than revitalization. Volunteers work best when supported by professional managers. In every downtown, at least one skilled person must have time to concentrate on downtown issues and to assure that policies and priorities are attended to.

Increasingly, governments and nonprofit corporations when seeking downtown managers stress business-related skills over design skills, as was earlier the case. This in turn reflects a second look at downtown priorities in many localities where emphasis on landscaping and signs has been replaced with a sober analysis of what the major needs really are. Job descriptions recently stress proven ability to organize and manage services benefiting businesses and some are looking for retail-related experience. Because so many communities recognize

Reprinted with permission from *New Jersey Municipalities,* Vol. 67, No. 4, April, 1990. Published by the New Jersey State League of Municipalities, Trenton, New Jersey.

recognize the competitive advantage of shopping malls, some are beginning to seek this experience among prospective managers.

Managers work most effectively with a broad-based policy-making body supporting and guiding them. Such a body, which can be governmental or nongovernmental, also needs to have downtown as its number one focal point. Conflicts arise and priorities are hard to establish when such a body also has communitywide or regional concerns.

The policy body should be composed of those with demonstrated commitment to downtown improvement and should represent the major interests required in order to be influential within the community. Downtowns include a wide variety of interest groups which have a direct, usually financial, stake in improved business conditions. These include persons who own property as well as those who use property for businesses and in some cases for residences. Even fairly small downtowns have lending institutions, professional offices and restaurants, as well as conventional retailing. Nonprofit interests may include hospitals and cultural facilities. Public sector interests include parking agencies and local economic development officials. Even consumers may have a role to play in rebuilding downtown economies. While the precise mix varies with the locality, successful downtown management requires participation through the policy entity of major stakeholders, such as these. Although it is advisable to draw from a wide range of nonprofit and governmental representatives for the policy body, the principal leadership should rest with the business community to assure that the commercial character of the system is sustained. The organization also needs to be able to exclude members from a decision when, as occasionally occurs, their personal or business interests conflict with downtown's interests.

Downtown management requires an assured source of funds. Not only must the manager be paid, but the downtown entity must be able to make commitments for essential services and other activities. Through the United States, communities are increasingly relying on what New Jersey calls "special improvement districts" as a means of assuring financing that is equitable and has the character of self-help. That is, the commercial interests within the district should bear all or most of the cost of the services that are designed to enhance commerce. New Jersey law authorizes a wide variety of property tax related financial systems and or a licensure alternative. A few communities have sufficient business support that they can depend on for multiyear contributions. Typically, however, this source of financial support produces less money with the passage of time.

The range of services that may be applied is limited only by the imagination and financial resources applied to the district's most urgent needs. The State's District Management Act, for example, identifies almost 20 authorized activities, including the following:

1. Fund the improvement of the exterior appearance of properties through grants or loans;
2. Fund the rehabilitation of properties;
3. Accept, purchase, rehabilitate, sell, lease, or manage properties;
4. Provide security, sanitation or other services supplemental to those provided normally by the municipality;
5. Undertake improvements to increase the safety or attractiveness of the district to business that may wish to locate there or to visitors. This may include litter cleanup and control, landscaping, parking, and recreational and rest areas;
6. Pubicize the district and its businesses;
7. Recruit new businesses;
8. Organize special events;
9. Provide special parking arrangements;
10. Provide decorative lighting;
11. Adopt and apply design criteria for signs and facades on privately owned buildings.

These authorities suggest the wide range of activities that may be undertaken whether or not a municipality applies the State District Management Act. To show how these have been applied in New Jersey localities, here are some examples.

The most evident business need in downtown New Brunswick was improvements in the supply and price of parking. The foundation for this set of reforms began with the appointment of the Parking Authority's manager to the board of New Brunswick City Market, Inc., the downtown policy body. Subsequent parking changes included the following: adjusted rates favoring shopper use over daily use by commuters; construction of a new parking garage; installation of parking location signs throughout the business district and especially at its entryways; and two hours of free parking for shoppers and diners. The latter, a validation program, has been widely promoted as an attraction for shoppers and merchants. The cost is shared by City Market, using its special improvement district funds.

Elizabeth's historic Midtown Special Improvement District is financing retail promotions and the creation of sign and facade design standards. Newark has orchestrated a project by which the downtown skyscrapers are lighted to help reestablish the area's visibility. Salem helped sponsor a rehabilitation project which will restore a handsome old commercial structure which has attracted the County College as anchor tenant. Englewood organizes and subsidizes advertising. The Summit Chamber of Commerce runs a highly successful direct mail campaign for its retailers. Some of these projects are supported by contributions and others by assessments.

Both Englewood and Trenton operate supplementary downtown cleanup systems and New Brunswick is supporting a supplementary security force. Both are applying the self-help district taxation feature of the state law. The statute prohibits use of district funds to make up for a cut in sanitation or police services. "Normal" services are expected to be continued. The law recognizes implicitly, however, that the standards of cleanup and security required of contemporary downtowns today exceed normal services. Thus, the Trenton Downtown Association operates its own street vacuum cleaners each morning and New Brunswick City Market contributes to the cost of a private security force which patrols the restaurant and cultural center areas after dark to assure their continued success.

The wide variety of manager skills, policy bodies, financing systems and services already represented among New Jersey municipalities has led Downtown New Jersey to encourage formation of a network of practitioners. Peter Beronio of the Englewood Economic Development Corp. is leading this effort. The group is preparing a list of technical assistance needs to which all those who are downtown managers or who aspire to become one may contribute suggestions.

Downtown New Jersey during its first two years has sponsored three statewide conferences, publishes a newsletter and recognizes special service to downtowns through an annual award program. Last year, five corporate leaders from throughout the state were recognized. In 1988, the awards went to Senator John Lynch and Assemblyman David Schwartz for their sponsorship of the District Management legislation.

Chapter 9

Public-Private Cooperation

BARBARA A. COE

Introduction

The City of Denver over the years has experienced its share of economic turbulence and of urban deterioration, as have most cities. In 1959, Denver's downtown business community formed an association called Downtown Denver, Inc. (DDI), to address downtown issues. The organization played a major role in establishing the Denver Urban Redevelopment Authority; the Auraria Higher Education Complex; and the Sixteenth Street Mall.

By the late 1970s, the city exhibited new problems, many of them stemming, ironically, from the success of its redevelopment program. Coupled with the demands for space of a then-vital energy industry, the redevelopment program had stimulated a proliferation of new high rise buildings. This created, in the views of many, a city of canyons with little aesthetic appeal and little public space. The city administration, under Mayor McNichols, had reduced the city's planning staff and was widely perceived as little interested in planning. Many in the business community were concerned about the likely effect of the lack of quality development on the continuing health of downtown.

Following twin tragedies—the severe illness of one and the accidental death of another director—Downtown Denver, Inc. reevaluated its ability to address contemporary problems. The board then reformed the organization, accompanied by extensive publicity, as a public-private partnership organization. It was to become a business leadership forum with a mission of working closely with government to address issues affecting downtown Denver and to coordinate planning and management of development. It was incorporated in March 1981, as the Denver Partnership, Inc.

4ry
Reprinted with permission from *The Western Governmental Researcher,* Vol. III, No. 1, Summer, 1987. Published by the Western Governmental Research Association, Long Beach, California.

The Denver Partnership

The Denver Partnership, Inc. has a unique structure. The Partnership itself is an umbrella organization designed to coordinate policy, with a board of about 100 that meets annually, and a Management Group that conducts the day-to-day policy business. Under it are two operating arms which actually do the work of the organization. One of them is the original membership association, Downtown Denver, Inc., which is now dedicated to political advocacy and downtown management. The other arm, Denver Civic Ventures, Inc. (DCV), is a charitable, public-purpose organization providing planning and development assistance for the downtown area. As a 501 (c) (3) organization, it is eligible to accept charitable contributions from foundations and corporations, giving it a capacity for revenue generation. These revenues must not be used for political activity, according to IRS rules, so activities of DCV must be kept clearly separate from those of DDI.

From the organization's perspective, the restructuring was indeed successful. Under the new structure, membership of Downtown Denver, Inc. grew to 400 from its 1980 membership of approximately 100. The budgets of both Downtown Denver, Inc. and Denver Civic Ventures grew to $3 million from the 1980 budget of $100,000. Staff grew from two and a half to a high of 26.

Perhaps as significantly, the organization's image was enhanced. Assisted by positive press coverage (some of this by such well-known syndicated columnists as Neal Peirce), and newsletters and other publications presenting the organization as polished, professional, newsworthy, and the focus of downtown action, the organization attracted attention and membership. The new structure provided the means for expansion of planning and other activities. Among downtown organization leaders in this country, it came to be widely considered as one of the most effective downtown organizations.

Four Projects

The research for this article examined numerous projects, but reviewed in depth the characteristics, processes, and outcomes of four of the most salient policy planning projects conducted by the Denver Partnership. These were the Mall Management District, the Downtown Plan, Cherry Creek Shopping Center Alternatives Plan, and convention center planning.

Mall Management District

One of the principal successes of the organization was the establishment of the "Sixteenth Street Mall." This included a transit/pedestrian retail mall, with active participation by the original Downtown Denver, Inc., (in partnership with the Regional Transportation District); and mall and downtown management through a Mall Management District administered by DDI. The mile-long mall is the spine of downtown, connecting Broadway near the Civic Center to the transit station at Market Street. The primarily retail-oriented Mall is bordered on one side by the financial district. It is popular, attracting, by 1984, 50,000 pedestrians and 40,000 shuttle bus riders daily. On many clear days throughout the year, groups gather at the benches, tables and chairs in the center island, dining, talking, resting, people watching, or just sunning.

When this mall was initially proposed (several versions have been proposed over the years), the local economy and building were lively. With growth had come traffic congestion, and the mall was considered to be a way to relieve the congestion. The opportunity seemed ripe for downtown improvements. The proposal aroused little opposition given that construction would be funded primarily by federal grants, and that most of the downtown property and business owners believed they would benefit.

One concern, expressed by Mayor McNichols, was the expected maintenance cost. To respond to this concern, DDI agreed to form a maintenance district of downtown owners, thus removing a major barrier to acceptance of the proposal.

Establishment of the district involved extensive networking and communication and an active leadership role by the business community. Downtown Denver, Inc. members communicated one-on-one with both the public sector and property owners, developing and enhancing the communication network among the stakeholders. They coordinated with government officials, including the Mayor, the City Council, and the Public Works Department. The latter was responsible for the establishment of the special district and for maintenance of city property. DDI circulated petitions and published notices in local newspapers and held informational meetings. The boundaries of the maintenance district were controversial. In order to move ahead, a decision was made to limit the district to a two-block wide area, but within a year to reassess it. The petition was supported by a majority of the involved property owners, but by only a narrow margin. After a year of operation, however, the proposed expansion was supported by property owners representing 72 percent of the property.

After formation of the District, Downtown Denver, Inc. then contracted with the District to provide management services, which initially included maintenance and policing and have since been expanded to include promotion and marketing. Virtually all those interviewed considered both the construction and the management of the Mall to be successful.

In the mall management district establishment, stakeholders were relatively few, limited generally to downtown property owners and to those directly involved in downtown management. With the exception of the City Public Works Department and the Regional Transportation District, a project co-sponsor, other organizations had few management responsibilities in the area, so turf conflicts regarding mall management were few. Furthermore, Downtown Denver, Inc. seemed the legitimate organization for these tasks, which seemed to fit clearly within its organizational mandate and within its geographic area of responsibility.

The goal of Downtown Denver, Inc. was clear. With most of the stakeholders to clearly benefit, the stakeholder group was relatively cohesive. Downtown Denver, Inc. members took an active and visible leadership role in establishing both the Mall and the District, working together and sharing leadership to accomplish the goal. The approach included extensive collaboration, networking, and communication.

Cherry Creek Shopping Center

The second project examined in this study was the Cherry Creek Alternatives Project. Proposed expansion of the Cherry Creek Shopping Center only three miles from downtown to a major regional shopping center (2 million square feet initially, followed by another 1 million later), office complex, and high-density residential area was viewed with alarm by the Denver Partnership Management Group. The center threatened to become a major competitor with downtown business and would create a major impact on residents of adjacent neighborhoods.

Taking a leading and adversarial role, the Denver Partnership initiated the formation of a task force, which ultimately included eighteen neighborhood groups, to consider the issue. The Denver Partnership commissioned an assessment of the impact of the development, which showed that the center could divert as much as $44,000,000 in sales receipts from downtown, and would negatively impact the neighborhood. Downtown Denver, Inc. then issued a press release critical of the proposed center. Both the developer and Mayor McNichols were displeased with the publicity. The Denver Partnership then commissioned consultants to prepare an alternative plan to present to the developer, but in the meantime, the proposed development seemed to be on hold.

About a year later, in 1985, it resurfaced. Over the course of the project's planning, several conditions had changed. The City was now experiencing declining revenues, which could be replaced by the retail dollars Cherry Creek would capture from the suburbs. To carry out its emphasis on planning, a new City administration had expanded its planning staff, thus limiting the planning role available to the Denver Partnership. This time, the City Planning Department worked closely with the developer and neighborhood groups to develop a plan acceptable to both, and did not formally involve the Denver

Partnership in the planning process. The resulting plan calls for a center somewhat reduced in scale, .9 million square feet of retail, a "high end" retail anchor, and a new parkway to at least partly accommodate increased traffic. For downtown business, this was an improvement over the original proposal, but would still mean substantial new competition.

The Cherry Creek project was less successful than the Sixteenth Street Mall project. In this situation, the stakeholders were numerous, including the owner, developer, neighborhoods, business owners, the City, the Denver Partnership, and residents near the area. Their interests were diverse, with some to lose and other to gain. The stakes were considerable, including the loss of downtown business, increased traffic and congestion, financial rewards for the developer and Cherry Creek shops, and shopping convenience for Denver residents.

The Denver Partnership was perceived to have a less than legitimate leadership role because the proposed development was beyond the geographic boundaries of downtown. The perception that the Denver Partnership's primary concern was its special interest, not neighborhood impacts as it indicated, was not conducive to development of mutual trust. The process used by the Denver Partnership was relatively closed, developing solutions in-house and then presenting them. Positions were generally communicated publicly by the president rather than by various business leaders, so widespread involvement was less visible, probably limiting the perceived strength and validity of the opposition to the proposal. Their communication of views through the one-way media channel, use of a confrontational approach rather than lobbying, collaboration, and communication with public officials and other stakeholders disturbed external stakeholders and led to future antagonism.

Proposed Convention Center

A plan for new convention facilities provided a third opportunity to review goal implementation by the Denver Partnership. In 1981, following a year-long discussion regarding the need for improved convention facilities, the Denver Partnership formed a Joint Convention Center Task Force, including leadership from the Convention and Visitor's Bureau, the Denver Chamber of Commerce, the Mayor's office, the City Council, the Denver Center for the Performing Arts, the *Denver Post,* and *Rocky Mountain News.* The group planned for a period of 18 months, holding more than 30 meetings. Because a public-private venture was considered desirable, the Task Force invited proposals from private developers. Of five proposals received, they recommended to the Mayor and City Council a developer who would construct a convention center, and as part of the arrangement, acquire the existing convention center for development.

The site was at Union Station, located in the Central Platte Valley. This is a vast, prime development area adjacent to downtown, largely undeveloped except for warehouses and railroad tracks. A new convention center at that site could be the catalyst for major redevelopment of the area. When the City Council began to negotiate with the developer concerning the terms of the agreement, however, negotiations fell apart amid allegations of collusion with the Denver Partnership leadership, and of financial instability of the developer. The project was widely seen as too heavily driven by the Denver Partnership representing business interests.

A second task force was then initiated by Mayor Pena with representatives from the City Council and the Mayor's office, the Convention and Visitor's Bureau and the Denver Chamber of Commerce, but excluding the Denver Partnership. After this task force's recommendation was presented and the City Council began its deliberations, the project again became highly controversial. Critics protested that the project would primarily benefit the interests of lower downtown businesses, while leaving taxpayers with the tab, a tab which they felt could run much higher than indicated. Several councilmembers demanded voter approval of the project. Upper downtown business interests, whose property values could be harmed by massive development at the opposite end, led a petition drive to force a special election regarding the proposal. After the special election was set, convention center proponents, including nearly every civic organization in the City, spent over $600,000 to promote the center, primarily with television ads, while opponents spent about one sixth that amount. Nevertheless, to the surprise and chagrin of the business community and city hall, the proposed convention center was defeated by a two to one margin, involving the largest voter turnout in any special election.

The convention center project seemed to be the least successful of the projects, given the sound defeat it received by the voters. In this situation, stakeholders were numerous and diverse: they included taxpayers citywide as well as downtown property owners, elected and appointed officials, and civic organizations concerned with the city's well-being. In spite of the project's salience to many stakeholders, however, the planning involved a narrow group, primarily the business community. The planning processes employed by both convention center task forces were relatively closed, with little input from ordinary citizens, and were characterized by a perception that the business community was manipulating the process. The Denver Partnership was seen as a legitimate participant in the issue but as one of many special interests in a situation affecting all citizens. Few individual business leaders from the Denver Partnership were highly visible in the process, even through the promotional phase. The convention center was promoted through an expensive media campaign, not a two-way communication process. At this stage, the business community's interest was perceived as more selfish than civic, and the media campaign did little to help build widespread support.

Downtown Plan

"Imagine a great city," was the campaign theme that helped Federico Pena become mayor of Denver in 1983. His election was viewed by the Denver Partnership leadership as a step forward, because of his strong pro-plannning stance. His theme was the catalyst needed to generate broad support for a major downtown plan. Such a plan, which had long been discussed by the Denver Partnership, was seen as an opportunity to build upon the success of the Mall and to bring the notions of public space and good design to the entire downtown. Another organization, the Urban Design Forum, helped to stimulate public interest and excitement by asking the public for creative ideas to help make Denver a "great city."

The timing was right for an exciting new planning effort. A recent internal evaluation of the Denver Partnership had identified the need for more focus, as well as the need to develop better relationships with other organizations. The economy was changing: the declining energy industry, overbuilding, and increased suburban commercial and retail construction had led to downtown vacancy rates of 25 percent. The revenues of the Denver Partnership were suffering: federal funds were scarcer, and contributors and members found it more difficult to participate because of their declining revenues. Both Downtown Denver and the Denver Partnership needed a shot in the arm if they were to retain their central roles.

The city's renewed interest in planning suggested that further planning by the Denver Partnership would need to be in partnership. After several months of negotiating, the Denver Partnership and the city established a joint venture to develop the downtown plan. The Denver Partnership embarked upon a major fund-raising effort to generate the estimated $2 million of foundation and corporate support estimated to be needed for the planning project, which would be primarily privately funded.

Because implementation of the plan was a major concern, Denver Civic Ventures suggested an innovative, collaborative process. Consequently, a 29-member steering committee was established with members from most of the major institutions concerned with downtown Denver. The group met about every two weeks for 18 months. The Steering Committee guided policy and design work by the Denver Civic Ventures staff to produce a framework plan addressing the major issues. The Steering Committee first identified 189 issues of importance, then reduced them to a list of five which incorporated many of the original 189: retail; connections between nodes and districts; access; districts; and transition zones.

The general public was invited to attend public meetings and regular steering committee meetings, and to visit the project planning center. On several occasions, the public was invited to respond to Steering Committee products.

The resulting concept plan was ambitious and exciting. It envisioned a new ringroad, a new transitway, a new transit mall intersecting the Sixteenth Street Mall, new pedestrian-only streets, a galleria with below-surface pedestrian walkways, and plazas, parks, and streetscaping. The plan also stressed the importance of Denver's site at the confluence of two waterways (Cherry Creek and the Platte River), and suggested the enhancement of this important resource through landscaping, fountains, gathering places, and water channels along pedestrian paths throughout downtown.

So far, the planning process can be considered a success, although projects have not yet been constructed. When it was presented to the City Council and numerous interested groups by the Steering Committee and staff, it generally was viewed favorably. Perhaps more important was that the planning process involved many stakeholders in an active, not simply titular way. The extent to which it is implemented obviously depends upon public and private financial ability as well as the extent to which implementors, both public and private, actually accept the ideas at the individual project level.

The downtown planning process used a collaborative approach. In this project, as in the two previous successful projects, stakeholders were numerous and their interests diverse. Few had reason, however, to oppose the preparation of such a plan—although the salience of the plan varied among the participants, producing varying levels of commitment. The design of the process, which involved virtually all the stakeholders, minimized turf battles over who should actually prepare the plan. The Denver Partnership was considered a legitimate leader in the process, paticularly in concert with the City. The approach was relatively straightforward and the goal relatively clear, although some interviewees expressed concern over perceived manipulative tactics. The openness of the planning process to the public allowed many participants to be involved at some level and to therefore support its purpose and outcome. The collaborative planning process produced a plan that is essentially a creation of all the participants. Its production meant extensive networking, communication, and the active and visible involvement of both business and civic leaders. The plan is therefore "owned" by them and more likely to be readily implemented than if the process were more unitary, elitist, or exclusionary.

Summary of Project Implementation Characteristics

The four projects discussed above were examined in depth to understand processes, relationships, and outcomes. Comparing the projects using matrix analysis and flow charts as well as narrative revealed the differences and similarities in both their contexts and their approaches. Each of the projects examined is complex, with numerous political and economic factors influencing their outcomes, and cannot easily be reduced to a few variables. But the goal of the research was to identify management processes that could assist in goal implementation success, given the complexities of the arena, not to assess which of all the possible variables were most significant in the outcome of particular projects.

The most successful of the projects, namely the Mall Management District establishment and the downtown plan preparation, involved relative openness and collaboration. In each case, the Denver Partnership goal was relatively straightforward, clear, and limited in scope. And in each case, leadership, was widely spread; stakeholders were urged to take active roles in the processes. Both projects included extensive two-way communication, including active and visible business leadership and involving most of the stakeholders throughout.

By comparison, projects that were less successful involved differences in the interorganizational management style and processes used by the Denver Partnership. In each of the less successful instances, the process was less open and collaborative. Participation in the processes was generally limited to those with similar views and interests. Business leadership was not particularly visible; rather the president was the primary spokesman. Neither of the projects was characterized by broad networking, communication, or relationship-building with political and citizen stakeholders, even though coalitions were established with various like-minded organizations. Communication often used a one-way media channel, limiting the opportunity for additional stakeholders to either provide information or to "own" the solutions.

Views of Successful Goal Implementation in the Public-Private Partnership

A second major part of the research leading to this article was the interviewing of top leaders in this arena to learn what they considered to be the key elements of policy implementation success. Forty community leaders from both the Denver Partnership organization and organizations working closely with the Denver Partnership supplemented document review and observation in providing information about implementation activities. In addition, these interviewees, plus officials of four other of the highest-regarded downtown organizations, reported their views of requirements for successful goal implementation in this type of public-private partnership arena. The results of those interviews were aggregated and are summarized below. This research emphatically supported the role of collaboration and openness in successful goal implementation in the public-private partnership.

Virtually all those interviewed stressed the need for focus, avoiding provincialism but not overreaching geographically. The tasks should be confined to those which financial resources, staff time, and broad attention are capable of supporting. The organization should keep its own mission clear and should not intrude into the areas of others' responsibility but accept these and work within that context.

Leadership was considered by interviewees to be a necessary attribute of the organization, in order for it to successfully initiate and carry out goals. Respondents outside the Denver Partnership indicated that such an organization is most successful, however, when leadership is widely shared, with others having an opportunity to lead and to receive recognition and credit for their efforts. Also, respondents thought that when the business leaders themselves take active and visible roles, the credibility and legitimacy of the organization, both essential to successful implementation, are enhanced. They emphasized the importance of a "reasoned" leadership style, avoiding arrogance or "muscle power," which is more likely to alienate than to enlist cooperation. Interviewees indicated that when the leaders are sensitive to the political process, working openly with the elected and appointed officials rather than being manipulative or Machiavellian, the public officials are more cooperative. They indicated that because accomplishments occur in partnership, strengthening relationships with others in the system is essential. Lobbying, building relationships, and working jointly on solutions are ways to enhance relationships.

The interviewees stressed the need for widespread communication and networking in implementing their goals, to purposefully communicate with a variety of stakeholders and cultivate strong relationships with officials of public agencies, and with both "non-traditional" and "traditional" groups, including neighborhood groups and citizens. They indicated the need to be sensitive to other organizations' constituencies and areas of responsibility and to publicly recognize others' contributions. Development of mutual trust and respect was indicated to be integral to effective relationships. Avoiding heavy-handedness and alienating other groups is essential to implementation success.

A collaborative, multi-organizational team approach to first identifying problems and then developing solutions was indicated to be important to success. Team efforts could take a variety of forms, including task forces, meetings or informal discussions with city agencies or other organizations, organization officials, neighborhood groups, and citizens. Openness of the processes to the media and to the public helped to dispel suspicion. The goal formulation process was considered most effective when honest and open to new solutions rather than an attempt to persuade others to adopt a pre-established solution.

For goal implementation, the most important variable seemed to be the goal formulation process itself. Although interviewees indicated they used common political practices such as alliance and coalition-building, lobbying, and mailings to help influence implementation, working closely with others at the solution development stage was very important, if not critical, to later successful implementation, because those who formulated solutions were then responsible for implementing them.

Open Focus: An Approach to Goal Implementation in the Public-Private Partnership, a Metaorganization

From these findings, the Open Focus model, a conceptual model of goal implementation success in this metaorganization arena, was derived. As an ideal model, in the tradition of Max Weber,[1] it shows what can be. It is a composite, combining the attributes of successful goal implementation indicated by the various sources, rather than simply presenting a picture of one existing organization or situation.

The public-private partnership operates in an exceedingly complex interorganizational arena, which includes a collection of numerous stakeholders, public and private organizations, informal groups, and individuals who have a stake or interest in decisions that affect them. They include public and private sector managers, employees and board members, elected officials, citizen and civic interest group members, and interested individuals. This arena could be called a "metaorganization." In most situations, partnerships must rely for implementation upon the various governmental agencies possessing implementation authority. The requirements of public decision-making are often at odds with the relatively rationalistic private sector view of the decision-making process. The partnerships themselves are likely to be fragmented, comprised as they are of representatives of many varied groups and viewpoints.

The metaorganization is amorphous and dynamic, reforming itself depending upon the topic or issue at hand. Stakeholders hold diverse interests and values and their involvement and interest vary depending upon the salience of the issue to their mission and commitments. Players and involvement change over time as other issues and activities capture their attention.[2] Because the system is composed of many groups and individuals, no one organization or individual generally has overall hierarchical authority. Authority is often unclear or overlapping, and power is shared. As such, lateral influence is more relevant than is hierarchical authority.[3] The requirements for successful goal implementation in such an arena are likely to be quite different than in a more "traditional" situation.

The "open focus" conceptual model has four attributes. They include: the open focus attitude, linking communication, evocative leadership, and collaborative vision. The open focus attitude is a foundation that supports the other three components. It includes the following:

OPEN FOCUS ATTITUDE

- Focused awareness of the entire metaorganization
- A longer time perspective, rather than immediate
- Alertness to significant external and internal events and trends, and flexibility in adjusting to changes
- Willingness to include broad stakeholder involvement and leadership
- Openness to a wide range of alternatives that may be initiated
- Clarity about the organization's mission and focusing on that mission, rather than willy-nilly moving from task to task.

As an attitude or stance, the open focus model provides the foundation for the goal implementation processes to be effective. No matter how carefully crafted, management and leadership processes alone are insufficient unless supported by a congruent attitude. Otherwise, the underlying attitude shows through, damaging the organization's credibility. Clarity of purpose also helps to clarify the organization's intent to the outside world, thus reducing ambiguity and uncertainty.

LINKING COMMUNICATION

- Linking with numerous others in two-way communication, which then links networks with networks, building information and support
- Including all stakeholders who are members of formal organizations and influential groups[4]
- Also including informatl groups or the "horizontal" society, which has the potential to decisively influence a given issue[5]
- Using supportive communication: listening, accepting, descriptive, honest, non-manipulative and non-controlling.[6]

Linking communication increases the information flow in both directions, but also helps to establish credibility and shared values, which in turn aid in the development of solutions and decisions that are acceptable to a broad spectrum of stakeholders.

EVOCATIVE LEADERSHIP

- Capable, committed leaders to provide vision, direction, and follow-through
- Encouraging others to participate but also to lead[7]
- Expecting others to lead, allowing them latitude, encouraging, prodding, and publicly recognizing them
- Exhibiting a clear sense of direction but not closely controlling.

In the multi-organizational setting, particularly given severe resource limitations, effectively using all the resources, including leadership resources, can help assure that more is accomplished for the community.

COLLABORATIVE VISION

- Includes the full range of stakeholders in the problem-solving process
- Assumes that all have something valuable to offer

- Participants are open to the ideas of others
- Participants together develop and share information
- Participants bring a variety of visions, ideas and inventions, synergistically stimulating ideas as a group.

Collaboration enhances the development of shared goals and values, a comprehensive understanding of the issues, and the creativity of solutions. If they have genuinely participated in the decisions, they are likely to be committed to assuring their implementation.

Collaborative processes vary. Not every decision warrants a lengthy, involved, formal planning process. Some may simply require networking and two-way communication discussed earlier, relegating to or informing other stakeholders. They are often difficult because individuals zealously promote their own solutions[8] and some stakeholders feel threatened by the process, especially if it seems to infringe on their traditional power. More time is usually required to formulate goals. The process is not usually straightforward and linear, but messy and dynamic, and unrealistic expectations may be raised. In spite of the difficulties, however, collaborative vision can contribute significantly to successful plan implementation.

Summary

As an exploratory effort, this study cannot purport to represent a comprehensive, generalizable theory of goal implementation. As a conceptual model, however, it is the first step in the formulation of a theory of goal implementation in this public-private partnership "metaorganization." The in-depth study of one public-private partnership organization, supplemented by interviews with forty-four leaders within and outside of that city, indicated one overriding dominant theme: within this arena, collaborative and cooperative planning processes are key ingredients for successful goal implementation.

NOTES

1. Max Weber, *From Max Weber: Essays in Sociology,* H. H. Gerth and C. Wright Mills, trans. and eds. (New York: Oxford University Press, 1946), pp. 196–203.
2. James G. March and Johan P. Olsen, *Ambiguity and Choice in Organizations* (New York: Columbia University Press, 1982), p. 26.
3. Myrna P. Mandell, "The Multilateral Brokerage Role: Strategic Management in the Public Sector," unpublished paper, p. 16.
4. Committee for Economic Development, Research and Policy Committee, *Public-Private Partnership: An Opportunity for Urban Communities* (New York: Committee for Economic Development, 1982), p. 21.

5. James A. Kent and Donald C. Taylor, Foundation for Urban and Neighborhood Development, personal communication.

6. J. R. Gibb, "Defensive Communication," *Annual Journal of Communication*, 1961, pp. 141–148.

7. James McGregor Burns, "True Leadership," *Psychology Today*, October 1978, pp. 46–58, 110.

8. Jeffrey L. Pressman and Aaron Wildavsky, *Implementation: How Great Expectations in Washington Are Dashed in Oakland* (Berkeley: University of California Press, 1973), p. xvii.

III : The Process

Chapter 10

General Planning

VIRGINIA L. WOLF

Midwest Research Institute (MRI) has assisted communities across the United States in setting up their own economic development programs. MRI's experience has shown that the key factors of a successful economic development program are well-defined goals and objectives, a focused marketing effort, and people who can make the best use of available financial and technical assistance programs.

Although mid-size towns and metropolitan areas have been involved in this process for many years and are competing effectively with their counterpart communities across the nation, many smaller communities and rural areas have just recently become involved in economic development efforts. Largely as a result of the changing role of agriculture, many of these smaller communities have chosen to promote their area's economic development as a way to expand or diversify the local economic base. This article discusses the process that should be followed by a community wishing to start an economic development program. Based on MRI's long experience, the process is essentially the same, regardless of the size of the community.

The first step in the process is to establish an organization to lead the effort. To be effective, the organization must be broad based so as to have the best possible financial and resource support. It must include representatives of the following groups: chamber of commerce, civic groups, educational institutions, elected officials, existing industry, financial institutions, labor, media, retail sector, utilities, and interested citizens.

The first task of this organization will be to establish goals and objectives. Matters to consider are:

What does the group want for the community?

Are some forms of economic activity favored over others?

Are some types of industry not wanted in the community?

This organization must set a clear direction, and a group which is represented by all sectors is in the best position to provide this direction.

Reprinted with permission from *Missouri Municipal Review*, Vol. 51, No. 2, February, 1986. Published by the Missouri Municipal League, Jefferson City, Missouri.

The next step in the process is to conduct a resource assessment which identifies community factors that either positively or adversely affect industrial development. These factors include the existing industrial base, industrial sites and buildings, labor force, population, transportation, and utilities. The material developed during this phase of the analysis can be used in preparing promotional materials and documents relative to prospect marketing. Among the questions to be answered are the following:

What is the current profile of the community's population and labor force?

What industries currently exist in the community; and historically, how have they grown or declined?

What is currently being done to promote the central business district?

Are there specific resources, such as tourism or education, which make the community particularly attractive?

What does the community have to offer in terms of industrial sites and buildings?

Does the existing labor force match the needs of prospective business?

Can the city's physical infrastructure meet the requirements of new industry?

What were the successes and failures of past economic development programs?

If a community already has organizations formed for economic development purposes, they should be reviewed. Usually, in both large and small communities there are too many organizations to be effective because of their overlapping purposes and memberships. The goals and objectives of each existing organization should be reviewed and, if possible, a single organization formed to promote industrial development. A single organization whose sole purpose it is to promote industrial development will more likely make the best use of community resources.

Once a community has assessed its resources for promoting economic development, the next step is to identify those industries which show the best potential for locating in the community. This identification process, called a target industry analysis, provides a focus to marketing efforts and makes the best use of community resources. At a minimum, a community should examine its own industrial base, the industries of the county in which it is located, and those of surrounding counties. Personal calls should be made on major area manufacturers to ascertain their expansion plans, the location of their supplier industries, and industries which use their finished products. A list of the state's manufacturers who are new or who have expanded should also be reviewed to determine the types of manufacturers who are choosing to locate in the state.

MRI recently conducted a target industry analysis for the Missouri Division of Community and Economic Development. The end result of this study was the identification of industries best suited for locating in metropolitan, in mid-size, and in rural areas. This information should provide the basis for a Missouri community involved in targeting efforts.

The last step that a community takes in promoting its economic development is to formulate a development plan. This plan should include, at a minimum, strategies, identification of persons or groups responsible for implementation, and a timetable for implementation. Some general areas to be included in the plan are:

Marketing: A marketing program must be focused and consistent. It does not have to be elaborate. The use of local resources such as academic institutions, newspapers, or existing industry can often help provide technical assistance in the development of marketing materials.

Industry retention: An average of about 80 percent of all economic growth across the United States is attributed to the expansion of existing industry. Communities are only recently starting to put resources into this important activity. An active and effective retention program is not only beneficial to keeping existing business and industry in the local area, but also it serves as an attractor for generating new industry. These new industries will perceive the community as pro-industry.

Local incentives plan: Local incentives include the latitude the community has in using state development incentives such as property tax exemption or industrial revenue bonds. Also, a community can utilize special arrangements on land, buildings, and utilities. It is important to have an established plan so that when the community representative approaches a prospect, the incentives that are available can be discussed at initial meetings.

Technical assistance: Many communities, both large and small, tend to isolate themselves from resources provided by state economic development organizations, utilities, and railroads. This is a mistake since these organizations are in daily contact with prospects and can serve as an important resource for referrals.

This article has outlined an approach to the structuring of an effective industrial development program that MRI has found to be highly effective. Attracting development to a community is a time-consuming process which requires considerable support from the entire community and active involvement and commitment from local leaders. If the proper organizational structure is in place, and it includes people and organizations that are committed to the program's implementation, a well-designed program can succeed. A focused, coordinated industrial development program can result in considerable economic gain for the smaller community that is willing to pull together.

Chapter 11

Capital Planning

RITA J. BAMBERGER
WILLIAM A. BLAZAR
GEORGE E. PETERSON

If economic development is to be restored to a central place in thinking about infrastructure choices, the capital planning and capital budgeting process would have to change. In this chapter, we offer some suggestions for planning reform.

The capital plan, as Harvey Perloff has written, is a community's connection between its future and its present.[1] A community that has given thought to its plans for the future is likely to have a "comprehensive plan" that lays out the land uses and physical allocation of space for 15–20 years from now. It may also have a statement of economic goals, including the types of economic activity it intends to encourage and the types of jobs it hopes to create. The capital investment the community makes will be instrumental in determining the way it moves toward the future. Nothing in the public sector's power will have more influence on the pattern of the development than the location and special characteristics of its infrastructure investments, and few, if any, public decisions will be as influential in shaping the kind of economic activity the community can attract.

Captial planning, of course, must do more than prod a community toward realization of its long-term goals. It must provide for the continued day-to-day delivery of reliable water, wastewater, and transportation services and respond to today's demands for infrastructure help from industry, whether or not these fit into any coherent plan for future development. Indeed, though today's infrastructure investment will serve as a bridge to the future, however investment decisions are made, the deliberate use of the five- or six-year capital budget to *achieve* long-term development objectives is rare. As Perloff notes, it is more usual to find the long-term comprehensive plan languishing in isolation, without any real influence on today's decisions, while the capital budget

Reprinted with permission from *Planning Advisory Service Report*, No. 390, September, 1985. Published by the American Planning Association, Chicago, Illinois.

becomes a *de facto* accumulation of individual investment items. Even where a community makes long-term capital needs projections, it typically prepares for the future only in the sense of calculating how much it will cost and what infrastructure management actions must be taken to perpetuate the present arrangement of infrastructure facilities and economic activities.

It is not practicable to retool the entire capital planning process around economic development. It is practical, however, to alter the planning emphasis to give more importance to considering how infrastructure facilities will support economic activities in the future and how this support role can be sharpened. One device for strengthening the economic orientation is to involve the business sector in capital planning. Business leaders have a sense of the growth opportunities for the local economy. They have opinions about the obstacles to growth, including deficiencies in the capital plant. And they bring to capital planning the habit of evaluating projects according to their probable economic payoff. It is true that business leaders have their own perspective on the future. Their counsel should be balanced by citizen and community involvement in the planning process. But most of the successes in planning for economic development involve collaboration between government and business and have succeeded because the joint effort has required both parties to take a longer view than found in the ordinary negotiations between government and business over granting tax breaks or improving road access.

Articulating Development Goals

Most communities do not have clearly articulated economic development goals. If they do, these most often are couched in such generalities that they provide little guidance in setting capital investment priorities. Perhaps a community's most practical contribution to strengthening the link between infrastructure and economic development is to articulate local development objectives with some specificity and to begin to identify the infrastructure base that can support them. Sometimes a negative approach is the fastest route to specificity. If a community identifies those types of development it does *not* value highly enough to encourage through public sector subsidies, it can narrow the range of infrastructure projects it considers.

Some successful examples of goal articulation will help illustrate this process.

San Antonio. Mayor Henry Cisneros and his advisory task force of public and business leaders have set a clear goal for San Antonio: to become a national leader in information, scientific research, electronic, and other high-tech industries. Feasibility studies show this to be a realistic goal. Private investment resources have been committed. The mayor's program provides a framework into which the individual investment pieces, public or private, can fit. Although a large volume of public investment is not currently planned in support of the private telecommunications network the very fact that the public sector has a clear course of development, and has promised to expedite private investment as effectively as it can, commits it to evaluating public infrastructure proposals in light of the support they would lend to San Antonio's overall development goals.

The strength of this version of goal articulation lies in the forceful and consistent expression of San Antonio's direction of movement, which now shapes all public and private investment decisions.

San Jose. In the mid to late–1970s, San Jose's citizens and public leaders decided that the city did not want to develop further as a bedroom community for households holding jobs elsewhere. It wanted to balance its population growth with job growth.

The city then adopted a clear-cut infrastructure policy to support this development objective. It determined that private residential developers would be required to install, at their own expense, virtually all of the private facilities made necessary by residential population growth. Where expansion of existing public facilities was required, developers (and ultimately new home buyers) would be required to pay the full incremental cost of the addition to the infrastructure base. In contrast, the public sector agreed to construct, expedite, and sometimes subsidize the costs of infrastructure to support industrial parks or other sites that would provide commercial and industrial jobs.

This policy, in turn, led to the establishment of two different standards for evaluating the economic payoff to public investments. For infrastructure in support of residential development, the city mandates the standards for streets, schools, wastewater removal, etc., that private developers must meet. The economic analysis needs only to establish whether there is sufficient demand for housing to pay both for the new homes and the public facilities that must accompany them. Most of the burden of this calculation is placed upon the private developer. For infrastructure in support of industry and commerce, the economic analysis is conducted by public authorities. It requires a projection of the payoff to the community that will be realized in terms of jobs, tax base, and future economic growth.

The development goals and associated infrastructure policies were incorporated in San Jose's General Plan in 1975 as follows[2]:

> The city shall actively promote economic development through the provision of industry-supporting capital improvements, with appropriate financing, and the provision of a simplified project review process.
>
> The city shall encourage the development of new industrial areas and the redevelopment of existing older and marginal industrial areas though appropriate financing to provide necessary public improvements.
>
> New [residential] development must provide for its own basic services and

facilities, based on the standards established by the city, without placing additional burdens on the existing population.

Louisville. One of the clearest capabilities of the local capital budget is to make some local sites more attractive for development than others by endowing them with superior infrastructure facilities. Used judiciously, this power can steer development to areas where it serves public purposes and also can provide in advance for the expansion requirements of local industry. Such advance planning is likely to bring rewards; the literature on firms' locational choices clearly establishes that the firms most likely to move out of the city to suburban locations are fast-growing firms that run out of building space, room for site expansion, and infrastructure capacity at their present locations.[3] These are just the firms that a city would like, above all, to retain.

Louisville's planning and economic development authorities made this kind of economic diagnosis and resolved to use the local capital budget in conjunction with the state's enterprise zone program to build up an area in order to hold expanding firms that would otherwise be likely to leave the city.

The site of the enterprise zone was selected, in large part, for its infrastructure facilities. It is a large tract of land (2,400 acres) stretching from the Ohio River to the Louisville airport, situated adjacent to the Port of Louisville and traversed by four major rail lines. Four interstate highways (I-64, -65, -71, and -264) are located nearby. Finally, an important potential development incentive has been the recent discovery that 40 percent of the enterprise zone sits on top of an underground aquifer. Preliminary feasibility studies suggest that the aquifer is ideally suited to support construction of a district heating and cooling system.

Supplementing these locational advantages, the city of Louisville is investing an estimated $58.5 million in public facility improvements, physical rehabilitation, and land clearance and assembly. The improvements represent a mix of replacement and upgrading of streets to provide interstate access, expansion and modernization of water and sewer lines to meet much greater capacity standards, and installation of local streets, sidewalks, etc., to support an industrial park. The city also has agreed to reduce water and sewer fees and connection charges and has pledged to give special priority to the connections, extensions, and maintenance required in the zone.

The Louisville Planning Commission, a joint city-county agency, performed the analysis preliminary to site selection. Four options were presented to the Mayor's Economic Development Advisory Committee, a private business group working with the city, which in turn made its recommendation for the most appropriate site to the mayor and Board of Aldermen. Louisville's plan explicitly recognizes that, to make the enterprise zone succeed, the city's capital budget will have to be reallocated to invest more in the enterprise zone and less elsewhere and to give priority to resolving capital-related problems in the zone as these arise. It also recognizes that infrastructure incentives will have to be coupled with tax breaks and financing subsidies if, as the city desires, the site is to gain a critical mass of industrial activities. In this sense, Louisville's plan does spatially what San Antonio's and San Jose's plans do sectorally: support some activities or locations to the exclusion of competing ones.

Setting Sectoral Priorities

Traditional capital planning and budgeting often break down in allocating investment resources between sectors. Most communities have no process (except political leaders' intuition and lobbying) for deciding how much of the capital budget should be spent on sewer repairs vs. the amount to be spent on road improvements, public buildings, or other uses.

The choice of sectoral emphasis within the capital budget is one of the most important to economic development and a logical point at which to involve the business community. Different industries may have competing priorities for public capital spending, but even the industries targeted for priority development are likely to give greater priority to removing bottlenecks in certain infrastructure support facilities than in others. The business community as a whole may even be able to agree upon sectoral priorities for the public capital budget. One instrument for determining sectoral priorities is the strategic planning process.[4]

San Francisco's strategic plan. Strategic planning is planning designed to force planners to relate public sector strategies to public goals and to translate future economic development objectives into current actions that will further their realization.

Infrastructure may or may not be an important element in the local strategic plan, depending on the kinds of development initiatives identified and the ability of infrastructure to support them. The steps in a typical strategic planning process include organizing; scanning the environment; selecting key issues; developing mission statements; conducting internal and external analyses; developing goals, objectives and strategies; developing an action plan; implementing the plan; and monitoring the plan in action. While all of these steps are important, there are several that seem to differentiate strategic from traditional comprehensive planning:

1. The environmental scan leads to identification of the major strategic issues to be addressed in the planning effort. The scan is based on an analysis of detailed historical and comparative data (e.g., industry growth rates; relative wage rates for different skills in the community; types and levels of jobs associated with different industries).
2. The external analysis and forecast identifies uncontrollable factors that may arise in the future that will be threats or opportunities. Using infrastructure as an example, this may involve dramatic increases in the cost of construction

as a threat that needs to be accounted for or, conversely, substantially higher federal funding or the elimination of what may have been inapplicable federal standards as an opportunity.

3. The internal analysis and assessment produces an understanding of strengths or weaknesses of the government for which the plan is prepared. This task includes identifying competitors and understanding their capabilities and advantages.

4. Strategy development involves capitalizing on important external opportunities, minimizing serious threats, taking advantage of strengths, and trying to improve on weaknesses.

San Francisco's strategic plan, subtitled "Making a Great City Greater" (corresponding to the plan's overall goal), was conceived in 1981 by the business community to address the city's future and to develop solutions to some of its major problems.[5] The plan was completed (at a cost of approximately $500,000) in 1983 through a process coordinated by the San Francisco Chamber of Commerce under the direction of a Strategic Plan Management Committee, with strong encouragement from the city government. The committee was composed of prominent business and community leaders. Arthur Andersen and Company was hired to actually prepare the plan.

The adequacy of the transportation system and job and business opportunities were identified through the environmental scan as two of four strategic issues to be addressed (housing and city finances were the other two). Transportation was singled out because of the city's geography and heavy dependence on good transportation linkages. Also, infrastructure investments in general were viewed as a key to San Francisco's ability to support job and business growth. Despite their importance, the city's expenditures on public works programs had been declining. Measured in constant dollars between 1975 and 1982, the city's total budget declined 7 percent; public works spending declined by almost 50 percent during the same period.

Having identified transportation as a key concern and having developed estimates of the magnitude of transportation need under different city growth scenarios, the planners went on to identify a series of future bottlenecks that would inhibit growth unless dealt with presently. For example, bridge capacity during commuting hours was projected to become a key constraint, as was transit capacity. The severity of both bottlenecks was projected to vary greatly by specific location.

San Francisco is now in the process of implementing the recommended transportation strategies, aided by a $40 million increase in 1984 over 1983 appropriations in city capital spending. Typical of most strategic planning efforts, this one is viewed as part of an ongoing process in which the priority issues are continually examined in the context of the city's strengths and weaknesses and its overall competitive position.

Enlisting Business Help in Locating
Infrastructure Bottlenecks

Once a community decides upon a specific development strategy, it can benefit from business's help in locating key bottlenecks that might jeopardize achievement of the strategy. This process involves using business as a source of information.

Planning efforts in the Delaware Valley. The Delaware Valley Regional Planning Commission (DVRPC) turned to business to help identify key bottlenecks in planning improvements for the U.S. Route 202/Pennsylvania Turnpike corridor, traversing Chester and Montgomery Counties in suburban Philadelphia.[6] About 44,000 or 20 percent of the estimated 210,000 jobs in the corridor are in high-tech firms. This amounts to a concentration of high-tech jobs — mostly in pharmaceuticals and computer services — five times greater than in the state as a whole. Land-use plans for the two-county area call for large amounts of additional growth on the remaining undeveloped tracts.

The objectives of the DVRPC study underlined the direct linkage the agency foresaw between having good transportation infrastructure and being able to realize the region's economic development ambitions. As noted by DVRPC:

> The transportation improvement recommendations that result from this study have the ultimate purpose of stimulating the growth of jobs in the corridor through the retention of present firms and the attraction of new firms. It is in the region's best interest to develop advanced technology in the region. Not only are jobs created by expanding high-tech firms, but productivity will be improved in the region's industries that buy high-tech products, improving their ability to compete and protecting the jobs of those in non–high-tech jobs.[7]

To identify the importance of transportation, DVRPC sought to identify the locational criteria that were most important to the high-tech firms in the corridor; firms' assessments of the advantages and disadvantages of the corridor as a location for high-technology firms; obstacles for future expansion and corridor growth; and differences between high-tech and other firms regarding transportation needs.

Such information was obtained in a three-step process. First, interviews were conducted with selected chief executive officers, developers, and other economic interests in the corridor. This was followed by a mail-back questionnaire to the 167 high-tech firms in the corridor (102 responded) and a selected sample of other firms for comparative purposes. In a third step, the corridor itself and some of its existing transportation problems were analyzed through site visits and a review of past studies and plans. The total planning effort was carried out with the support and cooperation of member governments in the corridor, transportation operators, the business community, and university researchers.

To identify the specific locations of current traffic bottlenecks, mail survey respondents were simply asked the question, "Are there locations in the vicinity of your firm with severe traffic problems?" Those locations cited more than once by different firms were mapped and then aggregated into transportation problem areas drawn to reflect their proximity and interrelationship to each other. Thirty-three highway segments or intersections were identified in this fashion and combined into 16 problems areas.

The survey also queried respondents on the quality and quantity of transportation modes other than roads, including transit services, paratransit, and airports. Here, confirming the results of other high-tech firm location studies, airport access was found to be very significant. Sixty percent of high-tech firms noted that Philadelphia International Airport was a "highly important" destination.

One other question of interest listed six major capital improvements under consideration in or affecting the study area and asked firm executives to identify those most important to their business operations. Figure 1 shows how these responses were presented for Chester County and Montgomery County. Of greatest general interest is the extreme variation in importance assigned to the different projects. Overall, the Schuykill Expressway capital improvement project was judged to be most important to the high-tech firms perhaps because, as DVRPC noted, "The expressway forms a tether to Philadelphia and its free flow is important to permitting Philadelphia to remain the focus of services to the corridor."

While using business insights to help determine priorities for highway investment can be a valuable tool, it should be noted that such insights may be limited in their ability to predict the improvements that would be most critical to future economic development. DVRPC's phrasing of the survey question on capital improvements yielded responses reflecting firms' views on highway investments that could help *current* operations. Since the programmed highway projects will be designed particularly to redress *future* transportation bottlenecks, the responses may not fully reflect potential economic development problems and opportunities. The informal nature of some of the questions also made the study more valuable in distinguishing broad investment priorities than in making close judgments between alternative projects.

Separating the Development Component of the Capital Budget

Only a handful of capital projects in each city are central to economic development plans. The rest of the capital budget consists of more or less routine projects, designed to keep the current infrastructure system working or to expand it to serve the needs of a growing population.

FIGURE 1. IMPORTANCE TO FIRMS OF PLANNED MAJOR PROJECTS

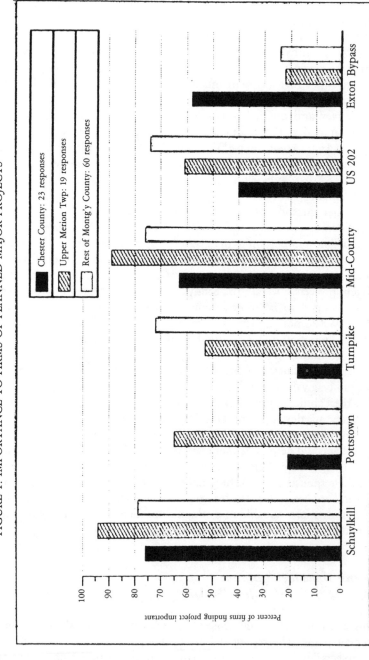

Source: Delaware Valley Regional Planning Commission, *Transportation Needs for High Technology Firms: Route 202 in Chester and Montgomery Counties* (Philadelphia, 1984).

Many cities have tried to give special treatment to economic development projects by separating them from the rest of the capital budget. The capital plans of New York City, Philadelphia, and Washington, D.C., now include separate sections devoted specifically to projects intended to promote development by adding to critical airport capacity, relieving port access bottlenecks, or building missing links in important highway networks. All projects were previously grouped by functional area (e.g., streets, water distribution system) regardless of their character or intended purpose. The new treatment recognizes that there is a class of investment projects where economic returns are especially important. Their separation from the rest of the capital budget may encourage thinking about these projects in relation to the alternative kinds of encouragements that the public sector can provide to stimulate business growth.

Some cities have gone further and have entrusted responsibility for capital planning in support of economic development to quasi-independent agencies or to independent authorities. A recent review of capital planning in different cities found that such agencies typically were created to speed up the investment process.[8] Economic development projects were able to avoid the citizen review that marked the rest of the capital budget. Ideas for projects frequently were initiated by developers and tied into "deals" that became conditions for the private investment going forward. Development agencies also differed from traditional capital budgeting agencies in that they looked upon infrastructure provision as one among many tools at their disposal. They expedited rezoning, helped secure environmental permits, issued or helped authorize tax-exempt revenue bonds for project financing, and otherwise tailored overall packages to stimulate development. Some of the development bodies took still greater initiative. The Port Authority of New York and New Jersey launched such activities as the New York Teleport and constructed the World Trade Center with its own capital.

As vehicles for injecting more concern for economic returns into the capital planning process, independent agencies of this type have several obvious advantages. They can act more swiftly than standard government agencies, have their own access to capital, and, in general, act as public sector entrepreneurs.

This strength can become a weakness, however. Such agencies can see themselves too narrowly as partners of the private sector unless there has been a clear enunciation of public sector goals for the development process. The capital plan for a community needs to be integrated into overall public sector policy, not parceled out so that the maintenance plan is developed by the public works department, the long-term capital requirements plan by the planning agency, and the economic development plan by a quasi-autonomous agency unrelated to the other two.

NOTES

1. Harvey S. Perloff, *Planning the Post-Industrial City* (Chicago: American Planning Association, 1980).

2. *General Plan* (San Jose; 1975).

3. Marc Bendick, Jr. and David W. Rasmussen, "Enterprise Zones and Inner City Economic Revitalization," in *Reagan and the Cities,* eds. George Peterson and Carol Lewis (Washington, D.C.: The Urban Institute, 1985).

4. James B. Hudak, "Strategic Planning for Large Cities," paper presented at the APA annual conference (May 1984); John B. Olsen and Douglas C. Eadie, *The Game Plan: Governance with Foresight* (Washington, D.C.: The Council of State Planning Agencies, 1982).

5. Arthur Andersen & Co., *San Francisco's Strategic Plan: Making a Great City Greater* (San Francisco, 1983). San Antonio's development strategy also emerged from a strategic planning exercise. See *Target '90: To Build a Greater City* (Report of the Target '90 Commission, San Antonio, 1984).

6. *Transportation Needs for High Technology Firms: Route 202 in Chester and Montgomery Counties* (Philadelphia: Delaware Valley Regional Planning Commission, 1984).

7. Ibid.

8. American Planning Association, *Local Capital Improvements and Development Management* (Washington, D.C.: National Technical Information Service, 1980).

Chapter 12

Strategic Planning

GUNNAR ISBERG

At the recent 60th annual Congress of Cities held in New Orleans, outgoing NLC president Charles Royer, mayor of Seattle, expressed "amazement" that some cities were cutting their planning staffs and budgets to cope with the current economic crisis, and said that this is the very time when planning should receive a major emphasis from cities.

A number of other conference speakers echoed similar messages, including Henry Cisneros, mayor of San Antonio, who predicted that those communities that are committed to the planning process would best be able to survive the crunch. He made clear, however, that he was not just speaking about traditional planning and zoning, but about a different type of planning called strategic planning.

Local communities have tried a number of different approaches to deal with the local economic crisis, including increased volunteerism, user fees, private-sector contracting, and delayed maintenance or other cuts in services. Some communities view planning as a "frill activity," one they can easily cut in times of hardship. Others maintain that this is the time when planning becomes most important, to help determine priorities in the competition for limited resources.

Discussions with local officials in both urban and rural areas indicate that the traditional comprehensive planning process has disappointed many of them, at least in helping them make day-to-day decisions about a community's future. Local officials give various reasons for not placing a great deal of faith in the comprehensive planning process.

They often charge that comprehensive planning lacks economic reality in terms of private development. Many developers characterize planners as "dreamers." Sometimes those charges are valid because many planners lack any formal training or understanding of land economics and development.

Critics also charge that the process usually lacks any meaningful imple-

Reprinted with permission from *Minnesota Cities*, Vol. 69, No. 4, April, 1984. Published by the League of Minnesota Cities, St. Paul, Minnesota.

mentation strategy, true in far too many cases. Many comprehensive plans contain voluminous background data but fail to indicate how to implement the plan. They often don't specify organizational arrangements, technical staff capability, or needed budgets.

And perhaps most importantly, many local officials are not committed to the planning process. This is especially true where planning primarily has fulfilled some governmental mandate or has been a condition of qualifying for a grant. The result of all this is that in one extreme city officials view planning as a mere exercise in data gathering, and in the other extreme as a means of justifying any and all development, no matter what the merits (or lack of them). In either case, planning has not been significant in influencing the type and quality of economic development in the community. A different approach is necessary to reconcile the relatively low esteem of the planning process with its importance to the future of local communities.

Strategic Planning

Strategic planning is a different approach from the traditional long-range comprehensive planning which began in the private sector about 20 years ago. One of its major characteristics is flexibility and adaptability to changing external environments. Strategic planners constantly ask "What if?" in developing future strategy. It is also a strongly focused process and emphasizes implementation. The process stresses:

- *Environmental scanning,* or identifying demographic, economic, technical, cultural, and political factors and their implications for the organization or community.
- *Determining goals.* Environmental scanning will bring out the issues and opportunities for new services or approaches, which will lead to establishing goals in a few key areas.
- *Analyzing strengths,* weaknesses, and resource limits, in which planners conduct resource audits for particular courses of action, including cost/benefit analyses.
- *Developing action plans,* including establishing priorities in key areas.
- *Developing implementation strategy,* including recommended organizational and staff changes or increases to implement objectives.

Environmental scanning ensures flexibility by focusing on the constantly changing external environment. The process also focuses on key issues, rather than on broad and general areas. The implementation strategy also includes potential organizational as well as staff changes, which enhances the likelihood of actual implementation of the plan. The important consideration of whether the development staff is adequate to implement the plan is almost never a factor in conventional comprehensive planning.

Strategic planning is only beginning its appearance in the public sector, and illustrative case studies are few as yet. However, it so far appears to be especially helpful in economic development planning as well as in annual operational and budget planning for cities, both crucial in the current economic crisis. The city of Northfield, for example, has recently developed some elements resembling strategic planning in its overall approach to planning.

Northfield has a history of commitment to the comprehensive planning process, which it first adopted in the 1960s after extensive citizen participation. Northfield, like many other Minnesota communities, has determined to emphasize economic development as a means to increase its tax base and employment for its citizens.

The city fully realized that its comprehensive plan would not by itself ensure economic development, but that it needed a more focused and action-oriented process. As a result, the city undertook several related programs resembling elements of the strategic planning process. For one, the city council, at a retreat conference in January 1983 to discuss city goals, adopted some major economic development policies which it had been kicking around for several years. Secondly, the city determined to enter the Star Cities program and received certification. Some of the elements of the Star Cities program include portions of a strategic planning process. This process brought out major issues regarding future economic development in the city.

What Type of Economic Development Should the City Promote?

The city needed to determine the type of economic development most suited to the city's size, location, existing land use, public facilities, environmental setting, and labor force. One of the early decisions was to cultivate existing industries to stay and expand, which in several cases has already happened.

Which Organization Should Be Responsible for Promoting Economic Development

There were three potential lead agencies: the city itself, the Chamber of Commerce, and the Northfield Industrial Development Corporation. After considerable discussion, the city took the lead role with the assistance and involvement of the other two agencies. A related issue dealt with the staff necessary to carry out the project, as well as a proposed budget. Obviously, the type, pay and commitment of the economic development staff will signal industries whether a city is really serious about economic development. The city hasn't resolved this issue yet but is making good progress on it.

What Implementation Method Should a City Use to Promote Economic Development?

Northfield recognizes that it needs an overall financial plan rather than the piecemeal financing approach of the past. In addition, the Star Cities staff, the city staff, and the planning commission are working on redevelopment that ties into the city's commitment to keeping the downtown area as the major retail, cultural, and entertainment center of the city.

Another area where Northfield is starting to apply the strategic planning process is in planning annual operations and budgets. For example, the city council holds an all-day meeting at the beginning of each year and invites key staff members. The meeting is in a retreat-type situation, with no interruptions, where participants can thoroughly discuss future goals and the coming year's projects. The council votes to assign priorities to the proposed projects and evaluates the goals and projects of the past year. This goal and priority-setting process later becomes major input for the budgeting process, including any recommended organizational or staff changes.

Proper development and implementation of comprehensive planning, can be very helpful to local officials in making development proposals; but it cannot by itself bring about economic progress. Strategic planning can help to focus city efforts in specific areas. In addition, it can help to determine the best organizational management, staff needed, and budgets needed to carry out programs, a process seldom part of normal comprehensive planning.

Chapter 13

Building Community Partnerships

RENEE BERGER

America is a nation of diverse communities shaped by many different forces. No force, however, is more powerful than a community's citizens.

Whether working alone or joining with other individuals or groups, informally organized or formally structured, operating on volunteer time, or a shoestring budget, these people share a vision that civic initiative can make a difference. They have proven their case in communities across the nation.

- Local units of the National Association of Letter Carriers have mobilized their members to monitor mail boxes of the elderly and handicapped. If their mail is not picked up, the carrier starts a procedure that notifies a relative or other person listed on the program sign-up form, alerting them to possible problems.
- Voluntary Action Centers in over 300 communities nationwide help to match volunteer resources with jobs that need to be done. VACs demonstrate innovative ways to recruit, place, manage, and recognize America's greatest natural resource, its volunteers.

What these activities have in common are people who are willing to commit resources to solving problems. The processes they set in motion require cooperation and as such are partnerships for community betterment.

There is no one "best way" to stimulate or nourish these partnerships. Indeed there are many good ways to create and sustain them.

Defining Community Partnerships

There is no simple definition of a community partnership. It is neither a particular structure nor a particular project.

Reprinted with permission from *National Civic Review,* Vol. 73, No. 2, May, 1984. Published by the National Civic League, Denver, Colorado.

Community partnerships describe a set of processes created by individuals or groups, acting alone or together, designed to benefit the community. To begin, they require *vision*; to be nourished, they require *cooperation*; to achieve their goals, they require *leadership and expertise*. The results of these efforts range from development of focused short-term projects, to the creation of an attitude that problems can be solved, to the formation of civic networks.

Building Blocks

Specific approaches to building partnerships need to be shaped in each community. The basic steps are discussed below. The examples emphasize the practicality and diversity of existing partnerships.

VISION
Community partnerships begin with a vision that a situation can be improved. This discovery stage has three steps:

Perceiving a need. Recognition that a problem exists, or that an opportunity can be encouraged, is the first step of the process. The numerous projects that have been created with this catalyst demonstrate that communities can act to address emerging problems.

In Jefferson, Oregon, local government realized the importance of including citizens in the development of an energy management plan for the county. Sponsored by Pacific Power and Light, this "Partnership for Progress" program assesses existing conservation efforts, identifies affordable energy savings approaches, evaluates the findings and makes recommendations, and promotes energy conservation fairs.

Communicating an idea. Needs will persist unless ideas for change are conceived and communicated. To gain momentum, there must be effective messengers.

For over 20 years, John Gardner has been focusing public attention on critical national needs. Now chairman of Independent Sector, a coalition of national voluntary organizations, corporations and foundations, Gardner was founder of Common Cause, chairman of the Urban Coalition and Secretary of Health, Education and Welfare.

Initiating an idea. Initiative can come from individuals or groups or the public or private sectors. An initiator who has a proven track record is essential for this step. This person will know how to define the problem and create an attitude that it can be solved.

James Rouse is both a successful developer and a neighborhood activist. His Enterprise Foundation wholly owns a for-profit commercial real estate firm designed to generate capital for innovative approaches to housing problems.

ACTION

For the community partnership process to continue beyond the vision state, momentum must be created and sustained.

Creating a structure. The structure of partnerships varies from city to city from ad hoc coalitions around specific problems to highly structured institutions. In the most effective stituations, the structure facilitates the involvement of all partners.

The Chicago Rehab Network has grown from eight neighborhood groups in 1977 to over 20 in 1983, with members drawing on each other's skills and experiences for housing rehabilitation projects. Mutual assistance services include financial counseling, legal assistance and consultation on property management.

Developing a management plan. The problem must be defined and common goals articulated. Strategies then need to be outlined. Since diverse input is often part of the partnership process, management plans need to keep lines of communication open.

Negotiated Investment Strategy is a unique program of negotiation and mediation which brings together representatives of government and the private sector to develop a coordinated local investment plan. The project was originated by the Charles F. Kettering Foundation.

The Volunteer Urban Consulting Group annually matches volunteers from corporations to over 350 nonprofit clients seeking management assistance. VUCG develops a management plan for each participating nonprofit client.

Identifying resources. Resources of people, technical expertise, funds, equipment, facilities, etc., can be found in both the public and private sectors.

Major insurance, banking and industrial firms have joined with private foundations to back the Washington, D.C.–based Local Initiatives Support Corporation. To date it has provided loans, grants and technical assistance to more than 140 community-based organizations nationwide.

The Neighborhood Housing Service grew from a grassroots effort in Pittsburgh to a federally supported program in over 100 cities. By creating working partnerships of residents, lenders and local government, NHS helps facilitate rehabilitation.

Employees of ACTION and other federal agencies in Washington, D.C., volunteer their time to help elementary school students with reading and math as part of the local "Operation Rescue" program. A continent away, employees of Atlantic Richfield participate in the Joint Education Project in inner city schools.

Building a network. Building support should be done systematically and continuously. The network also should be diverse. Key staff and volunteer leaders should be identified to perform this function.

The Citizens League of the Minneapolis–St. Paul Twin Cities area has been exploring alternative systems for the delivery of public service since the early 1970s. Focused originally on government's purchase of services, it now examines a wide variety of alternatives utilizing both profit-making and non-profit partners.

Opportunities for Civic Betterment

Both the private and public sectors face enormous challenges as we seek to address our critical human, social and environmental problems. One strategy for potential partners is to wait until the stakes are so high that survival depends on change. Alternatively, potential partners can start immediately, avoiding the wasteful effects of crisis.

No one would disagree that there are unmet needs in our nation. The conflict arises in allocating limited resources and setting priorities. The process of building community partnerships is not free of this conflict, nor are there such guarantees of success. To increase the likelihood of success potential partners can:

- Promote the importance of the idea of community partners.
- Communicate to their constituencies and to the total community that partnerships are achievable, with potential benefits for all.
- Create an atmosphere of discussion about civic betterment.
- Clearly identify problems to be addressed and inventory the human and financial resources that will be required.
- Recognize, respect and celebrate existing partnerships.

Civic Leadership Roles

In the community partnership process there are many leadership roles to be undertaken. The individuals and organizations that take on these roles can come from the private or public sector. Some of the roles are:

SEER — recognizes the need

VISIONARY — has the idea that promises to remedy the problem.

INITIATOR — communicates the idea and readies the process for initiation.

SELLER — markets the idea.

CONVENOR — offers neutrality to increase the likelihood of cooperation.

FACILITATOR — ensures that the lines of communication remain open.

BRIDGE BUILDER — constructs relationships with other groups to stimulate interest and gain support.

SUSTAINER — seeks to construct the building blocks of community partnerships, so they are self-sustaining.

Civic Leadership Action

Specific actions that can be undertaken to start community partnerships in your community include:

PROMOTING THE IMPORTANCE OF THE IDEA
- Either you or a designated senior-level staff person has this placed on the agenda.
- Time is specifically allocated to planning how to get the message out, e.g., a newsletter.
- Seek the assistance of key groups and individuals, e.g., civic associations, labor groups, religious groups, the media and business groups.
- Consider establishing a partnership group composed of key senior level people from the involved sectors.

RECOGNIZING EXISTING PARTNERSHIPS IN YOUR COMMUNITY
- Identify examples of partnerships.
- Generate a list of leaders and contacts.
- Establish a clearinghouse for this information, e.g., publicize a telephone number to call in partnership information.
- Plan a question and answer series to talk about community partnerships, what they are, their benefits and costs, and how they are packaged.
- Share information about existing local partnerships with the media and in public forums; ask civic leaders to publicly acknowledge their accomplishments.

IDENTIFYING THE PROBLEMS AND THE POTENTIAL REMEDIES
- Assess your own resources.
- Ask others to assess what they can contribute.
- Develop problem-solving seminars.
- Identify a neutral forum where problem-solving can be carried out, such as a community foundation, community-wide forum or planning body.
- Train people and provide technical assistance.
- Identify people with expertise who are willing to give time to specific projects.
- Establish volunteer technical assistance specialist groups.

Civic Benefits

A reasonable question to ask is why we should get involved in building community partnerships. Here are some of the answers:

PRIVATE SECTOR: FOR-PROFIT

- Business firms are interested in highly skilled labor and recognize that effective educational programs are vital for their work force.
- Business firms require adequate transportation, and other services to carry out their functions.
- Business firms are interested in good housing, quality education and stable neighborhoods to attract and retain their employees.
- Business firms are interested in the quality of life in the community for their employees.

PRIVATE SECTOR: NONPROFIT

- Nonprofits are interested in contributing their talent to achieving a high quality of life for all residents.
- Nonprofits share the same concerns as business about the need for housing, education and other aspects of community life.
- Nonprofits are interested in the most efficient and effective use of resources in providing services.
- Nonprofits are interested in building working coalitions to respond to community needs.

PUBLIC SECTOR

- Government seeks to limit the tax burden on its citizens.
- Government seeks alternative uses of resources to solve community needs and to take advantage of opportunities.
- Government is interested in stimulating local interaction to promote improved relationships between the private and public sectors.
- Government seeks to prevent unnecessary dependency, and, instead, provide opportunities for personal and civic growth.

Chapter 14

Downtown Revitalization

J. THOMAS BLACK
LIBBY HOWLAND
STUART L. ROGEL

This chapter attempts to summarize some of the basic factors that must be considered by any city attempting downtown retail development. Based on interviews with 40 experts on development and retailing, it describes some of the approaches that are being taken in cities across the country to reverse the declining trends in downtown retail.

Four categories of downtown retail projects are described: downtown shopping malls, specialty or festival retailing, mixed-use projects, and retail street innovations.

It stresses that cities must be realistic in assessing the markets for downtown retail. They are not what they used to be. While each city is unique, four basic submarkets for downtown retail services must be evaluated: close-in households, metropolitan residents, downtown workers, and transient customers such as tourists, conventioneers, and business visitors.

In addition to assessing the mix of customers from these four submarkets which a downtown retail development might attract, a city must take several other factors into account: the extent and location of competing shopping opportunities, the other attractions of downtown that might help attract customers, accessibility and parking convenience, the social character of downtown, the quality and character of existing downtown retail facilities, and the cost of land and facilities.

Such an assessment can serve as the basis for a realistic downtown retail development strategy. To implement such a strategy, both the public and private sectors in the downtown must be fully committed or most developers will steer clear of getting involved.

Several options exist in carrying out the strategy. A conventional approach can be taken in which public and private interests play traditional roles, or

Reprinted with permission from *Downtown Retail Development: Conditions for Success and Project Profiles*, 1983. Published by the Urban Land Institute, Washington, D.C.

codevelopment involving public and private interests as financial, development, and operating partners is feasible.

Whatever approach is taken, it should be chosen with the eyes of city hall and the civic community wide open to the real possibilities unclouded by nostalgia or unrealistic expectations.

By capitalizing on new opportunities rather than trying to restore the past, cities across the country are beginning to prove that downtown retail can be revitalized.

Reversing the Trend: Downtown Retail Revitalization

Throughout the 1950s, 1960s, and 1970s, the retail districts of many cities deteriorated as they lost their formerly dominant role in the metropolitan retail market to suburban shopping.

Yet, despite these trends and in contrast to the 1950s and 1960s, a significant number of cities, working with creative, entrepreneurial developers, have initiated new downtown retail revitalization projects since the early 1970s.

Boston and Baltimore, working with the Rouse Company, have developed the now famous Faneuil Hall/Quincy Market complex and Harborplace. The same developer, in cooperation with the city of Philadelphia, created the Gallery, a 250,000–square foot, 122-store mall connecting two department stores.

Developer John Portman developed a new 300,000–square foot retail center as part of a major office, hotel, and retail complex in downtown Atlanta. Urban Investment and Development Corporation developed Water Tower Place in Chicago—a project with 600,000 square feet of retail on seven levels arranged around an atrium.

The list of major downtown retail revitalization projects in small and large cities is impressive: the Crossroads Mall in Bridgeport; the Stamford, Connecticut, Town Center, a 900,000–square foot regional mall; the Grand Avenue in Milwaukee, a 245,000–square foot retail project; Town Square in St. Paul, 70 stores in a retail, office, and hotel complex; Louisville Galleria in Louisville, Kentucky; the list goes on. Planning, site acquisition, or construction has begun in cities as diverse as San Diego, St. Louis, Minneapolis, and Charleston, West Virginia.

Four categories of projects. The projects fall into several categories reflecting, in part, the retail market opportunities available to the downtown of each individual city:

1. *Regional shopping malls* downtown that include one or more department stores, are relatively freestanding, and in which retailing is the dominant activity. Such malls are the downtown answer to competition with suburban centers for a share of the metropolitan retail market.

2. *Specialty or festival retailing* containing no large store anchor and concentrating on food, entertainment, specialty, and boutique items in a festival or theme environment designed to attract tourists and conventioneers as well as metropolitan residents.

3. *Mixed-use projects* in which retailing is combined with at least two other components, most often hotel, office or convention facilities. Mixed-use projects may or may not contain major anchor stores and may also contain specialty or festival characteristics. They are designed to take advantage of a substantial on-site clientele of office workers, hotel guests, or conventioneers as well as to attract metropolitan customers.

4. *Retail street renovations* which are efforts to strengthen and improve an existing storefront retail district by enhancing its attractiveness and accessibility, often by creating a transit or a pedestrian mall.

By no means have all of these efforts proven successful. The financial disappointments with Detroit's Renaissance Center, a 375,000-square foot mixed-use retail center in a major office and hotel complex, is the best known example. The forces that led to the decline of downtown retailing are powerful and cannot be overcome by wishful thinking or the lack of analysis in advance of undertaking a project of the real market for downtown services.

Since there is a growing interest in and commitment to retail revitalization among developers, city, state and federal governments, civic organizations, and downtown associations, the time is right to assess why some of these downtown projects have succeeded while others have failed.

Differing views on prospects for successful retail development downtown. There is no uniform opinion among the developers and retail trade experts on all of the reasons for success or failure. Conditions vary from city to city and reasons that may be explanatory in one case may not apply in another.

Some experts are bullish. While recognizing the difficulties of pulling off successful projects, they feel that such factors as growing downtown office employment, increased middle- and upper-income interest in close-to-downtown housing in some cities, and tastes for more urbane recreation and tourism all augur well for downtown retail revitalization in selected cities.

Others argue strongly that conventional retailing can only occur downtown in cities where a close-in residential market exists of sufficient scale to support such development. They discount the recent growth in middle- and upper-income households in close-to-downtown areas as insufficient to generate significant buying power or to offset the losses of middle- and upper-income residents suffered by central cities since the 1950s. To make their point, they cite retail successes in Chicago, Stamford, Santa Monica, Glendale, San Francisco, and Manhattan—all cities with strong middle- and upper-income residential populations in and around downtown. To make the other side of their argument, they point to less successful projects in cities such as Detroit, Kansas City, and Springfield, Massachusetts, where there is less close-in buying power.

A third group takes the view that differences between cities are too great to draw general conclusions about what makes for success or failure in downtown retail revitalization.

Realistically assessing the potential market for downtown retail. Even if some retailers and developers are optimistic, some pessimistic, and some non-committal regarding opportunities for downtown retail revitalization, there is strong agreement on the factors which determine retail investment potential and, therefore, on the factors which must be assessed realistically in evaluating the potential for a major project in a given downtown area. The principal factors stressed by the experts interviewed were:

1. The size (buying power) of the market that can be attracted to a downtown retail center. Retail projects do not create customers. They must come from somewhere and there are constraints on the drawing power of any retail complex. In fact, that drawing power drops off sharply within 15 to 20 minutes travel time away from the project. Downtown retail projects must combine several different submarkets of customers to generate sufficient sales to make the project feasible. The submarkets include: (*a*) households living close in for whom the downtown is the most convenient location to shop; (*b*) the remaining consumers in the metropolitan area who might be attracted downtown occasionally if central city shopping opportunities and attractions outweigh the inconvenience of time and distance; (*c*) downtown workers; and (*d*) transients (tourists, business visitors, and conventioneers).

   Clearly many factors unique to each city influence the rate at which each individual downtown and retail project can capture a share of each of these four categories of potential customers. However, the size and character of these four submarkets establish the upper limits of retail space that can be supported economically.

   A tough-minded, realistic assessment of market potential must evalute each of these factors. City planning staffs are becoming more knowledgeable about retail markets, so proven, reputable, expert help should be brought in to assess market potential and other factors in advance of undertaking a retail development project. Failure is certain if plans for a project are pinned on hopes or nostalgia rather than hard-headed analysis.
2. The extent, location, and character of competing shopping centers.
3. The recreational/cultural attractiveness of downtown — its theaters, museums, sports events, fairs, or tourist attractions.
4. The accessibility, transportation, and parking convenience of downtown retail for the potential markets that it can serve.
5. The social character of downtown.
6. The extent, location, and character of existing retail facilities in downtown.
7. The availability and cost of land downtown.
8. The cost of construction and operations downtown.

The effect of one variable will depend on the conditions of eight or nine others and the interaction among them. For example, in most downtowns, parking is viewed to be a major problem for retail operations. There is not enough of it, it is expensive to construct and operate, shoppers often fear crime in parking structures, and fees drive customers away. Yet there are exceptions. The superstars of downtown retailing, in the opinion of one retail market analyst, are Manhattan, North Michigan Avenue in Chicago, and Union Square in San Francisco—all areas where parking is virtually unavailable or extremely expensive. Also, Faneuil Hall, one of the most successful of the contemporary downtown retailing projects, initially had little contiguous parking, illustrating that some factors can offset or override the influence of others.

The objective of a market assessment is to define the strengths and weaknesses of opportunities that are not being realized, but which *might* be solved through cooperative public and private action. In the assessment, the city should evaluate whether there are sufficient existing retail anchors that can provide the basis for a major new retail mall, or whether a shift in the location for optimal retailing calls for creation of an entirely new retail center, or whether tourist and convention business is or could be sufficient to support "festival" retailing such as that of Boston's Quincy Market or Baltimore's Harborplace.

Developers, investors, retailers—all should be consulted and involved in the assessment. They can tell the city whether the assessment is sound. In any event, their own views and their own situation must be part of any assessment.

Realistically assessing what the city can do. The assessment, if done well, will provide the city with an understanding of what opportunities there are to capture a larger share of the retail market and what is generally required to do so. It will identify problems to be overcome. And it will raise the questions of implementation. This places the ball in the court of the city government and downtown business and civic organizations. Two questions must be addressed: How willing are the city government and downtown business community to take steps to improve central city retailing? How effective can the city and downtown business and civic organizations be in coordinating and managing the downtown retail function as an integrated operation?

Developers and investors who sense that a leadership commitment is lacking or uncertain will not risk their time or money in working with the community.

There are downtown problems—physical, economic, and social—that can serve as obstacles to any retail development effort. Often downtown retail developments require management innovations comparable to those used in suburban malls. Sometimes the introduction of competition actually strengthens the pulling power of an existing store. The more diverse the shopping opportunities, the more customers are pulled in. The shopping center is a major social invention. By providing constant management over the retail area as a whole and by grouping shopping opportunities in close juxtaposition, a synergism among competing retailers results in which the sum is greater than the parts. Downtowns need to adapt this innovation to their own purposes.

There are added costs of doing business in many downtowns that can help make downtown retail development financially infeasible. Often, the only way to overcome these obstacles is through special incentives, concessions, or contributions to a retail development project that help make the financial arithmetic of a project come out right.

With limited public resources, cities are finding it advantageous and necessary to enter into new kinds of financial and business arrangements with private developers and financial institutions—arrangements which they had never previously contemplated, such as assuming the role of codeveloper.

Thus, in undertaking downtown retail development, a city must assess realistically what it can do. And the city, together with downtown business and civic leadership, must agree on the form and mechanism for ensuring close public and private cooperation in the formulation, planning, and execution of a retail development strategy.

Developing a basic retail development strategy. Once a general assessment of market opportunities and problems has been completed and an appropriate mechanism for close and stable public-private cooperation exists, a basic retail development strategy can be prepared and projects implemented.

What Can the City Do?
Getting the Civic Act Together

The *sine qua non* for a proposed downtown retail project, in the nearly unanimous opinion of the experts interviewed, is enthusiastic and aggressive local political and civic support. There are developers with much experience in downtown projects who will not consider going into a downtown project unless the city executive, the council, and the citizenry are demonstrably behind it. There are lenders who consider local government willingness to back a project as one of the key factors in their risk assessment. An almost universally cited worry of developers is that downtown projects can easily become political footballs. Therefore, they try to secure bipartisan support for proposals, or, preferably, to have at least day-to-day decisions removed from the political level and delegated to a nonpartisan, quasi-independent entity.

Downtown retail projects require an unusual amount of political and public support because they tend to be much more expensive and riskier to develop than their suburban competitors. As we have already seen, the additional expense and risk factors include land assembly problems, higher land costs, the need for parking structures, a longer development period, more stringent code requirements, and higher security and operating costs. Moreover, the success of a downtown retail project is more or less dependent on its physical or functional linkages with other downtown elements—offices, hotels, cultural or entertainment facilities, transit, and so forth. The forging of such links is of necessity a matter of cooperative arrangements between the project developer and the public sector and other business interests in the downtown.

In general, the city should expect to provide:

1. A sound and workable redevelopment or revitalization strategy and plan for downtown retail
2. Strong political support for the plan and its component projects
3. Assistance in site or property acquisition, if necessary
4. Financial support as required
5. Indirect support in the form of programs and policies to encourage the development of housing, amenities, and other attractions in and around the downtown that will help attract people to the area
6. A streamlined regulatory environment in which barriers to efficient financial and physical development are minimized.

Public-private cooperation. In addition to the public role, there is usually a need for a quasi-public body representing local interests and with financial powers that can provide financial support, stimulate private business and civic involvement in planning and decision making; carry out various entrepreneurial functions such as property acquisition, management, and development in an effective and expeditious manner; and provide financial participation when no other source is available. Projects in Philadelphia, Baltimore, Milwaukee, and San Diego have been carried out with the strong involvement of such quasi-public bodies.

In Philadelphia, for example, in order to minimize the risk to the developer, the Philadelphia Redevelopment Authority spent $18 million to build the shell for the Gallery retail project. In Baltimore, a quasi-public corporation, Charles Center/Inner Harbor, Inc., cleared the site and provided improved access and improved infrastructure for the highly successful Harborplace. The Milwaukee Redevelopment Corporation is a limited-profit corporation that can operate in a business-like manner to acquire land, work with consultants and city officials, and as any private developer, become directly involved in a project implementation.

Downtown retail management. The need for close public-private cooperation does not end with project development, however. One of the historical problems creating disadvantages for downtown retail relative to suburban malls has been the lack of effective central management. This problem has been recognized for some time, but it continues to plague most downtowns.

Under the "Main Street" program of the National Trust for Historic Preservation, there have been successes in providing voluntary coordination among merchants in some retail strips of smaller cities. A coordinator assigned to the project can assume responsibilities analogous to those of a suburban mall manager, but with these few exceptions, there is a lack of centralized management in downtown retail districts. Some of the retailers and developers interviewed were generally of the opinion that voluntary approaches to the creation of centralized management have not worked well. Many merchants are simply unwilling to cooperate.

The advantages of centralized management have been well demonstrated: coordinated operating hours, control of tenant mix, common design themes, common and coordinated advertising, and so forth. Though centralized management is clearly advantageous and widely recognized as such, little has been done in most downtowns to solve the problems of decentralized retail operations. Thus, the most effective solution and course of least resistance appears to favor development of a new retail center under single ownership — a centrally managed facility.

This is an issue warranting concentrated attention. There are no legal means to impose involuntary controls on downtown merchants, at least to the degree necessary to control tenant mix and operating hours. Some cities have used special districts as a device to provide special maintenance, promotion, security, and transportation services in the downtown area. These districts are typically funded through a special property tax assessment on downtown property owners.

Although the model may not be replicated in most cities, it is reported that retail property owners in Schenectady, New York, formed a downtown retail corporation and transferred their individual properties to the corporation in exchange for an interest in it. The central corporation then obtained a central management capability.

The time has come when it may have been proven necessary to invent for many downtown retail districts management mechanisms and professional staff that can serve as both counterparts and competitors to those in suburban centers.

Public incentives and financing. Rare is the contemporary downtown large-scale retail project that has been developed without significant public subsidy or financing support. The following examples of direct public participation are instructive:

- *Charleston Town Center, (Charleston, West Virginia)* — Public funds being used to write down land costs, construct a garage, and help construct the shell of the mall.
- *Faneuil Hall (Boston, Massachusetts)* — Public funds used for infrastructure improvements, property tax abatement, and advantageous (dollar-a-year) lease terms on the structure leased by the city to the developer.
- *Glendale Galleria (Glendale, California)* — Public funds used to write down land costs, upgrade infrastructure, and build a garage.
- *The Grand Avenue (Milwaukee, Wisconsin)* — Public funds used for public concourses, skyways, a parking structure, and underground utility improvements.

- *Harborplace (Baltimore, Maryland)* — Public funds used to assemble and prepare land which is then leased to the project developer.
- *Lexington Center (Lexington, Kentucky)* — Public funds used to develop an arena, convention center, the mall shell, and parking spaces.
- *Louisville Galleria (Louisville, Kentucky)* — Public funds used to build parking, a department store, and portions of the mall.
- *Plaza Pasadena (Pasadena, California)* — Public funds used for site acquisition and preparation and parking construction.

Most cities can expect to provide one or more of the following if a major downtown retail development project is to prove feasible:

1. Necessary improvements to streets and freeways to improve access and general environment
2. Subsidized parking
3. Acquisition and preparation of sites for new construction
4. Expeditious approvals of rezonings, street realignments, and the like
5. Legislation to allow the establishment of special downtown management organizations financed by special exactions
6. Financial assistance in the form of "soft" loans or "soft" leases for facilities
7. Obtaining state and federal financial assistance when available through urban development action grant or other grant programs
8. Providing financial assistance for the development of downtown housing.

Such substantial front-end public subsidies frequently become a matter of some controversy. Some observers argue that city returns should be accounted for by spinoffs such as increased employment, tax revenues, and the project's attraction of additional real estate investment to the area. This school thinks cities should stay out of the direct risk and profit aspects of the real estate business.

On the other hand, others point out that many recent projects have easily repaid the public investment in the project in a few years. Boston, for example, invested approximately $12 million in Faneuil Hall and has received well over $2 million per year in lease payments alone.

Other observers feel quite strongly that cities should structure business deals with developers in an effort to recover and even make a profit on their front-end subsidies. Municipalities as investors have participated in a good number of recent retail projects by receiving lease or cash flow income from the project (Faneuil Hall, the Grand Avenue, Harborplace, the Louisville Galleria, Rainbow Centre in Niagara Falls, the Gallery in Philadelphia) or parking revenues (Charleston Town Center, Plaza Pasadena, the Gallery in Philadelphia).

The precise form and participation of the city is very much an element in its basic strategy for downtown retail development.

The triangular partnership. Each partner in the development project, in addition to the local government, has special responsibilities.

The developer is the director and organizer of the process. He conceptualizes the project, initiates activity, assumes risk, invests money, and expects to earn a profit in return. When the local government is involved as codeveloper, it assists the developer in some of these responsibilities and correspondingly must share some of the risks.

The third group of participants in a development project are the investors and lenders. The developer is responsible for seeking out organizations or individuals willing to invest money in the project. These "equity investors" can expect three types of return: cash flow, tax benefits, and or capital appreciation. Many projects are organized as limited partnerships. A limited partnership consists of two kinds of partners: the general partner, normally the active member of the organization, has unlimited liability and must bear responsibility for any commitments or debts entered into by the partnership. Limited partners, on the other hand, are liable only up to a designated amount, usually the amount of their investment.

Lenders also have two important responsibilities in development projects: first, they are the source of debt financing; second, they carefully review a project's economic and financial feasibility. Almost every lender requires an economic feasibility study for any project. Lenders provide several sources of capital; construction loans that help cover construction and some front-end costs; and permanent financing for a completed project.

The local government, developer, and investors/lendors comprise a triangular development partnership, but civic organizations also become a vital part of the equation in most cities. Without broad-based support from civic organizations few projects can succeed. Active opposition will kill the chances for most major projects to either be implemented or succeed if they are.

Chapter 15

Using Urban Renovation Experts

WILLIAM HOFFER

One weekend in 1982, a "SWAT" team of urban-redevelopment experts descended upon Healdsburg, a town of 8,800 residents, located in the center of California's premium wine region. The team's analyses and recommendations for Healdsburg during that four-day visit led to efforts that have reinvigorated the city.

The vacancy rate of buildings in the downtown business district has dropped to 3 percent from 30 percent, and retail sales have tripled. Healdsburg's once-declining inner core has been refurbished and revitalized, its assessed valuation has nearly tripled, and development is continuing.

The urban-renovation experts who spurred those results are among the most prominent in their respective fields. R. Terry Schnadelbach, who served as team chairman, is a New York City landscape architect and ecologist. He coordinated the efforts of William Lamont, Jr., a community-development planner from Boulder, Colo.; Ernie Niemi, an economist from Eugene, Ore., who specializes in cost-benefit analysis of proposed development projects; David Stea, distinguished professor of architecture at the University of Wisconsin/Milwaukee; Milo Thompson, professor of architecture and urban design at the University of Minnesota in Minneapolis; and Raymond Trujillo, a development expert from Albuquerque, N.M.

These men went to Healdsburg to answer a call for help. In Healdsburg, as in a growing number of small U.S. cities and towns, the downtown business district was suffering from what some have called "mall withdrawal." Local officials had created a Redevelopment Agency in 1980 to bring shoppers back to their downtown, but it had accomplished relatively little.

The experts' visit was conducted under the Regional/Urban Design Assistant Teams (R/UDAT) Program of the American Institute of Architects.

Reprinted with permission from *Nation's Business,* Vol. 77, No. 1, January, 1989. Published by the U.S. Chamber of Commerce, Washington, D.C.

Healdsburg paid travel expenses for the team, and its members donated their expertise. Since the AIA program began in 1967, more than 500 men and women from more than 30 professional disciplines have donated an estimated $3.5 million worth of services to areas in 40 states with a combined population of 21 million. Their goal is to save a characteristic slice of American culture: Main Street.

In a nation with a 200-year heritage of innovation and growth, it is perhaps natural that old business districts have given way to modern merchandising methods. But look at what can be lost to progress. Main Street is a living history of the social and economic forces that created your town. If you let it deteriorate, you may lose that historical record forever. Furthermore, local businesses lose sizable investments when buildings are left idle on local Main Streets.

Another way to view the economic importance of Main Street is to think of the various small businesses as a collective industry. Could your town afford to lose an industry that employs 750 people? That is the typical Main Street job base in a town of 15,000 people. And it is an industry that attracts other industries. A clean, characteristic, thriving downtown shopping district is one of the most notable signs of a forward-looking local business community.

Frank McIntosh, coordinator of the Georgia Main Street Program, tells the story of a businessman and his wife who were searching for a suitable location for a new facility. Seeing the dilapidated downtown section of one town, the wife remarked, "I wouldn't live in such a place," and the couple drove on.

Look around the downtown district of your town. Chances are that there is much character behind the aluminum facades and the garish signs that have taken over. But does it show? Or does your Main Street need a face-life?

There may never be a better time to begin—for one very important reason: You can get help. Tax credits and low-interest loans are available, especially for historically significant locales. Low-cost or no-cost plans are already drawn up and ready for adaptation. State and federal agencies as well as private organizations offer information and assistance for every step of the process. Perhaps most important is the fact that customers are ready to return to Main Street.

Consider the fall of Rome—the one in northwest Georgia—and the town's rebirth. In 1834, two lawyers and a cotton planter founded Rome at the point where the Etowak and Oostanaula rivers combine to form the Coosa River. Over the years the downtown area, known as "Between the Rivers," became a commercial center for the local cotton industry.

Rome's first strip shopping center opened in the 1960s and spawned an economic exodus from downtown. When River Bend Mall opened in 1975, both of the town's major department stores left downtown to move into the new facility.

Rome was not rebuilt in a day. City officials hired consultants, but their recommendations were too costly. Progress began only when the city and the local merchants' association agreed to split the cost of a $30,000-a-year downtown manager, Janet Hackett. Under her leadership, Rome flourished. Five downtown blocks are now on the National Register of Historic Places, qualifying dozens of businesses for tax credits. Since 1982, a total of $8.2 million has been invested in downtown structures, more than half of that financed by low-interest loans arranged through the Downtown Development Authority. Property values are up 29 percent. The improvements have generated $80,000 in new taxes for the city.

Can you follow the same road that led to Rome's revival? The first step is to get some low-cost advice, which is available from R/UDAT. "We send in a team of 8 to 10 top pros," says Bruce M. Kriviskey, director of R/UDAT program. "There are planners, developers, landscape architects, economists, sociologists, lawyers, and financial experts. Their travel expenses are paid by the host community, but our guys donate their time." Initial contact is made during a four-day visit that runs from Thursday through Sunday. Team members agree in advance *not* to accept commissions resulting from their recommendations.

In Healdsburg, the R/UDAT team found City Hall at its disposal. Teenage volunteers stood ready to research facts and figures. The police chief cooked breakfast. Townspeople stopped by with snacks.

Local leaders had called in the team because they were frustrated. A decaying billboard on six acres of vacant land along the west side of the downtown plaza had long displayed on overdue promise: "Commercial Development Coming Soon." But various plans had foundered. Businesses were caught in a deadly cycle of declining property values, reduced occupancy rates, and ever-dwindling traffic. The question was whether Healdsburg could bring pride — and customers — back to Main Street.

"The R/UDAT visit was very stimulating," says Kurt Hahn, deputy executive director of Healdsburg's Redevelopment Agency.

"It forced fast decisions, a process that we in government are not particularly used to. Camping out in a conference room — not just going along at our own pace — was very beneficial. We have replicated that process many times since."

Because geography virtually barred the city from expanding, the R/UDAT team recommended that Healdsburg remain small. The town was advised to concentrate on building small commercial and service firms to provide groceries, drugs, and general merchandise as well as health care, insurance, and banking services. The experts also said that Healdsburg should not try to compete with a new mall down the highway in Santa Rosa.

Since Healdsburg is a natural stop for tourists traveling a major highway through California's wine country, R/UDAT recommended a two-part approach to capturing outside capital. Motels, gas stations, and fast-food outlets had already begun to spring up near the freeway exit, and the team strongly advised that such growth be restricted to that area. This would allow the downtown area to concentrate upon another type of tourist—the one attracted by the three wineries located in the city and the dozens more throughout the surrounding countryside.

The committee recommended that the vacant six acres on the west side of the plaza become the site of a "first class" hotel-and-restaurant complex, and the team advised that other such facilities be prohibited elsewhere. It further advised the adoption and enforcement of design guidelines to preserve the character of the area.

The urban redevelopers' recommendations resulted in a new street pattern for Healdsburg, the placement of parking facilities on the outskirts of the downtown circle, and the opening of the plaza to pedestrians, enhancing its function as a community gathering place.

In subsequent years, Healdsburg implemented what Hahn calls "the more practical aspects of the recommendations." One of the first tasks was to persuade the developers of the proposed Vineyard Plaza Shopping Center to re-site its project, from outside the town to a new location only two blocks from the central plaza. The necessary encouragement came from $5.2 million in Redevelopment Agency Certificates of Participation, guaranteed by Safeway Stores, Inc., of Oakland, Calif.; $1 million of developer equity; $1 million invested by Thrifty Drug; a $1.3 million loan from the city to the developer; and $700,000 of city investments in off-site improvements. For its participation the city receives 20 percent of rental income and resale appreciation as well as full interest on the loan.

With this visible evidence that business was committed to the downtown area, Healdsburg set to work vigorously. Major face-lifting projects began throughout the plaza, restoring original architectural features and replacing signs to conform to new design regulations. Utility lines were buried, streets were repaved, and period lighting was installed in the common areas. A major north-south thoroughfare is 80 percent complete.

And what about the vacant six blocks and the aging sign promising commercial growth? The town bought the land, took down the sign, provided two square blocks of fresh downtown parking, negotiated an agreement with San Jose builder Barry Swenson to develop a commercial office project, and began soliciting an owner or tenant for the major hotel recommended by R/UDAT.

"That weekend did a great deal to build enthusiasm for change and to bring together diverse viewpoints," Hahn says. The work is not finished, but six years after the "SWAT" team's visit, $93 million in new construction has been completed. Net assessed valuation has grown from $133 million to $331 million. Retail sales volume is growing at the fastest rate of any locality in Sonoma County.

Success stories like Rome and Healdsburg are now being told across the land, thanks largely to a coalition of business and government officials. In 1980 the National Trust for Historic Preservation established the National Main Street Center to assist localities in finding effective, affordable solutions to the problems of deteriorating central commercial districts. In seven years it has helped local business people revitalize the downtown commercial districts of more than 350 small and midsized U.S. towns.

This encompasses far more than construction work. Improving local economic management, strengthening public participation in community affairs, and making downtown an enjoyable place to visit are as critical as rehabilitating buildings, recruiting new businesses, and expanding parking facilities.

The short-term goal is to produce visible results that enhance the quality of the downtown commercial district, but the long-term goal is to foster cooperation among merchants, bankers, public officials, the chamber of commerce, and civic groups so that the refurbished Main Street will remain vital over the years.

In its first three years, the National Main Street Center concentrated on demonstration projects in 30 small towns and cities in six states. NMSC staffers met with local leaders to assess needs and capabilities. In each town they helped to organize an inter-disciplinary team of bankers, retailers, designers, advertising executives, small-business specialists, parking experts, real-estate developers, and financial analysts.

The efforts resulted in nearly 600 individual rehabilitation projects in those towns, representing an investment of nearly $64 million. All told, 1,051 businesses were started in these renovated areas.

Similar stories can be found from state to state. In Colorado, shortage of capital was a chronic problem. But the Colorado Main Street Program, working with civic and business groups, helped convince the state legislature to authorize $150 million in bonds to finance small-business development. It also pioneered the development of revolving loan funds to finance local projects. As a result, the five Colorado demonstration towns have seen 310 downtown businesses open this decade.

The Massachusetts Main Street Center, in addition to providing technical assistance, supplied each of five selected communities with $4,500 in seed money to underwrite the cost of local promotions that returned the investment many times over.

In North Carolina, the state Main Street Center decided to emphasize partnerships between small-business people and bankers, and it found a willing partner in North Carolina National Bank, which provided not only funding but also technical assistance to localities. In Selby, population 17,000, business leaders pioneered the use of a tax-exempt $1 million commercial loan pool that is partly responsible for the 58 new businesses that have opened in the downtown area since 1981; the program is now a statewide model.

In Texas, a consortium of 19 state agencies meets each February to discuss the coordination of that state's Main Street Program, which now has ongoing projects in 19 towns. The state's first five demonstration projects resulted in the opening of 155 new downtown businesses, creating 380 jobs.

Experience has shown that a local community must commit to a minimum of three years in order to make a Main Street renovation project work, and in order to establish the ongoing support that will keep Main Street vital once it has been restored. This can best be accomplished by a coordinated and committed local steering committee. It is not necessary for a local committee to know what it wants to do, or how to finance it. Rather, the key is a strong sense of togetherness, a determined attitude that Main Street must and will be revitalized.

Though presumably any local business person could renovate one downtown store, the community approach has obvious advantages. An individual shop owner is more likely to participate if all or most other shop owners become involved. In many towns, considerable thought must be given to the preservation of history. Written standards and guidelines are essential if the finished project is to retain an essential character. Planning should be coordinated before individual plans are drawn and construction contracts negotiated. Historians, building inspectors, and local residents must have as strong a voice as architects and engineers.

For more information about public and private Main Street rehabilitation projects, contact the National Main Street Center, National Trust for Historic Preservation, 1785 Massachusetts Avenue, N.W., Washington,D.C. 20036; (202) 673-4219. The National Center offers various types of assistance, such as publications, slide shows, video cassettes, computer software, seminars, and personal consultations. To get started, community leaders may wish to buy a copy of *Revitalizing Downtown,* a 115-page looseleaf handbook outlining a complete methodology. It costs $35.

Another source of information is the Regional/Urban Design Assistance Team Program of the American Institute of Architects, 1735 New York Avenue, N.W., Washington, D.C. 20006; (202) 626-7452. AIA's *Urban Design in Action,* documenting the achievements of R/UDAT, is available for $25, plus $3 for shipping.

When you begin, however, you should not expect miracles overnight. Whatever the current state of your Main Street, it probably is the result of decades of change that cannot be reversed quickly. If you resolve to revamp Main Street, you must dig in for the long haul. "Don't try this unless you have a long-term perspective," says Kurt Hahn, in Healdsburg. "It takes patience and persistence."

Chapter 16

Rethinking Economic Development Planning

WILBUR R. THOMPSON
PHILIP R. THOMPSON

This combination essay, theoretical exercise and progress report on current research reconsiders the conventional and popular industry-targeting approach to local economic development planning, and offers a new, *complementary* "occupational-functional" perspective. This new approach, which goes beyond a local economy's immediate export base, focuses on a locality's long run basic capabilities, especially the quality and potential of its human resources.

This article offers some early estimates of tentative indicators with which to judge the comparative position and prospects of a local economy on five alternative, or complementary, or sequential local economic development paths. The principal value of this work to economic development strategists is that the occupational-functional approach is likely to be more amenable to long range policy initiatives and responses than the conventional industry-targeting approach. But no hard choice is forced. Rather, the synergism of the two approaches can produce deeper insights into the local economic development process and greater returns from the practice of development planning.

The Conventional Approach

In contrast to mainstream or national economics, which draws on over 200 years of thought, local economic growth and development theory has an intellectual history of barely three decades. Moreover, it has subsisted largely, and barely, on two major ideas: export base theory and comparative advantage, both with roots in international trade theory.

Reprinted with permission from *Commentary*, Vol. 9, No. 3, Fall, 1985. Published by the National Council for Urban Economic Development, Washington, D.C.

The local economy is defined as a cluster of workplaces together with the area around it which is within a reasonable commute to that work and is seen as primarily dependent on those local businesses that sell to outsiders. It is these local export industries that pump new income into the local economy, income that both circulates inside the local economy and ultimately leaks out to pay for needed imports.

Export base theory sees local businesses that sell to customers residing *within* the local economy — retail grocers, family physicians, bankers, etc. — as derivative activity linked to the export base in almost fixed proportions. If the local export base grows, then more new income will be generated, thereby supporting more retailers, doctors, bankers, etc. The seeming corollary and the guiding principle in area development policy and practice is that if the export base contracts, then the lost jobs simply must be replaced, roughly one for one, or else that local service superstructure will shrink, and roughly proportionately. But if a local merchant fails, a new one will rise automatically to take his place. (The new one may, in fact, have driven the old one out through superior business practices.)

The public policy implications would then seem clear: areas losing export manufacturing should place the highest priority on identifying replacement export industries and target their local economic development efforts on firms in those industries. Indeed, export industry targeting has been the principal thrust of almost every local economic development committee and the central focus of each new state commission on employment and economic development.

The local development strategy that flows from the export base logic begins by identifying those industries that are: (1) relatively large, (2) fast growing and (3) compatible with local resources, especially skills in excess supply. The dilemma that this simple, direct approach faces, especially in mature manufacturing economies, is that very few manufacturing industries are now growing or are projected to grow at even the national average rate of growth, and even rarer are those that are projected to add large numbers of semi-skilled, blue-collar workers that are in such excess supply. Unfortunately, the development analyst can spend many hours in near fruitless search, combing that long list of manufacturing industries — 200-odd SIC four-digit industries — for a promising target.

But dark as the employment picture is, especially for displaced lower-skilled manufacturing workers, the export base logic unduly constrains our thinking about alternative paths to local economic development and unnecessarily restricts our policy options. Concentrating on the local export sector tends moreover to lock one into a very short range development perspective and makes light of a venerable concept from mainstream economics: "comparative advantage" as the very foundation of local growth as well as international trade. In the long run, *basically,* the fortunes of the local export sector depend on the efficiency and creativity of the full local economy and especially on the performance of certain *key local service* industries.

Local Services

So much of the local service sector is largely derivative (passive) in nature and that part is so readily seen — so close to our daily life — that we tend to lose sight of that relatively small set of local services which are so critical to export industries' vitality. To broaden our policy options, we need to distinguish carefully between routine "derivative local services" and the critical "local development services," as portrayed in Figure 1. We could choose to approach the stimulation of the local export sector *indirectly* by focusing more on key development services that largely determine the efficiency and creativity characterizing our local export industries, that is, services that determine local comparative advantage and disadvantage in inter-regional competition and trade.

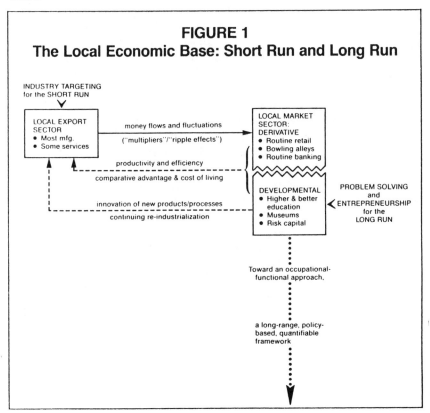

FIGURE 1
The Local Economic Base: Short Run and Long Run

Fully as important as efficiency is the role that the development services play in ensuring that wholly new export industries will be formed; new products and processes must be invented and innovated, or captured from outside, frequently and regularly enough to ensure the periodic regeneration of the local export base — "industrial renewal." Indeed, these key local development services are the true local economic base, and the current set of local export industries are the intermediaries that pump income into the economy at any given time and thereby *finance* these "basic services." Most export industries come and go; the key local services abide.

Subsidies

Those who argue most strongly for targeting export industries over local trade and service activity point out the wastefulness of using scarce resources to assist some business like a national, fast-food chain when its success can only come at the expense of an alternative, existing, family restaurant, yielding little or no net gain in local employment and a net loss in local income after accounting for the public subsidy. In contrast, the use of those resources to attract a new export-oriented manufacturer is seen as a *local net* gain. (The fact that this is still a zero sum game at the national level is not their concern.)

But the cards are stacked in their illustrations. Public resources used to increase the efficiency or quality of local education, transportation, utilities, fire and police, or health care reduces the cost of doing business locally, thereby strengthening the competitive position of all local exporters. Or, raising the quality of life locally could serve the local interest by holding or attracting scarce talent, again strengthening the hand of all local business including exporters. Moreover, the fact that this is a *positive* sum game at the national level should be of concern to all. At its very best, free market competition argues that individual firms pursuing their own self-interest can increase the national well-being. And the same can be true in inter-regional competition to produce a better product — urban efficiency and amenity.

In general, careful attention to the structure and performance of the internal economy, at least in large metropolitan areas, offers the promise of the greatest gain both locally and nationally, just as surely as misguided subsidies of such businesses as fast-food restaurants have led to the worst of both worlds. Targeting a particular manufacturing export firm or even an industry that falls in between is a minimum risk strategy at best (except perhaps for the smallest places). The challenge then is to integrate local economic development and urban planning: land use, transportation and capital investment strategies.

A New Approach

A complementary, rather than alternative, approach is to turn from the typical gleaning of fields for new industries to look more deeply into the nature of the local *occupational* base created by the local industry mix. If we think of the local economic base as both the local industry-mix and its reflection in the local occupation-mix, we can *leverage existing local occupational strengths* as surely as we can *target new national industries.*

Anyone who has ever taken the trouble to compare the very different occupational profiles of various industries is struck by the almost unbelievable variation between the proportion of the total workforce employed in, say, professional and technical work. For example, scientists and engineers account for less than one-half of 1 percent of the workforce in apparel and wood products, more than 7 percent in the chemical and electrical machinery industries and twice that in the aircraft industry. (This tightly linked family of occupational indexes should be a critical component in any standard definition of high-tech industry.)

Each local economy would find on careful self-study that its industrial history has left behind an occupational legacy that opens wide some paths to local economic development and, if it does not fully foreclose others, at least cautions that other local development strategies may mean a steep uphill climb.

We have devised five occupational-functional rows that encompass and aggregate the scores of occupational classifications devised by the Bureau of the Census:

1. routine operations, ranging across manufacturing, trade and services;
2. precision operations, focusing on industries that employ more craftsmen and technicians;
3. research and development, serving as a center of science and technology;
4. central administration, performing the headquarters function and
5. entrepreneurship, capturing the propensity to start new businesses.

The routine operations row is centered on the census classification "operators, fabricators and laborers." Precision operations emphasizes the classification of "precision production, craftsmen and repair." Research and development keys to "professional specialty occupations," and central administration to "executive, administrative and managerial." The Census does not use entrepreneur as an occupational classification, much as one would like to know about it.

This occupational-functional approach captures in a broader and tighter framework many of the recurring perspectives and concerns that have appeared in recent articles in this journal. For example, the R&D row addresses the call to focus policy more on technological processes and infrastructure rather than

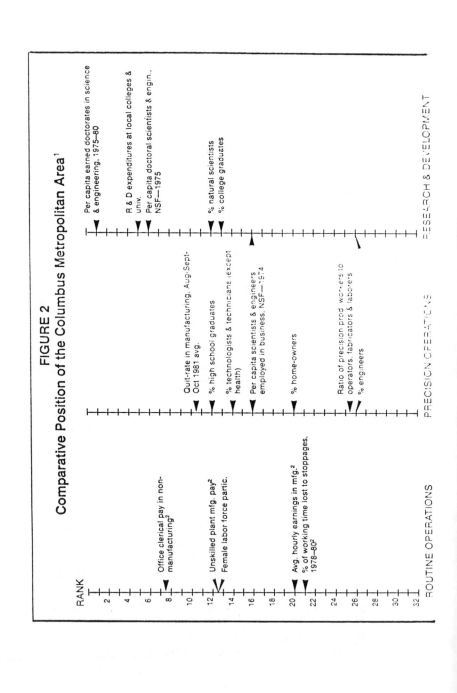

FIGURE 2
Comparative Position of the Columbus Metropolitan Area[1]

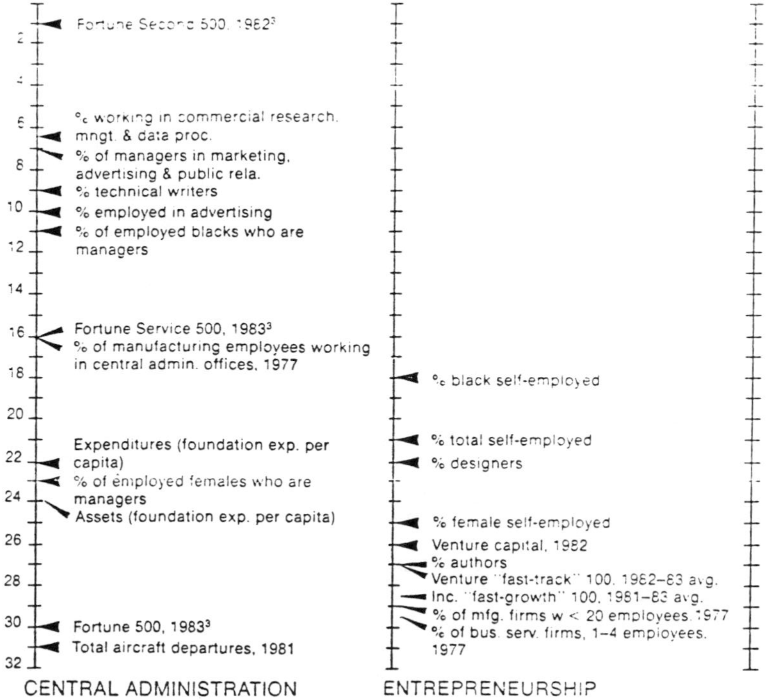

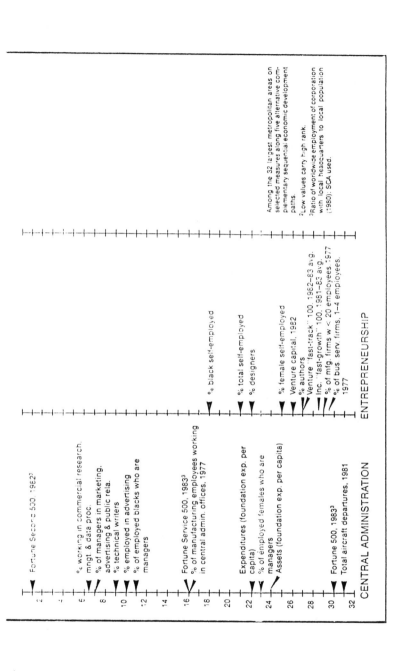

Fortune Second 500, 1982[3]
% working in commercial research, mngt. & data proc.
% of managers in marketing, advertising & public rela.
% technical writers
% employed in advertising
% of employed blacks who are managers
Fortune Service 500, 1983[3]
% of manufacturing employees working in central admin. offices, 1977
Expenditures (foundation exp. per capita)
% of employed females who are managers
Assets (foundation exp. per capita)
Fortune 500, 1983[3]
Total aircraft departures, 1981
CENTRAL ADMINISTRATION
% black self-employed
% total self-employed
% designers
% female self-employed
Venture capital, 1982
% authors
Venture "fast-track" 100, 1982–83 avg.
Inc. "fast-growth" 100, 1981–83 avg.
% of mfg. firms w < 20 employees, 1977
% of bus. serv. firms, 1–4 employees, 1977
ENTREPRENEURSHIP
2
4
6
8
10
12
14
16
18
20
22
24
26
28
30
32

Among the 32 largest metropolitan areas on selected measures along five alternative complementary sequential economic development paths.

[2]Low values carry high rank.

[3]Ratio of worldwide employment of corporation with local headquarters to local population (1980): SCA used.

on particular industries; the entrepreneurship row adds to "high-tech" that even newer, magic word in contemporary local economic development strategy.

The important distinction between regenerating a local economy and re-employing its inhabitants is integrated into development strategy through explicitly considering routine and precision operations across all industries, with associated lessons for manpower training and relocation. Finally, the head-quarters row provides an especially incisive perspective on the locality's growing role in international trade and its place in the global economy.

Early Returns

The occupational-functional approach can be illustrated by discussing the early research returns from using it in Akron and Columbus, Ohio. The position of the Columbus metropolitan area on each of the five paths is ranked relative to others in the 32 metropolitan areas with 1980 populations of 1 million or more, employing some 50-odd indicators, as shown in Figure 2. Using the same five paths, the Akron metropolitan area occupational-functional profile was ranked among the 40 metropolitan areas of between one-half and 1 million population.

By studying these profiles we can learn that the Columbus metropolitan area ranks first within its peer group of the 32 metro areas in the per capita number of doctorates awarded in science and engineering between 1975 and 1980 (see Figure 1, R&D path). The Akron metropolitan area ranks first within its peer group of 40 metro areas in the number of *Fortune 500* corporations with headquarters in its metro area (weighted by their world-wide employment), relative to population.

Overall, these indexes form distinctive patterns. Columbus is strongest in research and development, weakest in entrepreneurship: Akron is strongest in precision manufacturing operations and central administration. Of the seven Ohio metropolitan areas of over one-half million population in 1980 (Akron, Cincinnati, Cleveland, Columbus, Dayton, Toledo and Youngstown), all are weak in entrepreneurship with the exception of Dayton, which shows only average-performance. Indeed, it appears that entrepreneurship is weak across most of the industrial Midwest. (An extended discussion on the nature of and reasoning behind the various indicators is available on request from the authors.)

This occupational-functional approach provides a new framework within which to review all location theory, one that seems likely to produce at least as many new insights as the conventional industry rubric. For example, industry-based location theory compares product to raw material transportation cost in weighing the relative pull to the mines and fields versus the product market—

leaning one way in material processing industries and the other way in the later stages of fabricating. But headquarters operations are much alike across industries and much more locationally sensitive to the ease and cost of air transportation, especially the offices of national and international companies. Again, wages and taxes are most relevant to routine operations whereas amenities may off-set these costs and dominate the location of research and headquarters facilities.

In many industries, if not most, a research-doctorate university is almost a necessary and sufficient condition to attract research centers. And local supplies of risk capital are critical to new entrepreneurs but of little or no consequence in the location of branch plants (routine operations) or large corporations, drawing largely on internal sources of capital (depreciation reserves and retained earnings). Perhaps location theory will turn out better the second time around.

Industrial Filtering

The promise and immediate return from the new perspective emphasizing occupations is especially striking in the new insights it offers into industrial filtering.

Briefly, the theory of industrial filtering argues that industries age and descend through a hierarchy in the national system of cities, ranked by their industrial sophistication. New products and processes are created in the larger, industrially mature centers where technical skills, specialized facilities and risk capital are easiest to find.

In the beginning, the central question is: where can this new work be done? But with time and growing experience, the production process becomes rationalized and routinized. As the maturing industry slides down its learning curve, lesser skills bring greater competition and product price pressure to seek out cheaper labor markets. The central question changes to: where can this now familiar work be done most cheaply?

The very act of sliding down the learning curve of a given industry is expressed neatly in our occupational categories: beginning with research and development, followed in time by precision operations and leading finally to routine work. And the entrepreneurial function, or occupation, is the means by which a firm, industry or place moves from one learning curve to the next to avoid sliding down a given curve too long and too far. Entrepreneurship becomes an act of self-preservation for places too.

The itinerary of the maturing industry—from Chicago to Memphis to Tupelo to Ciudad Juarez—is less interesting than the process by which a given locality along the way gains, loses and replaces industries—individual elements in the chain of succession. The best scenario for a major research center is shown

FIGURE 3
Industrial Filtering and Local Re-Industrialization

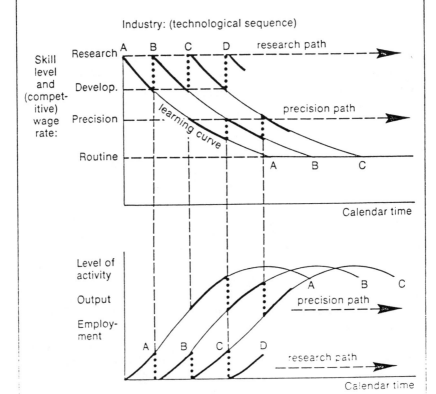

Industry: (technological sequence)

Skill level and (competitive) wage rate:

Research
Develop.
Precision
Routine

research path
precision path
learning curve

Calendar time

Level of activity
Output
Employment

precision path
research path

Calendar time

—————— Industry life stages
━━━━━━ Local occupational-functional path
•••••••• Exercise of local entrepreneurship
(including corporate acquisitions)

by the uppermost heavy solid line in Figure 3: at the point in time industry A has descended from the research to the development stage and moved perhaps out of its university birthplace to an engineering complex, that research center has already moved on into a new frontier of science or technology. And this place may remain at the cutting edge of science and technology while delegating the second-phase business of refinement to others.

Again, an advanced manufacturing center, the lower heavy line on the figure, can escape sliding down into routine work (and lower wage rates) by exercising local entrepreneurship, expressed here by stretching upward aggressively to capture the new precision work flowing out of the development stage—pilot plants—of industry B.

The lower half of the figure correlates in time the routinization of the skills required in the aging industry with the slowing growth of its output and employment, giving double meaning to the concept of maturing. Note, for example, that the precision workplace typically acquires industries during their growth phase and holds them until they have slowed to near stagnancy. Places relegated to routine operations tend to acquire industries only when they are poised at the edge of decline, becoming in effect industrial hospices. Every place runs to stand still (hops across the family of growth curves), but some places run for higher stakes (hop across the family of learning curves on a higher plateau of skill).

Much of this theory of industrial filtering and the correlate process of local re-industrialization was developed almost two decades ago (Thompson, 1968, "Issues in Urban Economics": 1969, *Contemporary Economics Issues*). The contribution here is that the newly created occupational-functional framework has opened the way for much more precisely quantifying and testing those hypotheses, and applying the ideas in the pragmatic business of local economic development planning, which should especially interest the practitioner.

If one can even only roughly place a local economy in the spectrum ranging from research to routine operations, the nature of the demands on local entrepreneurship are more clearly seen. And if one can estimate the vigor of local entrepreneurship, including that in local corporate headquarters, the likelihood of responding to continuing crises of local re-industralization can be more soberly and honestly appraised. Building elegant superstructures of local development practice will not suffer for the patient implanting of stronger theoretical foundations.

Crossing Boundaries

A local economy may grow and change over time in either of two ways. It may remain specialized in the same industry and progress in its functional role from simple to more complex operations—from routine to precision work, and even on to becoming a major center of research and development in related fields. Strictly speaking, if this center of research moves beyond developing new processes to creating and innovating products, then the place has crossed boundaries to a new industry. But it is useful here to distinguish between this economic development path up the occupational ladder and a very different sequence in which a locality may, through the practices of some specialized occupation—riding some functional role—progress from one industry to another. These alternative development sequences are shown in Figure 4.

FIGURE 4
The Industrial-Occupational-Functional Matrix

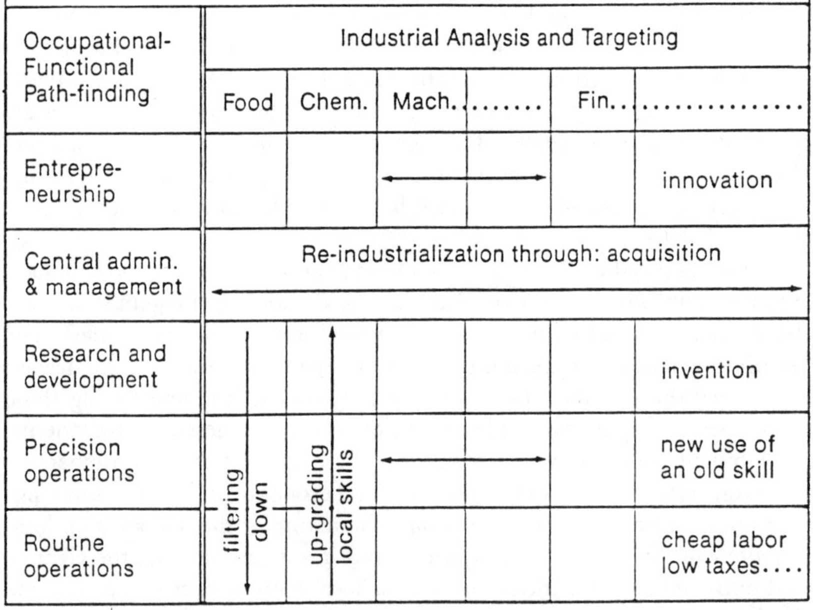

Occupational-Functional Path-finding	Industrial Analysis and Targeting					
	Food	Chem.	Mach.	....	Fin..	....
Entrepre-neurship			←————————→		innovation	
Central admin. & management	Re-industrialization through: acquisition ←————————————————————————————————————→					
Research and development	↑		invention			
Precision operations	filtering down / up-grading local skills		←————————→		new use of an old skill	
Routine operations					cheap labor low taxes....	

This abstract thesis may be dramatized by using individual case histories as analogies. For example, the president of Apple Computer illustrates the thesis of shifting between industries by being proficient at a given occupation. John Scully, the former president of Pepsi Cola, was hired by Apple presumably because of his management and marketing skills rather than his knowledge of computers.

It is also possible to shift occupations within a given industry through upward mobility. For example, the late Alfred Hitchcock began his career in the movie industry by putting titles and credits on movies (routine operations); he proved so adept at this he was promoted and assumed more technical duties in film production (precision operations), from there he innovated techniques of filmmaking, such as better camera angles and back-lighting (research and development). After innovating techniques, he directed movies (management) and finally attracted investors and produced his own movies (entrepreneurship), so that when he died in 1980 his estate was worth over $20 million. And individuals carry communities with them as they move across industry and occupational boundaries.

Local Re-Industrialization

Corporate acquisitions are one of the most common routes by which localities cross industry boundaries in the course of economic redevelopment. When a local headquarters company acquires an existing company in a different industry, even if no transfer of production facilities takes place, the host locality will in various ways begin to reflect the technology and industrial culture of the new industry. Some personnel changes are inevitable and ordinarily a significant flow of technical information takes place between the new subsidiary and the local headquarters. A corporate conglomerate enlarges the community's experiences and awareness of other economic possibilities.

Local corporations may instead carry their host locality with them along the *entrepreneurial* development path by acquiring patent rights. In further work in greater depth, the analyst may find good reason to distinguish between local corporate acquisition of existing companies with established track records, regularly reported in balance sheets and income statements, and merely acquiring the right to take the risks of introducing a new product. The boundary between aggressive management and market innovation may be imprecise in practice, but this dual focus may be very productive in policy-based research.

For example, General Motors has recently acquired partnerships in a Japanese robotics firm, purchased outright a leading computer software company and three new, small machine-vision firms. While these are all linked to their motor vehicle specialization, they all have the potential of carrying General Motors and southeast Michigan into new technical fields and new industries. When local corporations with millions, even billions of dollars of liquid assets go shopping, they can carry their host communities with them across industry boundaries, up occupational ladders and into new technologies. But local industrial development data bases do not typically extend beyond numbers employed and rates of growth to range of skills and knowledge.

Assuming, for example, that more precise measurement were to confirm first impressions that Akron and Columbus rank high in headquarters activity and low in entrepreneurship, Figure 3's logic would argue that the re-industrialization of these places will originate more through corporate acquisitions than through pure entrepreneurship—that is, individual proprietorship. Corporate headquarters entrepreneurship could take the form either of acquiring patents at the end of the research stage or buying control of new companies at the end of the development stage from venture capitalists who had acquired control earlier from the original inventor-entrepreneur.

Even such tentative conclusions pose as many new questions as they answer. Should local development strategists lean more toward accommodating and assisting local corporate venturing or more toward nurturing their individual underdeveloped invention, innovation and risk-taking—that is, leverage their strength or remedy their weakness? But at least the analysis would have progressed in that unending sequence of critical questions. We leave for another time and place an extended discussion of how corporate entrepreneurship and intrapreneurship—individual creativity and risk-taking within large organizations—best fit into the five-path framework so summarily discussed in this brief chapter.

Functional Selection

Each of the many industries performs each of the five functions somewhere. But just as a particular place may host some industries and not others, so too it may practice more of some occupations or functions and less of others. Colloquial language reflects this: headquarters cities, factory towns and research centers are just as familiar descriptions as their industry counterparts: apparel towns, wholesale centers and state capitals.

Again, this simple cross-classification reminds one that just as there are "sunrise" and "sunset" industries, so too there are occupational-functional sectors that are expanding and ones that are contracting. And this is especially true when we adjust for national boundaries and the substitution of capital for labor. Routine work may not be contracting world-wide, but employment in it within the United States *is* shrinking, either because it is being transferred to other countries or increasingly performed by machines.

We argue in another paper (Thompson & Thompson, in press, *The Future of Winter Cities*): "A serious shortcoming of industry targeting, as typically practiced, is that the development strategist too often acts as if it is necessary to target the whole industry, from the headquarters through the laboratories to the assembly line. The local economy may not have the hub location from which to carry on headquarters work or, enjoying that favored, but high cost location, it may have to accept the decentralization of routine operations in that target industry to smaller, low wage, low rent places, or the local university may attract only the R&D function to its campus setting. The occupational approach reminds the developmental strategists that an industry can be disassembled and only part of it targeted to take advantage of the special locational needs and preferences of the many different operations.

"For example, mature industrial areas could seriously consider some fast growing industry despite that industry's characteristically low wages for routine operations (e.g., surgical and medical instruments with one-half the auto plant wage) but only if local strategists target the headquarters, research or pilot plant operations where low skill wages count for little in the location decision. Local development strategists would do well to look to the intersection of a growth industry column with their best-shot occupational row. Remember the worldly wise Mr. Robinson in the Hollywood movie *The Graduate,* who whispered 'plastics' into the ear of Dustin Hoffman? This industry tip still left the ambitious youth to ponder the occupational choice of technologist, manager or entrepreneur—a path through the laboratory, the accounting class or cheap loft space."

Conclusion

The national industry-targeting approach would seem on first blush to have a nice touch of humility to it, as if the community were saying that it will do whatever the nation most wants done. Local responsiveness to the national market becomes a regional economic variation on the classic theme of "consumer sovereignty." Or one could see it, instead, as an act of incredibly high confidence: a perhaps too easy presumption that the local economy can do whatever needs doing as well or better than other places. Any and all industries are fair game for this "renaissance place."

The local occupational-functional approach could also be interpreted as some undetermined mix of community security and insecurity in its skills and experience. The local economy that begins by identifying with great care its productive skills and experience is, in effect, saying: this is what we do best, and the call is mainly to develop or attract new industries for which our current strengths are the critical locational attractions—industries other than those now in hand that built this base. This would seem to include both the simple shoemaker who out of humility "sticks to his last" and the metal trades worker who either out of timidy or obstinacy rejects relocation, retraining or a wage cut and also sticks to the last. A major, recent industrial redevelopment study in the Detroit area was self-constrained in its search to only "metal bending industries" simply because that was and still is the nature of the local skills in heaviest excess supply.

The local occupational-functional approach is most relevant and powerful in places where the skills are the greatest and most transferable. For both individual workers and for localities as a whole, the greater the skill, the more reluctant the person or place is to write off the heavy investment in that skill. But we do need to distinguish carefully between specialized skills and general education, and between these two characteristics and the venturesomeness of the person or place. The higher the level of basic or general education, and the broader the economic experience, the more we would expect the person or place to seek the best bets across the board—the fastest growing and most rewarding industries, even if some adaptation is called for on their part.

One might, in fact, argue that the occupational approach is highly professional and is expressed in a reluctance to consider any industry that does not protect the local investment in current skills and experience—only "appropriate work" is considered, at least for the first few passes at local economic redevelopment. Conversely, a local economy that includes any and all industries in its targeting field shows a predisposition toward almost pure entrepreneurship with current skills expendable. All in all, individual and institutional attitudes and behavior serve to reinforce our strong and growing preference for a combined and coordinated industrial-occupational-functional approach to local economic development analysis and action.

IV : The Incentives

Chapter 17

Business Incubators

THOMAS RESSLER

Business incubators, as their name implies, are "mother hen" programs and facilities that help "hatch" new and fledgling companies by providing support services and professional advice the firms might not obtain otherwise.

Business incubation programs usually are housed in facilities which offer start-up companies space at below-market rental rates. In some cases, however, incubation programs provide professional services and advice, but not space, operating as "incubators without walls."

Highly adaptable to meet the needs and goals of their founders, incubators' missions range from bringing jobs to (and increasing the wealth of) inner cities, to diversifying rural economies, to transferring and commercializing technology from universities and major corporations.

Business incubation is a relatively new concept: In 1984, there were only 50 business incubators in the United States; today, there are more than 500 in North America, with new ones opening at a rate of four or five per month.

In California, where business incubation is just beginning to gain momentum, the first incubators opened in the mid–1980s; today, there are more than 25 incubation programs, with another dozen in various stages of development. In addition, California is one of only a handful of states to have a state incubation association, the California Business Incubator Network (CBIN), founded in 1990.

Given California's current economic climate, business incubation makes a lot of sense, says a national authority.

"Business incubators are proven tools for creating jobs, encouraging technology transfer and starting new businesses, all of which can help reverse California's economic downturn," says Dinah Adkins, executive director of the National Business Incubation Association (NBIA), a professional organization of more than 690 incubator developers, managers and industry friends.

Reprinted with permission from *Western City*, Vol. LXIX, No. 7, July, 1993. Published by the League of California Cities, Sacramento, California.

Business incubators accelerate the successful development of entrepreneurial companies, Adkins adds, by providing hands-on assistance, a variety of business and technical support services, and milestones for start-up and fledgling firms during their most vulnerable years.

"An incubation program's main goal is to produce successful graduates, businesses that are financially viable and freestanding when they leave the incubator, usually in two to three years," Adkins says, observing that about 30 percent of incubator clients "graduate" each year.

In all, more than 6,000 developing businesses are part of incubation programs, with the latest NBIA research showing that 35 percent of those are service companies; 27 percent, light manufacturing; 22 percent, technology products and research and development; and, 17 percent, other kinds of firms.

"The earliest incubation programs were focused on technology in general or on a combination of light industrial, technology and service firms. Today these programs are referred to as 'mixed use/general purpose' incubators," Adkins says.

"However, in more recent years, new incubators have been developed to target specific industries, such as food processing, medical technologies, space and ceramics technologies, and wood working," she adds.

"Incubators also have been created for arts and crafts people, for retail firms and for software development, as well as for women and minorities, and microenterprise creation."

Incubator sponsors include local governments, economic development agencies, four-year universities, two-year colleges and combinations of these groups, as well as for-profit incubators launched by individuals or corporations. There also is a growing segment of nonprofit and for-profit incubators.

North Carolina First Flight, Inc., operates 12 business incubators scattered around the state. Originally a state agency charged with boosting the state's economy, the organization recently became a nonprofit agency. The agency's offices are located at George Mason University where one of its incubators, focusing on high-tech businesses, is located. Businesses incubated in First Flight have included a software firm, a company which manufacturers a thermal faces identification system which allows business security systems to recognize the faces of individuals who are authorized to enter, a geographic information system company which makes use of NASA technology, and an auto repair firm. One company, which provides a central reservation system for hotels grossed $300,000 last year, but revenues surpassed $3 million in just the first quarter this year. While the incubator located at George Mason focuses on high-tech companies, most of First Flight's incubators are located in more rural areas of the state where the focus is on textiles, consulting services, and crafts. One incubator has helped launch a small city's only travel agency.

Incubated Companies Have High Success Rate

Whatever their mission or location, business incubators share a common bottom line: success in helping new firms.

"Studies show that new businesses are most vulnerable during their first several years of operation, during which time 60 percent fail," Adkins says. Not so, however, for new businesses affiliated with an incubator.

"Research shows that more than 80 percent of firms that have ever been in an incubation program are still in operation," Adkins says, describing research conducted by state government agencies in Michigan and Pennsylvania. "Furthermore, Coopers & Lybrand, the accounting and business consulting firm, has found that 'graduates' of incubators—firms that have left incubators for their own commercial space—are increasing revenues and creating jobs."

For some incubator graduates, the sky's the limit: at least two of the firms included on *Inc.* magazine's most recent *Inc. 500* are graduates of incubator programs. One, MapINFO Corp., a spinoff of Rensselaer Polytechnic Institute, recorded $15 million in revenues last year on its business mapping services. The other, Restek Corp., is a fast-growing business in State College, Pennsylvania. With $6.5 million in revenues in 1991, it manufactures capillary columns and accessories for analytical labs.

Adkins explains that incubators are achieving success by providing precisely the assistance many start-up businesses need.

"Most start-up companies are launched by an entrepreneur who has a great idea, but no business or management experience," Adkins says. "Incubators—through their own expert staffs and a wide array of outside consultants and advisors—can provide assistance in every aspect of running a business, from developing a sound business plan to marketing the product or service."

Equally important is the financial assistance incubators can provide.

"Through a variety of programs, incubators can help their clients and tenants obtain the financing and capital required to grow their businesses," Adkins observes, noting that, in addition to helping clients qualify for loans from commercial lenders, many incubators also have their own micro-loan and seed capital funds. Further, many incubators help match young firms with venture capitalists and other private investors, and some incubators take equity or royalty positions in their companies.

Business Incubators: A Model for Urban Revitalization

In California, inner-city business incubators are operating, or are being developed, a trend Adkins says can help restore hope in such neighborhoods as those of South Central Los Angeles.

"Business incubation programs have a proven track record of being able to help revitalize inner-city neighborhoods," Adkins says, noting that one of the best examples of this type of facility is Wisconsin's Milwaukee Enterprise Center (MEC), which opened in 1986.

Housed in a six-story, 195,000–square foot former Nunn-Bush shoe factory, MEC was founded and is owned by the Wisconsin Foundation for Vocational, Technical and Adult Education (WFVTAE) and Milwaukee Area Technical College (MATC). The building, donated to WFVTAE by Nunn-Bush, had been vacant 10 years and was in serious disrepair; it has been renovated section by section.

MEC's accomplishments are impressive. According to Julius Morgan, MEC's director for entrepreneurial development, the incubator's 70-some tenants employ some 400 people and generate monthly revenues of $1.6 million. Minority ownership accounts for more than 70 percent of the tenants. (Of the 30 percent "majority" — white — owners, many commute to MEC from the suburbs.)

Almost one-half of the tenants' employees live within a one-mile radius of MEC, where the unemployment rates are the city's highest. In addition, MEC recently opened a second facility, a 120,000–square foot former Square D battery factory.

To meet the needs of inner-city entrepreneurs, MEC provides extensive educational and training programs, including those offered through its Basic Literacy Center, which helps companies and their employees develop literacy, math and computer skills.

Business Incubators: What's New in California

Although business incubator programs in California are fewer in number than those in Northeastern and Midwestern states, they do reflect the diversity common to the industry nationwide. Examples include:

Rural economic development. In Winton, located in rural Merced County, Winton Business Adventures occupies a new, 18,000–square foot facility built specifically as an incubator facility and sponsored by the Central Valley Opportunity Center.

"Our objective is to bring jobs to a rural community with a 70-percent minority population," says Thomas Abdul-Salaam, economic development specialist and facility manager.

Open since late 1991, the incubator, which is designed for light manufacturing and office use, is meeting its objectives: it is 90 percent occupied, and its 10 tenants employ 41 people. The incubator has not yet produced any graduates, but it also has not had any failures.

"Our tenants range from a bakery equipment repair company to the publisher of the community's minority newspaper, with others in sales and marketing and service businesses, and we also have one high-technology firm," Abdul-Salaam says.

The incubator also assists external clients by providing them with all the services available to incubator tenants, including counseling and technical assistance.

"Our external programs are an excellent way for us to service entrepreneurs and small firms that basically don't need office space, but rather, office-type support services, as well as the counseling and technical assistance," Abdul-Salaam says.

"The truth is," he adds, "we did not anticipate as many people wanting office space and the associated services, so these programs give us a way to reach these people."

Food processing incubator. Among only three such incubators nationwide, the Foodworks Culinary Center in Arcata is flourishing.

"I thought that in a rural, isolated area such as ours, where food is the natural resource, there could be a type of vertical integration, including growers, processors, wholesalers, and retailers," says Cindy Copple, executive director of the Arcata Economic Development Corp., Foodworks' owner and operator.

Growers, wholesalers and retailers, of course, were in place, but local processors were not.

Copple, whose background includes working in the food industry, began to hear about incubators while serving on a national food cooperative and realized an incubator might be a way to help establish local food processors.

She began to plan the incubator with a group of some 30 potential tenants, which over time "self de-selected" to nine committed tenants. After a combination of public and private funding was obtained, Copple oversaw the design and construction of a 20,000–square foot incubator facility.

Foodworks opened in July 1992 and was fully occupied — with the original nine companies plus three more — a month later. In addition to food processors, who produce a wide range of products, tenants include a labeling and packaging firm and an assembler of gift baskets filled with tenants' products.

For-profit/technology transfer. A good example of a for-profit business incubator is the Technology Development Center (TDC), founded in 1991 in Davis by partners Mary Ferguson and Charles Soderquist.

"Our focus is on technology transfer from the University of California at Davis, where there are many ideas and patents that have not been commercialized," says Ferguson, who serves as the incubator's executive director.

Ferguson and Soderquist bring a winning combination of experience to the incubator: she served 14 years as program manager for two major research grants at UCD; he is a well-known Davis-area entrepreneur with a Ph.D. in agricultural and environmental chemistry who in 1985 helped engineer a complex triple merger that resulted in a national network of laboratories known as Enseco, Inc.

To assist companies with high growth potential, TDC has established a $1 million seed fund, financed by private investors. TDC retains an equity interest in the businesses it helps get started.

TDC has worked with 10 client companies, three of which have graduated. The incubator also is managing a company, which commercializes technology spun off by another incubator firm. Ferguson is president of this company, which is field-testing a naturally extracted product that repels beavers from trees in areas where beaver dams are not appreciated.

An inner city focus. The business incubator, San Francisco Renaissance, focuses on assisting inner city minorities and women in forming new businesses. An outgrowth of an intensive entrepreneurship training program, the incubator offers business consultation, phone answering services, a place for enterpreneurs to network, and other assistance.

Now in its fifth year, San Francisco Renaissance has assisted the start-up of 11 businesses including a general contractor, a firm which assists newcomers to the area in locating rental housing, and a Spanish-language book seller. The companies had gross revenues of more than $1 million in the past year, and the budget for the incubator itself runs between $100,000 and $130,000 annually with funding coming from Community Development Block Grant funds and from contributions from such private-sector sources as Bank of America, the San Francisco Foundation, Pacific Gas & Electric and Pacific Telesis.

Business Incubation: A Brief History

While there have always been shared spaces, services and management in the real estate market, business incubators as we now know them in the United States came into being in the late 1970s.

The industry began in the industrial northeast, where the "rust-belt" economic conditions of the late 1970s and early 1980s prompted not only a renewed entrepreneurial spirit, but an emphasis on economic development and job creation.

This emphasis resulted in three simultaneous movements. The first was the attempt to use old, abandoned factory buildings in distressed areas of the Midwest and Northeast by subdividing them for small firms; the second was begun as an experiment funded by the National Science Foundation to foster entrepreneurship and innovation at major universities.

The third movement arose from the initiatives of several successful individual entrepreneurs or groups of investors who sought to transfer their own new venture experiences to new companies in an environment conducive to successful technological innovation and commercialization.

America's First Business Incubator

The oldest U.S. incubator on record—which, decades ahead of its time, reflects the movement to "recycle" old buildings—was launched in 1959 in Batavia, N.Y.

Known as the Batavia Industrial Center (BIC), this incubator grew out of one family's desire to offset an economic downturn.

"In 1957, Massey-Ferguson, the farm implement manufacturer, closed its 850,000-square foot plant, putting almost 2,000 employees out of work," recalls Joe Mancuso, who with his four sons manages BIC.

"In a town of only 17,000 people, this was a tremendous blow, and my family, who owned a number of retail businesses in town, decided to buy the building in an attempt to attract new industry and create jobs."

During its 30-year history, BIC has had more than 600 tenants, virtually all successful, representing a wide range of business and industry, from traditional manufacturing firms to high-technology companies.

Chickens Help Hatch a Name

Mancuso believes he may have coined the term "incubator."

"In our first year, one of our tenants was a chicken company, which had about 400,000 chickens in 80,000 square feet of space," Mancuso says.

"We were out on the road a lot of the time, trying to interest investors and attract companies to the center, and in a joking way, because of all the chickens, we started calling it 'the incubator.'

"The name caught on and we continued to refer to the center as 'the incubator' throughout the 1960s, long after the chickens were gone."

Mancuso's claim carries some weight: throughout the 1960s, he was extremely active in economic development circles—he was president of New York State's economic development association in 1967—telling one and all about the success of his new idea, the business "incubator."

Despite the BIC and a couple of other early examples, it wasn't until the mid–1980s that incubators came into their own. The impetus, Adkins recalls, was from the U.S. Small Business Administration (SBA), which promoted incubator development from 1984 until 1987 through its Office of Private Sector Initiatives.

Under the direction of John Cox, now SBA's director of finance and investment, the agency held a series of regional conferences to disseminate the word on incubation; SBA also published a newsletter and several incubation handbooks. As a result of this activity, incubator development grew from just over 20 openings annually in 1984 to more than 70 in 1987.

NBIA, which was formed by industry leaders in 1985 and which initially had but 40 members, today serves 690 members with training programs. It also offers a clearinghouse for information on incubator management and development issues. The association, which by 1987 had become the primary source of incubator information, also publishes a wide range of "how-to" materials to assist incubators and their start-up and fledgling firms.

Chapter 18

Community Reinvestment Act

VIRGINIA M. MAYER
MARINA SAMPANES
JAMES CARRAS

The Community Reinvestment Act, commonly known as the CRA, was enacted as Title VIII of the Housing and Community Development Act of 1977. Its passage was the culmination of years of grassroots community activism, research, and regulatory protest dealing with bank lending practices in cities around the country. Financial institutions in Chicago, Cleveland, New York, Boston, Baltimore, and other cities were accused of "redlining," or refusing to make mortgage loans in lower-income, often minority, inner-city neighborhoods.

The vigorous community and activist scrutiny of the banking industry led the Senate to hold hearings to investigate the redlining allegations and determine if the industry was discriminating against certain communities. During the course of the hearings, Congress was told that bank disinvestment, coupled with a decline of basic services such as transportation, health care, public safety, and retail stores, intensified the decline of older urban neighborhoods. This trend of large-scale disinvestment and shifts in racial and ethnic mix heightened the urgency for financial institutions to ensure that they meet the banking needs of their communities.

The Community Reinvestment Act reinforced the message, spelled out in bank charters, that federally insured and regulated financial institutions have the inherent obligation to meet the convenience and needs of their communities. The CRA reinforced this basic tenet and required that financial institutions not only meet depository needs but also credit needs of local communities, including low- and moderate-income communities (see box on the next page). The CRA applies to all federally chartered and insured depository institutions: bank holding companies, national banks, savings and loan associations, and federal savings banks (all referred to as "banks" in this

Reprinted with permission from *Local Officials Guide to the CRA,* 1991. Published by the National League of Cities, Washington, D.C.

THE COMMUNITY REINVESTMENT ACT

The CRA, enacted in 1977, requires each federal financial supervisory agency to use its authority when conducting examinations to encourage the financial institutions it supervises to help meet the credit needs of the community. Specifically, a regulatory agency conducting an examination of a financial institution must:

(1) assess the institution's record of meeting the credit needs of its entire community, including low- and moderate-income neighborhoods, consistent with the safe and sound operation of the institution; and

(2) take that record into account in evaluating an application for a charter, deposit insurance, branch or other deposit facility, office relocation, merger, or holding company acquisition of a depository institution. 12 U.S.C. § 2903.

Simply stated, the CRA and the implementing regulations place upon all financial institutions an affirmative responsibility to treat the credit needs of low- and moderate-income members of their communities as they would treat any other market for services that the bank has decided to serve. As with any other targeted market, financial institutions are expected to ascertain credit needs and demonstrate their response to those needs.

Source: Joint Policy Statement.

chapter). In addition, some twenty states have developed similar CRA statutes.

The CRA gave communities the opportunity to help modify bank lending practices. The law encouraged every bank to identify the credit needs of its community, including low- and moderate-income neighborhoods; develop or adapt products to respond to those needs; and market the services to those communities.

While the CRA was a helpful first step toward increasing bank investment in low- and moderate-income communities, several problems limited its effectiveness: the language was vague, giving few specific guidelines; the law had no teeth—there were no concrete incentives for complying and no immediate penalties for not complying; and scrutiny and enforcement were often lax. In an effort to spur full enforcement of the act, community-based organizations and coalitions challenged or protested bank applications for mergers, acquisitions, and branch openings. Since 1985, with the advent of interstate banking, community organizations used the regulatory system to leverage more than two hundred lending agreements, most of them with large regional banking institutions. These agreements spelled out specific commitments for mortgages, affordable housing, and small business lending.

Two factors brought renewed attention to the CRA in the late 1980s. The lack of federal funds for affordable housing and community development forced local development agencies and community-based organizations to intensify their search for private financing resources. In their efforts to gain financing, they often used CRA as a leveraging tool to encourage bank participation in community investment programs and partnerships. During the same years, new studies of bank lending patterns in several major cities, alleging that redlining and discriminatory practices continued to exist, received extraordinary press coverage (for example, in Atlanta, Boston, Detroit, and New York). The renewed public focus on investment practices resulted in an important regulatory policy statement in March 1989, and then in August 1989, in new legislation that increased the enforcement and power of CRA.

Federal Regulators' Statement on CRA

In March 1989, the four federal bank regulatory agencies—the Federal Reserve Board, the Federal Home Loan Bank Board (since replaced by the Office of Thrift Supervision), the Office of the Comptroller of the Currency, and the Federal Deposit Insurance Corporation—issued a Joint Statement on the Community Reinvestment Act to clarify the responsibilities of banks and community-based organizations. The significance of this policy statement extends beyond the printed words. It was the first comment by regulators on the CRA since a brief informational statement in 1980.

The document was carefully crafted to detail regulatory expectations and guidelines to both financial institutions and their communities. The twenty-three page Joint CRA Statement details:

• The basic components of an effective bank CRA policy;
• The need for periodic review and documentation by lenders of their CRA performance (use of expanded CRA statements); and
• The need for ongoing communication with community organizations.

The Statement noted that all federally regulated financial institutions (referred to as "banks" throughout this book) must be far more proactive in communicating with their low- and moderate-income communities and "assessing their credit needs." In other words, financial institutions must have a better understanding of their communities' credit needs, resources, and concerns—and banks must respond to these needs with responsive loan products and programs. Effectively, banks need to look at the CRA from a strategic point of view and develop a plan of action.

Components of an effective bank CRA policy. A bank's CRA Statement, available to the public by law, generally outlines the description of its lending community and the types of credit offered (see box on next page). In their 1989 policy, the regulators encouraged financial institutions to expand their CRA

CRA STATEMENTS OF FINANCIAL INSTITUTIONS

CRA Statements describe the financial institution, its community, and the products and services offered. Federal regulators strongly encourage financial institutions to expand the contents of these Statements, which are reviewed by bank management on an annual basis. CRA Statements must be available to the public at all branch locations.

Cities should review the CRA Statements of local banks and thrifts to keep informed of how the institutions view themselves and what they are doing in the community. Basic elements of a CRA Statement include:

Description of the financial institution and its branches;
Delineation of its community (with a map) and how it was determined;
List of specific types of credit and services the institution is prepared to extend within each community;
Copy of its CRA Notice;
Minutes of the Board meeting in which the Statement was approved.

In addition, an expanded CRA Statement may include the following:
Methods used in ascertaining community credit needs;
Results of the credit needs assessment process;
Steps taken to meet identified credit needs;
Special programs (i.e., educational or technical assistance)
Community outreach efforts;
Product development efforts;
Marketing techniques to reach low- and moderate-income communities;
Results of the institution's Internal CRA Review;
Community development projects in which it is involved;
Community leadership activities with community-based development organizations;
Charitable contributions to support community-based activities for low- and moderate-income communities.

Statements to elaborate on CRA efforts and describe their CRA performance, including:

• The methods and results of ascertaining the community credit needs;
• Steps taken to meet the needs, such as special credit-related programs, educational or technical assistance programs; and
• Descriptions of their outreach, product development, and marketing efforts, plus a summary documenting their results.

The regulators also recommended including a summary of the results of the bank's Internal CRA Review. Such documentation in the CRA Statement serves as the framework for public comment on an institution's CRA performance. American Security Bank of Washington, D.C., and Bank of America, California, have expanded CRA Statements that can serve as models for other institutions. The CRA Statement may be a good first step to learning of the activites and community philosophy of each bank. A note of caution: not all banks have expanded their CRA statements, which may indicate a lack of awareness on their part.

Bank/community relationships. The most effective community investment initiatives have come from discussions among lenders, local government, and community groups. In many cases, these discussions or negotiations have resulted from either challenges to bank expansion applications or publicized mortgage lending studies done by grassroots community advocates and coalitions.

The Joint CRA Statement encourages banks and community groups to engage in dialogue and establish ongoing relationships without the acrimony of past CRA protests of bank applications for mergers or acquisitions. Interested parties, such as city governments and community groups, are "strongly encouraged" to comment on bank performance and to bring their concerns and issues "to the attention of the institution and its supervisory agency at the earliest possible time."

One method of communicating concerns to a bank is to use the bank's Public Comment File. Banks must maintain a Public Comment File containing any CRA statements in effect during the past two years, a copy of the most recent CRA Performance Evaluation (conducted on and after July 1, 1990), and all comments on bank performance; copies must be sent to the appropriate federal agencies. This file is open for public review.

Financial Institutions Reform, Recovery, and Enforcement Act of 1989 (FIRREA)

In August 1989, five months after the regulatory statement was issued, Congress passed the Federal Institutions Reform, Recovery, and Enforcement Act (FIRREA), focusing attention on its role in restructuring the nation's thrift industry and the cost to taxpayers. The hefty document also included new CRA disclosure provisions that could have a profound impact on communities around the country and their quests for increased bank involvement in their minority and low- and moderate-income neighborhoods. FIRREA amended the CRA and the Home Mortgage Disclosure Act (HMDA) to increase the amount of information available to the public by

- Revising the CRA rating system,
- Requiring disclosure of CRA ratings and evaluations, and
- Expanding HMDA reporting requirements.

New CRA rating system. The regulators use twelve assessment factors to review bank CRA performance. These assessment factors are grouped into five performance categories:

- *Ascertainment of community credit needs:* activities conducted by the institution to determine the credit needs of the community, including efforts to communicate with the community about credit services, and the extent to which the institution's board of directors participates in formulating policies and reviewing performance with respect to the purposes of the CRA.
- *Marketing and types of credit offered and extended:* the extent of marketing and special credit-related programs to make members of the community aware of the bank's credit services; origination of residential mortgage loans, housing rehabilitation loans, small business or small farm loans, and rural development loans, or the purchase of such loans originated in the community; participation in governmentally insured, guaranteed or subsidized loans programs for housing, small businesses, or small farms.
- *Geographic distribution and record of opening and closing offices:* geographic distribution of credit extensions, credit applications, and credit denials; the record of opening and closing offices and providing services.
- *Discrimination and other illegal credit practices:* any practices to discourage applications for types of credit set forth in the bank's CRA statement; evidence of prohibited discriminatory or other illegal credit practices.
- *Community development:* participation, including investments, in local community development and redevelopment projects or programs; ability to help meet community credit needs based on its financial condition and size, legal impediments, local economic conditions, and other factors; any other facts that bear upon the extent to which the bank is helping meet community credit needs.

In the past, banks received a numerical rating for each of the five categories, from which a composite rating (from one, the best, to five, the worst) was derived. The grading criteria for each category were not specific, and the weighted value of each category in relation to the composite rating was not clear. The lax enforcement of CRA was demonstrated as the composite ratings tended not to reflect much analysis; virtually every institution received a passing grade. Less than 3 percent of all banks received less than passing grades. The regulatory agency's evaluation process and ratings for each institution were not publicly disclosed.

The FIRREA amendments changed the grading system to replace the earlier numerical scale with a four-tier descriptive rating system. The new ratings are:

- Outstanding record of meeting community credit needs
- Satisfactory record of meeting community credit needs
- Needs to improve record of meeting community credit needs
- Substantial noncompliance in meeting community credit needs

All four regulatory agencies now use this uniform set of CRA disclosure guidelines and the same rating system. These new guidelines provide consistent and better defined parameters for the new ratings. For example, CRA

CRA RATINGS GO PUBLIC UNDER FIRREA

As of July 1, 1990, CRA ratings are no longer on a numerical basis; rather they are written evaluations using a four-tier descriptive system:

Outstanding record of meeting community credit needs
Satisfactory record of meeting community credit needs
Needs to improve record of meeting community credit needs
Substantial noncompliance in meeting community credit needs

Each financial institution will have its performance reviewed in five major categories:

1. Ascertainment of community credit needs;
2. Marketing and types of credit extended;
3. Geographical distribution and record of opening and closing offices;
4. Discrimination and other illegal credit practices; and,
5. Community development.

An "outstanding" rating will be achieved only by financial institutions that demonstrate certain qualities, including leadership in ascertaining community needs, participation in community revitalization, and affirmative involvement in planning, implementing, and monitoring their CRA-related performance. Most CRA observers agree that "outstanding" ratings will be difficult to achieve.

CRA Evaluations can be found at an institution's main office and designated branch in each of its local communities. They are not, however, required to provide free copies.

evaluations now include findings and supporting facts for each category, as well as overall conclusions. In addition to being more qualitative, the ratings are now disclosed to the public.

Disclosure of the CRA ratings and evaluations. The new disclosure policy created by FIRREA is important to city officials because it provides a new tool for increasing bank community investment. Under the new regulations, lenders are required to make the CRA evaluations public within thirty business days of their receipt from the regulator. The evaluation must be placed in a financial institution's CRA public file at its main office, and also at one designated office in each community it serves. It must be made available to anyone who requests the information. The institution may also include its response to the evaluation in the public comment file, if it so chooses.

Expansion of the Home Mortgage Disclosure Act

The Home Mortgage Disclosure Act was passed in 1975, early in the debate over redlining, to create a national system under which regulated financial institutions were to report mortgage loans.

The lack of home mortgage availability, especially in urban areas, resulted in charges of discrimination or "redlining," the systematic exclusion of certain geographic areas as viable communities for bank investment. The allegations of redlining centered around minority communities. Community leaders used creative but elementary means to demonstrate bank disinvestment through maps of neighborhoods marked where mortgages had been made. Lenders had no systematic method to indicate where specific mortgages had been made. Early in the debate, the Home Mortgage Disclosure Act (HMDA) emerged. HMDA instituted a national reporting system of mortgage loans by regulated financial institutions.

HMDA required financial institutions to disclose information on their mortgage originations and purchases. Banks were required to submit summary reports of their mortgage loan activity by geographic area. The reports, however, lacked detail in reporting information to reflect loan activity with respect to expressed demand (loan applications). Also, rapid investment in lower-income communities often resulted in gentrification, displacing residents for newer, more affluent buyers and investors. Financing for gentrification alone does not fulfill institutions' obligations under the Community Reinvestment Act.

HMDA's limited effectiveness as an analytical tool resulted in efforts to amend the Act. Eventually, changes to the HMDA were implemented through the Financial Institutions Reform, Recovery, and Enforcement Act (FIRREA) of 1989. The changes to HMDA will make it a valuable tool for cities and towns as they define their community needs.

Reporting requirements. HMDA now requires financial institutions to disclose the race, gender, and income level of all applicants as well as borrowers by census tract. Institutions must also report on the disposition of each loan request and may, if they choose, indicate the reason if the application is denied. Loans sold to the secondary market must be noted according to the category of purchaser.

The first set of expanded reports is due to the supervisory agencies by March 1, 1991. Each agency, in turn, gives the data to the Federal Reserve, which will produce a series of data tables for each reporting institution. Each bank's report will be sent to the bank; the bank will subsequently make the report available to the public upon request. As in the past, the regulators will also continue to provide these reports to local HMDA depositories in each metropolitan statistical area, where copies of the HMDA data for each local institution are available for inspection or copying by the public.

These reporting requirements extend to virtually all mortgage lenders, including mortgage and home finance companies, banks, savings and loans, and credit unions. The only financial institutions exempt from these new requirements are those with assets of less than $30 million (including assets of the parent organization). In addition, the U.S. Department of Housing and

Urban Development (HUD) requires all FHA lenders, regardless of size or affiliation, to comply with the new HMDA requirements. FHA lenders must report HMDA data on all FHA activity to HUD, regardless of reporting to any other regulatory agency.

Bank Activities/Responses Encouraged by Regulators

In their 1989 statement and their subsequent actions, the regulatory agencies have encouraged financial institutions to undertake many activities in their banking and CRA efforts.

In general, the following actions are encouraged:

- Participate in various government-insured lending programs and other types of lending programs, such as conventional mortgage loans with private mortgage insurance to help meet identified credit needs.
- Develop and advertise services to benefit low- and moderate-income persons, such as government check cashing and low-cost checking accounts.
- Target an advertising and marketing strategy to inform low- and moderate-income groups of the loan and deposit services available to them. Identify means to reach these groups (for example, small newspapers, radio, television, community/church organizations, non–English literature).
- Establish a process involving all levels of management in efforts to contact governmental leaders, economic development practitioners, businesses and business associations, and community organizations to discuss the financial services that are needed by the community.
- Participate and provide assistance to community development programs and projects.
- Invest in state and municipal bonds.

Some bankers need to be reminded that CRA-related loans and activities are safe and sound investments in the community. The agencies discourage "give-away programs" that would place an institution at undue risk — and they offer many approaches lenders can take to address community credit needs. City government should evaluate local lenders' CRA programs using their own criteria.

CRA evaluations for all CRA examinations commenced by bank regulatory agencies after July 1, 1990 will be made public. This is a large number of evaluations, and it will take some time before evaluations for all banks are available. As examinations are completed, the public evaluations will be sent to the banks by the regulatory agency. The bank will then have thirty business days in which to release the evaluation to the public.

To determine whether a particular bank's CRA Evaluation is available to the public, contact the bank directly or consult the bank's primary supervisory agency. Each supervisory agency now periodically publishes lists of those banks for which public CRA evaluations are available.

The New CRA Environment

The efforts by community organizations to change policy to mandate public disclosure of CRA ratings were opposed by the banking industry. Proponents for public disclosure (community organizations, state and local governments, and the National League of Cities) say such information will be helpful in several ways.

- Disclosure places pressure on regulators to make their examinations more thorough.
- Public disclosure provides communities with more information and encourages banks to be more active.
- Disclosure will make CRA efforts a more competitive element among local lenders.
- Lenders with solid CRA programs will be duly noted and can promote their record.
- The descriptive information in the evaluation identifies the strengths and weaknesses of an institution's CRA program and policies.
- The public can assess its impact on the financial institution's CRA policies.
- Access to such information indicates the emphasis on and interpretation of certain elements of CRA by the supervisory agencies.

In opposing public disclosure, the banking industry claimed that ratings could be misinterpreted by consumers (possibly confusing CRA with safety and soundness evaluations, which are not disclosed publicly) or misrepresented by others to cast aspersions on an institution's community record.

As more examinations are released, it seems certain that some financial institutions will incorporate them into public relations and marketing strategies. For instance, Bank of America in California, which was rated "outstanding," issued a press release and aggressively distributed copies of its examination findings. The public may request a meeting with the regulators and place letters to financial institutions in their public comment files (with copies sent to the regulatory agencies) prior to the anticipated examinations. All of the effects of public disclosure have yet to be seen, however.

What the New CRA Environment Means Locally

The new CRA environment spells opportunity. It also means more information, more communication, and more collaboration among the public, private, and nonprofit sectors.

Implications for lenders. Many lenders must now respond to the new CRA environment. Lenders are seeking to minimize the politicizing of the CRA issue by institutionalizing community reinvestment practices as a normal course of business. This is accomplished through aggressive community outreach that facilitates dialogue and that can in turn help identify and take advantage of sound market opportunities. A receptive bank attitude fosters goodwill and cooperation between the lending institution and its community. All this can result in good business for the lender and economic growth and vitality for its community. As the First National Bank of Chicago discovered, a neighborhood lending operation can be a strong profit center.

Local officials who give increased attention to the CRA, however, should view it in the context of today's uncertain economic climate and the banking industry's losses, especially in real estate lending. The declining financial condition of many institutions has increased federal regulators' scrutiny of loans. In turn, lenders have reduced all types of lending. As a result, many lenders feel they are receiving mixed signals from regulators who are, on one hand, scrutinizing all lending and, on the other hand, encouraging banks to undertake community development lending. Though the two are not mutually exclusive, this environment appears to be somewhat confusing for lenders.

Implications for local governments. Together, the CRA Policy Statement, increased regulatory enforcement, and disclosure of CRA ratings and HMDA information provide new tools to help local governments and community organizations make sure that financial institutions invest in low- and moderate-income areas.

The need for ongoing dialogue across the interested sectors is an obvious part of identifying needs and developing responses to those needs. Local government officials can establish a constructive process to work on community reinvestment issues with local lenders and community representatives. Local government and the lenders share the mutual interests of complying with federal regulations while building the local economy and community development base. Armed with more complete information on local lenders' performance and a local credit needs assessment, city officials can work confidently with the banking community on specific issues affecting targeted low- and moderate-income neighborhoods.

The Role of Local Officials

Often, public offices, functions, and programs are generalized under the catch-all category of "government." Different government interests identify priorities, needs, and solutions based on their respective interest or expertise. For instance, the priority "development" issues of the Mayor may differ from the immediate concerns of the City Council, while the Planning and Community Development departments may be focusing on different phases and elements of the community economic development process. Government is always blending political agendas with planning, policy, and programmatic policies. It is important, however, not to send mixed messages to residents, banks, and other interests. Making sure that all parties are working under the same message is a key element in success.

Notwithstanding the different perspectives, functions, and concerns, city leaders need to take advantage of the current CRA climate by assuming a variety of roles. Leadership takes many forms, depending on the local personalities and political climate of the community.

City as advocate. City officials can be the advocates for community reinvestment, raising the credit issues that need to be addressed by financial institutions. The city can increase awareness of the need for investment initiatives through studies, such as a community credit needs assessment and or analysis of HMDA data; planning documents; public hearings on issues; and community meetings. The city can provide uniform demographic data to all financial institutions so that all are working from the same base when they develop their plans. As an advocate, the city should be prepared to ask the questions and exert pressure on local financial institutions to respond to the community credit needs.

City as architect. The city may also choose to be the architect of a comprehensive community investment strategy or specific program. With the needs of the community identified, the city can develop an investment strategy that maximizes the city resources by investing with private sector actors. Get a head start by formalizing the goals, objectives, and potential responses discussed within local government. Through these efforts, the city sets the agenda and framework for discussion. The resulting strategy or plan can be the basis for discussion with local lenders and community-based organizations.

City as facilitator. City leaders can serve as the facilitators and brokers, building bridges between the local financial institutions and community-based organizations and building consensus based on common interests. The city assumes this role by sponsoring hearings, forums, and smaller meetings among interested parties. Community-based organizations know what their needs are, and the financial institutions need to understand them. The education that comes from discussion among the public, private, and nonprofit sectors helps construct a community investment program that is doable and beneficial. As facilitator, the city can build consensus among groups with very different perspectives.

City as provider. Local government can be the provider, as well, of public resources to be used with new bank commitments to increase their impact and reduce the risk for private lenders. Such participation can include loan guarantees, loan programs, loan participations, technical assistance services, and community outreach.

City as partner. Most important, in all situations, and along with any other roles it may take on, the city can be a partner in the development and implementation of a comprehensive community investment program. Working with all interested groups, the city can establish a process, participate in the process, and help get a community investment program off the drawing board and into the community. Local officials can help create new vehicles and intermediaries that facilitate bank participation in community economic development.

Prepare for your roles. Whatever role or roles the city chooses to assume, the greatest success will occur when city officials are prepared. Being prepared in the following areas can demonstrate the local government's leadership in the community reinvestment process.

- *Get the facts.* Know your community and its credit needs.
- *Set the agenda.* Armed with the knowledge of the needs in the community, local officials should identify their goals and plans for the city. Specific projects in which participation by the private sector can leverage precious public dollars can be used as the initial areas of focus for discussion with local lenders.
- *Dedicate staff time.* As with any city plan or program development, consider committing staff time to working on this process in two areas: meetings with local lenders and community organizations; and program/product development to consider for your city.
- *Research product and vehicle options.* Financing products require creativity and resourcefulness. Learn what is working and what has not worked elsewhere; explore initiatives in other communities. The National League of Cities can serve as a peer-to-peer referral resource for local officials interested in learning from colleagues in other areas.

Chapter 19

Directing Capital
to Small Firms

THOMAS P. DOUD

There is a growing awareness among economic development practitioners that traditional approaches to economic development can no longer be counted on to produce desired growth in jobs, income, and tax base. This awareness is particularly acute in the nation's urban areas and the heavily industrialized Northeastern and Midwestern regions. In these regions, economic developers increasingly look to government intervention in capital markets to spur economic development.

The attraction of capital markets for economic development professionals is based on the fact that without buildings and equipment, the means of production commonly referred to as capital, economic development could not take place. Increases in per capita income are largely dependent upon increases in the productivity of labor. Labor productivity is for the most part a result of the quantity and quality of capital goods available to work with.

It is important to understand that while capital is a necessary ingredient for the success of a firm, it is not a sufficient condition. In other words, the proper amount and type of capital cannot make a bad business deal good. It cannot make up for a lack of adequate labor, raw materials, markets for the product, or management ability. However, the wrong kind of money, debt instead of equity, for example, or short-term debt instead of long term, can lead to the downfall of an otherwise good business deal.

Recent studies have shown that many enterprises cannot get the funds they need because of imperfections in the capital markets as they exist. Sometimes this failure manifests itself in a firm having to pay an unnecessarily high return to attract capital. Other times, it shows up in a complete rationing away of credit at any price. In either case, capital is effectively unavailable. These studies indicate that capital market imperfections do, in fact, cut off

Reprinted with permission from *Economic Development Review*, Vol. 5, No. 3, Winter, 1987. Published by the American Economic Development Council, Rosemont, Ill. All rights reserved.

access to capital for those young, small, profitable firms who produce over half of our society's new jobs.

This article examines how states and local governments are beginning to take steps to intervene in capital markets to increase the flow of funds to these young, growing, small firms.

It is acknowledged that the list of state development initiatives discussed is incomplete. The field is so dynamic that some of the newest innovations surely may be omitted, but enough have been included to transmit an understanding of the role of intervention in capital markets for economic development purposes.

Theoretically, four strategies for attempting to alter the flow of capital within a state can be identified. Two of these strategies revolve around the power of the state to regulate private financial institutions and other financial intermediaries. The state charters and regulates private financial institutions, which in turn invest private capital under private management in pursuit of profit which aids in the creation of economic activity. Two additional strategies involve intervention by the State Government in private capital markets. These involve the most cost and greater risk to State Government. Both state regulation and intervention have passive and active modes. The four strategies can be thought of conceptually this way[1]:

	Passive	*Active*
Regulation	Passive Regulation	Active Regulation
Intervention	Passive Intervention	Active Intervention

These four options vary from passive regulation, which is the least costly and least risky alternative, to active intervention, the most costly and risky alternative.

Passive Regulation of Capital Markets

As the level of government which charters state commercial banks, savings and loan institutions, insurance companies, and state and local pension funds, states can impose regulatory requirements which influence the cost and availability of funds (liabilities) to financial institutions or influence the nature of their investments (assets).

Historically, regulation of state-chartered private financial institutions has given short shrift to the objective of fostering state economic development. The goal of regulations has generally been to insure the safety of deposits, preserve the profitability of the institution, and protect against mismanagement. Regulations on the liability side of the balance sheet could have a powerful effect on the asset side because uses of funds are constrained by sources of funds. As a general rule, loosening restrictions will increase competition among them and tend to force them to look for more creative ways to lend or invest their assets. Allowing N.O.W. (Negotiable Order of Withdrawal) accounts, which are, in effect, interest bearing checking accounts, is a good example of this sort of passive regulation which could have implications for capital markets. When N.O.W. accounts were allowed, savings and loans, and savings banks in the Northeast, began to compete aggressively for new sources of funds. These new sources of funds increased the institution's cost of doing business, which in turn has tended to make these institutions look for higher return investments (which are also higher risk). This led these institutions to seek consumer loans as well as higher risk and longer term industrial and commercial mortgages, or to push for regulatory changes that will permit them to lend in new riskier markets such as commercial lending. This, in turn, tends to fill one of the capital gaps identified for small firms, namely longer-term debt capital, small, young businesses find difficult to obtain.

Being more creative in regulating the liabilities of financial institutions could encourage more aggressive risk taking on the asset side. It could directly improve capital market performance and stimulate the flow of crucial capital to these small, young firms.

Regulation of assets, what financial institutions loan to and invest in, would also appear to hold some promise in directing capital to small, young firms, but perhaps not as much as first thought. Attempting to mandate investments by financial institutions could prove to be counter productive, as capital can freely flow out of the state to the detriment of all. Asset regulations, which might show some promises, are those which would offer tax incentives for investment in small, young firms, or relaxing existing constraints on lending to or investing in profitable enterprises.

It could be that there is an important opportunity for state banking and insurance commissions to examine regulatory policy from an economic development perspective. Facilitating the flow of state chartered banks, savings and loans, credit unions and insurance companies' investments to profitable, small firms could be the cutting edge of innovative state economic development policy. However, at this time, it does not appear to be.

Active State Regulation of Capital Markets

If a state is to pursue a policy of active regulation, it must pursue a policy more aggressive than simply reviewing current regulatory practices in order to remove barriers to the flow of capital. Active regulation of capital markets calls for the promotion of publicly chartered, but privately capitalized and privately managed, development institutions which improve capital market efficiencies. The states take an active role by creating a regulatory framework in which these private institutions can operate profitably yet achieve public good. When states do this they are moving from a passive regulatory mode to an active one. With this move, some costs to the state are incurred. These include any administrative costs that the state may have for regulatory services performed and tax expenditures which might be necessary to induce private investors to invest capital in these organizations.

The best example, historically, of state active regulation is the Business Development Corporation. Originally chartered in Maine in 1949, about thirty states have development corporation legislation on their books, with about twenty-seven currently with active corporations.[2] Business Development Corporations were intended to lend to firms who had been refused credit by conventional lenders. They are chartered by the State Government, but capitalized entirely from private sources. Management is also provided privately.

The Business Development Corporation offers a number of possibilities for being a market-perfecting financial intermediary. First, it can do things other institutions are prevented from doing by law. For example, it can make business loans on an unsecured and subordinated basis. Second, Business Development Corporations offer banks, insurance companies, and other financial institutions a vehicle to pool the risk associated with small business loans. These institutions would be allowed to hold a smaller piece of a larger number of small business loans than would be the case if they loaned directly to risky small businesses. Third, the Business Development Corporation can reduce information and transaction costs associated with small business lending by specializing in this particular type of loan.

In terms of the capital market failures discussed above, these corporations seem to be well designed institutions. However, they have had a limited degree of success. In 1977, for example, there was an average of only four new loans made per Business Development Corporation, for a total value of $1.1 million, and over half of this value has been accounted for by just five of these institutions: Kansas, New Hampshire, Massachusetts, North Carolina, and New York.[3] Legally, these institutions could be doing a great deal more than they have done to provide capital to young, small firms. The most often-cited reasons for difficulties reaching target firms are problems with: (1) risk-adverse management; these staffs have tended to be quite small and not aggressive in seeking loans; (2) competition with conventional lenders who own the development corporations and would rather carry the loan themselves after credit approval by the development corporation; and (3) too high of debt equity ratio has forced the corporations to avoid riskier and thus more profitable loans, let alone equity financing, because of the need for cash flow to service the debt from other financial institutions.

An alternative explanation for why the Business Development Corporations have not been overly successful is that there are no credit-worthy firms in the market place who have been denied capital. However, the experience of a recent second generation active regulation institution, the Massachusetts Capital Resources Corporation, indicates that this is probably not the case.

The Massachusetts Capital Resources Corporation, in its first five years of operation, has managed to invest $89 million dollars in 78 Massachusetts-based companies creating approximately 6,000 jobs in the Commonwealth.[4] The Corporation represents the largest and most successful example of active regulation operating in the United States. It is a privately owned and managed debt and equity-providing institution capitalized with $100 million of equity capital provided by the eight life insurance companies of Massachusetts on a pro rata basis depending on asset size. The Corporation was capitalized by the life insurance industry in return for a $100 million state restructuring and reduction of taxes on the insurance industry. The state designated categories of investment in small firms in which the Corporation could invest and investment goals. Failure to meet these guidelines would result in taxes being reimposed. As noted above, the Massachusetts Capital Resources Corporation has been very successful in providing capital to Massachusetts business, particularly the small business sector which has traditionally had difficulties gaining access to high risk debt and equity capital in Massachusetts and elsewhere in the United States.

The Massachusetts Capital Resources Corporation is a good example of how capital markets can be improved. It reduces risk aversion by pooling high risk investments and spreading them among the eight life insurance partners by asset size so each has the same negative burden. It reduces information and transaction costs for the life insurance companies by creating an institution which is specialized in the high risk of small business and thus expert in their analysis and handling. It also circumvents legal constraints which life insurance companies have concerning the type of investments they can make. From all accounts, it appears to be an outstanding example of an economic development innovation.

The Maine Capital Corporation is another example of active regulation. The Corporation is a publicly chartered venture capital company authorized by the Maine legislature because the lack of equity and debt capital presented severe obstacles to statewide economic development. The Maine Capital Corporation is legislatively mandated to make equity investments in new Maine businesses or in existing businesses which are in need of expansion capital. To induce investment in the Corporation, the state allowed a fifty percent tax credit against personal and corporate income taxes. In each year for five years, an investor can credit the lesser ten percent of his investment in the Corporation, or fifty percent of his total tax.

The Maine Capital Corporation fills a gap in the Maine capital market by providing equity financing to small firms which export their production from Maine. The Corporation supplements its equity financing with long-term debt provided by a subsidiary small business investment company. Thus, the Corporation can provide comprehensive financing packages to deserving small businesses in Maine, including both equity and debt. The legislature has placed only broad limitations on the Corporation's ability to invest its funds. It can make investments only in Maine firms and cannot invest more than $200,000 in any single firm.[5] The Maine legislature has chosen to use tax credits as a carrot rather than after-the-fact sanctions, as was the case in Massachusetts with the Capital Resources Corporation.

In 1981, the Indiana legislature authorized another example of active regulation, the Corporation for Innovative Development. The impetus for creation of this corporation was the realization that the state's comparative economic advantage was the creation of innovative small businesses to develop productivity in improving technologies for the state's durable goods sector and to take over subsidiary operations of large manufacturers.

The new corporation is privately capitalized and privately managed. As is the case in Maine, a key attraction to investing is that investors who purchase stock receive a credit on their income tax liability equal to thirty percent of the purchase price of the stock. It will assist small business in three ways. First, it will invest in high risk start-ups. Second, it will invest in SBIC's which finance small business. Third, it will finance leveraged buy-outs of subsidiary manufacturing plants being spun off by parent corporations because profits are not adequate.

Passive Intervention in Capital Markets

States can passively intervene in the capital allocation process through the use of economic incentives. This usually takes three forms: (1) decreasing the cost of economic development investments, (2) decreasing the risk of small firm investments, and (3) providing a secondary market to increase liquidity of lending institutions.[6] All three of these interventions can cost the state money, but they are administered passively through financial institutions.

The most common attempt to decrease the cost of economic development investments has generally been to reduce the cost of capital through subsidy. The forms these capital subsidies take are known to all economic development practitioners. They are usually in the form of tax credits, exemptions, or interest subsidy programs. The most common form of subsidy is not a state subsidy at all but rather a federal subsidy—the interest subsidy associated with tax exempt industrial revenue bonds.

The risk associated with economic development investments in small business can be decreased through the use of loan guarantees and credit insurance. A guarantee is a commitment of the state to fund defaults. Insurance involves the purchase of a premium which forms a reserve fund which stands behind the loan. Guarantees and insurance help reallocate capital in favor of small enterprises that have faced obstacles in acquiring funds. If designed and implemented properly, loan guarantees and insurance could be a very cost-effective job creation tool. To do this, fees and premiums must be set to reflect the true cost of providing the insurance or guarantee. This will help screen out both too healthy and too weak of firms.

The liquidity of institutions making economic development investments could be improved by developing a secondary market for such investments. Having a secondary market could greatly increase the availability of capital to small business borrowers. With a secondary market, a financial institution could make a loan to a small business, sell that loan in the secondary market, and thus replenish its ability to make another small business loan. While this would appear to offer some possibilities for increasing capital availability to small businesses, few states have attempted to use this incentive.

Active State Intervention in Capital Markets

The most risky and highest cost option for a governmental entity that wants to intervene in the capital allocation process is active intervention through the creation of state development finance institutions which are publicly chartered, publicly capitalized, and publicly managed. These institutions operate as direct financial intermediaries lending or investing in projects that are believed not to have access to private financial markets. These intermediaries provide equity or debt capital, or both. Currently, there are only a few equity-providing institutions which are publicly chartered and managed in the country. The oldest of these is the Connecticut Product Development Corporation.[7] The Corporation was created to stimulate the development of new products and technologies to be produced by Connecticut firms. It seeks to stimulate new products by providing grants to finance development costs in existing small firms. In return for the grant, which can be up to sixty percent of development costs, it receives a royalty, usually at five percent of sales. The Corporation does not finance start-up situations and thus avoids the need to provide managerial assistance. Rather, it emphasizes funding new products of existing Connecticut firms. If the product fails but the company grows in other areas, the corporation receives no return. Since its inception in 1975, 39 products have received support from the Corporation. The average funding has been approximately $120,000, with the maximum to date being $300,000. Many of the 39 recipients are still engaged in development work and their products have not yet come to market. However, the Corporation's royalty income has begun to increase at an exponential rate and profitability has been demonstrated.

The Product Development Corporation has a number of desirable attributes: (1) it provides patent money, no payments are made until sales begin; (2) it leaves complete control of the company in the hands of the company, thus avoiding the public ownership problem; (3) the royalty agreement allows for substantial returns on successful products, although the Corporation limits its return to five times the initial grant; and (4) payment of royalties comes out of pre-tax income, which is more attractive to the firm.

The Massachusetts Technology Development Corporation is somewhat similar to its Connecticut cousin. It is an independent public agency which provides venture capital financing to early-stage, high risk technology-based companies in Massachusetts. Its purpose is to provide a source of capital to new and expanding technological enterprises which have the capability of generating significant employment growth but which have been unable to secure conventional sources of capital. The Corporation is geared toward providing equity to young companies which have already engaged in product development to the point of needing production and distribution financing. It seeks more direct job creation benefits than does the Connecticut corporation, and stresses the notion that the state's comparative advantage lies in high technology. The Corporation deals with both start-ups, through a subsidiary, and early-stage expansions. It has been in business for several years of operation and has committed over $3 million to Massachusetts, small businesses, which has leveraged additional investments of approximately $18 million. It is estimated that the assisted companies will create directly almost 1,900 new jobs.[8]

As a result of concern for the long-run decline of an economy based primarily on oil, Alaska has created the Alaska Renewable Resources Corporation. The Corporation is to use a small portion of the proceeds from oil leases and royalties to finance the transition of the economy to one based on renewable resources.[9] The Corporation has broad powers, and is able to make research grants, participate in royalty agreements, take equity interest, provide convertible debt, or make loans. The resources Corporation, with a potential investment pool of $150 million, is much larger in relation to its state's economy than other similar corporations. The Corporation's investments have mostly been approximately sixty percent straight debt and forty percent equity, subordinated debt and convertible debt. The investment goal for the corporation is to invest between $15 and $20 million per year.

Both the Kentucky Highlands Investment Corporation and the Massachusetts Community Development Finance Corporation focus their equity investments in a different manner. They invest in new or expanding ventures that are located in economically depressed target areas. Kentucky Highlands, founded in 1971, operates solely in a nine county area of southeastern Kentucky containing approximately 180,000 mostly poor and unskilled people. The Community Development Finance Corporation can provide funding only to ventures sponsored by local community development corporations.[10] Firms receiving capital must be located in low income areas and provide employment above the minimum wage.

Encouragement about the success of public equity institutions can be found in the record of the Kentucky Highlands Investment Corporation. It currently has eleven major business investments in its portfolio, employing several hundred people. Kentucky Highlands has provided over $3.1 million in debt and equity financing to these firms and has leveraged an additional $3 for each it has committed.[11] Kentucky Highlands has been able to attract to southeastern Kentucky with its distance from markets and suppliers and lack of skilled and experienced labor, good entrepreneurs with sound business ideas. This ability is based on one thing available in southeastern Kentucky and not typically available in other locations. That is the rarest form of ventures which are not high technology firms.

In sharp contrast to equity providing institutions, publicly chartered and managed debt institutions are present in almost every state. The most common source of funds for public debt intermediaries is the sale of Industrial Revenue Bonds to finance business enterprises.

Some of the New England states' development finance institutions have innovated a market-perfecting mechanism to assist young, small firms with their debt capital needs. The Umbrella Revenue Bond is a mechanism for increasing capital availability to firms normally excluded from private market financing. Under this concept, a pool of loans to several small businesses is packaged into one revenue bond secured by the revenue stream and assets of each firm. Each borrower provides mortgage insurance premiums to fund a reserve which stands behind each loan in the bond package. The Connecticut Development Authority was the pioneer in adapting the revenue bond mechanism to the needs of small businesses through such a program. Massachusetts and Maine have followed suit.

Conclusion

Traditionally, state and local economic development efforts have attempted to direct tax and capital incentives to larger firms, hoping to influence plant location and expansion decisions. These incentives were designed under the assumption that large businesses were the real source of net job creation and increases in tax revenues. However, recent economic investigations underscore the critical economic development role played by expanding small and medium-sized businesses. Small businesses are an important source of new jobs and technological innovation and tend to be at least as profitable as larger firms.

Because of the importance of the role of small business in the job generation process, increasing research has been devoted to the problems confronting the small businessman. This research has found that the birth and expansion of independent single establishment firms is seriously impeded by their inability to acquire sufficient capital because of imperfections in capital markets. Some of these capital market imperfections are inadequate mechanisms for spreading and pooling risk, high information and transaction costs, various forms of prejudice, excessive market concentration, and unintended consequences of federal and state regulation of capital markets. These imperfections cause smaller firms to have difficulty in raising debt and equity capital.

To counteract these capital market imperfections, the states are beginning to move on two fronts: state administrative regulation and economic incentives are being used to influence the investment behavior of private financial intermediaries and individual investors; states and localities are beginning to create public financial intermediaries.

These emerging state actions indicate a growing concern for assisting small businesses with their capital availability problems. It is anticipated that these actions will move from the states which were responsible for their innovation in the 1970s to become the state of the art in economic development by the end of the 1980s. If this prediction comes true, state legislatures will become the battleground in the 1980s for the way in which capital is allocated in the economy and the consequences will appear in the way states regulate financial institutions. Restrictions on the price, term, and nature of liabilities will be loosened, increasing competition among financial institutions and encouraging higher risk investments. Restrictions on branch banking will be eased and new special purpose, private financial institutions designed to fill existing capital gaps will be chartered.

Many states, and even localities, will create their own financial intermediaries. This should manifest itself in the form of: (1) industrial revenue bond issuing authorities being transformed into small business finance authorities by providing security in the form of mortgage insurance or full faith and credit backing of bonds issued for small business finance; (2) creation of Public Equity Capital Corporations which will supply capital in return for some share of an uncertain future income of small businesses; and (3) increasing pressure to use state and local employee pension funds to finance debt and equity programs for small business.

NOTES

1. Beldon Daniels, Nancy Barbe and Harry Lirtzman, "Small Business and State Economic Development," in *Expanding the Opportunity to Produce: Revitalizing the American Economy Through New Enterprise Development*, ed. Robert Friedman and

William Schweke (Washington, D.C.: The Corporation for Enterprise Development, 1981), p. 42.

2. Litvak and Daniels, *Innovations in Development Finance*, p. 83.

3. Ibid.

4. Massachusetts Capital Resources Corporation, 1982. Annual Report, (Boston: Massachusetts Capital Resources Corporation, 1982), p. 4.

5. Interview with Belden Daniels, President, Council for Community Development, Inc., Boston, Massachusetts, 23 June 1983.

6. Daniels, Barbe, Lirtzman, "Small Business and State Economic Development," p. 47.

7. Interview with Thomas P. Munson, President, Connecticut Product Development Corporation, Indianapolis, Indiana, 23 September 1983.

8. Massachusetts Technology Development Corporation, Annual Report 1982, (Boston: Massachusetts Technology Development Corporation, 1982), p. 4.

9. Belden Daniels, *Development Finance in Alaska,* (Washington, D.C.: Council of State Planning Agencies, 1979), p. 73.

10. *Financing Enterpreneurship,* (Washington, D.C.: Council of State Planning Agencies, 1981), p. 7.

11. Ibid., p. 12.

Chapter 20

Enterprise Zones

GLENDA GLOVER
J. PAUL BROWNRIDGE

Enterprise zones are depressed areas, specifically designated as such by the state, and involve the application of tax incentives and regulatory relief to encourage private investment, redevelopment and economic well-being in these specific, geographic areas. The purpose of enterprise zones is to revitalize economically distressed areas and to increase employment opportunities, particularly for zone residents. The enterprise zone concept requires less government intervention by removing regulatory barriers which restrict market entry. Ideally, the private sector would be encouraged to locate in the zones, thereby generating income which would be used to revive the existing neighborhoods and create new jobs.

Currently, 35 states and the District of Columbia have enacted enterprise zone legislation and have established 3,172 enterprise zones. Within these zones, 11,658 firms are participating in the various state programs, have invested more than $40 billion and produced 663,885 new jobs.

The eligibility requirements for a geographic area to be selected as an enterprise zone vary from state to state, but an overwhelming number of states require high unemployment, low income levels, pervasive poverty and population decline as major eligibility criteria. Similarly, the states offer a variety of tax incentives to firms located in enterprise zones. The most common incentives include employer tax credit, sales or use tax credit, and property tax credit.

This research presents an analysis of the enterprise zone program in South Central Los Angeles and a determination as to whether enterprise zones, when used as an instrument of urban policy, represent viable incentives to encourage participation from firms in the South Central Los Angeles area.

Reprinted with permission of the Government Finance Officers Association, publisher of *Government Finance Review*, 180 N. Michigan Ave., Suite 800, Chicago, IL 60601 (312-877-9700). Annual subscriptions: $30. Chapter originally published in Vol. 9, No. 3, June, 1993.

California Enterprise Zones

The California enterprise zone program was established in 1984 and amended in 1989. It established two concurrent programs: the Enterprise Zone Act, which was introduced by Assemblyman Pat Nolan, and the Employment and Economic Incentive Act, which was introduced by Assemblywoman Maxine Waters. Of the 34 areas of the California enterprise zone program, 25 are enterprise zones (Nolan) and 9 are incentive areas (Waters). California zones had created 7,041 jobs and $382 million in business investment by the end of 1990.

Both the Nolan and Waters programs offer incentives for companies that locate or expand in the enterprise zones or incentive areas. Some of the incentives included in the Nolan or Waters programs are as follows:

- Tax credits for hiring unemployed individuals for at least three months or for hiring individuals enrolled in a job training program,
- Tax credit equal to the amount of sales tax on purchases of manufacturing machinery,
- Employee tax credit of 5 percent of wages earned up to $10,500,
- Lender income tax deduction of interest income for loans to enterprise zone businesses,
- Income tax deduction of 40 percent of real and personal property in the year purchased of up to $100,000 per year (Waters) or $10,000 per year (Nolan),
- A 15-year carryover of net operating losses applied against taxable income, and
- Local fee waivers and other development incentives.

In addition to state tax credits and state assistance services, the City of Los Angeles also offers business assistance when applying for loans, additional support with building permits, job training linkages and management assistance.

Eligibility for enterprise zone or incentive area designation differs between the Nolan and Water programs. To be eligible as a Nolan enterprise zone, an area must have a population of at least 1,000 and generally must meet the criteria for Urban Development Action Grant program for each census tract in the area. For the Waters incentive area program, the area's population must be at least 4,000 if within a metropolitan statistical area (MSA) or 2,500 if non–MSA and it must have unemployment and poverty rates of at least 150 percent of the national average.

Registration in incentive area. Firms located in the incentive areas (Waters) must register to participate in the state enterprise zone program, and a determination must be made by the California Department of Commerce as to whether the firm meets the prerequisites for participation. To qualify for certification, a business must meet one of the following criteria:

- At least 50 percent of its employees are residents of high-density unemployment areas; or

- At least 30 percent of its employees are residents of high-density unemployment areas, and the business contributes to an approved community service program; or
- At least 30 percent of its owners are residents of high-density unemployment areas.

Only certified firms in the incentive areas can take advantage of the tax benefits offered by the state enterprise zone program. Another advantage of registering with the program is that a familiarity is developed with the zone managers which often facilitates problem solving aspects of the program.

Studying South Central L.A.

There are five zones in South Central Los Angeles, consisting of two enterprise zones—Central City and Pacioma—and three incentive areas—Eastside, Greater Watts and Wilmington/San Pedro.

The purpose of this study was to identify the factors related to business activity and employment in these zones, as well as the socioeconomic characteristics of businesses located in the enterprise zones.

Zone administrators provided data pertaining to the economic, social and demographic factors of the enterprise zone they administer. This information included the number of firms, designation date of the zone, new business investment, number of new jobs, new business licenses and zone population. Data received from the zone administrators for Central City and Pacioma included all firms located in the enterprise zones; while data received from the three incentive areas—Eastside, Greater Watts and Wilmington/San Pedro—are available only for those firms which have formally enrolled as participants in the incentive area program. Participation from firms in these three zones generally is higher than from the enterprise zones, which do not require registration.

Another set of data was obtained from the business firms. A list of firms within each of the five zones in South Central Los Angeles was obtained from the five zone administrators. A sample of 447 firms was then selected from the population of 4,015. During the months of November and December 1992, each firm was telephoned and questioned regarding the number of employees, revenue of the firm, investment in capital assets, and the types and amounts of credits taken by the firms. Of the firms contacted, 373 supplied data used in this analysis. Of the sample, 31 percent of the responses were from Central City, 10 percent were from Pacioma, 19 percent from Eastside, 22 percent from Greater Watts and 18 percent from Wilmington/San Pedro. Based on the information from the zone administrators and the survey of businesses, profiles of the enterprise zones and incentive areas were compiled; these profiles are presented in Table 1.

Exhibit 1
PROFILES OF LOS ANGELES ENTERPRISE ZONES AND INCENTIVE AREAS

	Central City	Pacioma	Eastside	Greater Watts	Wilmington/ San Pedro
Designation date	1986	1986	1988	1986	1989
Number of firms	2400[1]	1200[1]	148[2]	143[2]	124[2]
Number of new jobs[1] (from 1987- 1990)	220	212	157	159	89
New business licenses	863	683	786	756	206
Firms using credits	43	19	*	12	*
Credits taken	$326,767	$196,940	*	$80,779	*

*Information not available.
[1]Includes all firms located in the enterprise zone.
[2]Includes only firms which are registered in the incentive area program.

Businesses in the Zones

Table 2 breaks down the data on the 373 firms of the sample by zone, type of firm, number of employees and sales volume. Table 3 shows how the firms of the five zones took advantage in 1991 of the incentives offered through the Nolan and Waters programs. Thirty-seven percent of the firms surveyed in all five areas were actively participating in the enterprise zone or incentive area programs. It is important to note that, in the incentive areas of Eastside, Greater Watts and Wilmington/San Pedro, all of the firms surveyed are certified and registered with the incentive area program.

Enterprise zones. Both Central City and Pacioma were designated as enterprise zones in 1986. Most of the firms in the two zones are involved in retail trade, have 10 or fewer employees, and earn between $500,000 and $2 million. Most of these firms were started between 1981 and 1990 — 59 percent in Central City and 50 percent in Pacioma. More than 85 percent of the firms surveyed in these zones do not take advantage of the credits offered by the enterprise zone program.

Incentive areas. As in the enterprise zones of Central City and Pacioma, most of the firms in the incentive areas of Eastside, Greater Watts and Wilmington/San Pedro are retail with 10 or less employees. Most of the businesses in all three areas have sales between $100,000 and $500,000; however, while at least one-fifth of the firms in Eastside and Wilmington/San Pedro earn between $500,000 and $2 million, only 8 percent of the Greater Watts businesses have sales in that range. The majority of the businesses were started between 1981 and 1990.

It is clear that, while some differences exist between the enterprise zones

Exhibit 2
PROFILES OF 373 FIRMS IN LOS ANGELES
ENTERPRISE ZONES AND INCENTIVE AREAS

	Central City	Pacioma	Eastside	Greater Watts	Wilmington/ San Pedro	All Zones and Areas Total
Number of Respondent Firms	116	37	71	82	67	373
Type of Firm						
Retail	49%	42%	46%	52%	41%	47%
Personal/Business	13	17	13	15	14	14
Engineering	8	6	8	11	18	11
Food	15	8	29	22	16	18
Manufacturing	10	8	2		11	7
Other	5	19	2			3
No. of Employees						
1–10	77%	83%	89%	85%	78%	72%
More than 10	23	17	11	15	22	28
Sales volume						
Less than $100,000	20%	27%	19%	31%	25%	20%
100,001–500,000	27	19	38	40	43	27
500,001–2,000,000	32	36	29	8	20	32
2,000,001–10,000,000	18	18	13	18	7	18
More than $10,000,000	3		1	3	5	3

Exhibit 3
SUMMARY OF CREDITS TAKEN BY 373 FIRMS
IN LOS ANGELES ENTERPRISE ZONES AND INCENTIVE AREAS

	Central City	Pacioma	Eastside	Greater Watts	Wilmington/ San Pedro	All Zones and Areas Total
Number of respondent firms	116	37	71	82	67	373
Percent of firms using credits	12%	9%	45%	38%	54%	37%
Amount of credits in 1991	$8,851	$5,358	$13,385	$4,211	$7,895	$39,700
Sales/use tax–%	40%	43%	25%	30%	31%	36%
Sales/use tax–$	$4,166	$2,565	$5,252	$1,561	$2,562	$16,104
Hiring credit–%	38%	34%	38%	55%	47%	42%
Hiring credit–$	$3,885	$2,118	$6,885	$2,650	$3,858	$19,396
Property ded–%	6%	10%	8%	—	18%	12%
Property ded–$	$800	$675	$1,250	—	$1,475	$4,200

and the incentive areas, businesses in the two programs are fairly homogeneous in terms of type, size and sales. Significant differences, however, occur in terms of utilization of incentives. While barely 10 percent of the firms in the enterprise zones use the tax incentives available to them, between 38 and 54 percent of the firms in the three incentive areas take advantage of the credits (see Table 3).

Conclusion

This study focused on firms operating in designated enterprise zones and incentive areas of South Central Los Angeles and the extent to which they are taking advantage of the incentives available to them through the enterprise zone and incentive area programs. The firms in the three incentive areas showed higher participation rates than those in the areas classified as enterprise zones. This is attributed to the fact that, in the three incentive areas, firms must register before they can participate; therefore, zone administrators work with a smaller number of firms and usually can have more successful marketing efforts. In the two enterprise zone areas, no registration is required. Zone administrators keep track of all firms located in the zone and must extend greater efforts to record the activities of the various firms.

Thirty-seven percent of 373 enterprise zone and incentive area firms responding to the authors' survey were participating in the enterprise zone program. Participation rates ranged from 9 percent for Pacioma firms to 54 percent in Wilmington/San Pedro. In 1991, 42 percent of the firms took advantage of the employer hiring credit, 36 percent used the sales/use tax deduction and 12 percent used the enterprise zone property tax deduction. These data represent only about 9.3 percent of the 4,015 firms located in the zones.

The authors conclude that enterprise zones and incentive areas have contributed to business development and have created new jobs in South Central Los Angeles; but the areas designated as enterprise zones need continuous attention, increased funding and a complementary federal enterprise zone bill to achieve the level of revitalization needed in South Central Los Angeles.

Chapter 21

Leveraging Private Investment

KENNETH P. FAIN

Small communities throughout the country are highly diverse in size, history, population, economic base or potential. But in varying degrees, all face the same fundamental economic development problem: How to foster economic growth, revitalization and new employment opportunities with limited public resources.

Put another way, how can towns help facilitate business expansion, new business development or downtown revitalization when funding sources for even basic services are at a premium? The answer is surprisingly easy to state: leverage private investment and financing with public capital. At its core, leveraging is simply a process of attracting additional funds for a program or project by making an initial investment.

Though easily said (and said often these days by federal and state officials) prescriptions that "ye shall leverage" are not so readily understood or carried out, especially in towns having little experience in committing public funds to stimulate private investment. In many such towns, neither town officials, the local business community nor local financial institutions have clear-cut notions about the need for leveraging, its many benefits or how best to go about doing it.

Matching grants, familiar to most town and township officials, represent one obvious form of leveraging, though strictly from public sources. Two or more funding sources are combined to help do a job for which one source would be insufficient.

In economic-development finance, the principle of leveraging prevails and local government's role is precisely the same as it is in matching grants. Through provision of a limited amount of public funds, the business development or downtown revitalization program stimulates private investment, both debt and equity. That private investment, in turn, helps create employment opportunities, tax base and economic vitality.

Reprinted with permission from *NATaT's Reporter* (No. 40, March 1984), the news journal of the National Association of Towns and Townships, 1522 K Street N.W., Suite 600, Washington, DC 20005-1202.

Indirect Leveraging

There is nothing mysterious about the concept of leveraging for economic development. In fact, most towns probably use one form of indirect leveraging for economic development, regularly. Every time a sewer line is constructed, a road is built, or a bridge goes up, there is an incentive for the private sector to take advantage of these facilities. When businesses take advantage of public facilities to expand operations or hire more employees, indirect leveraging for economic development is at work.

All of these publicly funded activities stimulate or induce the investment of private capital, often in amounts far in excess of the public funds spent. Houses are built and purchased, businesses expand or locate, jobs are created — because the town chose to make an investment of its own.

Indirect leveraging for economic development is most effective when it is planned and when the public expenditures are phased to provide orderly development based on overt economic objectives and targeted benefits, such as in industrial park development. That's a tall order, even for the most sophisticated or largest local governments. But even if it were standard operating procedure in small communities to leverage funds for economic development, it would still be only "indirect" leveraging at its best.

For most communities, the strategies and techniques of indirect leveraging may need further refinement, but the concept of stimulating private investment through the provision of public facilities, improvements or tax benefits is well known and accepted. It is part of the traditional approach to economic development, one that demonstrates a "good fit" with the expected and accepted functions of local government.

Passive Approach Is No Longer Enough

Indirect leveraging is, however, a generally passive approach and does not usually involve the township in what may be the most critical part of the business decision-making process: matching affordable financing to business plans.

Though there are times when business expansion or location decisions are contingent on provision of certain public improvements or tax breaks, even the most aggressive use of these inducements may not be enough. If the businesses involved cannot obtain sufficient financing under acceptable terms and conditions, no expansion, construction or business start-up will occur.

Similarly, if main street merchants cannot afford the cost of financing storefront facade improvements, upgrading and expanding inventory, and additional advertising, then the benefits of those expensive street, curb and gutter improvements, tree plantings, etc., may not be so self-evident.

Community preparedness programs, good planning and provision of public facilities are important and should not be avoided. But to make things happen in local economic development in the 1980s, local officials can and must reorient themselves and develop additional approaches to using public funds. Officials must become part of the business development, deal-making process through direct participation in business financing.

Direct Leveraging

Use of public funds to provide additional capital, lower-cost debt financing or guarantees for debt financing is often called direct leveraging. Direct leveraging may not be a role with which town or township officials are comfortable or familiar. Nevertheless, it is a role that is increasingly necessary to help foster economic development and revitalization.

A township's willingness to use direct leveraging to facilitate business development and revitalization provides many benefits—some immediate, others over longer periods of time.

Probably the most important of these benefits is that direct leveraging allows the town to help shape its own economic destiny rather than passively waiting for the uncertainty of market forces to mystically implement the town's economic development plans. Other key advantages and benefits of using public funds (which include federal or state grants, tax revenues and local dollars) as part of the package of business financing include:

Flexibility. Direct leveraging is potentially, by definition, the most flexible economic-development tool town officials have at their disposal. Public funds can be used to help tailor special investment and loan programs that fit the specific and immediate needs of the town, businesspeople and lenders. Public funds can be used to reduce interest rates, extend terms (repayment schedules), increase capital investment (downpayment amounts) or do any combination of these activities to assist business.

Maximum return on investment. Direct leveraging almost always provides the most benefits for the least expenditure of public funds.

A $100,000 Community Development Block Grant (CDBG) could be used to provide ten $10,000 grants for storefront rehabilitation. The work might be done, ten properties might be improved, but the businesses might have no more customers than before. More importantly, the $100,000 will have virtually disappeared, from the town's perspective, except perhaps for some minor increases in property tax assessments.

On the other hand, that same $100,000 could be used to create a $400–$500,000 below-market-rate loan pool that would facilitate storefront rehabilitation and provide working capital to help 30 to 50 businesses expand, add new lines of merchandise or services and construct buildings. In addition, the funds used to support the pool can, as loans are paid down or paid off, be returned to the town for other economic development activities.

Federal and state funds are precious commodities: to pass those funds through in the form of grants for private use may be easy but it's extremely wasteful, especially when direct leveraging opportunities are available.

Funds retention/recycling. Many of the best direct-leveraging programs feature uses of public funds that eventually enable the town to recoup all or part of its investment. Loan repayments, the sale of rehabilitated buildings and the sale or lease of industrial shell buildings are examples of actions that can result in return of the town's CDBG or Urban Development Action Grant (UDAG) funds for reuse in other economic-development activities.

Timeliness. A low-cost loan program can be planned and operational in much less time than can public facilities projects which might not produce much private investment. In fact, once lenders understand the town's objectives, they can help set up such a program in a matter of weeks, if necessary. Also, some state and federal programs are moving toward multiple funding cycles. Many states administering CDBG programs have established quarterly application and funding cycles for economic-development projects.

Increased community confidence. Direct-leveraging agreements with local lenders serve as evidence that the town is not standing still, is willing to work with the business community in an active partnership and has experts in finance committed to the town's future.

Enhanced grantsmanship capacity. Competition for many grants has increased dramatically without any corresponding increase in the total grants authorized. Consequently, federal and state grant programs are increasingly emphasizing leveraging and private sector participation. In reviewing grant applications, federal and state officials continue to add weight to leveraging private resources as a factor in determining grant awards.

Advantages of Leveraging for the Lender

Financial institutions in small communities are very much "anchored" businesses. They are tied to their communities and local market areas by their charters and often by state law that specifies how and where they can conduct business. Consequently, for most smaller banks and savings associations, the social, physical and economic health of the communities they serve directly affects their own fortunes. When a local economy is stagnating or in severe decline, deposits flow out of the institution and loan demand is low. Hence the profit potential for the financial institution is, in a very real sense, tied to the potential for growth in the community.

Although this general consideration can provide powerful incentives for community banks to participate in public-private leveraging programs, there are several other major benefits local lenders could enjoy:

Enhanced image in the community. Participation in local, economic development programs helps local financial institutions strengthen their ties to the community and their claims that small banks know and serve their customers best. This is no small accomplishment given the fact that small financial institutions are being threatened by competition from large banks and S&Ls from out of town and even out of state.

Opportunity to expand customer base. Through provision of subsidized, low-interest-rate loans, use of loan guarantees or other leveraging tools, lenders can provide financing to customers who might not have qualified under normal credit standards or who simply could not have afforded financing at market rates. In essence, these loans would not have been made and a potential customer that might have become a loyal, longstanding one, would be lost. Leveraging programs allow the lender to expand the market.

Immediate income generation. Putting leveraged loans on the books, especially when economic conditions may have kept loan demand low, makes money for the financial institution. Usually, the lender obtains a market rate for his or her part of the loan; the subsidy is provided by using public funds.

Secondly, lenders also receive loan origination fees and servicing fees. If participation in public-private financing programs was not profitable, few financial institutions would even consider it.

Both small communities and their small financial institutions can benefit tremendously by combining resources in public-private partnerships for economic development. To develop that partnership, however, towns and townships must be willing to commit public funds for use in direct leveraging. They must become a direct party to the business financing process.

Chapter 22

Public/Private Partnerships

ROBERT B. PENDER
FRANK C. SHAW

State, county, and local government leaders throughout the country are grappling with a perplexing predicament: how can their governments provide essential services when their constituents consistently oppose spending the money to pay for them? Many crucial services—hospitals, roads, jails, solid waste disposal and wastewater treatment—require vast capital intensive facilities. Legal or political limits on taxes and borrowing, however, prevent governments from raising the enormous investments these facilities demand.

Fortunately, creative financing techniques developed in the last decade can help many governments meet these conflicting obligations. The capital resources needed for crucial services can be raised by applying principles of project finance developed initially in the energy field. Through partnerships with the private sector, governments can raise private funds to build or operate expensive facilities and, thus, ease the burden on debt ceiling and on taxpayers.

Project finance is similar to financing special purpose bonds: the project's revenues are pledged to and ultimately retire the debt. However, project finance often uses private, not public dollars. A large, capital intensive project can be financed by private lenders if the project will generate a continuous, predictable stream of revenue sufficient to operate the project and serve the debt incurred to build the facility. If the demand for the service and the cost of providing it can be predicted accurately for the period of a long-term contract—and if the risks of the project can be minimized—the project will be "financeable." Private lenders will put up the cash.

These creative finance techniques work best when public bodies join private businesses in partnerships. The public and private sectors have distinct skills and resources, particularly differing abilities to bear certain crucial types of risks. By allocating responsibilities and risks to the party most able to bear them, public/private partnerships can increase the predictability of the revenue

Reprinted with permission from *Texas Town & City,* Vol. 78, No. 6, June, 1990. Published by the Texas Municipal League, Austin, Texas.

stream generated by a project and can perform with less strain, while private business can profit by providing the service.

The private sector's most significant contribution to public/private partnerships is its ability to raise large sums quickly in private capital markets. The more crucial the facility, the more readily will private banks lend the funds. Such lenders can be certain the demand will remain high for the service provided by the facility and that the community will continue to support the project. For example, an Indiana county recently found itself under a federal court order to renovate its overcrowded jail—or else. Other demands, however, competed for the county's resources. The solution was a lease-purchase.

A private leasing company bought the jail and leased it back to the county. The proceeds raised by the sale were dispersed to finance the reconstruction ordered by the federal court. The installments on the lease, appropriated annually, were used to purchase the jail back from the leasing company. Moreover, the service was crucial—too many inmates, too few cells—and a state statute mandated appropriations for the lease. These factors reduced the risk to the lessor. The lease payments were tax free, reducing the overall cost. The county thus obtained money for a crucial service at a reasonable cost. Such creative techniques allow many communities to meet a pressing need while avoiding a political fight over a new bond issue.

Public/private partnerships must be structured with care to take full advantage of the partners' differing contributions. For example, Florida communities, running out of solid waste disposal options, are turning to private developers of municipal waste-to-energy plants. Private owners often can obtain depreciation and other tax benefits that reduce the overall cost of a public facility. However, public participation may be crucial to a project's economic viability.

Florida's new solid waste management statute requires utilities to purchase electricity from waste-to-energy plants at higher rates if the plant is "owned or operated by or on behalf of" a local government. With proper tax planning and careful contracting, private developers should satisfy both the IRS and the state regulators. Private ownership creates tax benefits, and public involvement brings higher electric revenues. The result is profitable new facilities and reliable waste management at less cost.

Private involvement can benefit the community in other ways. The long-term contracts necessary to finance a solid waste facility may give the community a guaranteed price. This price stability may reduce the community's long-term exposure to market fluctuations, such as skyrocketing landfill disposal costs. In addition, muncipalities often negotiate to share in the up side of projects, further cutting service costs when the developer does well.

The private operator also can guarantee performance. If a purely municipal facility fails to work properly because of faulty technology or cost overruns, the community may face the difficult choice of living with substandard performance or suffering unexpected expense. By contracting with a private developer, however, the community shifts these risks from its taxpayers to the private party. In a well designed long-term contract, the private operator will perform to certain standards, or else pay a financial penalty to the community. Ultimately, if a private developer fails to perform, the municipality may proceed against the developer by recourse to negotiated security enhancements (e.g., letters of credit, guaranties or revenues) or may seek a new partner.

Additionally, private enterprise is less confined by regulatory and political pressures than local governments, and can procure materials faster and more cheaply. Pure competitive drive—the private venturer's fear of losing business—can improve service while reducing costs. A corporation that specializes in a particular service, such as construction and operation of power plants that burn waste, can bring to the partnership a breadth of experience and a depth of expertise that local governments simply may not have.

Finally, if the community and operator build an oversized facility, the community can share further in the up side. For example, solid waste facilities can accept waste from surrounding areas, and the municipality will share in the increased profits from disposal fees and electricity revenues.

A private/public partnership works best when government continues to bear certain key risks and responsibilities.

Government most often ensures the predictability of the revenue stream. In some cases, government creates the demand for a service through its power to compel. For example, a key component in many municipal solid waste projects is the power of a municipality, granted by state law, to exercise control over the waste stream within its borders. Local ordinances directing delivery of trash to a single disposal facility assure both a predictable stream of revenue from tipping fees and a long-term supply of fuel. By eliminating the risk of interruptions in the waste stream, government secures the market—and this assures financeability.

In other cases, the stream of revenue comes directly from the local government, which purchases a service in annual installments through ordinary appropriations. Because such contracts are pay-as-you-go, the government avoids the difficulties of raising large capital sums initially.

Public involvement brings more benefits than merely controlling cost, of course. Through long-term contracts the community exercises control and oversight over the manner of performance of the municipal service. Whether addressing the communities' concerns regarding quality of construction, efficiency, compliance with laws, or other specific local needs, the contract can protect the municipalities through tailored covenants, review procedures and mechanisms.

Government participation also can remove legal barriers to joint activity. One of northern Virginia's booming counties found its county government rapidly outgrowing available office space in the county courthouse. The county wanted to build new office space, but competing demands prevented it from raising large sums for construction.

The county examined alternate approaches, including a sale–lease-back of county land to a private developer.

However, state law did not expressly authorize leases of county land to private builders.

The county appealed to the state legislature for statutory relief. The legislature responded, and the county now has arranged a lease of land to a developer, who leases office space back to the county.

Key to the new office building was the financial flexibility offered by the private developer. The building is large enough to permit the developer to lease additional space to private tenants.

This higher density use allows the lessor to give the county a break on the county's own rental of office space. Moreover, the county has retained options to expand its floor space as the government's own needs grow, saving the county the expense of building unneeded space now or seeking higher-priced additional space in the future. Because of the private partner's flexibility, the county was able to share in the benefits from its own real estate development, lowering the total cost to the county.

Similar techniques soon may be applied by a nearby Virginia state university seeking to expand its urban campus. State funds for such projects are limited.

However, legislative reform initiatives may soon permit state universities to apply creative financing techniques like those employed by the county government. By allowing universities a direct return on the public's investment in the community, these creative solutions will enable the schools to fulfill their educational missions at less public cost.

In construction of offices or classrooms, in operation of prisons, in disposal of solid waste and in many other areas, governments are finding creative solutions to pressing financial demands.

Public/private partnerships, and the techniques of perfected finance, allow local governments to manage demands of public resources and to meet the growing needs of their constituents at a lower cost.

Properly constructed, such arrangements provide a net benefit to both the public and private sectors.

Public/private partnerships no longer are restricted to contracting out a few marginal services: they are essential to the art of governing.

Chapter 23

Urban Infill Development

M. LEANNE LACHMAN
DEBORAH L. BRETT
LEWIS BOLAN

Urban infill has been the subject of much interest on the part of both the public and private sectors in recent years. Central cities and mature suburban communities have begun to recognize its importance as a strategy in their development arsenal. Likewise, developers and builders have begun to realize its profit potential. Despite this interest, little has actually been known about infill land: its magnitude, its characteristics, or its potential.

Recognizing this lack of information, the U.S. Department of Housing and Urban Development commissioned Real Estate Research Corporation (RERC) to undertake a comprehensive analysis of infill opportunities and constraints. The primary focus was detailed case studies of infill parcels and their development potential in three diverse metropolitan counties—Dade County (Miami, Florida); King County (Seattle); and Monroe County (Rochester, New York).

In all, approximately 500 parcels were examined in terms of their size, ownership, zoning, physical characteristics, availability for development, neighborhood dynamics, and marketability. A comparative study was also made of development costs on infill sites and at the urban fringe. Although generalizations about national potential or about development economics certainly cannot be made on the basis of three in-depth case studies, especially for a phenomenon as multifaceted as infill, commonalities emerged in the three metropolitan areas that provide guidance for cities and developers alike.

This chapter highlights some of these findings without explaining the detailed research methodology. Several companion volumes present in-depth findings, quantitative analyses, and descriptive guidelines for inventorying local infill potential and stimulating development on available parcels.

Reprinted with permission from *Urban Infill: Its Potential as a Development Strategy*, 1981. Published by the Real Estate Research Corporation, Chicago, Illinois.

Identifying Infill Land

Simply stated, infill land consists of vacant parcels that are already served by utilities and are surrounded by urban development.

A wide spectrum of infill parcels was examined in the three case studies, ranging from lots suitable only for individual homes to bypassed tracts of 20 acres or more. These sites were both privately and publicly owned, located in built-up suburbs as well as central cities, and carried any zoning or planning designation other than permanent open space. As long as the parcels were within already urbanized areas and served by (or close to) water and sewer lines, they were considered as part of the infill land supply.

Every city in the country contains land that has remained vacant despite successive waves of development. This evolutionary process is illustrated in Figure 1, which shows the sequential stages by which land becomes urbanized and available for development.

How large is the supply of infill land? How much of that land is usable? How much new development could it support? The answers will vary among metropolitan areas and within individual cities or suburbs, but untapped opportunities exist in virtually every community.

Our research indicates that significant quantities of infill land free of environmental constraints exist in most regions—and in attractive locations. Whether this land supply is, in and of itself, sufficient to handle projected future growth is important but somewhat academic. In some areas it could be sufficient; in others it will not be. Of greater concern is whether builders will find it profitable to use the infill land supply that exists, and whether local governments will create an environment that encourages builder interest.

Market Trends Encourage Infill

Infill locations may not capture all of a region's demand for vacant land, but they should be able to attract a far larger share than they have in the past. A number of urban market trends now favor centrality, and developers are looking at developed as well as developing areas. Simultaneously, local governments are interested in increasing their tax bases without further expanding their infrastructures. Thus, as demonstrated by the 15 points listed in Figure 2, contemporary market and fiscal trends favor infilling.

Two real estate "givens" underlie development direction at any particular juncture: The key to success in real estate development is location, location, location; timing is everything.

In combination, the point is that developers are looking for the right project at the right site at the right time. The times are auspicious for infill because continued outward growth is slowing in many metropolitan areas, environmental

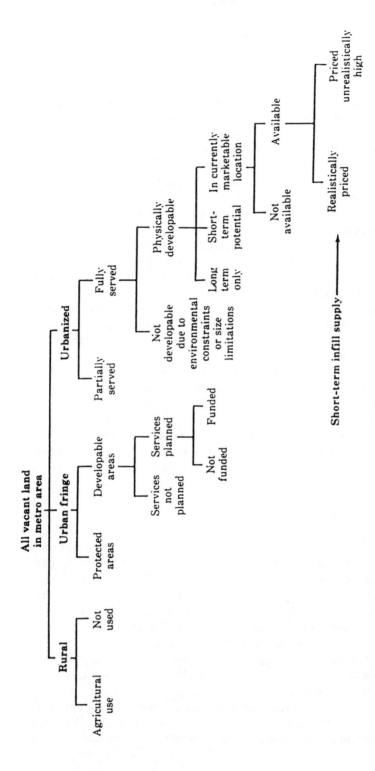

Figure 1. The Vacant Land Continuum

Figure 2. Trends Encouraging Infill Development

1. Rising energy costs reinforce the advantages of close-in locations
2. Decreasing capability of local governments to expand infrastructure at the urban fringe
3. Escalating costs of land preparation at the urban fringe
4. Increasing interest in public transit accessibility
5. Growing costs in money, time, and "aggravation" of obtaining approvals for development on raw land
6. Rising local government need for tax base expansion
7. Strengthening service economy and growth in centrally located office employment
8. Declining proportion of child-oriented households
9. Rising interest in accessibility to urban amenities and multiple uses
10. Expanding multiuse nodes in cities and suburbs
11. Increasing scrutiny of excess land in public ownership
12. Growing pressures to preserve environmentally sensitive or agricultural land
13. Need to maximize use of inplace public facilities
14. Strengthening of older neighborhoods through preservation and rehabilitation efforts
15. Capitalizing on development opportunities that do not require substantial public expenditure

and fiscal constraints discourage raw land from being urbanized, and individuals and businesses are increasingly attracted to accessible, closer-in locations.

Infill development should not be viewed as a panacea that will accommodate all future growth. Infill potential can vary significantly among metropolitan areas, as suggested in Figure 3. Building will continue at the urban fringe, but at a slower pace than in the '50s, '60s, and '70s. Rehabilitation and redevelopment of underutilized land will also capture a significant share of development demand. However, public officials willing to promote their infill inventories should encounter positive responses from the real estate community. Unlike many historic urban development programs that sought to counter trends, infill activity is very much in the mainstream of developer interest and supports current trends.

Being realistic, infill also faces obstacles:

1. Land costs may be high.
2. Parcels are generally small.
3. Many sites are being held off the market by the owners.
4. Neighbors may resist new construction, especially if zoning changes are involved.

Oftentimes, the obstacles can be mitigated, and tools for doing that are listed in Figure 5.

Figure 3. Factors Affecting Infill Potential

Factors	Markets with highest potential	Markets with lowest potential
Growth	Rapidly growing population; extensive demand for new housing	No population growth; limited new household formation
Employment centers	Strong CBD and local employment nodes; long commuting distances from the urban fringe	Weak CBD; dispersed employment centers; short commutes from the fringe to jobs
Building conditions	Extensive investment (public and private) in neighborhood preservation and upgrading	Little investment in existing building stock or public facilities
Resident incomes	Infill land located in a variety of neighborhoods serving many income groups	Infill land concentrated in low-income neighborhoods
Land prices	Shallow land price gradient from urban fringe to inner city or significant density differences to balance steep gradient	Steep land price gradient from urban fringe to inner city and little variation in land use densities
Growth controls	Limits on outward spread of development operating regionwide	No growth guidance or coordination among jurisdictions
Availability and cost of services	Developers at the fringe pay costs of service extensions and assist with school and park requirements; limited preservicing	Extensive preservicing; little in the way of impact fees charged

Infill Land Characteristics

Magnitude of opportunities. In total acreage, vacant infill land represents 37,000 acres in urbanized Miami (Dade County), 70,000 acres in Seattle (King County), and 66,000 acres in Rochester (Monroe County). After eliminating clearly nonresidential sites, property currently unavailable for development, and parcels with physical or market limitations, RERC found that there are approximately 10,000 acres of residential infill land in Miami, 24,000 acres in Seattle, and 13,000 acres in Rochester.

These properties could theoretically accommodate two-thirds of Miami's, nearly all of Seattle's, and all of Rochester's residential growth for the next 10 years. It would not be advisable, however, to force all future growth onto these sites because there is also a market need for development at the urban fringe.

To avoid unacceptable inflation of land prices, the market must remain competitive in terms of locational choice and quantity of supply.

Parcel size and assembly potential. Infill parcels range from less than one-quarter acre to 20 acres or more. There are relatively few individual parcels with more than five acres. Over half the lots in all three areas are a quarter acre or less — the equivalent of the average single-family detached home site. The size patterns are similar from city to city, but there are more smaller parcels in the Miami area, which has the strongest and highest value real estate market of the three. Clearly, there has already been intense development pressure on the larger parcels that existed five or ten years ago.

The capacity of small infill parcels to meet market demand may be substantially enhanced by land assembly. In Seattle and Rochester, between 50 percent and 60 percent of the sampled infill parcels were observed to be adjacent to other vacant land. In Miami, infill sites are slightly more isolated, with only 40 percent bordered by another undeveloped property. Most of this land is not in single ownership. RERC staff also found numerous instances where infill parcels abutted underutilized properties that could be redeveloped in conjunction with a project on the vacant site next door. Consolidating infill parcels into larger, more easily developable sites will, in most cases, call for coordinated land assembly involving multiple owners. This adds to the complexity of development but may increase the rewards as well.

Physical attributes. The vast majority of infill sites are free of severe physical limitations to development. Certain vacant sites — such as remnants from highway construction or long but narrow abandoned rights-of-way — will not be developable. Other limitations, such as steep slopes or flood prone locations, can be corrected through careful design. New site planning and construction techniques are enhancing the attractiveness of difficult-to-develop parcels that were "skipped over" ten or even five years ago. However, sensitive sites cannot be developed at the same densities that are possible for unconstrained land; per unit construction costs can be high.

Infrastructure conditions. Although infill sites have access to roads, utilities, and other public services, their condition is not always adequate to support new development — especially large-scale, high-density projects. Fifteen percent of the sampled infill parcels in urbanized King County lack direct frontage on public roads. In Dade County, one-third of the sites have public water lines with diameters smaller than the standard six inches needed to maintain pressure and fire flow for development at urban densities. One can find water and sewer lines that are over 50 years old serving infill parcels.

Maintenance practices vary considerably among jurisdictions. Fiscal limitations, especially in older central cities, result in deferred spending on capital upgrading and replacement. These problems need public attention, not only to encourage infilling but also to stimulate and reinforce investment in existing buildings in older neighborhoods.

Zoning. In all metropolitan areas, some degree of "mismatch" exists between market demand and the zoning designations of the vacant land supply. Communities "over zone" for industrial or commercial uses in the hope of attracting tax ratables. Multi-family housing, which can make efficient use of expensive infill sites, is often viewed as less desirable than low-density single-family homes, especially in the suburbs.

In a rapidly changing real estate market, it is impossible to achieve a perfect balance between zoning and the demand for land. Community preferences must also be considered. Nevertheless, inappropriate zoning can be a deterrent to infilling. Of the owners of available infill properties interviewed as part of this study, roughly 25 percent in all three case studies felt that some change in existing zoning would improve the marketability of their land. In weak markets, downzoning is suggested as a way of reducing artificially high land prices. In desirable areas, density bonuses may be needed to make development more economical. Modifying site planning standards for sideyards, setbacks, and off-street parking can also be helpful.

Location of infill lots. In all three urban counties examined, a majority of infill lots are located in the suburbs. Lots in Miami/Miami Beach accounted for only 28 percent of all infill parcels; for Seattle, the central city share was 41 percent. Lots in the city of Rochester were more numerous, accounting for 47 percent of the total. City lots are often clustered in low-income neighborhoods, thereby limiting their marketability.

More important is the considerable size disparity between infill parcels in central cities and those in the suburbs. Suburban sites are far larger. As a result, they account for over 90 percent of the infill acreage in all three cases. If unconstrained by zoning or physical limitations, these larger suburban tracts will be more readily marketable.

Land ownership. Infill land is owned by a multiplicity of small-scale entrepreneurs and private citizens. In all three metro areas, more than half of the sample parcels are held by private individuals. Business entities control far fewer of the vacant parcels than many observers would expect. Government owners are overrepresented in the Monroe County sample because many vacant properties there are tax delinquent or were cleared years ago by the Rochester Urban Renewal Authority. If government properties are excluded from the inventories, the proportion of parcels in individual (as opposed to business) ownership is 69 percent in Monroe County and 71 percent in the Seattle area. This means that of privately held sites, about two-thirds are controlled by individual citizens.

Only one-fourth of the infill parcels examined in RERC's investigation are owned by people who are engaged primarily in real estate. Speculators who purposefully hold property off the market are not the dominant holders of vacant urban land. However, major corporations or institutions can control the larger properties that are most attractive to the big suburban builders.

The vast majority of infill parcels are owned by individuals and businesses located within the metropolitan area—not foreigners or corporations located in another part of the country. Ownership by outsiders accounts for less than one-fifth of all parcels.

Land availability. Not all of the infill land supply is available for development. In fact, just over half of the approximately 500 parcels surveyed are or would be on the market within five years. Availability of land is highest in Rochester (62 percent); where as in Seattle and Miami, the figures are 50 percent and 53 percent respectively.

The real estate knowledge and sophistication of infill land owners vary considerably. However, owners of sites who would make their properties available for development voice strong optimism about future development potential. Fully half to three-quarters of infill site owners believe that the market for their land will improve over the next five years. This may help to explain the fact that only half of all privately owned infill sites are currently available for purchase.

Owner motives. Motivations for property ownerships are difficult to isolate, but RERC's research suggests that there are three dominant reasons for holding infill land:

1. Future appreciation / investment—the primary motivating force for both individuals and businesses.
2. Personal use—most significant for vacant parcels adjacent to existing residences.
3. Future expansion—providing future reserves for both business and residential development. This is also the motivation for government agencies' retention of land for anticipated facility needs, though some of those needs may no longer exist in cities with stable or declining populations.

The properties being held for appreciation or investment, and some of those reserved for expansion, could be made available for development, given positive market conditions, workable financing, and "the right price." Overall, about half the parcels examined could be deemed available.

Land prices and housing costs. Infill land in stable, middle-income neighborhoods can be as much as 15 times as expensive, on an average per unit basis, as raw land at the metropolitan fringe. Statistical averages mask important realities within any market area. High land prices are a function of desirability (quality of the surrounding neighborhood, absence of development obstacles, and perceived market strength).

New infrastructure costs can be significantly less for infill housing than for identical units at the suburban fringe, but the savings will usually be insufficient to offset higher land prices in stable mature neighborhoods. Small infill parcels that can make maximum use of existing in-place utilities will have minimal site improvement costs. Larger infill projects require creation of on-site roads and utilities, so their costs per dwelling unit will not be dramatically lower than for development at the urban fringe.

High land prices, per se, will not necessarily limit development. The key factor is what can be built and sold or rented on the land and the relationship between sales prices or rental rates and land cost. In other words, the developer will pay high land prices if the final package of land and building will command high rents or a high sales price.

For housing consumers, price parity is often achieved between central-city and fringe locations when commuting and total transportation costs are taken into account. For example, an average household living at the urban fringe in Rochester could be expected to spend $3,100 more per year on commuting and auto ownership than the same household in the city of Rochester. This equation is being considered more and more as energy costs escalate.

Neighborhood attitudes. City governments that want to encourage infill will have to anticipate, plan for, and resolve conflicts between builders and local interest groups. One of the most common neighborhood concerns is compatibility of new building design with the surrounding structures. Sensitive design solutions are often possible — using similar facades and setbacks, for example. However, if the initial proposal is for a wrenchingly incompatible structure, nearby property owners may be righteously indignant and force expensively unpleasant confrontations.

Residents and local business owners may be extremely aware of aging sewer and water systems that lack the capacity to handle additional loads or to withstand the jarring of heavy construction. Again, opposition can be reduced if the city and or developer address these problems first.

In middle-income neighborhoods — especially those that have recently been upgraded through the initiative of individual homeowners — infilling may be opposed because the new structures will generate more traffic, exacerbate parking problems, or introduce an incompatible scale or design. In low-income neighborhoods, residents may view infilling as the beginning of gentrification and displacement — depending on the type of development proposed.

Many developers who are accustomed to building at the urban fringe are extremely apprehensive about neighborhood protests. Thus, they look to local governments for help in obtaining approvals and mitigating neighborhood opposition.

Roles for Local Government

Efficient processing can go a long way in allaying builders' fears and creating a positive environment for development. This is particularly important, given the fact that most infill parcels are small and therefore appeal to the small- or medium-sized developer. Such individuals and companies typically have limited staff time and are relatively inexperienced in dealing with a wide range of government agencies. Because time is money in development, expediting permit processing is essential.

As interest in infill heightens, local public agencies should take steps to identify, classify, and become familiar with vacant parcels within their jurisdictions. Most local governments remain only vaguely aware of the location and extent of skipped-over properties.

Infill is a fairly new concept and most developers are not actively scrutinizing urban areas to locate individual buildable parcels. Cities can prepare inventories and market analyses for available sites, particularly those that fit the general description in Figure 4, and then distribute the information to local real estate brokers and developers.

Figure 4. The Optimum Infill Site

The context	The property
Viable market area	For sale at realistic price
Compatible, well-maintained surrounding properties	Sufficient size for intended use
Receptive neighborhood	Perceived market for intended use(s)
Helpful city government	Adequate utilities in place
Absence of environmental problems	Street frontage
Workable building code	Regularly shaped developable parcels
Good public services	No major topographic, drainage or subsoil problem
	Appropriate zoning
	Potential development profitability comparable to alternative sites

Local agencies also play an important role in determining project feasibility, mainly through traditional activities such as zoning and planning reviews and by capital investment programs to build roads, sewers and water mains. Techniques that can be used to encourage infilling range from "passive" efforts at technical assistance (for both builders and neighborhood groups) to modified codes and review procedures or more conscious targeting of capital improvements. Creative liaison with neighborhood groups that oppose new construction projects is emerging as a legitimate public activity. Other techniques being used to encourage rehabilitation and redevelopment—such as tax abatement or tax increment financing—can also be used to assist infill projects.

Needed actions	Possible incentives	Target opportunities	Cautions
Stimulating developer interest in infilling	Training programs/seminars/publicity campaign	Outreach to builders, developers, and realtors through professional associations and the news media	May have to go outside the region for speakers who have had success with infilling
	Parcel files; information on prototype projects	Comprehensive; or only for special uses (multi-family; industrial)	Needs careful staff supervision
	Design competitions	For scattered small lots; for large areas offering unique opportunities	Needs volunteers to serve on review committees and needs funds for prizes
Removing obstacles created by government			
Reducing delays in project review	Reform of staff review procedures	Small-scale projects	Must assure adequate citizen participation
	Elimination of unnecessary hearings	Projects requiring variances or special use permits	Requires cooperation of many city departments and staff members
	Creation of ombudsman or expeditor	All projects; or just those involving assisted housing or employment generation	Obstacles in state enabling legislation
Correcting excessively high or inappropriate standards	Reexamination of code provisions; encouragement of performance-based requirements	All infill projects; could also be important in redevelopment and rehabilitation	May encounter resistance from city staff, building trades, or neighborhood groups; results will not be immediately visible
Improving zoning balance (not enough multi-family land; over-zoning for industrial use)	Comprehensive review of zoning map and/or regulations	Citywide or in designated neighborhoods as part of the neighborhood planning process	May encounter resistance from neighborhood residents and property owners depending on the types of changes proposed. Must be based on sound market analysis

Figure 5. Tools and Techniques for Encouraging Infilling

Needed actions	Possible incentives	Target opportunities	Cautions
Creating neighborhood support for infilling	Inclusion in neighborhood plans of strategies for dealing with vacant lots	All neighborhoods (especially those with high potential)	Neighbors must see advantages for existing housing and businesses as well as the developer if they are to be convinced; developers must be flexible and willing to listen
	Project review meetings with developer in advance of official hearings	All projects likely to generate controversy	May also need to meet neighborhood groups in advance
Addressing market weakness or uncertainty/poor area image	Demonstration projects involving local development corporations and neighborhood interests	Low- and moderate-income neighborhoods, especially for projects providing jobs and/or increased shopping or services	Builds confidence if successful; high risk; limited expertise in dealing with risky situations
	Loan guarantees	Projects in areas with poor image but location advantages (i.e., near jobs, transit, major institutions)	Risk of unsuccessful projects requires expertise of experienced builders and banks
	"Below-market" financing through mortgage revenue bonds or industrial bond programs	Target neighborhoods and projects where special financing terms can act as a "magnet" to households or businesses who would otherwise locate at the urban fringe	Recent federal legislative limitations; need for careful market studies
	Greater attention to maintenance and rehabilitation	Low- and moderate-income neighborhoods	Concern over long-term displacement of the poor
	Visible public commitment to upgrading public works	Target neighborhoods	Resistance to targeting on a neighborhood basis
	Interim uses (parking, gardens, play areas)	Areas with established neighborhood organizations that will assume maintenance responsibility; areas with open space or parking needs	High maintenance burdens; resistance to future change

Addressing site-specific problems

Reducing the high cost of infill land	Land price write-down	Unique opportunity to achieve public purpose	High costs if used extensively; adverse political impacts from using public funds to subsidize strictly private projects
	Tax abatement	Definite project with committed developer	
	Leasing of publicly owned land	Varies; generally used for housing developments priced for low/moderate-income occupancy	Careful lease structuring needed to protect public interest
	Density bonuses; permitting variances from sideyards or setbacks to allow greater coverage	Mixed-use projects; projects incorporating assisted housing	Need to assure design compatibility with surrounding areas; possible opposition of neighbors
	Forgiveness of delinquent back taxes	Definite projects with committed developers	Legal obstacles in some states
	Downzoning	Areas where permitted densities do not match local housing market preferences	Objections of landowners
	Fee waivers	All infill projects	Fees are not a high proportion of project costs; effects are more psychological than financial
Increasing land availability	Property tax "disincentives" —site value taxation —higher taxes on vacant land	Vacant land in marketable locations (targeting will be difficult if not impossible)	Adverse effects on vacant property owners in deteriorated areas; adverse effects on existing buildings in "hot" neighborhoods
	Land assembly (vacant land only or vacant and underutilized sites)	Definite projects with committed developers	Expensive; legal limitations on use of eminent domain powers

Needed actions	Possible incentives	Target opportunities	Cautions
Increasing land availability (continued)	Land banking	Areas with extensive scattered parcels; high incidence of tax delinquency	Expensive; may require enabling legislation; land may not be marketable in the short run, especially in weak markets
Correcting infrastructure problems	Public funding of off-site capital improvements (minor street and utility extensions or upgrading)	Small-scale infilling, especially for industrial use	Reluctance of elected officials to target limited CIP dollars to new development; need for flexibility in CIP administration
	Tax increment financing	Larger projects, especially mixed use	Legal limitations in most states
	Special improvement districts	Commercial and industrial areas covering both infill and rehabilitation	Taxpayers must be willing to participate
	Greater flexibility and creativity in plan review	All infill projects	Resistance from city public works/ engineering staff to deviation from "standards"

Figure 5. Tools and Techniques for Encouraging Infilling

These and other techniques that have been in specific localities and are suitable for encouragement of infill are listed in Figure 5. The list is representative rather than comprehensive, and few of the techniques are unique to infill usage. Most of them are familiar to city planners and building officials, but they may not have been targeted as yet to this application.

Reconciling the competing concerns of private developers, neighboring property owners and local governments is not an easy task. But there is ample evidence that it can work, and that market conditions are now more favorable for infilling than they have been in the last 20 years. Opportunities are available for the private sector to make a profit while acting in concert with public goals for sound urban development.

Chapter 24

Ways to Revitalize
Your Downtown

DELORES PALMA

Downtown revitalization is enjoying a surge in popularity. All across the country, in large and small cities alike, a new emphasis is being placed on rejuvenating what was once the heart of the community.

This renewed emphasis can be seen in a pilot program recently begun by the National League of Cities. Entitled "Accepting the Challenge: The Rebirth of America's Downtowns," the pilot is receiving widespread interest. At the regional level, chambers of commerce and utility systems, once immersed solely in industrial development, are turning their attention to downtowns. And, at the local level, there has been a surge in the creation of special assessment districts which generate hundreds of thousands of dollars a year to fund downtown revitalization programs.

Downtown revitalization is not new. Twenty years ago, those who tried to revitalize their downtowns were pioneers. Today, however, hundreds of communities across the country have on-going downtown revitalization efforts in place. These communities provide a tremendous amount of information about how to ensure that a downtown revitalization effort is successful.

A recent survey of 210 U.S. communities that have active downtown revitalization programs attempted to determine what types of activities are being used—and which of these seem to bring about the greatest success—in revitalizing downtowns.

The results of the survey and follow-up discussions by Washington, D.C.–based Hyett Palma, Inc., showed that downtown revitalization initiatives in use today primarily fall into two categories. First, there are initiatives that could be viewed as "tried and true" downtown activities. These activities were revealed in the survey as having been in use for many years and are typically thought of as "the backbone" or foundation of most downtown revitalization programs.

Reprinted with permission from *American City & County,* Vol. 107, No. 11, November, 1992. Published by Communication Channels, Inc., Atlanta, Georgia.

The "tried and true" activities that are used by a majority of downtown programs include:

- Seminars for downtown business owners, typically on topics such as window display, merchandising and marketing techniques;
- Technical assistance for building and property owners on topics such as writing a business plan, making loan applications, business computerization, and using in-house mailing lists;
- Public property enhancements such as streetscape improvements, lighting and landscaping;
- Technical information, assistance or incentives to encourage private property improvements;
- Informally working with the local media by issuing periodic press releases; and
- Producing print pieces—such as downtown directories, maps, walking tours, etc.—to promote the downtown itself and the downtown program.

"Progressive" Initiatives

In addition to the survey, follow-up discussions with downtown professionals revealed that a second category of initiatives—"progressive" activities—are gaining popularity in downtowns. These activities differ from the tried and true initiatives in that they have not been in use for as long a period of time and they are proactive in nature. The follow-up discussions revealed that, downtown revitalization programs which are experiencing a great deal of enthusiasm and success, seem to have these "future thinking" initiatives in place.

The 10 progressive initiatives, which are gaining widespread acceptance across the nation, and that seem to stimulate downtown revitalization's success and enthusiasm are:

Private-Public Partnerships. During the last 20 years, many communities have formed private-public partnerships whose mission was to enhance downtowns. In these partnerships, the public sector, the business sector and the civic sector joined together, made decisions together, and each carried their weight to reinvest and reinvent their downtown areas. Going beyond that, the most successful downtown revitalization programs today are forming private-public partnerships.

What is new about these partnerships is that they are driven by the private, rather than by the public sector. The Heart of Corpus Christi, Inc., is one such partnership. Created in 1987 with the private sector taking the lead and the city as a strong partner, "The Heart" has stimulated the rehabilitation of 199 buildings, the creation of 1,267 new jobs, and the absorption of 262,020 square feet of downtown building space.

Downtown Vision. Waiting until the handwriting is on the wall and then reacting to it is the old way of doing business. The newer, more proactive and successful way of revitalizing downtown is to define a clear vision of where downtown needs to go—a realistic vision that is shared by the business community, the local government and the citizens—and then to aggressively pursue that vision. The city of Falls Church, Va., with a community divided over growth/no growth issues, spent almost a year conducting an out-reach effort to define a shared community vision for its traditional downtown—the Washington Street Corridor. That effort resulted in a vision that has been embraced by residents, the civic sector, the business community and City Hall, and a partnership has been formed to make that vision a reality.

Market-Driven Actions. Market analysis is the critical first step for successful downtown revitalization. The *Field of Dreams* approach to downtown revitalization—"if you build it they will come"—has been proven not to work. Instead, the successful approach is much more business-oriented—know who the customers are, who potential customers are, what they want today, what they will want tomorrow—and provide those things.

For greatest success, this market knowledge must drive all downtown improvement actions—all of the private sector's business decisions and the public sectors governance decisions—including how to market the downtown, which business hours to keep, which types of streetscape improvements to make. Fairfax, Va., realizing the importance of market knowledge, is undertaking a comprehensive retail market analysis that will identify not only the retail potential for downtown (Old Town Fairfax) but for four other commercial areas in the community as well. This community wide approach will ensure that each commercial area has a clear economic identity and that these complement rather than compete with each other.

Business Plans. Businesses that operate according to a business plan are more successful than those that do not. The same is true for business districts. The most proactive downtown partnerships are starting their programs by defining a clear, aggressive course of action. Thousand Oaks, Calif., one of the communities participating in the downtown pilot program of the National League of Cities, has recently started an effort to revitalize its traditional commercial core—Thousand Oaks Boulevard. To do this, the community defined a vision for the area and then charted a clear, aggressive course of action to attain that vision.

Dare to Be Different. In the most successful downtowns, the business community knows that it cannot out mall the mall and it cannot out discount the discounters. Instead, for downtown to succeed it must create, carve out and become known for its own particular niche in the marketplace. It must dare to stand out from the crowd.

While it is true that downtown cannot out mall the mall, it's also true that the mall cannot out—"downtown" downtown. Downtown leaders must become intimately familiar with the competition—which is constantly changing—and then focus upon what is not being offered that downtown can offer best.

Downtown Tupelo, Miss., is taking this bold approach. An abandoned shopping mall and an underused fairground site that could have been seen as liabilities were viewed instead as downtown opportunity sites. The shopping mall is being converted into a downtown coliseum and plans are under way to develop a portion of the fairground site as a downtown housing, office and lodging complex. By daring to be different, downtown Tupelo's traditional core will soon include two new niches.

Old-Fashioned Values. The most successful downtowns in America are—and will continue to be—those that have realized that their strength lies in doing business the old-fashioned way. This means a return to personalized customer attention; providing quality for money; standing behind the products; promoting the special, historic appearance of downtown; promoting downtown as the community's social, cultural, entertainment, residential, professional office and family center; and stressing the community pride that results from a healthy downtown.

In Murfreesboro, Tenn., situated on the town square, downtown leaders have used old-fashioned values that remain in place—hometown loyalty, locally owned small businesses, personalized customer attention—as the foundation of their successful revitalization program.

Remembering what once made it so successful, downtown Murfreesboro is again providing these qualities better than any local commercial facility.

Management Techniques from the Malls. While downtowns should not try—and are not able—to compete head-on with malls and win, the most successful downtowns are those that have learned and borrowed the best management techniques from the malls. These include:

• Have the downtown partnership function in a way that is similar to a mall management company;
• Hire a full-time, professional, experienced downtown director who would be the equivalent of the mall manager;
• Define and implement a leasing plan for downtown so businesses that can share customers are clustered together;
• Make sure downtown is appealing by keeping high standards of maintenance for both private and public spaces;
• Put into place a financing mechanism that will ensure adequate, predictable and reliable funds that will be available to implement the downtown revitalization effort.

In 1986, the Boise Business Improvement District in Idaho was created. The district is operated by the downtown Boise Association in partnership with the city of Boise, the Boise Redevelopment Authority and the chamber of commerce. The district has borrowed sound ideas from the mall by bringing sound management, paid staff, a retail leasing plan, a parking validation system, a promotion and advertising program, and a long-term financing mechanism to downtown Boise.

Economic Themes. In the past, downtown leaders often thought that the way to compete with malls was to create a physical "theme" that would make downtown distinct. However, current thinking is that—to stand out in the mind of the customer—downtown must create and market economic themes. These are created by clustering together businesses, such as apparel and antiques or restaurants and home furnishings, that appeal to a particular customer group. By clustering similar businesses, these businesses become more convenient for customers and downtown becomes known for those businesses. In this way, downtown takes on an economic theme that makes it distinct.

The Traverse City Downtown Development Authority in Michigan is aggressively creating economic themes in its downtown. Using the results of a retail market analysis recently completed for downtown, the authority has formed a committee to identify and recruit businesses to a variety of downtown "clusters," each with a unique economic theme.

Focus Groups. A tool long used in the advertising industry, focus groups are now widely used in the most aggressive downtown efforts. The downtown partnership should assemble a small focus group of downtown customers or potential customers and ask what they like and dislike about downtown. The lesson here is, for success, don't try to guess what customers want. Rather the best course is to just ask them.

In New York, the City of Poughkeepsie Partnership, a nonprofit organization whose mission is to revitalize downtown Poughkeepsie, has done just this. The organization regularly holds focus groups of downtown customers and potential customers to evaluate its promotions and marketing activities. And, most importantly, the partnership acts on the recommendations made in the focus group.

Formal Marketing Campaigns. Downtown's customers and potential customers are sophisticated and smart consumers who have many shopping options. And they are constantly bombarded by sophisticated marketing messages. The most progressive downtown efforts in the country today are those that have realized the need to implement a marketing campaign that is every bit as professional and comprehensive as the competition's. For greatest success, the campaign must be of high quality, professional, and must stress a downtown's economic themes and overall image.

CITYCENTER Danbury in Danbury, Conn., recently decided to take the plunge into a professionally crafted marketing campaign. The organization hired a professional to help them define a strategic marketing campaign and, after successfully raising the necessary funds, the organization retained a public relations firm to implement that campaign in conjunction with the group's marketing committee.

The message from downtown professionals across the country is clear: a proactive, self-help attitude will be essential for successful downtown revitalization efforts in the 1990s. By learning from the successes of other downtowns and using these 10 progressive initiatives, community leaders can make great strides in revitalizing their downtowns.

V : The Application

Chapter 25

Community-Based
Economic Development

JAN STOKLEY

This chapter is the result of a recent survey of twenty CDBG entitlement cities to learn more about the programs and institutions being developed by local governments to support community economic development. Needless to say, in several cities no such programs or institutions existed. The explanation generally offered for their absence was that programs to support community-based organizations would unduly politicize the city's use of scarce economic development resources.

The three cities described in this chapter, however, have succeeded in supporting community-based economic development (CED) in a financially responsible way. Recognizing that neighborhood-based economic development organizations can play a role in the city's economic development that cannot be filled by either the private or public sector, these cities have attempted to design ongoing programs of support for CED that lead to rational, merit-based funding decisions. Of course, funding community economic development can never be an entirely a political process because community organizations play an important role in the city's political life. But as the following three case studies show, cities have many different options in designing effective and fiscally responsible programs of support for CED.

Most community-based organizations (CBOs) would urge a city to design a program of support for CED that is as politically neutral as possible. Politically neutral programs protect CBOs from the unpleasant experience of having city funds pulled out of their projects at the last minute because of election results or other changes in the political winds, after years of hard work by the CBO to develop the project and get matching funds from other sources. Many community organizations have had this experience in cities where CDBG funding

Reprinted with permission from *Economic Development & Law Center Report,* Vol. 15, No. 2/3, March/June, 1985. Published by the National Economic Development & Law Center, Oakland, California.

is held out as a political plum, and most would want to avoid ever having it happen again.

A second reason that community organizations support merit-based funding of community economic development is that it gives them greater freedom to criticize city government and work for change in the city's policies. Many community organizations have had to give up their role as strong advocates for low-income people in order to become effective development organizations simply because in the 1980s most funding for community development is controlled by local governments. To the extent that a city's community development funding is based on rational, merit-based criteria, community organizations retain greater freedom as spokespeople for low-income neighborhoods.

CBOs also support rational, merit-based programs of funding for their projects because such programs are viewed as a stable base of support by national and regional foundations and corporations, making it easier for CBOs to obtain operating and venture support from sources other than the city.

The programs examined in this article represent experiments in supporting CED by the cities of Portland (Oregon), St. Paul, and Pittsburgh. All of these programs are in their early years but are generally heralded as successes by city government officials, community organizations, and neighborhood residents. The diversity of the programs reflects the uniqueness of each city's political structure, neighborhood life, and general approach to economic development. Although very different from each other, all of the programs point to the same conclusion: city governments can design effective, merit-based programs for supporting community-based economic development that can enable community organizations to make their own unique contribution to the city's revitalization and growth.

Portland's Neighborhood Self-Help Program

Portland is a city where, for many years, people held the view that city funds and community-based economic development should not mix. Now, however, thanks to the city's unqualified success with a rather modest program, the Neighborhood Self-Help Program, a different view on the subject is developing.

Founded in 1982, the Neighborhood Self-Help Program is administered by a single coordinator, Dee Walsh, within the city's Bureau of Community Development. Funded with $50,000 of CDBG funds annually, the program provides one-time grants of up to $5,000 to nonprofit community-based organizations for projects which address a basic community need. Service projects must directly benefit low- and moderate-income people, while physical improvements must be located within targeted low- and moderate-income neighborhoods.

In the first year of the program, seven projects received $39,000 of CDBG assistance. Those seven projects leveraged $170,000 of private contributions and in-kind donations in addition to many hours of sweat equity, prompting HUD to award the city a Certificate of National Merit for the program in its "Working Partners" competition.

The city accepts applications in the fall for January funding. A committee consisting of city staff and two representatives from a Citizens Advisory Committee make funding recommendations based on a number of criteria, including the applicant's ability to demonstrate that the project will inspire a high degree of community involvement, generate volunteer labor and donated material, and encourage neighborhood residents to participate. When funding decisions have been made, the city staff works with the community organization to bring together all the pieces of the project.

Some of the projects funded by the Portland Neighborhood Self-Help Program include:

- **Cooperative housing rehabilitation by REACH Community Development, Inc.** REACH, an economic development corporation in the Buckman neighborhood, received a grant of $5,000 to help rehab 35 housing units. REACH uses volunteers to do light construction work, and residents contribute their own sweat equity. The Neighborhood Self-Help grant funded a part-time coordinator to oversee the unskilled construction work and to encourage participation by neighborhood volunteers and residents.
- **Home gardening support by Lents Neighborhood Association.** Neighborhood Self-Help awarded $5,000 of its funds to Lents Neighborhood Association to pay for gardening materials and a project coordinator. The community organization worked with low- and moderate-income households to build twenty raised-bed vegetable gardens. With volunteer assistance from other service organizations, residents built their garden boxes and learned how to grow their own vegetables.
- **Senior energy assistance by Warm, Inc.** A nonprofit energy assistance organization for seniors, Warm, Inc. received $9,875 of Neighborhood Self-Help funds to pay for a project coordinator to bring together community resources and establish a good volunteer system. Warm, Inc., distributes seasoned firewood to seniors and provides information on low-cost energy conservation.
- **Community gardening by Brooklyn Action Corps.** Brooklyn Action Corps., a nonprofit neighborhood association, received $1,535 of Neighborhood Self-Help funds to convert a vacant lot into a community garden. The funds paid for land preparation, a water system, and fencing, with labor provided by neighborhood residents and the land leased for two years by the Portland General Electric Company. Seventy percent of the 63 garden plots are tended by low-income families, with 8 plots reserved for Indochinese refugees.
- **Development of a model energy house by Responsible Urban Neighborhood Technology (RUNT).** RUNT, a nonprofit organization in northeast Portland, acquired a burned-out abandoned building from the Portland Development Commission. The Neighborhood Self-Help Program provided $3,548 to pay

for a construction and volunteer coordinator to help the group turn the building into a model urban energy-conserving and recycling house. Almost all of the renovation work was done by volunteers with recycled or donated materials.

When asked to evaluate the program from the city's perspective, Dee Walsh cites as one of its major benefits the positive media image that the program has generated for Portland. "A city where community residents get support and encouragement for their work to build their neighborhood is attractive to a lot of people," she said. The other major benefit of the program, according to Walsh, is that even the modest level of funding and technical assistance that the city's emerging community development organizations have gotten from the program has made them stronger and more effective.

As the capacity of the city's community development organizations grows and the successes of the program mount, Portland may seek to expand its program of support for community-based economic development. In the meantime, the modest Portland program, requiring an annual CDBG commitment of only $50,000 and approximately one-fourth of one staff person's time, offers a workable model for other cities that wish to take a first step towards local government support of community economic development.

St. Paul's Neighborhood Partnership Program

The St. Paul Neighborhood Partnership Program is a $3.65 million fund for neighborhood self-help projects, administered by the St. Paul Department of Planning and Economic Development. Every six months, community organizations as well as small businesses can compete for funding from a pot of $700,000, and all of the city neighborhoods can participate since the program is funded by both CDBG funds and the proceeds of capital improvement bonds. Thus, it is much more ambitious, both in size and design, than the Portland program.

The NPP funds can be used for three types of projects. The first, minor capital improvements, includes planting trees, putting in new street lights and benches, or putting up neighborhood identification signs. The second, rehabilitation, encompasses improvements of housing and commercial buildings. The third type of activity, economic development, includes building new housing, expanding existing businesses, or bringing new businesses into the neighborhood.

In order to get funding for a project, a CBO must form a "partnership committee" that is representative of all of the neighborhood people who may be interested in the project, including neighborhood residents, businesses, and community organizations. This partnership committee develops a formal proposal and submits an application for NPP funding. The application must provide for a neighborhood match, which can be in the form of other loans and grants, sweat equity valued at $10 per hour, or in-kind contributions including exterior improvements to housing and commercial buildings. The amount of the neighborhood match depends on the neighborhood's income level. Neighborhoods with higher incomes—at least equal to the city's median—must contribute three dollars in neighborhood resources for every dollar from the NPP fund. Moderate-income neighborhoods—where the income is between the median and 80 percent of the median—must raise two dollars for every dollar of NPP funding. And lower-income neighborhoods— where most residents have an income that is 80 percent or less of the city's median income—have to contribute one dollar in neighborhood resources for every dollar of NPP funds.

Although any neighborhood can apply for NPP funding, the program imposes some conditions on how the NPP funds are used in different neighborhoods. CDBG funds, which make up two-thirds of the NPP pot, can only be used in low-income neighborhoods or for projects in other neighborhoods that benefit low-income people. And capital improvement bond proceeds, which make up one-third of the pot, can only be used for physical improvements of public areas. As a result, lower-income communities have somewhat more flexibility in developing proposals for funding under the NPP program.

When the neighborhood's "partnership committee" has developed a formal application, it applies for funding on NPP's six-month funding cycle. Over a two-month period, the proposals are initially reviewed by the St. Paul Planning Commission and the Capital Improvement Budget committee. With their recommendation, the proposals are submitted to the Mayor and City Council where the final funding decision is made.

To limit the conflicts that might arise if a neighborhood submitted several proposals during a single funding cycle, the program requires each district council to prioritize the neighborhood's proposals. From the city's perspective, proposals that fare best in the competition are those that involve significant participation by the neighborhood residents that are consistent with district and comprehensive plans. All projects must be capable of completion in 18 to 24 months or of becoming self-sustaining within that period.

Once a proposal is selected for funding, a city planner assigned to the neighborhood and other city staff help the partnership committee develop a full program and secure the matching pledges. Proposals selected for NPP funding have priority for funding under other city programs, and the city staff help the partnership committee use this priority to the project's advantage.

The St. Paul Neighborhood Partnership Program is not limited to funding the community development projects of community-based organizations, but those organizations have been leading participants in the program. The program is now in its fifth funding cycle. Twenty-nine projects have been funded, and the City Council is now reviewing seventeen more applications.

Some of the projects funded by the Neighborhood Partnership Program include:

- The Lowertown Artists Cooperative obtained a $200,000 loan to help develop a 28-unit housing/studio cooperative.
- Lexington-Hamlin Community Organization obtained a loan of $114,000 to purchase and rehab a number of single-family residences that the Housing Authority had placed on the market because of increasing maintenance expenses. The units are now managed by a residents' cooperative.
- Highland Business Association, a neighborhood commercial association, obtained a grant of $234,000 for a street and facade improvements project that cost $1.75 million. The organization assessed the member businesses for the balance of the project cost.
- Hispanos of Minnesota obtained a $12,000 grant to establish a revolving-loan fund so that low-income people could borrow the damage deposit necessary to obtain an apartment lease.

The St. Paul program has been successful for several reasons. By setting aside funds for several funding cycles, the city signalled an ongoing commitment to the program. Because the program has a strong set of merit-based funding criteria and requires that competing projects be ranked in order of priority at the neighborhood level, it minimizes political showdowns about funding decisions. The program has generated a city-wide base of support for community economic development by using the proceeds of capital improvement bonds to finance participation by all of the city's neighborhoods, decreasing the likelihood that the program would be viewed as simply a hand-out for low-income communities. Finally, by requiring community organizations to form neighborhood "partnership committees" and to satisfy strict leveraging requirements, St. Paul ensures that the projects it funds have a strong base of community support.

St. Paul's partnership with community organizations has been so successful that when the city received $2.2 million in 1983 Emergency Jobs Bill funds, it immediately turned to community organizations for proposals to put people to work. The city sent notices to some 40 community organizations and published newspaper notices advising the organizations of the availability of the funds and the constraints on the city's use of the funds. After a general orientation meeting, the city received 50 proposals for funding from community organizations, of which 17 were funded.

Because of the requirement that the city quickly commit the Emergency Jobs Bill funds to job-producing activities, the city did not develop stringent competitive criteria like those that govern the Neighborhood Partnership Program. This had its advantages, according to Bob Hammer, the program administrator, because the city funded some very creative proposals that might have had difficulty competing under the Neighborhood Partnership Program.

Projects funded by the Emergency Jobs Bill money include acquisition of an abandoned warehouse to serve as a business incubator that will provide low rent and technical assistance to 13 new business employing 44 full-time and 6 part-time employees. Community-based drug rehabilitation centers obtained funds to provide employment counseling for clients. And other community groups, including five neighborhood health clinics, were able to hire additional staff to expand their services.

Pittsburgh: A Multi-Faceted Support System for CED

The city of Pittsburgh has helped to organize and support five different programs that finance or assist community-based economic development. The variety of these programs reflects the city's response to the different levels of experience of the community development corporations and the range of their needs, whether for technical assistance, operating support, or venture funding.

To provide technical assistance to community-based organizations, the city in 1981 helped organize the Community Technical Assistance Center, Inc. (CTAC), an independent nonprofit corporation that provides technical assistance and support to all of the city's community-based organizations. The city now contributes $130,000 to CTAC annually, which represents over one-half of CTAC's budget. Although CTAC is available to help all community-based organizations, its policy is to devote at least 75 percent of its time to low- and moderate-income neighborhoods. CTAC provides organizational development, resource development, financial management (including a computerized accounting system), and general legal assistance to community organizations. It has also helped neighborhood groups publicize their activities. CTAC is now in the process of hiring a staff person to specialize in community economic development.

In another approach to technical assistance, the city has recently organized the Neighborhood Fund to which it has committed $150,000 of CDBG funds this year and will commit another $100,000 of CDBG funds in the next round of competition. Under the Neighborhood Fund program, community organizations apply for grants for technical assistance to develop specific projects. The purpose of the fund is to permit an emerging organization to assess the feasibility of a project and its own organizational capacity to perform it. The Neighborhood Fund is specifically targeted at emerging groups that have not previously been able to obtain city or other financial support to engage in economic development.

The city has also recognized the need of community organizations for operating support. Rather than throwing up its hands at the political spectre of city-supported "grant colonies," the city has attempted to meet the legitimate need of CBOs for operating support by supporting the organization of and contributing CDBG funds to the Pittsburgh Partnership. The Pittsburgh Partnership is an independent nonprofit entity funded by the Ford Foundation, Mellon Bank, the Pittsburgh Foundation, and the city. It now provides operating funds for five Pittsburgh community development corporations for a period of two years and is in the process of committing continued funding for the CDCs for two additional years.

The city has also developed two programs to provide venture funding for CBOs. The first, the Neighborhood Economic Development Investment Fund, was originally proposed by a consortium of community development organizations who asked the city to use its 1983 Emergency Jobs Bill allocation to fund business and economic development loans.

The loan program, as it was eventually worked out, is a true partnership between the economic development department of the city's Urban Redevelopment Authority and the CBOs. The city targeted $1 million in Emergency Jobs Bill funds for the program and designated seven community organizations from seven low- to moderate-income neighborhoods to act as brokers for the program in their neighborhoods. The CBO's role is to market the loan program to small businesses in its neighborhood, to help the businesses develop a viable loan application, and then, if the city funds the loan, to monitor whether the loan actually results in job creation. For these services, the CBO receives 25 percent of the loans paid back by the businesses; the loan payback gives the community organizations unrestricted funds to help finance other activities and ventures.

To qualify for a loan from the Neighborhood Economic Development Investment Fund, the borrower must create one job for every $5,000 borrowed, come up with three dollars of other funding to match every dollar borrowed from the program, and possess equity equal to at least 10 percent of the total project cost. The minimum loan from the Neighborhood Economic Development Investment Fund is $10,000, and the maximum loan is $100,000. Interest on the loan is 6 percent, and the term of the loan is usually consistent with the term of the borrower's other financing.

CBOs as intermediaries. What are the benefits to the city of using seven community-based organizations to broker loans under the Neighborhood Economic Development Investment Fund? When asked this question, Dave Feehan, Executive Director of East Liberty Development, Inc., one of the CBOs participating in the program, responded with six reasons why it makes sense for the city to implement the program through community-based organizations.

The first reason identified by Feehan is marketing. "The city staff does a pretty good job of marketing million-dollar UDAGs to large developers, but neighborhood-based organizations like ELDI are much better at marketing business and economic development loans to small neighborhood businesses," he said.

A second reason, according to Feehan, is that "CBOs can do a much better job of evaluating the small businesses. We know the people in the business, their capabilities, and their role in the community and can look beyond the dollars and cents on the business's financial statements in assessing the benefits and risks of the loan."

Using the CBOs as intermediaries also enables the city to impose a leveraging requirement on the borrower. If the city staff people had to help the small businesses meet the leveraging requirement, the city would simply not have the staff time to fund more than a few loans. But, Feehan explained, "with the staff people of seven CBOs working on the loan applications, it is really feasible to require small businesses to develop other resources and satisfy the leveraging requirement, so that the city can get a lot more bang for its buck."

A fourth reason for using CBOs to implement the program is that they are in a position to help monitor the borrower's financial situation after the loan is made. Without the participation of CBOs, the city staff would simply make the loan and would have little capacity to monitor the borrower's situation or intervene in a timely manner with support when the borrower encountered unexpected difficulties.

Fifth, because the CBOs are entitled to 25 percent of the loan payback, the transaction now includes a player with a real financial stake in the success of the loan. "City staff people are certainly committed to making feasible loans," Feehan explained, "but their degree of interest just cannot compare to ours, because we are counting on our share of the loan payback to help us finance our own projects and stay afloat as an organization."

Finally, Feehan points out, by charging the community organizations with the responsibility of monitoring the job creation results of the loan, the city increases the likelihood that the borrower will actually meet the job creation requirements. "Because we're here in the neighborhood and in daily contact with the business, the borrower simply cannot ignore the job creation requirement the way it could if it were accountable to some downtown city staff person with a hundred loans to monitor all over the city."

Feehan's points are illustrated by an example of one loan that ELDI brokered for the city. ELDI helped a minority entrepreneur start a new business, a small owner-operated fabric store called And Sew On. With ELDI's assistance, the entrepreneur developed a $40,000 loan package to provide funds for inventory, leasehold improvements, and working capital. Ten thousand dollars was borrowed from the Neighborhood Economic Development Investment Fund and $30,000 was obtained from the city's minority-business enterprise program. ELDI leased space to the new business in its own building. ELDI was in a much better position than city staff to market the loan program to the entrepreneur, to help it develop an application, and then to monitor its ongoing financial and job creation performance.

The Neighborhood Economic Development Investment Fund has been such a success that the city has added $425,000 of CDBG funds to its capital. The program will continue to be funded by the 75 percent of loan payments that are recaptured by the fund and by additional CDBG monies.

The success of the Neighborhood Economic Development Investment Fund alone has more than justified the city's provision of funds for technical assistance and operating subsidies for community development corporations. At least seven of the city's CDCs are now playing an important role in the city's economic development program, performing a job that city staff people simply could not perform as effectively.

The city's newest program of support for community-based organizations is the Community Development Investment Fund. Recently approved, the program will initially be capitalized with $400,000 of CDBG or UDAG recapture funds. The program will be used to provide grants to community organizations for real estate projects on more flexible terms than are available under the existing Local Initiatives Support Corporation (LISC), CDBG or UDAG programs. The CBO can then grant or lend the funds to the partnership or developer of the project. One of the purposes of the program is to enable the CBOs to obtain an earlier return on investment than would otherwise be possible and thereby increase their self-sufficiency. Applications will be submitted on a quarterly basis to the Pittsburgh LISC, which will make decisions on funding subject to ratification by the Board of Directors of the city's Urban Redevelopment Authority.

Characteristics of Successful City Programs

As these diverse case studies show, the success of local government support for CED does not depend on the size of the program but whether the program provides predictability, satisfies criteria of fairness, respects the independence of the community-based organizations, and takes advantage of the CBOs' strongest assets.

Predictability is a critical ingredient of a successful program. When CBOs have some assurance that a program will continue to exist a couple of years down the road, they can undertake more sophisticated projects that promise a greater community impact but also require a longer pre-development time-line.

Another benefit of predictability is that it induces major foundations and corporations to make supporting grants and loans to the CBOs and to develop major funding partnerships with the city, as in Pittsburgh. It is much easier for CBOs to leverage other financing or operating support when the city government is perceived to have made an ongoing commitment to community economic development.

Predictability can be enhanced by designing a program that is not entirely dependent on the city's annual budgeting process to survive. This can be accomplished by making an initial funding commitment sufficient to keep the program going through several funding cycles, as in St. Paul, and also by targeting UDAG recapture to the program in cities like Pittsburgh where large UDAG loans are beginning to be paid back. To the extent it is feasible and consistent with the other goals of the program, the CED support program itself should make loans rather than grants to the CBOs, so that the loan payback can be recycled to keep the program going.

Fairness and the appearance of fairness are also essential to a successful program of support for community economic development. The local government and the CBOs must design a CED financing program that satisfies three tests: fairness among neighborhoods, merit-based criteria for funding, and a fair review procedure.

Fairness among neighborhoods is important to prevent the perception that the program only benefits certain groups of people. The St. Paul Neighborhood Partnership Program places great emphasis on equal neighborhood opportunity. All of the city neighborhoods are eligible to participate, and each neighborhood must choose the project it most wants funded. At the same time, the St. Paul program takes account of the economic differences in neighborhoods by adjusting the leveraging requirements to reflect a neighborhood's median income. Fairness among neighborhoods is also a critical ingredient of the Pittsburgh Neighborhood Economic Development Investment Fund, where CBOs in each of the city's seven low-to-moderate-income neighborhoods have been allocated a pro rata share of the Emergency Jobs Bill funds to administer.

The fairness of the competitive criteria is also important. The more specific the criteria and the more clearly the criteria relate to the merits of the project, the less likely it is that the city officials will make a funding decision that is politically motivated or otherwise arbitrary.

The review procedure itself should satisfy a fairness test. This can be accomplished by having relatively disinterested city staff people prepare a careful factual evaluation of each proposal on the merits. Then, even if the Mayor and City Council retain control of the ultimate funding decision, they must justify their decision in light of the detailed factual analysis developed by the city staff.

It must be recognized, however, that fairness in allocating operating support is more difficult to achieve than fairness in allocating venture funding. Decisions about venture funding lend themselves to merit-based analysis, but decisions about whether to allocate operating funds to this group or that group do not. Cities should not respond to this difficulty by simply refusing to provide operating support to CBOs, but should consider supporting an independent entity to make these awards on the lines of the Pittsburgh Partnership.

The degree to which a city's CED financing program respects and builds on the independence of the community organizations is also important to its success. If city government is perceived to have co-opted a CBO to accomplish a political or other agenda, the CBO loses credibility in the neighborhood, its ability to engage in community economic development is seriously compromised if not lost, and the whole purpose of the program is defeated.

Independence of the CBOs is promoted by structuring a program that satisfies the three fairness tests described above and also builds up the financial resources of the CBO. For example, the Pittsburgh Neighborhood Economic Development Investment Fund gives each participating CBO 25 percent of the loan funds that are paid back. This aspect of the program gives the CBO a strong incentive to make sound loan recommendations, while it also contributes to the CBO's future financial independence.

Designing a program that is based on leveraging is another way of promoting CBO independence. This requirement assures the city that it is funding groups with a strong base of support in the community. It also prevents the CBO from yielding to the temptation to become a colony of city government. Leveraging requirements, however, should always take account of the shortage of capital in low-income neighborhoods.

Finally, a successful program of support for community economic development should be designed to capitalize on the CBO's strongest assets. Local government officials should ask themselves: "What are the assets of community-based organizations that distinguish CBOs from our staff, traditional lenders, and private developers?" These assets typically include the CBO's ability to leverage foundation support and volunteer labor, familiarity with small neighborhood businesses and the neighborhood's housing needs, and the knowledge of the market for goods and services in the neighborhood. After identifying these assets, the city government is in a better position to identify the economic development strategies that are best implemented by CBOs. The benefits of capitalizing on the CBO's assets are demonstrated by the Pittsburgh Neighborhood Economic Development Investment Fund where the city gave the CBOs a job—making loans to small businesses—that the CBOs could do better than anyone else in the public or private sector. This point is also illustrated by the Portland and St. Paul programs where the funding criteria emphasize the use of neighborhood volunteers and contributions, and the satisfaction of basic neighborhood needs.

A local government interested in developing a program to support community economic development should recognize that it must consult with community organizations to design a program that provides the necessary degree of predictability, satisfies basic criteria of fairness, respects the independence of CBOs, and capitalizes on the CBOs' strongest assets. Each city must design a program that satisfies these basic criteria but also makes sense in light of the city's own unique circumstances. The three approaches in St. Paul, Portland, and Pittsburgh demonstrate that, although there are no cookie-cutter solutions to the design of a partnership between local governments and community-based development organizations, an effective program of local government support of CED can produce measurable benefits for the city and its neighborhoods.

NOTES

• For more information on Portland's Neighborhood Self-Help Program, contact Program Development Specialist, Bureau of Community Development, 1120 S.W. Fifth Avenue, Room 1120, Portland, Oregon 97204-1963.

• For more information on St. Paul's Neighborhood Partnershp Program, contact James Zdon, Department of Planning and Economic Development, 25 West Fourth Street, St. Paul, Minnesota 55102.

• For general information on Pittsburgh's programs, contact City Planning Department, 7th Floor, Public Safety Building, Pittsburgh, Pennsylvania 15219, (412) 255-2221. For detailed information about the Community Development Investment Fund and the Neighborhood Economic Development Investment Fund, contact Evan Stoddard, URA of Pittsburgh, 200 Ross Street, Pittsburgh, PA 15219.

Chapter 26

Developing the Contaminated City

TOM ARRANDALE

During the booming 1980s, malls and commercial buildings filled up the western New Jersey farmlands along the eight-mile stretch of U.S. 1 between Trenton and Princeton. At the same time, near the state capital down by the Delaware River, Trenton's once formidable steel, porcelain, ceramics and rubber product factories were rusting away behind padlocked gates and high chainlink fences.

Trenton officials want to rebuild the city's manufacturing economy by attracting new firms to an urban enterprise zone in those downtown industrial neighborhoods. But New Jersey's tough Environmental Cleanup Responsibility Act holds the seller responsible for removing contaminants before a property can be sold. The city cannot afford to clean the area up itself, and financial and legal uncertainty discourages investors who otherwise might jump at the chance to redevelop what once were prime industrial sites.

Trenton's plight underscores a troublesome paradox confronting government environmental and economic development policy all across the country. New Jersey's own statewide land use plan calls for limiting suburban sprawl while revitalizing the state's decaying cities. But state and federal pollution cleanup laws are thwarting redevelopment in the old core cities.

As they stand, "existing environmental regulations make it almost impossible to recycle one of our greatest assets—our old industrial cities," complains Detroit developer Ted Gatzaros. Gatzaros thinks there is a market for suburban-style subdivisions in downtown industrial districts, but the cost of removing contaminated foundry sand and other pollutants probably will stymie projects for redeveloping riverfront and lakeside lands once occupied by Detroit's mighty manufacturing companies.

Before the University of Pittsburgh and Carnegie Mellon University began

Reprinted with permission from *Governing,* Vol. 6, No. 3, December, 1992. Published by Congressional Quarterly, Inc., Washington, D.C.

building a technology center on the site of an abandoned steel mill, consultants raised the possibility that the institutions could be held liable if future tenants or workers were to sue over ill effects from contaminants on the property. Contamination from the past is making it difficult to find new uses for a shutdown Chicago steel mill, shuttered New England textile plants, abandoned western mines and smelters, and obsolete petro-chemical plants, metal-plating factories and machine shops in aging manufacturing centers such as Toledo, South Bend and Baton Rouge. Even in smaller cities, such as Bennington, Vermont; Wyandotte, Michigan; and Davenport, Iowa, the cost of cleaning up industrial contamination may make it prohibitively expensive to redevelop the sites of old factories and mills.

That situation poses "a very important issue that anybody who has an urban agenda, especially in our older urban areas, has got to address," says Jeffrey Tryens, deputy director of the Center for Policy Alternatives, a Washington, D.C., think tank.

When pollution is found, environmental groups and neighboring homeowners have good reasons for demanding that governments step in to keep contaminants from blowing with the wind, soaking into playground soils or flowing into drinking water supplies. But some severely polluted industrial lands may never be fully cleansed, at least under current scientific knowledge and decontamination technology. So some environmental regulators suggest that it makes sense to contain the pollutants—as quickly and cheaply as possible—and then put industrial lands back to work under tight land use restrictions guarding future generations against health-threatening exposure levels.

Just north of Boston, for instance, city officials in Woburn, Massachusetts, are working with federal and state regulators to build a regional commuter and industrial center atop one of the most contaminated Superfund sites in the country. A dying Montana copper town is pinning its hopes for a tourist boom on building a championship golf course over arsenic-laced soils surrounding a ruined smelter. Meadville, Pennsylvania, and Commerce, California, paid for cleaning up abandoned industrial plants so they could be converted to new uses.

As those communities have found, it can be possible, in the words of Charles W. Powers, a Boston-based consultant on managing contaminated lands, to turn a polluted industrial site or toxic waste dump into "an asset, both private and social, not simply an albatross or a liability."

Before those liabilities can be turned into assets, however, there are formidable legal and regulatory obstacles to be overcome. The fact that human health is at stake vastly complicates what on the surface would seem to be a relatively simple matter of matching the level of cleanup to a site's intended use.

So far, the U.S. Environmental Protection Agency has listed more than

1,200 hazardous waste sites in all 50 states that qualify for cleanup under the federal Superfund program. In addition, state governments are contending with contamination at thousands more facilities, ranging from giant factories to leaking landfills to corner gas stations with rusting fuel tanks underground.

Among other industrial states, New Jersey, Connecticut, California, Illinois and Michigan have enacted measures requiring that landowners remove or at least disclose industrial contamination before they can sell their property. Those laws have forced some cleanups, but they have also left some old industrial sites sitting idle. As Trenton has discovered, the merest hint that land is polluted can scare investors off from vacant sites in downtrodden city neighborhoods with a history of nearly 200 years of intensive industrial development.

State environmental cleanup programs move slowly enough, but some communities have come to see the federal Superfund cleanup process as a virtually permanent local institution. By the fall of 1992, EPA had finished cleanup plans at just 150 listed facilities. Some properties have been in limbo for a decade while EPA or state scientists study the contamination and draw up remedial plans. The Superfund process "is one which virtually everyone tries to avoid getting sucked into, for once in it, no one knows the way out," Powers says.

Following the principle that polluters ought to pay, the Superfund program requires responsible companies to bear the cost of cleaning up contamination they created. The average cost of cleaning up a site has been $30 million, and the process of tracking pollution sources and assigning blame almost always bogs down in protracted legal squabbling as companies and landowners try to shift blame and minimize their own liability.

In legislating the Superfund program, Congress has never answered the question "How clean is clean?" EPA sets cleanup goals on a site-by-site basis, relying on time-consuming investigations of contaminants at each site that attempt to estimate the threat they pose to human health. Generally, regulators base remedial plans on the worst-case danger that people would face if they lived on a site in the future; state cleanup programs follow a similar scheme. But just because a site isn't safe to live on doesn't mean it can't be made to serve some useful economic purpose.

As things stand, a company that buys or rents an old factory site is risking open-ended costs in complying with cleanup requirements that can change with the whims of regulatory politics. "People are not going to buy a piece of property if they're taking a crapshoot on what those costs will be," notes Lee Webb, executive vice president of the New York State Urban Development Corp.

Some sites no doubt will remain so toxic that they may never be fit for redevelopment. But a few communities already have found ways to clean up contaminated industrial lands and put them back into use as productive economic assets.

Rather than wait a decade for the federal government to complete a Superfund cleanup, for instance, the Wichita, Kansas, city government has launched its own $20 million effort to remove industrial solvents beneath virtually its entire downtown business district (see *Governing*, October, 1992, page 36). By tackling the job itself, the city has gotten the cleanup going three to five years ahead of the usual Superfund schedule, salvaging an urban redevelopment program that had been threatened when state officials discovered the pollution. Minneapolis spends $5 million a year to buy contaminated industrial sites, accepting the risk of cleanup liability, for redevelopment as light manufacturing or research facilities. Davenport, Iowa, bought and cleaned up a failing farm equipment plant property to provide a downtown site for the local *Quad City Times* newspaper to build a printing plant and distribution center.

Even after a property is declared a Superfund site, some local officials are recognizing that cleanups will cost less and move more quickly if they step in, right at the start, to decide what polluted lands eventually will be used for. Instead of digging out a contaminated municipal landfill, for example, Denver and suburban Aurora are collaborating on a less costly plan to cap the Superfund site and turn it into protected open space off-limits to development. In Montana, ARCO's environmental remediation office has commissioned pro golfer Jack Nicklaus, with Anaconda–Deer Lodge County planners' approval, to design a championship course over a capped Superfund site laced with arsenic and other contaminants near a Montana copper smelter shut down since 1902. The depressed mining community will get a tourist attraction; ARCO, still liable if any contaminants leak out, "can be sure that the remedy will stay in place for the long term," says Sandy Stash, the company's Montana Superfund manager.

No community in the country may have more reason to fear toxic contaminants than Woburn, an industrial suburb 12 miles north of downtown Boston. After all, chemicals found leaking into two city wells a decade ago have been blamed for giving 28 Woburn children leukemia. Nonetheless, in the fall of 1992 Massachusetts officials announced plans to turn a different Superfund site a mile and a half away into a major commuter rail station.

Part of the 245-acre tract, which is listed fifth on the national Superfund priority list, is contaminated by tannery and chemical wastes dating back to the 19th century. The major landowner could not afford to clean up the polluted lands, blocking redevelopment of the entire property. So EPA, state officials and the city government worked out an innovative plan that turned the land over to a custodial trust, managed by a Boston-based consulting firm, to prepare a redevelopment strategy that works hand in hand with the Superfund cleanup effort.

Known as the Industri-plex site, the land sits on a commuter rail line near where Boston's Route 128 circumferential highway crosses Interstate 93. Massachusetts transportation officials are designing a new interchange along with a $15 million commuter station with a 2,500-car parking lot. Coupled with light industrial development, the plan will "take a complete wasteland and turn it into an economic high point," says Woburn Mayor John W. Rabbitt.

EPA's remediation plan will capture poisonous hydrogen sulfide gas given off by decomposing tannery hides still piled on the site, along with plumes of benzene and toluene, two toxic petroleum derivatives, moving through groundwater. Instead of digging out soil contaminated by toxic heavy metals, including lead, arsenic and chromium, the plan will cover them with 30 inches of clean dirt, possibly combined with plastic membranes. The commuter station, parking lot pavement, and other structures planned for the site will be integral parts of the cover that will keep contaminants in place and isolate them from the environment.

In the same stroke, the transportation development will ease traffic congestion and contribute to controlling air pollution. The state will be saving as much as 80 percent of the cost of building the station at another location, and it has been estimated that proceeds from the sale of the rest of the land would exceed $20 million. The city of Woburn stands first in line for revenues to pay off back taxes on the property, while other income will go toward cleanup expenses.

Some Woburn residents have advocated fencing the site off and barring any development. But fences can fall down, and joggers and bikers may ignore signs warning them about health hazards, notes Jack Marlowe, a Woburn native who a decade ago helped found a local group, called For a Cleaner Environment, to push for cleaning up hazardous wastes in the city. Marlowe prefers to have a state agency control the most contaminated tracts, with governments making sure that remaining contaminants lie undisturbed by imposing strict controls "over what can be done on the site five or ten or twenty years from now."

To make the plan work, state and local officials will have to convince the public that deed restrictions or similar measures can keep future owners from drilling wells, building schools and homes, or taking other steps that might expose people to long-buried contaminants. "I don't see how anything could go wrong," Mayor Rabbitt says. "It will be probably one of the most controlled areas in the whole country."

Powers, the Boston consultant whose firm is acting as custodial trustee for the Industri-plex site, contends that creative mechanisms for tailoring cleanup goals to a site's ultimate use will be essential for reclaiming contaminated property. "You've got to make sure that your land use planning is good enough to keep residential use from happening," he says. In Woburn, he maintains, "the

Industri-plex process is working because the full range of governmental functions and levels has become involved" in matching remediation at the site to how the land will be developed. But because banks and businessmen remain wary of the risks, he adds, "for the next several years, the process of making sites come alive will depend on government involvement."

If the Woburn plan works out, the Industri-plex tract could be the first large-scale Superfund site redeveloped for new economic purposes. Meanwhile, environmental regulators in other industrial states are preparing to adjust pollution cleanup programs to encourage similar projects.

New Jersey is one of the states with the most to gain from such an approach. The state already has 113 sites listed as national Superfund priorities, and its Environmental Protection and Energy Department has identified more than 600 major sites that need to be decontaminated; thousands more may require at least partial cleanup action. In addition, more than 17,000 New Jersey industrial plants are subject to the state law requiring that contamination be removed before lands are sold. For landowners, "it becomes a very daunting task" to determine what those laws require them to do to comply with cleanup standards, acknowledges EPED Commissioner Scott A. Weiner.

Governor James J. Florio is backing proposals to simplify the Environmental Cleanup Responsibility Act's restrictions on property transfers and grant financial aid to small businesses and municipal governments facing heavy costs in meeting the law's requirements. To expedite small-scale cleanups, EPED has set up a program to grant a clean bill of health to a property when the owner voluntarily complies with state requirements.

New Jersey regulators also are developing generic cleanup standards to replace site-by-site determinations of cleanup goals. That will give landowners a clear idea of what levels of contamination the state will accept after a cleanup is completed, making remediation costs more predictable. For properties that will be dedicated to industrial purposes, the new regulations will set an alternative standard, one less stringent than what is applied in residential areas.

The alternative standard will give urban governments a chance to accept higher contaminant levels in return for opening idled industrial property for new commercial development, Weiner says. "In balancing all these things, the problem of economic development and jobs is a very important one," Weiner says. "Shouldn't the decision really be the community's?"

Given public alarm about toxic wastes, rethinking environmental cleanup goals will not be an easy matter. But it could be a key step toward restoring inner city economies, while saving governments billions of dollars by concentrating economic growth near existing highways, sewers, electric power lines and other urban infrastructure. EPA has commissioned Resources for the Future, a Washington, D.C., research organization, to assess whether the slow pace of federal Superfund cleanups in inner cities plays a role in forcing economic growth into suburban and rural areas.

The conclusions are due next summer. Right now, it seems clear that the tradeoff for idling old industrial sites will be continued metropolitan sprawl that creates even more serious environmental problems. "That's an excellent example of the sometimes perverse effect of our laws," says William K. Reilly, the Bush administration's EPA administrator.

"We do not really want as a matter of national environmental policy to encourage companies to locate in greenfield locations, with all of the infrastructure and transportation and other consequences that has," Reilly adds, "when there are job needs and development needs and land that can serve those needs located in developed areas in cities."

Chapter 27

Diversifying the
Local Economy

KJELL RODNE

Since 1982, Duluth, Minnesota, has undergone a physical, economic, and spiritual renaissance that has lifted the community out of despair seemingly deeper than Lake Superior, the traditional economic cornerstone for the city. Believing that each and every resident is critical to community success, Duluth turned to its citizens for advice on needed steps to turn their city around and then followed that advice. Work began immediately on several projects — parks renovation, downtown redevelopment, waterfront development, and housing. Efforts built on such positive strengths as health care, education, industrial development, and tourism.

In the early 1980s, demand for northeastern Minnesota's famed iron ore sharply declined. Because Duluth is adjacent to the Iron Range, the city's economy also suffered. During the same years, Duluth lost a U.S. Steel plant that shut down completely, as well as an air base and a major pizza manufacturing plant. Duluth's population dropped from 100,000, a figure that had remained steady for 40 years, to around 85,000. The city's unemployment rate exceeded 20 percent, and the *Wall Street Journal* named Duluth one of the 10 most economically distressed cities in the country.

The city's housing stock was aging and deteriorating. Almost no new construction was undertaken. Vacancy rates soared to 14 percent and higher despite natural attrition and the demolition of houses for a new freeway project.

A New Direction

Duluth's transformation began in 1982 with a series of six public forums entitled "Future City, Duluth Tomorrow." These sessions dealt with such

Reprinted with permission from *Public Management*, Vol. 73, No. 3, March, 1991. Published by the International City/County Management Association (ICMA), Washington, D.C.

subjects as economics and human services, demographic changes, and quality of life and helped Duluthians forge a new direction. This new direction called for a shift in the city's economic base from mining and shipping, legendary resources rooted in the past. Iron mining is unlikely to rebound as an industry, and Duluthians knew they had to diversify their local economy.

The Downtown Renaissance

Duluth's downtown renaissance demonstrates the city's diversification. Formerly a typical urban downtown, suffering from declining market base, unacceptable storefront vacancies, unattended aging buildings, and an exodus to the suburbs, Duluth has revived itself. The city and the Greater Downtown council formed the answer: a public-private partnership. Unexpended federal highway monies were a basic resource for a major $16 million streetscape project. Creative use of tax increment funds provided for a storefront renovation project. All projects were carried out with a community game plan in mind. Duluth's downtown was to retain its historic character, and the city was to tap and expand an emerging economic resource—tourism.

A citizen design review committee studied storefront renovation designs, which were provided free to participating building owners. Low-interest loans were provided for storefront renovation, building cleaning, skywalk extensions, and building code upgrading. Today, newly constructed buildings have blended the character of the past with the freshness of the future. In total, 51 buildings have participated in the downtown renovation program.

Duluth's streetscape program is one of the most attractive and comprehensive in the country. Some citizens question using bricks to pave streets, but, the city needed a renaissance of fact and spirit, and the streetscaping project was its beginning. The Greater Downtown council coordinated more than 30 organizational meetings, which were held at least once a week during the two-year construction phase. Police, engineers, transit authority, contractors, and citizens worked together to create solutions. The project's 3.5 million bricks built a dramatic new image for downtown Duluth.

Revitalizing the Waterfront

Duluth's lake, open spaces, and parks—the essence of the city's charm—stood silent for years, waiting to be rediscovered. Because the city lacked physical and visual links with the lake, the waterfront's potential was lost. Until the city turned around to face the lake by encouraging redevelopment of incompatible land uses, made landscape improvements, and provided access to lakeshore open spaces, people were unable to appreciate their link with Lake Superior.

The Downtown Duluth waterfront plan, "Rediscovering a Waterfront Heritage . . . Downtown," was completed in 1984. It received the Minnesota American Planning Association Chapter award for excellence. The ambitious redevelopment of 350 acres of land along two miles of the Lake Superior harbor basin includes a mix of new and old development. In May 1985, the state legislature approved $16 million for the construction in Duluth of a major state convention center, which was added to the existing arena-auditorium. The *William A. Irvin,* a 610-foot Great Lakes iron ore carrier, was purchased by the Convention Center Board to serve as a drawing card for the city. The extension of I-35 has provided convenient freeway access to the downtown waterfront. Today, Bayfront Festival Park, Corner of the Lake Park, Lake Superior Plaza, and new freeway park decks successfully bridge what was once a gap between the city and the waterfront.

The city also built a two-mile waterfront promenade called Downtown Lakewalk on land donated to the public by six adjacent property owners and on excavated rock from the I-35 freeway project. Lake Place, located above the Lakewalk, is a 2 ½-acre urban park on top of the newly constructed 1,000-foot freeway tunnel.

By 1985, Duluth was booming with new economic development projects. More than $715 million in new public and private investments stimulated the local economy, and by 1990 Duluth's strong commitment to economic diversification had resulted in more than $1.2 billion of new investment in Duluth. Lake Superior Paper Industries' $400 million paper mill, one of the most sophisticated plants in the country, stands out as the biggest single industrial investment in the city since U.S. Steel's plant went up in 1916. In addition, $119 million in major capital investments by the Duluth medical community and $56.5 million by AT&T and US West Communications brought even more diversification to the local economy.

Meeting Local Housing Needs

Duluth seemed to be caught in a Catch-22: how would it maintain a healthy stock of affordable housing during aggressive economic development efforts?

In 1986, Mayor John Fedo announced several new programs to replace decreasing state and federal dollars for local housing needs. A housing trust fund now stimulates new housing opportunities and combats the deterioration of existing housing stock, especially for low- and moderate-income residents. As a coordinating body, the Duluth Housing Trust Fund reviews the city's housing assistance plan and the comprehensive homeless assistance plan to ensure that they reflect the community's housing needs. The fund also works with local agencies, nonprofit organizations, and funders to ensure efficient and effective use of available resources. The trust fund reviews applications for low-income housing tax credits and recommends their allocation to the city council. The fund issues periodic requests for proposals in its initiatives. Criteria for assisted housing programs emphasize long-term affordability. In most instances, the fund allocates funds on a zero- or low-interest loan basis but also awards grants when appropriate.

Using the same investment incentives that had proven effective in commercial retail revitalization, the housing trust fund and the city began to accomplish the goals and objectives established by consensus. The first success story came with foundation support exceeding $500,000 to acquire and rehabilitate deteriorated single-room occupancy units.

Since its inception four years ago, the Duluth Housing Trust Fund has successfully leveraged three dollars for every one dollar invested. It has initiated and implemented numerous local housing programs, including the following.

Contract for deed buy-out program. A zero-interest loan for $100,000 was recently issued to Neighborhood Housing Service, a nonprofit agency providing rehabilitation services for owner-occupied and rental units in Duluth's West End. The funding supports a contract for deed buy-out program, so that income-eligible purchasers under contract may upgrade their homes. After three years, funds will be returned to the Duluth Housing Trust Fund's loan pool.

Homeownership for low-income Native Americans. The Duluth Housing Trust Fund secured $16,000 to underwrite downpayment and closing costs for five low-income Native Americans purchasing homes through the Minnesota Housing Finance Agency (MHFA) Indian Housing Program. In an excellent example of partnership participation, the MHFA provided low-interest mortgage loans, a local savings and loan association oversaw the loans, and the Ordean Foundation provided escrow and closing cost assistance.

Family housing in the Central Hillside. A deferred repayment loan of $20,000 was issued to Center City Housing Corporation for the rehabilitation of a vacant triplex located in Duluth's Central Hillside neighborhood. The triplex will provide three three-bedroom units for low-income families, clearly one of Duluth's pressing housing needs.

Single-room occupancy loan fund — Housing for very low income individuals. The trust fund has successfully secured $850,000 for the single-room occupancy (SRO) loan fund, a joint program of the fund and the Downtown Housing Commission. The program was designed to develop, upgrade, and preserve SRO housing, including maintenance and support services for very low income residents. More than 294 housing units were upgraded through homeowner, renter, and single-room occupancy rehabilitation programs in 1989, despite the loss of federal assistance for housing. In addition, 972 households received energy conservation assistance and or major repairs through the community action program weatherization grants and the city of

Duluth's energy conservation loans. The use of low-income housing tax credits has also helped stimulate construction of 57 new units. These accomplishments illustrate the efforts of the city of Duluth and its subgrantees to utilize new, innovative sources of funding to provide quality, affordable housing for low- and moderate-income residents.

West Duluth single-room occupancy housing development. In the fall of 1989, the Duluth Housing Trust Fund provided a $2,000 loan to the community action program to study the feasibility of converting a vacant former West Duluth community facility into 29 single-room occupancy units and commercial space. The housing trust fund has provided an additional $17,000 no-interest loan to insure, heat, and protect the center over the winter.

West Duluth Home Start Program. The Duluth Housing Trust Fund provided $75,000 in community development block grant funds and $5,000 from its community investment fund to a neighborhood development association for the Home Start Program. This program stimulates construction of affordable, new, single-family homes throughout West Duluth neighborhoods. Three area lenders provided financial support and assistance to the Home Start Program. Duluth Housing Trust Fund assistance has been used to cover title insurance, site improvements, and downpayment and closing costs for low- and moderate-income families. To date, three Home Start houses have been constructed, four are underway, and approximately ten are currently securing financing, title to land, or bids from builders.

Low-income housing tax credits – An important development tool. The Duluth Housing Trust Fund acts in an advisory capacity to the city on the preservation of low-income housing tax credits for eligible local housing projects. Since 1987, the Duluth Housing Trust Fund has recommended the allocation of approximately $175,000 in tax credits. The program will provide 252 apartments, affordable for low-income people, for at least 15 years.

The trust fund also has begun preparing a capital campaign to raise $1 million by encouraging the leadership and participation of key business and professional sectors of the city. The fund will continue to establish partnerships with the private sector and coordinate with other local housing organizations to minimize duplication and maximize communication. The goals are to create additional family housing units providing three or more bedrooms; to establish a $700,000-plus revolving loan fund to assist with up-front costs of home ownership, including downpayment, closing costs, and utility deposits; and to develop additional single-room occupancy housing in downtown.

An Aggressive Strategy

During the 1980s, Duluth initiated an aggressive public-private economic development strategy that has had much success. Today, the city has expanded five medical facilities in the older Central Hillside neighborhood. This expansion collectively represents more than $45 million in investment. Although the development is important to Duluth's economy and job base, it is impinging on the availability of housing in the neighborhood. The Duluth Housing Trust Fund is involved in a fund-raising campaign driven in part by contributions and investments from the medical institutions. Those resources will assist in replacing housing lost through the expansion of the medical facilities by providing no-interest loans from an equity fund. Nonprofit developers will thus be able to finance the development of low-income housing in the area.

Economic development does not have to occur at the expense of vulnerable low-income housing. It can and should occur in a symbiotic win/win environment in which jobs are created and the housing stock is upgraded at the same time.

Duluth's Housing Trust Fund uses contributions and investment capital. Other public funding, such as low-income housing tax credits and state low-interest mortgage financing, matches the private assistance. Resources are leveraged in this way to accomplish housing goals, and housing is not sacrificed in the process.

Economic development objectives cannot continue to be met if housing opportunities are not available. The Duluth housing vacancy rate has now dropped to about 4 percent, and prospective industrial developers need to know that the market can accommodate an influx of employees. Duluth is meeting this need through the joint efforts of the Housing Trust Fund and the newly created economic development authority.

Duluths economic development authority began in 1989 to explore public partnership with the private sector to oversee and stimulate economic development activity. The economic development authority has established a program to utilize tax increment financing to stimulate housing development at all income levels, representing a "Robin Hood" approach to financing.

Duluth has market-rate housing developers who have not been able to finance their private projects because of a lack of available utilities or a low overall market rent structure that will not support new construction. The city of Duluth agreed to fill the financing gap by the use of the tax increment generated by the projects on a pay-as-you-go basis, which eliminated any risk to the city or economic development authority. Projects are expected to generate more increment than is necessary to fill that gap. The additional increment will then be pledged to assist low-income housing development elsewhere in the project areas.

Duluth continues to create new resources through the economic development authority. They can be used along with resources coordinated by the housing trust fund, to accomplish low- and moderate-income housing development that had been impossible previously.

The Minnesota State Legislature is changing the manner in which tax increment financing can be used, a move that may hurt low-income housing development in the future. Duluth Mayor John Fedo, Chairman of the U.S. Conference of Mayors Subcommittee on Housing, has a strong commitment to housing and is working diligently to preserve what has been a useful and creative financing tool.

All public officials are challenged in this era of diminishing federal and state resources and must become especially creative. At a time when known resources are shrinking, local governments must look for opportunities to create new resources. They also must coordinate the resources available with imagination and a determined vision to succeed.

Duluth now has the foundation for a sound future, a future that will be built through cooperation. Affordable housing can be accomplished in concert with economic development, especially if the private sector can be recruited as partners.

Chapter 28

Inner-Habor Development

BARBARA BONNELL

Baltimore is one of the nation's great cities, with a regional population of 3.5 million and a port which ranks fourth in tonnage in the United States and among the top 12 in the world.

According to the New York Times, "Baltimore City is achieving one of the most successful renewals of any aging city in the country."

Baltimore has received national recognition for the success of its sustained downtown redevelopment program, which has succeeded in reversing negative urban trends and created an appealing environment for private investment. This recognition includes 24 national awards for excellence in design, planning, and architecture, and selection by the International Federation for Housing and Planning as the American city with the best urban revitalization program.

The city's downtown redevelopment program began in 1959 with the 33-acre Charles Center Project, which is now complete. A public investment of approximately $35 million created a setting which attracted a private investment of approximately $145 million. The public share includes landscaped plazas with fountains and sculpture and overhead pedestrian walkway systems. The private development has resulted in the construction of 16 major facilities, including 1,750,000 square feet of commercial office space; 400 apartment units; 335,000 square feet of retail or related commercial uses; 4,000 parking spaces; a 1,500-seat legitimate theatre; and a 700-room Omni Hotel.

The success of the Charles Center Project sparked additional private development and renovation efforts which created other buildings containing 1,800,000 square feet of office space adjacent to the project area.

In 1965, the city recognized that the Inner Harbor Basin, an unappreciated and under-utilized resource in the heart of downtown, represented a dramatic opportunity for massive scale redevelopment. The Inner Harbor Plan, covering 240 acres surrounding the historic portion of the old harbor, was

Reprinted with perission from *Lawyers Title News,* May/June, 1986. Published by the Lawyers Title Insurance Corporation, Richmond, Virginia.

adopted by the City as a 30-year blueprint for renewal and recycling. Because of the vastness of the area, the redevelopment effort was divided into five separate urban renewal projects.

Since 1965, the City has transformed the shoreline around the water's edge into a regional playground featuring a wide variety of cultural and recreational attractions. A brick promenade circles the water and functions as a working bulkhead where visiting ships from around the world can be anchored for public display. New finger piers accommodate sightseeing vessels for the public, and a 158-slip marina accommodates yachtsmen and pleasure boaters. Small boat rentals are available and several historic vessels — the City's replica of a Baltimore clipper, the U.S. Frigate *Constellation* (the oldest vessel in the U.S. Navy), and an authentic Chesapeake Bay skipjack, among others, are on display.

The Maryland Academy of Sciences' museum and planetarium are open to the public on the south shore. Other cultural attractions include the $21.5 million National Aquarium; the Six Flags Power Plant family entertainment center; and a public observation deck and exhibition facility atop the World Trade Center.

The public attractions and landscaped open space at the water's edge have created an environment appropriate for public events of regional and national significance; a regular program of festivals and celebrations reaches a crescendo on New Year's Eve, when hundreds of thousands flock to the waterfront for a spectacular fireworks exhibit and dancing.

A new 500-room Hyatt Regency Hotel opened for business in 1981 on a square block facing the western edge of the Inner Harbor, the first of 17 new or remodeled hotels supporting the $42 million, 185,000–square foot Baltimore Convention Center, which opened in the fall of 1979 on a site immediately to the west of the hotel.

The Rouse Company has developed "Harborplace," two pavilions containing 150,000 square feet of specialty, leisure-oriented retail and restaurant space in the shoreline area. Harborplace has been phenomenally successful, prompting further private development of new fashion retailing in the Brokerage, a mixed-use complex opening in 1987.

In the fall of 1984, the Rouse Company broke ground for a $200 million mixed-use project including a 650-room luxury Stouffers Hotel, retail space, office space, and parking for 1,200 cars. The Gallery at Harborplace will be completed next year.

These facilities enable Baltimore to compete successfully for the first time for large national and international meetings and conventions. Most of them are connected physically by landscaped pedestrian walkways and overpasses above the most heavily traveled street systems. Additionally, since the summer of 1985, a fleet of 12 trolleys provides area transportation for 25 cents a ride!

Eleven major private office buildings have recently been completed in the Inner Harbor area, including the 40-story home office of the United States Fidelity and Guaranty Company; the new headquarters building for the Equitable Bank Corporation; the Baltimore Federal Financial Corporation, and the Union Trust Company; a regional office center developed by the IBM Corporation; the new headquarters building of the Chesapeake and Potomac Telephone Company of Maryland; the World Trade Center—an office building developed by the State for the Maryland Port Administration and port-related private businesses; a new federal courthouse and office building; and an office tower developed by Cabot, Cabot and Forbes of Boston.

The Federal Reserve Bank has also completed a new branch building to serve the Baltimore-Washington area on a seven-acre site just west of the Inner Harbor area.

In addition to the major development projects, the Inner Harbor area is experiencing a renaissance of smaller, but cumulatively important projects. Chart House Restaurants, a California concern, has rehabilitated two warehouse buildings into a 300-seat restaurant, and Borel Restaurants, also of California, has opened a $2 million Rusty Scupper Restaurant adjacent to the new Inner Harbor Marina. Other commercial activity involves the recycling of existing buildings, and development groups are proceeding with the renovation of historic old structures, such as the 80-year-old former Fish Market, which is being renovated as a restaurant/cabaret establishment.

In addition to the cultural and commercial development, the Inner Harbor area contains a significant quantity of new housing. Inner Harbor West Venture, a limited partnership including the National Corporation for Housing Partnerships, is constructing 250 townhouses, garden apartments, and a midrise apartment building on a 10-acre site west of the shoreline area. The Murdock Development Company of California has completed construction of a luxury condominium and first-class hotel on a dramatic site facing the Inner Harbor basin.

Other residential development near the Inner Harbor includes the renovation of a number of nineteenth century houses in the Otterbein area under the City's nationally known homesteading program, in which individuals obtained derelict structures from the City for a nominal charge in exchange for the obligation to renovate in accordance with strict design standards. Within the Otterbein area there are also an additional 100 units of in-fill housing both as new construction and conversion of existing commercial structures.

Overall, the 30-year redevelopment program is well ahead of schedule, with $1.5 billion worth of public and private projects either completed or under construction. Each year more than 22 million visitors come to Baltimore to enjoy the sparkling new attractions.

Clearly, it was necessary to change the self-image of Baltimore's citizens before changing the attitude of the rest of the world toward the city. Today, the new image is firmly entrenched and the city has embarked on the greatest growth period in history, due in part to public-private cooperation and active encouragement of development by the City through writing down land costs and providing parking and other public improvements and amenities.

Baltimore's downtown redevelopment program is the result of a unique partnership between the city government and the private sector. The unique aspect of this public-private partnership is its implementation arm—a private, nonprofit management corporation working under the direction of the city's Department of Housing and Community Development, now called the Neighborhood Progress Administration.

The city government establishes the policies under which the corporation conducts its activities, including: (1) the preparation of planning concepts, project plans, and implementation programs; (2) the supervision of land acquisition, relocation, and site preparation; (3) the recruitment of and negotiation with private developers; and (4) its role on behalf of the City in the design of ongoing public improvements.

The nonprofit corporation's contract with the City enables it to conduct confidential negotiations with developers who are interested in buying or leasing City-owned property in the renewal area, and to negotiate joint public-private ventures between the City and private developers, when appropriate.

Unlike a city agency, with a permanent function and existence, the nonprofit corporation provides specialized service to the City on a year-to-year basis. The contractual agreement has been continued under the administration of six different mayors, including Mayor William Donald Schaefer, who took office in December 1983 for a fourth four-year term.

In summary, there is hardly a block within the central business district that has not been touched, and in many cases, totally transformed by renewal activity. Truly Baltimore is a city revitalized.

Chapter 29

Main Street Projects

JULIE SINCLAIR

Generally, historic preservation and economic revitalization are terms applied to the downtown projects in Baltimore and Boston, or, closer to home, Mobile and Montgomery. Rarely does any local official think in terms of his community participating in what appears to be an enormous capital program. The reason is simple: lack of money. What can a community with a population of less than 5,000 do to generate the kind of investment needed to make such a program work? local officials ask. The answer, according to LaFayette (population 3,647) is plenty!

In the last three months the City of LaFayette has received commitments and grants totally $1.425 million. This combination of programs and funding will bring 100 new jobs to LaFayette's downtown business district together with half a million dollars of Central Business District public works improvements. David Schure, Director of the Alabama Main Street Program, says "LaFayette provides the state with a sterling example of how the Main Street approach can work in a small city. LaFayette is one of the smallest communities in the entire country involved in this type of downtown revitalization." Through the hard work and joint efforts of the Mayor, Council, Historic Preservation Authority, and the Main Street Project Manager, the city has turned its declining downtown into an economically renewable resource.

Mayor Ed Yeargan and the City Council actively pursued designation as one of Alabama's first Main Street Cities eighteen months ago. The downtown business district was on the National Register of Historic Places and the economic vitality of the area was declining. Threatened by larger shopping centers in Auburn, Opelika, and Columbus, Georgia, together with the advent of regional shopping malls, LaFayette's downtown merchants were losing more and more of their local patrons. Not many went downtown unless they had business at City Hall or the Courthouse.

In Spring, 1982, Robert D. Long was selected to become LaFayette's Main

Reprinted with permission from *Alabama Municipal Journal*, Vol. 51, No. 3, September, 1983. Published by the Alabama League of Municipalities, Montgomery, Alabama.

Street Project Manager. He moved into offices downtown and began surveying the city. Mr. Long discovered several problem areas but also found many strengths. Because LaFayette never participated in the urban renewal projects of the 1960s and 1970s, the downtown square remains basically unchanged from the late nineteenth century. With such a unique historic foundation, LaFayette had a giant headstart over many communities which must undo the damage of over-zealous urban renewal before beginning to recruit new business to their downtowns. The personal commitment of Mayor Yeargan and several local businessmen to revitalizing downtown led to the incorporation of a Historical Preservation Authority last year.

According to Mr. Long the Main Street Project in LaFayette is working to make downtown economically viable again by focusing on four areas: organization, promotion, design, and economic restructuring. The organization area includes developing a strong business association, increasing cooperation, strengthening the public-private partnership, and improving downtown's ability to compete with other shopping areas. The promotion area involves developing effective advertising, improving the quality of special events, and improving the overall image of downtown LaFayette. The design phase is the most visible because it involves storefront design, window and merchandise displays, signs, and public improvements. The economic restructuring phase involves recruiting new businesses, utilizing vacant or underutilized space in productive ways, market analysis, and improving business skills and expertise.

On June 27th of this year, the hard work and dedication of concerned public and private residents came to fruition. On that day Mr. Glenn McClendon, President of Glenn McClendon Trucking Company, announced that the corporate offices of the company would relocate in downtown LaFayette. The Historic Preservation Authority will issue a single bond sale to cover the $750,000 McClendon project plus another $425,000 in other downtown restoration projects. Construction is expected to begin this month and be completed in February 1984. The McClendon Company will relocate 65 employees to the new headquarters downtown from their current facility. A total of thirteen improvement projects will be funded from the Authority's bond issue, believed to be the first such package issued by a Historic Authority in Alabama.

At the same time, Mr. Jonathan Jay Crowder, Chairman of the LaFayette Historical Preservation Authority, announced that the Authority had obtained a $20,000 grant from the State Historical Commission to stabilize the Hightower Building. The Authority signed an option to buy the historic centerpiece of downtown and is negotiating with interested individuals to revitalize this building.

In August, the United States Department of Housing and Urban Development awarded a $219,400 UDAG grant to LaFayette for use in the general renovation of the downtown business district. HUD officials reviewed the Historic Preservation Authority's bond issue, private commitment to downtown, and the city's offer of $54,600 in matching funds for the grant in deciding to approve the UDAG money for LaFayette. The majority of the UDAG money will be spent on five projects: sidewalk reconstruction, new street lighting, acquisition and development of off-street parking areas, pedestrian plaza construction, and paying the administrative costs of the Authority's downtown revitalization project bond issue. The remainder of the UDAG funds will be used to pay architect and engineer's fees, project inspection fees, construction supervision, new pavement markings, and contingency and administration costs. All of the downtown public works improvements are scheduled to be completed by late summer of 1984.

Lasting Benefits

Thus, nearly $1.5 million will be invested into LaFayette's downtown business district in the next six months, bringing an expected 100 new jobs and $500,000 in new revenue into the community. The construction and public works improvements will create many short-term jobs downtown. The long-term effects of this substantial influx of money and construction cannot be measured exactly, but the City of LaFayette expects to be reaping the benefits of a reviving downtown economy for years to come.

However, the city cannot stop here. The city council recently adopted an innovative sign control ordinance for the downtown area that already is being used as a model for other municipalities in Alabama. The Council's Police and Fire Committee is investigating the possibility of replacing the downtown parking meters with a two-hour parking program. This procedure has been praised for its beneficial effect on downtown retail sales. The overall image of downtown improves as the meters are removed, customers generally feel more inclined to linger in stores, more frequent police patrols through the parking areas tend to insure safety and security, and more employees and patrons utilize off-street parking, thereby leaving more downtown parking open for infrequent visitors and other customers.

Mayor Yeargan is convinced that the activities begun this summer mark "the beginning of a new era for downtown LaFayette." Mr. Long predicts more public-private cooperation and involvement in revitalizing the downtown economy. In the past, most small town local officials believed that historic preservation and economic revitalization could not work in their municipality. LaFayette is disproving this belief. Through dedication, hard work, and perseverance small cities and towns can improve their failing downtown economy using historic preservation tax incentives, federal and state grants, and public-private investment and cooperation. It's working in LaFayette, and it can work in your community too.

Main Street Program

The Alabama Main Street Program is managed by the Alabama Historical Commission. According to the Program Director, David Schure, there are only two requirements for municipal eligibility in the program. To be eligible, a municipality's downtown must be listed on the National Register of Historic Places and the population of the city must be between 3,000 and 50,000. When the program was first announced nearly two years ago, twelve municipalities met the requirements. Now there are only ten communities not already in the program that meet the requirements. However, in the last few months several municipalities have begun the process of getting their downtown listed on the National Register. Perhaps by next year, the Commission will have as many as thirty municipalities from which to choose Main Street participants.

The Alabama Main Street Program consists of a 50/50 match of funds for two eighteen-month cycles totaling three full years of support to each participant. Brewton, Eufaula, and LaFayette were chosen as Alabama's first Main Street cities. Selma was added late last year and the Commission plans to announce two more additions to the program by December.

Although there are only two formal criteria for eligibility, the Commission carefully reviews many factors in choosing participants. Due to the broad scope of the program and its three year limitation, the Commission feels that a municipality must have a strong commitment to historic preservation and reviving the economic vitality of downtown before coming into the Main Street Program. Mr. Schure noted that if a city has a combination of city government support, merchant support, and private support that city will stand a much better chance of being chosen to participate than a city with only one or two vocal proponents. Broadbased support does not necessarily mean having lots of money as much as it means having a strong local foundation of interest and commitment upon which the Main Street Program can build.

Chapter 30

Negotiating Business Developments

CHERYL A. FARR
LAWRENCE D. ROSE

The following case study describes how the city of Mercer Island, Washington, negotiated a particularly novel land development deal, and how the city manager functioned as an effective broker in the negotiations.

Background

The city of Mercer Island is a lovely island in the middle of Lake Washington, linked to Seattle on the west and its sprawling suburbs to the east by the bridges of interstate highway I-90. In 1978, the city's population of 22,000 was predominantly well-to-do; recent sales of island homes had a mean value of $146,000. Mercer Island's winding roads, lovely vistas, and breathtakingly attractive residences had earned it a reputation as a wealthy community.

The city government, however, was far from being comparably wealthy. This can be traced in some measure to the fact that the business district was quite small and contained mostly service enterprises such as service stations, grocery stores, dry cleaners, and drug stores; sales and business taxes produced limited revenue. But in even larger measure, the economic straits of the city can be traced to a state law, passed in 1973, which effectively deprived the city of much of the value of the rich and expanding assessment roll that had been the basis for property (ad valorem) taxes, the former keystone of Mercer Island's revenue system. That law limited all cities in the state to collecting no more than 106 percent of the property tax dollars received in the preceding year. Accordingly, tax rates became merely an expression of dollars, not a measure of revenue to be produced.

Reprinted with permission from *Municipal Innovations Series Report*, No. 34, 1981. Published by the International City/County Management Association, Washington, D.C.

Mercer Island has faced the problems of inflation and rising costs with a property tax revenue base that expands slowly and, correspondingly, with an increasing interest in the revenues to be gained from utility taxes, business and operating taxes, and the 0.5 percent sales tax the city receives from local sales. In evaluating the avenues that would provide needed revenues, local officials saw few real choices. Because of the property tax cap, residential development was not an encouraging option. Development had spread south in waves across the island for two decades, leaving few available residential sites. Since the city had developed over the years the image of a place that valued attractive amenities and quality of life attributes, officials did not consider industrial uses as an option for revenue development. City officials became convinced that attractively designed commercial and office development was the only means to increase local sales tax revenue and thereby provide needed services for residents. They believed that Mercer Island's location (ten minutes from downtown Seattle), as well as its affluent market, would encourage such development.

In the early seventies, the city drafted its first master plan. Among the stated goals was the development of a healthy economy in the main business district, an eleven-block area containing a fragmented collection of buildings heavily punctuated with parking lots. Most of the buildings were occupied by wholesale, retail, and professional office uses. While the vacancy rate was low, much of the commerce was marginally successful and the turnover rate was high.

The major undertaking proposed in the master plan to generate a healthier economy in this central business district was the construction of a city hall and community center. A fourteen-acre parcel of land belonging to the school district, which was vacant and not expected to be needed in the future, was pinpointed as the appropriate place. For years it had been zoned exclusively for public purposes. The schools had no need for the site, but the city had no means to acquire it or to develop something on it even if the site were acquired.

At one point, it seemed that what was called for in the master plan—a new city hall and community center, and downtown revitalization generally—could be accomplished. The city had submitted a grant proposal to the Economic Development Administration (EDA) and the school district's board had agreed to lease the property to the city for a token amount if the EDA grant came through. It did not, however, and the idea of a new city hall went on the back burner. Occasionally city officials speculated about doing something with four acres owned by the city immediately adjoining the school property. But "doing something" required money, and the city treasury was conspicuously missing the resources needed to do anything. A portion of the city-owned four acres was being used by the city's water and sewer utility, but this was seen as an inefficient use of valuable property and was considered a temporary situation until the resources needed to develop the site materialized.

Repeated efforts during the seventies demonstrate the city's continuous commitment to the economic development goal the master plan had set. The city implemented commercial development design controls which enhanced the aesthetic appeal of the central business district by setting design standards for the service and convenience businesses that were built. The city also committed the business and occupation tax revenues it collected to a business district beautification fund. Through the fund utilities were placed underground, attractive street lighting was purchased, and plantings and street furniture were placed in easements along property edges. For council members, new and old, city manager Larry Rose consistently highlighted the master plan's goal of economic growth and kept alive an awareness of the central business district's sales tax potential. The political commitment to economic development downtown remained strong, with officials awaiting the right opportunity.

Summer of 1979: The turning point. In the summer of 1979, Mercer Island's officials faced twin problems. The first, and most difficult, was that the city's corporation yard, housing the public works facilities, was located on leased space in the path of highway construction and had to be vacated. As the officials looked for new space, they realized quickly that Mercer Island's little remaining vacant land was too expensive to purchase; furthermore, no available sites would adequately screen this unattractive use from nearby residential areas. The only available city-owned land was the four-acre parcel in the central business district. City officials believed that the corporation yard would be an unwise use of valuable property, and even began looking for a site in an adjacent community.

It was at this point that a phone call to the mayor presented a second, less difficult problem. In retrospect, however, this call precipitated events that are seen as a turning point for the expansion of Mercer Island's economic base.

That historic call came from Charles Bershears, then president of one of Mercer Island's major employers, Farmers New World Life Insurance Company. He was seeking help from Mayor Ben Werner in solving a problem his company had (and one the city would have liked to have had): how to manage business growth. The problem that Bershears presented to the mayor had to do with expanding the company's parking facilities into the residential zone. The understandable opinion Farmers had received from city staff was that it was unlikely that the zoning law would be amended for this purpose. Bershears asked the mayor if anything could be done. The mayor, in turn, suggested that city manager Rose talk with Bershears to see what help, if any, could be offered.

From the city's perspective, as Rose initially saw it, the departure of the company would have very little impact. Insurance companies and banks in the state of Washington are regulated and taxed totally by the state, so the city received no direct revenues from this business. Although there were almost 800 people working in the Farmers office building, its freeway location meant that the vast majority of employees went to and from work on the freeway, and seldom used the services in the business district. As this was a conclusion that nobody disputed, there simply seemed to be no justification for a time-consuming effort, even for a firm which for years had been a respectable corporate citizen.

Then, it dawned on Rose one day. If Farmers could stay on the island but be relocated to the central business district, its payroll of 800 employees and the purchasing power they represented could provide a dynamic boost for the entire economy of the city. The fourteen-acre property belonging to the school district suddenly, once again, loomed as critically important.

The plight of Farmers, a subsidiary of Los Angeles–based Farmers Insurance Group, was real and becoming more onerous day by day. The spectacular growth of the business compelled it to expand almost immediately. The company had sufficient land at the present site, which had been bought in the mid–1950s, but zoning bisected it. The front 4.8 acres, on which the Farmers building was situated, were zoned commercial/office; the southerly nine acres were zoned residential. The company had failed to seek a change in the zoning classification at the time of purchase, when it probably would have been simple to do so. This was not the case in 1979.

Farmers had engaged the services of a respected local land attorney to explore the possibility of the rezoning early in 1979. After talking with city officials and residents in the neighborhood surrounding the site, the attorney advised Farmers that there was substantial opposition, that the process might consume the better part of a year, and that the outcome was uncertain. Farmers could not wait a year, especially for an unpredictable result. Already bulging at the seams, the company had to begin at once to provide for expansion, and the only certain alternative was to go elsewhere—out to the suburbs, where land would be inexpensive and plentiful. In fact the board of directors had already decided to relocate to the suburbs at the time the city had come on the scene. This was not a promising situation for the city to try to change the course of destiny.

Negotiating a Public-Private Partnership

Assuming that the fourteen-acre school property would still be available at the generous terms agreed to when the city had applied for the EDA grant, Rose discussed with Mayor Werner the idea of making available to Farmers the school site plus the adjoining four acres owned by the city. On this land Farmers could build its headquarters and a city hall which the city could lease back. Or the city could build the complex, using revenue bonds, and lease space to Farmers.

Mayor Werner urged Rose to make the proposal to Bershears, which he did. Bershears, who wanted to remain on the island for sentimental as well as practical reasons, discussed it with his directors. Later he told Rose there was some interest among board members, and asked Rose if he would be willing to go to Los Angeles and lay the plan before the full board of the parent company. Informal discussion and casual suggestion had suddenly taken on a serious note.

Rose needed not only authority to proceed; he needed a competent endorsement of the validity of the plan. At a meeting arranged by Mayor Wener, key members of the city council were joined by James Ellis, a distinguished Seattle bond attorney. Ellis, a champion of public-private cooperation who had put together some nationally renowned projects, gave enthusiastic support to the proposal. And the council members approved the idea of having Rose make the offer to Farmers' board of directors.

At the board of directors' meeting, several issues were critical in bringing about the positive response Rose received:

1. The city manager was able to be frank about why Mercer Island was offering its proposal: 800 warm bodies with discretionary income to spend would be working daily in the downtown area.
2. The city had "done its homework," having gone to a reputable lawyer for legal advice *before* it went to the Farmers Insurance Group's board of directors. A key board member who knew Ellis told his colleagues, "If Jim Ellis says it's a good deal, I believe it is."
3. The insurance company knew that if it left Mercer Island it would lose roughly 25 percent of its existing employees. Insurance companies are labor intensive, with a heavy dependence on relatively low-paying clerical jobs. Employees were unhappy at the thought of a longer drive, which would increase both commuting time and expenses. Mercer Island provided a broader labor market to draw from than a distant suburb, and the downtown site had the added advantage of being on an intercity bus route. The company preferred to find a site close enough to its present location to enable it to keep most of the employees, rather than face extensive training of new employees.
4. The city manager emphasized that Mercer Island wanted to keep Farmers and would work cooperatively with the company, while many of the distant suburbs were antagonistic toward business development. He mentioned that Farmers could face environmental restrictions and citizen scrutiny in a developing community, whereas because Mercer Island's site was in a developed commercial area where the master plan called for additional growth, the likelihood of such problems was much lower.

The Farmers Insurance Group's board of directors was interested, and agreed that Mercer Island's officials should negotiate with the school district for its fourteen-acre parcel. However, Farmers would continue evaluating alternative sites for its new facility in case the Mercer Island site did not come available.

Mercer Island is unusual in that the school district and city borders are conterminous, but it is not unusual in having a weak relationship with the school board. Because much of the school board's budget is provided through the state of Washington, it was relatively unconcerned about the local government's revenue needs or economic development goals.

After three months of negotiations with the school board, Mercer Island's officials concluded that the proposal they had made to Farmers was not going to work. The school board did not want to part with its land without receiving a substantial payment—perhaps as much as $3 million. Because the school board had never obligated itself to sell its fourteen acres to the city at the time of the EDA proposal for a new city hall, the city did not have any choice but to pay the asking price or give up hope of getting the site. (The school district's land was zoned for public use and could not be sold for commercial use by the school board.)

City officials were frustrated at not being able to bring the school district's site into the deal, but were unwilling to give up hope. They searched for another way to bring the Farmers payroll into Mercer Island's central business district. Taking a fresh look at the situation, local officials came up with another idea. On the side of the city's four-acre parcel opposite the school district's property was a two-acre site occupied by a bowling alley. The city manager remembered hearing that the owner wanted to sell. Could a building meeting Farmers' need be accommodated on six acres?

The city decided to try to make it work. Mercer Island's city council made a bold move: it voted $20,000 to hire an architectural firm called TRA to do a massing study to determine if a building suiting Farmers' needs could be accommodated on a six-acre site. Farmers had hired TRA to do preliminary drawings of buildings suiting its need, although no site had been chosen. The prospective building would have to meet the requirements of the local design review board, provide on-site parking, and not block the views of Lake Washington that were a selling point for unit owners in the adjacent condominium complex. At the same time, the council voted to take a one-year option to buy the bowling alley site. The $5,000 earnest money deposit would be forfeited if the site was not purchased.

City manager Rose told Farmers president Bershears what the city intended to do, but did not try to elicit any promises from the company in exchange. The city council believed that bringing a major employment center into the central business district was important enough to the community to merit risking some of the city's limited funds. Farmers was impressed with this public-sector commitment.

Developing public support. While the TRA massing study was being developed, the manager and mayor put together a "crisis team" composed of representatives of the design review board, the planning commission, and the city council. The crisis team was briefed on the city's proposal to Farmers and the plans in the works. When TRA completed its efforts the crisis team, under the guidance of Jerry Bacon, director of community development, met with the manager and the mayor to discuss the six design alternatives that TRA had proposed. Working from the six sketches, the crisis team and TRA created a building design that met the criteria of Farmers, the design review board, the planning commission, and the city council.

Hoping that when TRA had completed its massing drawing one or more of the concepts would prove attractive to Farmers, local officials continued to ruminate about an alternative deal to be negotiated. A new city hall could wait, but a new corporation yard could not. Finally, the city settled on the idea of trading the city's six acres for Farmers' fourteen acres. While it could be postulated that land values were about equal because the city's six acres had more valuable zoning, the Farmers office building was obviously an asset of enormous value. So what the city finally focused on was not the value of the building as part of a trade, but its value if Farmers had to sell that building and property and pay capital gains taxes on it. Why not give the building to the city and create a tax write-off?

City officials again sought out the best resource person available to help evaluate that possibility. The city manager called on Hugo Oswald, a corporate tax attorney and a former member of the city's planning commission. Explaining the negotiations that had taken place, Rose asked Oswald to review the tax consequences for Farmers of a land swap combined with a donation of its building to the city for use as a city hall. While Oswald obviously did not have information on Farmers' particular tax situation, he was able to provide a generic analysis of the proposal's tax consequences.

Oswald's analysis highlighted several options providing favorable tax consequences for the business. For all the options, the crux of the analysis was this: because Farmers had owned the property since the early fifties and property values had risen dramatically in the intervening years, Farmers would face a large capital gains tax upon the sale of its property. By giving its building to the city, Farmers would be able to take a charitable deduction off its tax liability. The deductions could be taken over five years, so the high value of the property could be written off against corporate tax liabilities in increments. By swapping Farmers' land for publicly owned land of equal value, no gain or loss would be recognized from the land swap by the Internal Revenue Service.

With the documentation from the massing study and the corporate tax analysis backing up its proposal, the city was ready to offer Farmers an attractive package. The city would exercise its option in buy the bowling alley property by issuing a $3 million councilmanic general obligation bond for a new city hall and corporation yard. Seven hundred thousand dollars would be used for purchasing the bowling alley site, $1.5 million would finance construction of a new corporation yard, and $400,000 would be held in reserve by the city. The city would clear the two adjoining central business district sites and trade them for Farmers' two adjoining sites (i.e., the commercially zoned and the residentially zoned parcels). The parcels would be assumed equal in value, so no gain or loss would be recognized from the land swap. Farmers would donate its building to the city as a charitable gift, and the city (as it thought at the time) would renovate it for use as a city hall. The city's corporation yard would be built on the nine-acre parcel behind the old Farmers building. Farmers would build its new building on the central business district site.

As the deal moved from idea toward reality, city officials worked to anticipate and avoid problems. Early on, the city manager met with the local newspaper editor to brief her on the city's negotiations. Appreciating the fact that private corporations shy away from publicity about inconclusive negotiations and might be scared off by premature public speculation—and thus be lost to the city as an economic boon—the editor agreed to hold back the story until negotiations were firm. However, she did write a stirring editorial that stated that Farmers was thinking about moving because of its expansion needs and that urged city officials and residents to work together to keep a fine corporate citizen on the island. This timely editorial was effective in nurturing public support for the city's efforts and in increasing Farmers' understanding of its local support.

After the city received preliminary drawings from TRA and met with the crisis team to pick a good design, the community development director and the city manager began meeting with the condominium associations from buildings near the site to explain the proposal and its impact on the condominium sites. Thanks to the geographical configuration of the island (the central business district sits low near the shore and is surrounded on the other three sides by terraced slopes), the proposed five-story Farmers building would not obscure the condominiums' lake view. In addition, the new development would replace the city's utility company facility and an old bowling alley with an attractively designed employment center. This public relations effort paid off; the condominium associations were, on balance, not opposed to the project.

As the negotiations evolved into a legal agreement for the exchange of property, the deal wavered on the edge of an abyss. Lawyers for both parties worked to hammer out an agreement, but their inclinations to protect their clients threatened to smother the deal in layer upon layer of clauses and exceptions. City manager Rose called Harold Gingrich, the corporate vice president for real estate investments, who had taken charge of Farmers' end of the negotiations. Backed by the knowledge that the city council had given him the power to negotiate the deal to its conclusion, Rose was able to come quickly to the point.

"Harold," Rose said, "the lawyers are asking for all kinds of things we never discussed. Can you tell me exactly what you want?"

Gingrich replied, "We'll swap the lands and give you the building."

"You've got a deal!" said Rose.

There was a long pause. "I have?" asked Gingrich.

"Yes," said Rose. "Now would you please call your lawyers and tell them that's the deal and nothing else?"

Gingrich did just that.

The legal agreement. The agreement that developed between the city and Farmers focused on three major issues: the property exchange, the charitable gift, and the building permit and closing date.

Property exchange. The city of Mercer Island and Farmers agreed that their lands were equivalent in value, and so qualified as a tax-free exchange under the provisions of Section 1031 of the Internal Revenue Code of 1954, as amended. This was important to Farmers because it allowed the company to avoid a capital gains tax. It was advantageous to both the city and Farmers because it resulted in a direct exchange with no cash involved, and both parties were getting property more valuable to them than the property they were giving up.

If the downtown parcel proved to be unsuitable for Farmers' proposed development as a result of soils and engineering tests, the city would receive Farmers' nine-acre, residentially zoned site in exchange for the two-acre bowling alley site. The city would be able to build its corporation yard, and Farmers would be able to sell or lease the cleared bowling alley property at its discretion. The location of the bowling alley site made it a valuable piece of real estate for investment purposes; on the other hand the nine acres Farmers owned were unusable for corporate purposes, and too close to offices and the highway to yield a quick sale for residential use.

Charitable gift. Farmers, "because of its long and beneficial association with the Mercer Island community," and because it "was aware of the desperate need of the city for adequate municipal facilities," gave its existing building to the city as a charitable gift. This gift, the agreement noted, "was neither a part of nor consideration for the property exchange." In this way, the city received a building to use for municipal facilities and Farmers was able to offset other corporate tax liabilities with the value of its gift. It should be noted that a gifting like this will only appeal to companies with enough tax liability to make the gifting worthwhile, *and* with enough funds available to cover new construction without selling its existing building. For Farmers, this was the case.

Building permit and closing date. Because no guarantee was given by the city that Farmers would get the permits necessary to build, the agreement was made contingent upon Farmers receiving a permit and turning its building over to the city by a specified date. If, for any reason, Farmers did not receive a permit, the deal would revert to the exchange of the residentially zoned site for the bowling alley site. The city required a specific closing date to ensure that Farmers carried out its end of the bargain in a timely fashion.

The agreement was signed, and soon construction began on Farmers' new building, and on the city's new corporation yard. A $15,000 sculpture jointly commissioned by the city of Mercer Island and Farmers New World Life Insurance Company was erected in the plaza in front of the new Farmers headquarters as a monument to the public-private partnership that had made the new development possible.

Afterword. As the city evaluated its space needs, it concluded that the old Farmers building was not suitable for a city hall because its floor space of 37,000 square feet was 20,000 square feet more than the city would be able to use. There was also concern that the former corporate headquarters was a bit too ostentatious for a city hall.

The city officials decided to seek a tenant to lease the building. An independent real estate company estimated the lease could bring in as much as $270,000–$300,000 per year. The city would be required to pay a 12 percent leasehold tax on any lease revenues since the building would be leased for private purposes, but the right tenant might also provide a high sales tax revenue for the city. Sales tax in the state is levied at the point of sale, so a corporate office can provide significant sales tax revenues; and the local share of 0.5 percent of sales taxes collected could add significantly to local revenues. The council decided to make a serious effort to market the building, and dedicated a major portion of the city manager's time to it. It was expected that revenue from the lease would service the debt on construction of a new city hall when a suitable site became available.

Mercer Island's ownership of the old Farmers building theoretically gave the city the capability to choose a desirable tenant, but the effects of the recession in 1981 and 1982 made it impossible to find any tenant able to afford the space at the estimated rate. Unwilling to leave the building empty until the economy improved, the city council leased the space to the state department of transportation for five years at a below-market rate (which would nonetheless produce over $1 million). The council planned to rent the building more profitably later to a commercial tenant.

In the meantime, however, a surprising new land swap has been negotiated. The city council agreed to exchange the old Farmers building for the school district parcel located in the central business district — the fourteen-acre parcel that the city first identified in the early seventies as the appropriate site for a city hall and community center. The school district urgently needed income, and the council voted to make the exchange "for the good of the schools."

Now the city is faced once again with the problem of what to do with an undeveloped, but valuable, property in the central business district, without money to do much of anything. The school parcel is still zoned for park and public uses only. It is the largest undeveloped parcel in the central business district, and the council is aware that its development will have a profound influence on the economic, social, and cultural health of the city.

Once Farmers moved into its new building, downtown land values began to rise, from $6–$7 per square foot in 1979 to $8–$12 per square foot in 1981, to $18–$20 per square foot in 1984. Pressures have mounted to rezone contiguous single-family parcels to multi-family. Although 1,000 people are now employed by Farmers at the new location, the effect on shops and stores nearby has been difficult to assess.

The city council would like to use the large downtown property it now owns to give the still random business community a strong, colorful, and distinctive character, supportive of and supported by a magnetic civic, cultural, and social presence. A joint public-private venture that would give the city the financial wherewithal it needs to develop the property seems the most likely option available. Whether the citizens of Mercer Island will tolerate any commercial use of the site (probably an inevitable result of public-private development) is an unanswered question at present. With land values up (partly because of the new Farmers headquarters) the city does not judge it economical to sell the property and go into the market for another site for a city hall complex. Another question complicating the city's planning is whether the central business district can tolerate competition from new commercial office space. If the city should build commercial office space on its new property, would it ruin the market for private interests? To find some answers to these questions and plan the best use for the new parcel, the council has appointed a committee that includes representatives of the city's business interests. The council is determined to pursue the public-private approach, which proved so successful four years ago in relocating the city's corporation yard and keeping a valuable business in the city.

Evaluation Team's Assessment

Shortly after the exchange of the old Farmers building for the city's six-acre site in the spring of 1981, an evaluation team sponsored by ICMA visited Mercer Island to evaluate the transferability, to other small and medium-sized cities, of elements that were critical to this public-private land development process. The team looked at the project from two perspectives: the deal itself and the role of the manager as a broker in land development negotiations.

The deal itself. In considering the transferability of elements in the deal itself, the team believed that this project exemplified the use of three techniques:

Land swap. Two publicly owned sites and two privately owned sites considered equal in value were traded. The exchange of such sites qualifies as a like-kind exchange under Section 1031 of the Internal Revenue Code of 1954, as amended. (This section provides that no gain or loss is recognized when properties of like kind are exchanged.) Since Section 1031 does not state that both parties must be taxpayers normally subject to taxation, involvement of a municipal tax-exempt corporation as one of the parties to the agreement does not affect the usefulness of Section 1031. The review team noted that there was no requirement for a professional appraisal of the land value to determine similar value.

Mercer Island's land swap took place so that the city and the insurance company could construct buildings on sites that were more appropriate for their new development than the sizes the parties originally owned. But this is not the only situation in which swaps can be effective. For example, land swaps also can be used by communities to *prevent* the development of a specific site. This can be done by exchanging a publicly owned parcel that is considered appropriate for private development, for a privately owned site, and then restricting the use of the newly acquired site to public open space.

A technique similar to land swaps is transferring air rights to offer investors developable space while maintaining public control of the site. In some cases local governments have then used the land at or below ground level to provide a development incentive (e.g., building a public parking garage underground). This will reduce development costs for the developer by providing on-site parking, and will provide revenue to the community. Lease payments and property taxes on the air space and improvements can provide communities with additional revenues, and at the same time the communities can retain control of the land.

Charitable gift. The review team noted that the large, successful private corporation involved in the Mercer Island deal had been unaware of the favorable tax consequences that would result from donating its building to a municipality. The team noted that such deductions on taxable income can be very attractive to corporations that have tax liabilities to offset yet do not need cash from the sale of their buildings for other purposes.

City officials frequently assume that private corporations are familiar with every trick in the book as far as development goes, but that is not always the case. The review team emphasized that local officials should realize that since businesses move infrequently they may welcome ideas for different approaches that can be used for development. The team noted that companies make mistakes just as cities do, but because they do not operate in the public eye their errors are not as well publicized as the public sector's.

School district–local government cooperation. Although the negotiations between the city of Mercer Island and its school district broke down, the concept of communities acquiring excess school property is transferable. Many school districts had projected higher population growth rates than have materialized and are left with both buildings and undeveloped sites that exceed their future needs. School districts may be willing to sell or lease these properties to the local government at minimal cost.

The manager as broker. In evaluating the manager's role as a broker in public-private land development negotiations, the review team highlighted several points as being important for other communities and managers undertaking similar activities.

A positive manager–council relationship. First and foremost in importance for successful negotiations is the need for a strong, supportive mayor-manager relationship. The manager in Mercer Island had the trust of the council, and particularly of the mayor. Decisions were made through continuous consultation between the manager and the mayor. The council members trusted the mayor to keep an eye on the day-to-day proceedings, and at every critical point the full council discussed its members' concerns and made the decisions. Without the knowledge that the council had given him its approval to negotiate a deal, the city manager could not have functioned effectively.

A willingness to get the facts that make good ideas persuasive arguments. Cities should not expect the private sector to do its own homework. If a project or a deal is important enough, the public sector should be willing to risk some of its own funds to explore options and to buttress its ideas with facts. Team members agreed that it is worth the expense to buy the best expertise the community can afford. Talented, imaginative resource people provide credibility that reduces the perceived risk in novel undertakings. Each time Mercer Island's local officials came up with what they thought might be a good approach they sought professionals, who were known in their field, to back up the city's ideas with facts, and this paid off. The city also put its own money at risk—in the option to buy the bowling alley site, and in commissioning TRA's massing study.

Being honest and following through on promises. Private sector representatives often are wary of involvement with the public sector, either because they have been "burned" once before or have heard of another business that was mistreated in a public-private partnership. Continued demonstration of good intent and not promising what cannot be delivered are the cornerstones for building public-private partnerships. The city manager's efforts to conclude negotiations quickly and efficiently through careful preparation and follow-through avoided the costly bureaucratic delays that the private sector often associates with government "help."

Implementing established policy. A consensus on the need for economic growth should be developed well in advance of any specific deal. If managers wait until the opportunity presents itself, it can be too late to mobilize support. When deciding which deals are worth investing the time and trouble to negotiate, the first question should be: "Is it in the master or comprehensive plan?" If not, said the review team, either it should be put in the plan or it isn't worth a major effort. When the type of development under negotiation is in an approved master plan, that document backs up the manager's stand. Then he or she is simply implementing established policy. City manager Rose recognized the need for consensus building, and directed his efforts toward orienting new council members to the master plan's economic development goals, and also reminding longtime council members of these goals.

Negotiating requires a team effort. Council support in negotiating public-private partnerships is one key ingredient; a second is staff support, needed to overcome minor obstacles that can torpedo an otherwise perfect proposal. Unless the task has been designated to a specific staff person, the manager should provide leadership in brokering public-private partnerships and set the tone for the staff's approach. At some point in most public-private land development negotiations someone from the public sector needs to tell naysayers, "We want this to work. Don't tell me why it can't work, show me how it *can.*" For important deals it is also useful to develop a team that can expedite the project through the procedural slowdowns that inevitably occur.

Retaining existing businesses makes sense. Keeping industries that are already located in a community is easier than bringing in new ones. More time should be spent by communities in helping existing industries stay or expand than in chasing down new leads. Recent studies show that very few businesses actually relocate each year, and the likelihood of a positive outcome is much higher when the business has a vested interest in the community.

Learning the art of negotiating. Regardless of the amount of legwork the manager does, the council is taking the public risk, and council members deserve the lion's share of credit for deals the manager successfully brokers. It is also important to keep in mind that some deals just will not work, and creating a crisis can harm a manager's future in a community. Managers can function effectively as brokers of public authority and property only in a harmonious environment; they must develop an intuition not only for when to call it quits in fruitless negotiations, but for when to get out of the limelight.

Anticipating roadblocks. There are many powers to contend with in public-private partnerships: the client, the staff, the city council, the media, the legal counsel, the citizens affected by the deal, the common good, and the manager's personal desire to mold the deal. Managers need to be imaginative, both in identifying their communities' negotiating strengths and in anticipating potential stumbling blocks. There were several points in Mercer Island's negotiations where the city officials might easily have thrown in the towel. Perseverance, imagination, and hard work helped them win their fight.

Negotiating land development deals takes time. On Mercer Island the private corporation was unable to handle its business without additional space, and the city faced eviction from its leased corporation yard. The deal came together quite easily because both sides needed to close the negotiations quickly. Even so, it still took nearly a year to get a signed agreement. The manager must have the council's backing to spend an inordinate amount of time negotiating the details of a project, or must have a staff person available to do the legwork.

Conclusion

Communities interested in encouraging local economic growth through public-private land development partnerships must make a long-range commitment of staff time, political support, and local funds to reap the rewards they seek. Mercer Island's project shows that cities can negotiate successfully for desired business development without using tax abatements or industrial revenue bonds, and without relying on federal or state funding.

Local government administrators who have worked as public-private land development brokers emphasize that the key to their effectiveness is council support. This frees them from much of the crisis management of day-to-day administration of their communities, and allows them to commit the community to a deal. They also note that negotiating land development deals is enjoyable and challenging; the bricks-and-mortar results give a different sense of accomplishment than most other tasks local administrators undertake.

The need for imaginative approaches for revenue development is likely to increase the opportunity for local government administrators to be the front runners in entrepreneurial cities. It is the responsibility of managers to communicate the need for a team approach to their councils, and to develop and maintain with them the positive relationships that are critical in successful public-private land development negotiations.

Chapter 31

Organizing for
Economic Development

DAVID H. ROEDER

In the middle of downtown Chicago, within sight of the city's famous Picasso sculpture, sits a civic embarrassment. It is a square block of vacant space that was to be the centerpiece of the North Loop redevelopment plan. All but one of the buildings on the site—including several that were historically or architecturally significant—were torn down four years ago and a glassy new office and commercial complex promised in their stead. Then the market for office space deflated, and last winter the site known ruefully to local planners as "Block 37" became a makeshift ice-skating rink. During the summer, tents have been erected there for high school students working on art projects.

Block 37 typifies the economic hangover in Chicago's central business district. Almost 40 percent of the downtown office space went up during the wild 1980s, when banks were eager to lend and city officials, dazzled by the promise of added tax revenues, welcomed almost any project. Today, with a 20 percent office vacancy rate in the region, some of the gleaming new towers are more than half-empty and downtown is pockmarked with vacant lots, legacies of a time when developers received demolition permits before their projects had secured financial backing.

Just west of Block 37 is city hall and the office of Mayor Richard M. Daley. Recent months have been rough on "The boss's son," who was first elected in 1989, 13 years after his legendary father, Richard J. Daley, died in office. The mayor spent much of his political capital last year seeking approval of two big projects: a new commercial airport at Lake Calumet on the far Southeast Side and a massive casino and entertainment center for an as-yet-undetermined site. Daley repeatedly said his motivation for seeking both projects was simple: "Jobs, jobs, jobs." In both cases, he could not win the necessary assent of state lawmakers.

Reprinted with permission from *Planning,* Vol. 59, No. 4, April, 1993. Published by the American Planning Association, 1313 E. 60th St., Chicago, IL 60637.

Fighting Back

Early last year, in an effort to make city government more responsive to business needs, Daley merged his separate departments of planning and economic development and installed a new commissioner, Valerie Jarrett, to run the superagency. But there was little she could do as companies with a strong Chicago presence—Spiegel, Sears, United, USX, Ameritech, Amoco, American Can, R.R. Donnelly, IBM—one after the other announced plans to reduce or eliminate payrolls in the region.

Jarrett was embarrassed in the case of Spiegel when the catalog retailer, citing a need for more space, said it was pulling out of its inner-city location and moving to Ohio. The new planning and development department hurriedly found a parcel of vacant land on the Southeast Side that it thought would meet Spiegel's needs but, when the company checked it out, it found that some of the acreage was under several feet of water at the edge of Lake Calumet. Jarrett said the city could have drained the property quickly, but Spiegel officials were unconvinced.

In the last year, however, the department has made progress on the development of seven new industrial parks to answer manufacturers' demands for modern, secure space. Jarrett has also instituted a new program called SNAPP—for Strategic Neighborhood Action Pilot Program—that concentrates city resources on selected communities. The $8 million initiative fixes potholes, clears abandoned buildings, constructs housing, plants trees—anything deemed likely to spur private investment in depressed areas.

The consensus among planners and community activists is that Jarrett works hard and is accessible to neighborhood groups, but is hobbled by her boss, the mayor, who remains focused on the megaprojects. They argue that Daley hasn't grasped a reality of the current economy—that the city's economic salvation lies in supporting smaller enterprises in the neighborhoods.

This is, after all, the city that lives by Daniel Burnham's credo—"make no little plans." A century ago, that attitude led engineers to reverse the flow of the Chicago River, ensuring the quality of the Lake Michigan water supply. That spirit survives today in a recent proposal for a 125-story building that would be the world's tallest (and which would arise from a lot so skinny as to make it the world's first anorexic skyscraper).

The big projects are all right, says Ted Wysocki, executive director of the Chicago Association of Neighborhood Development Organizations, but they won't replace the 200,000 or so manufacturing jobs the area has lost in the last 20 years. Wysocki suggests that Chicago should change Burnham's words to "make a lot of little plans." "The mayor needs to understand that each Chicago community has its own version of a megaproject," says Wysocki, whose organization embraces 65 neighborhood groups with concerns ranging from establishing day-care centers to finding occupants for abandoned factories.

Wim Wiewel, director of the Center for Urban Economic Development at the University of Illinois at Chicago, says he's been impressed by the commitment of Jarrett and her staff. "What seems to be lacking is clear strategic direction and purpose. Her department was out of the loop on the airport and the casino," he says. Indeed, both projects essentially were lobbying campaigns run directly from the mayor's office, although Jarrett insists that was appropriate and that her department would have become involved had either proposal advanced beyond the state legislature.

Both Daley and Jarrett sharply deny that the big projects have consumed planners' attention. "It's an ongoing fight to keep cities alive in America," Daley says. "It's not just one project or two projects." As evidence of his administration's concern for the neighborhoods, Daley points to efforts to clean up graffiti, revoke liquor licenses for nuisance taverns, and install bigger street signs at major intersections.

Such programs "are the nuts and bolts of the city. But, at the same time, you have to have some vision" for the future, Daley says. His motivation for creating an omnibus planning and development department was to improve communications with the neighborhoods, he says. "You can't have planning on the left hand and economic development on the right hand. Government is too divided," Daley says, adding that with the new system, he's "trying to coordinate things and tell people what's going on."

The Commish

For her part, Jarrett says the notion that city hall is biased toward megaprojects is "terribly unfair" and that there is no tension between her department and the mayor's office over priorities.

A 36-year-old attorney who has done some real estate work but has no background in planning, Jarrett at first worried neighborhood groups, who feared that the development part of her department would run roughshod over the planning part. It hasn't happened that way and Jarrett now jokes about the concern. "In this economy, we have plenty of time to plan," she says. During her watch, the department has issued longterm guidelines for industrial development on the North and West sides. She also has joined forces with the Chicago Park District and the Cook County Forest Preserve District to begin drafting an open space plan for the city, a program funded by a $400,000 grant from the Chicago Community Trust, a major local foundation.

In February, Jarrett and Daley announced a concentrated attack on blight in Kenwood-Oakland and Woodlawn, two impoverished South Side areas. With $1.2 million in seed money from the Chicago-based MacArthur Foundation, the city will draft a broad framework for redevelopment, including plans for 5,000 new housing units geared to various income levels. The hope is that banks and private investors will provide the capital to carry out the improvements. Jarrett says the project is promising because 70 percent of the land in those communities is vacant, with the city holding title to most of it.

She also hails it as an example of planning done in concert with local residents, including both the Woodlawn Organization and the Kenwood-Oakland Community Organization, whose executive director, Robert Lucas, says he believes Jarrett and Daley are sincere in their stated aim to upgrade the South Side without spawning gentrification.

Still, in Chicago, others invariably disagree. Robert Starks, a veteran activist in black politics, views the development scheme as "top-down planning" with racial overtones. "Daley does not trust African-American citizens to make their own decisions," says Starks, who teaches political science and inner-city studies at Northeastern Illinois University.

Since taking over the department, Jarrett has reorganized the chain of command, consolidating sundry functions into eight divisions, including one offering "one-stop shopping" for businesses seeking license and permit information. She has also divided the city into seven planning districts, assigning staff to each. With an annual budget of $39 million, Jarrett asserts that the vast majority of her 240 employees work on neighborhood issues, as opposed to the central business district.

One controversial organizational change merged the Commission on Chicago Landmarks, an independent city agency since its creation in 1967, with Jarrett's department. The new landmarks division is headed by deputy commissioner Charles Thurow (a former APA assistant research director). Preservationists criticized the merger, which saves the city about $100,000 a year. But Jarrett says the commission "functioned in a vacuum, without addressing owners' abilities to rehabilitate some of our landmark buildings."

Some outsiders contend that the department's reorganization has caused confusion. "Valerie Jarrett has high ideals but I think she needs at least a couple more years to make that department work," says Willie Lomax, leader of the Chicago Roseland Coalition for Community Control, which serves a neighborhood plagued by crime, joblessness, and abandoned housing. Another source familiar with the department says, "Morale is very poor and you've got people just bumping into each other all the time."

Daley's reshuffling of city hall did not stop with the planning unit. In early 1992, he changed the name of the public works department to transportation, adding some duties and subtracting others. Maintenance of the 90-year-old network of freight tunnels in the downtown area was transferred to another department, a decision Daley may have come to regret.

Last spring, contractors driving a pile into the Chicago River unknowingly breached a section of the mostly unused tunnels. By April, the hole was big enough to admit a torrent of river water, flooding the basements of numerous downtown buildings and prompting concern that the water would spread to the subway system. The ultimate damage was less than feared, although some buildings and businesses were out of commission for days. But in the aftermath, there were indications that, because of bureaucratic confusion, city officials had not responded quickly enough to early warnings of a leak.

Then in September, a span of the Michigan Avenue bridge, gateway to the city's showcase shopping district, snapped open during a reconstruction project and had to stay that way for several weeks while officials gauged the damage and the cause. The bottom line in both incidents was that little harm was done, although liability questions for the flood are unresolved. However, they made the once-vaunted City That Works look more like the City of Snafus.

Such problems aside, North Michigan Avenue exhibits a retail energy that is the envy of other central cities. Meanwhile, State Street is showing renewed vigor as a commercial and cultural nexus, with the city preparing to begin a $30 million "demalling" project that will reopen the street to car traffic. Unemployment in the city is down to 8.4 percent, a sharp drop from the 10 percent of a year ago. The 1990 census revealed that housing prices in large sections of the city rose 150 percent during the 1980s.

The Bigger Picture

In the region, too, there are many signs that the Chicago area has been spared the worst of the national real estate bust. While housing prices on the East and West coasts have declined, values here have consistently risen from year to year. New office parks continue to emerge on former farmland, although the 20 percent commercial vacancy rate in the suburbs is virtually identical to the city's figure. In most parts of the metro area, which now stretches past distant, independent cities such as Waukegan and Aurora, planning agencies are more concerned with managing growth than encouraging it.

On the negative side, each new demographic study confirms that Chicago not only has some of the nation's wealthiest suburbs, most to the north and west, but also some of the poorest, notably Ford Heights and Robbins to the south. For economic salvation, Robbins has seized upon a controversial plan to build an incinerator and collect fees from burning the trash of its more prosperous neighbors.

Throughout the metro area, the overriding issue is the efficient use of land, says Phillip D. Peters, AICP, executive director of the Northeastern Illinois Planning Commission, whose offices are in Chicago. Peters notes that in the last 20 years, the region's population rose only 4 percent, but the amount of land devoted to residential use increased by 46 percent. During that period, the population of Chicago and its close-in suburbs declined by 770,000, while the outer suburban ring gained a million people.

NIPC's priorities are reflected in the comprehensive plan for the region that it issued last year. It calls for preservation of open space, improved suburb-to-suburb transit, and greater coordination among local governments. This last task is made more difficult by the multiple layers of local government for which Illinois is notorious. In the metropolitan area, there are more than 1,400 agencies empowered to levy property taxes, ranging from cities and school districts to library boards and mosquito abatement districts.

Thus, municipalities fight each other to annex every piece of developable property. Some have had second thoughts about unchecked growth, however, and now are assessing impact fees on home builders within their boundaries. Peters says NIPC wants a state law that will ensure that the fees are shared by jurisdictions affected by a development, not just the host municipalities.

It's widely assumed that the booming suburbs have stolen jobs from the city, but state labor department statistics indicate that most of the manufacturing jobs Chicago lost either vanished or went to another state; the suburbs have had only a negligible increase in manufacturing employment since the 1970s. What is clear is that Chicago has a smaller share of the regional jobs. It had about half the region's workers as late as 1980; today, the figure is under 40 percent.

Reason for Cheer

That trend is likely to continue but it may be deceptive, especially if a rising economic tide lifts everyone, suburb and city. On this point, economists are sounding almost cheery. "Not having relied on the defense industry, we're not being pulled down by it," says Robert Dedrick, executive vice-president and chief economist for the Northern Trust Company. Dedrick points to recent upticks in the confidence levels of Chicago area purchasing managers.

John Skorburg, chief economist for the Chicagoland Chamber of Commerce, estimates the region gained 50,000 jobs in the last half of 1992, bringing the total of 3.35 million jobs even with the previous year. In contrast, Skorburg estimates that Los Angeles has a jobs deficit of 50,000 from a year ago and New York City 25,000. "It's a tough economy but our good transportation system and our central location has helped. Also, the labor force is good and highly trained," Skorburg says.

Most of the new jobs have been on the service side, and Skorburg acknowledges that the area's 500,000 blue-collar jobs are down about 200,000 from 20 years ago. But, he says, "the manufacturing that is still here is leaner and meaner and more high tech."

Diane Swonk, senior regional economist and vice-president of the First Chicago Corporation, assigns major importance to Chicago's role in the automotive and heavy machinery industries. She notes that when Caterpillar's

12,600 workers in Peoria were on strike last year, the effect on local suppliers was chilling. But now that's over and there is evidence that American car companies are staging a comeback. Ford's Taurus, which has won bragging rights as the best-selling car in the U.S., is built on the city's South Side.

Chicago's City of Big Shoulders reputation was based in part on industries that are severely diminished—meatpacking and steel production. The Union Stockyards closed in 1971. If the old industry has a modern equivalent, it's probably the city's four exchanges—the Board of Trade, the Mercantile Exchange, the Midwest Stock Exchange, and the Chicago Board Options Exchange—which regularly set records in their frenzied trading of stocks, bonds, futures contracts, and agricultural commodities. A 1986 study said the exchanges employ 33,000 people; that number is thought to have risen at least a third since then. To the world, Chicago sets the price of the pork belly even if it no longer slaughters the pig.

According to the U.S. Department of Labor, 187,000 steel-related jobs vanished from Chicago and neighboring Lake County, Indiana, from the late 1950s to the mid–1980s. Last April, the U.S. Steel South Works plant, which employed 20,000 people in its post–World War II heyday, closed for good, leaving unused 585 acres along the lakefront near the city's south end. The parcel would cover downtown if laid on top of it and its future use poses a grave challenge to its neighbors and city planners.

Convention City

In the meantime, industries that Carl Sandburg could not have envisioned when he ennobled his "stormy, husky, brawling city" in verse have taken up some of the slack. The Pullman plant was closed long ago, but Chicago remains a transportation hub, thanks to O'Hare International Airport's status as the world's busiest and to the city's popularity with conventions and trade shows. While the coastal cities lost some convention business during the last recession, Chicago actually saw an increase of about 13 percent, according to the Chicago Convention and Tourism Bureau, and remains the country's number-one convention city, last year hosting more than 30,000 events. The bureau views the less-than-65-percent hotel occupancy rate as only a blip in the larger picture.

The city has taken steps to protect its flank in this crucial area. The prime exposition center, McCormick Place, is undergoing a neary $1 billion expansion that will increase its space by about 80 percent. The same board of state and city appointees that controls McCormick Place also is proceeding with a renovation of Navy Pier that will bring shops, cultural attractions, and festivals to the underused space. The projects are being financed largely by taxes on hotel bills, car rentals, restaurant meals, and the like.

At this point, the plan for a new airport at Lake Calumet is going nowhere but Daley has exploited one victory from that imbroglio. In October 1990, he obtained congressional authority to levy a $3 charge on every passenger using O'Hare and Midway airports. The tax was to be a funding mechanism for the new airport; now the money is being applied to improvements at O'Hare and Midway Airport on the Southwest Side. Work at O'Hare includes construction of a new international terminal and a people mover to whisk passengers from one far-flung terminal to another. The work at both airports is under the direction of aviation commissioner David Mosena, AICP, formerly Daley's chief of staff and a onetime APA research director.

As for the likelihood of the mayor's megaprojects being revived, Daley himself sends mixed signals. At one point last year, he declared his Lake Calumet airport "dead, dead, dead." Yet, in interviews, he makes it clear that all he needs is a shift in political winds to start promoting it again. The project, which could cost anywhere from $5 billion to $25 billion, probably would spur about 50,000 new jobs. At 9,400 acres, it would be larger than O'Hare International Airport. However, the city itself counted 28 landfills or toxic waste dumps within the proposed site and about 50 businesses and thousands of residents would have to be relocated.

The mayor stopped lobbying for the Lake Calumet site last June when it failed to pass the Illinois Senate for lack of two Republican votes. The Republicans took control of the senate in last November's election, and their leader, new airport opponent James "Pate" Philip, became the senate president. The mayor says he can't do anything as long as Philip is in charge. Meanwhile, Republican Gov. James Edgar, who had originally sided with Daley on Lake Calumet, has shifted his airport endorsement to a rural site near Peotone, some 35 miles south of the Loop.

Prospects are also dim—but not dead—for the casino, which Daley and his supporters refer to as the "international theme park and casino." The $2 billion complex proposed by Hilton Hotels, Circus Circus, and Caesars World promised to net the city 38,000 jobs. The casino never came to a vote in the legislature, but Daley says, "It's still on the agenda. It's still there." In this case, the opposition comes from Edgar, who contends that a casino would hurt the state's racetrack industry and even its lottery, and would benefit organized crime. In addition, legislators from downstate districts regard a Chicago casino as a threat to their towns' riverboat gambling franchises.

In the last few months, Daley has turned his attention from the megaprojects to issues such as crime prevention (including his proposal to create cul-de-sacs in some neighborhoods). With a new Democratic administration in place and several Daley allies close to President Bill Clinton, the mayor also is looking to the federal government for aid, traveling to Washington with other big city mayors in February.

One area where Daley says help is needed is in environmental cleanup, particularly in connection with the South Works plant, where no one is sure what's left in the soil after more than 100 years of steel making. "We need great flexibility in EPA rules if you're ever going to bring the land back to where people can go to work," Daley says. A bill pending in Congress would provide $300 million over three years for environmental cleanups. In Daley's view, its passage would signal a new concern with urban needs. "America has treated its cities like foreign governments," he says. "Great countries have to have great cities and America better believe in that."

Neighborhood Power

Greatness in Chicago still means the neighborhoods, from the sturdy bungalow belt to the rows of chic townhouses. On the community level, Chicago, proving ground for Saul Alinsky, is hyperorganized, a result perhaps of the days when city hall was machine-run and people needed to demonstrate strength to get a hearing. "Around Chicago, the joke is that when two people are mad about something, they form a community organization," says Martin Berg, an associate director of the Chicago Association of Neighborhood Development Organizations. Many of those organizations are pursuing their own "megaprojects." Some examples:

- In a North Side Hispanic community, local groups are taking over space in a commercial strip of tawdry liquor stores and starting a day-care center.
- A community group in the impoverished Englewood area on the South Side has convinced one of the city's largest developers to construct a mall along 63rd Street, a moribund commercial artery, and to pay for rebuilding a sorely needed firehouse nearby.
- On the West Side, the Argonne National Laboratory is providing job-training advice to Bethel New Life, an active group with interests ranging from housing development to loan packaging and recycling. Indeed, with a new, privately financed basketball and hockey arena being built and other industrial and residential projects ongoing, there's more happening on the West Side than there has been in years.

Also on the West Side, there are several construction projects on the campus of the University of Illinois at Chicago. Three other city universities—DePaul, Loyola, and the University of Chicago—also have major projects under way even while the overall construction market is taking a breather. Another institution, Northwestern Memorial Hospital, also has mustered the wherewithal for an expansion. Such projects say something about the current Chicago marketplace. Speculation is out, but you can still get something built if the use of the property is assured.

Yet speculation—on a large and small scale—has always played a major part in this city's development. Otherwise, the late novelist Nelson Algren could not have been moved to call Chicago a "city on the make." The phrase implies a robust machismo — building, tearing down, scheming, selling, sweating — all of which have done great things here. That tradition has also saddled the city with Block 37 and other failures of urban planning, such as a horrendous concentration of high-rise public housing.

Today, as Chicago joins other U.S. cities in a competition for global markets, it may be served best by leaders who can identify its core strengths and capitalize upon them. The day for making "many little plans" has dawned.

Chapter 32

Reforming Zoning Regulations

Bruce W. McClendon

Over the years, zoning has been a subject of major local controversy in Beaumont, Texas (pop. 118,000).

The city adopted its first comprehensive zoning ordinance in 1948 and repealed it the same year when it was recalled by special election.

In 1955 a compromise zoning ordinance was adopted with the support of the local development community. Three years later a national consulting firm was hired to prepare a comprehensive plan and to update the zoning ordinance. The consulting firm concluded that the 1955 ordinance was "very defective" and recommended adoption of a completely new ordinance.

Subsequently, a new zoning ordinance which reflected the consultant's recommendations was prepared and submitted to the city council for adoption. However, this ordinance was rejected by the council and the original 1955 ordinance was left basically unchanged until the present time.

Justification for Change

Since 1960 the population growth of Beaumont has been minimal despite glowing predictions to the contrary. Over time, regulatory reform became recognized as an important contributing factor for economic development. It was generally agreed that revising and updating the zoning ordinance was necessary to ensure that the community remain competitive with other development markets, while also providing local residents and developers with the opportunity to take advantage of more efficient or economical types of development.

A review and evaluation of the Beaumont zoning ordinance convinced the city planning staff that its many inadequacies were seriously discouraging and restricting local economic development. The planning staff classified over

Reprinted with permission from *Texas City & Town*, Vol. 70, No. 8, August, 1982. Published by the Texas Municipal League, Austin, Texas.

40 major deficiencies in the zoning ordinance into the following general categories:

1. Defects in the original ordinance
2. Deficiencies created by improper or lax administration and subsequent amendments to the original ordinance which were inconsistent, conflicting, or ambiguous
3. Inconsistency with state statutes or judicial decisions
4. Failure to reflect current public opinion and prevailing community values and
5. Failure to reflect current zoning concepts and innovative development practices.

The list of deficiencies ranged from poor organization and lack of clarity to exclusionary zoning practices and outright conflicts with state enabling legislation. Where limited provisions had been made for such innovative development techniques as cluster housing, the regulations were overly restrictive and time consuming, and they unnecessarily hampered opportunities for flexible creative developments.

The deficiencies in the zoning ordinance were having an obvious negative impact on local economic development. New types of development were being discouraged and many times, development costs were being inflated by unnecessary and excessive regulation. For example, the minimum lot sizes for single-family residential development were larger than necessary, which contributed to making the cost of housing in Beaumont higher than the regional average.

Many new developments and uses were not provided for in the list of permitted uses. This meant that the zoning officer could not always immediately respond to informational requests from potential developers. Often the staff had to confer with the legal department or undertake analytical studies to determine whether a proposed use would be permitted in a particular zoning district.

Compounding this problem was the fact that no list of permitted uses existed for the heavy industrial district and each and every proposed heavy industrial use had to be approved by the board of adjustment. The uncertainty and delay caused by this situation had an adverse effect on the city's ability to compete for industrial prospects.

Interestingly enough, while the ordinance was unnecessarily hampering development, the lack of certain minimum regulations to protect existing single-family development from the consequences of other forms of development was making it increasingly difficult to obtain public support and council approval for rezoning. Failure to require any side or rear yard setbacks or any type of screening for commercial and industrial development resulted in increased residential incompatibility and opposition to development.

The deficient list of permitted uses in the numerous multi-family and commercial districts also increased rezoning difficulties. The permitted uses in the various districts had not been prepared according to related areas of similarity, compatibility, external effects, or functional interrelationships. As a result, many rezoning requests were being denied even though the city council, planning commission, and adjacent property owners were in support of the applicant's intended use for the property.

Applications were denied because the requested zoning district also permitted uses which would have been harmful to the neighborhood. The failure to have more functionally compatible districts and the inability to ensure development compatibility with a specific use permit had led to rejection of development proposals ranging from shopping centers to beauty shops.

The increasing public opposition to rezoning and the surge in citizen complaints about new developments that were taking place, together with a growing desire to remain competitive and encourage more economical and efficient development opportunities, all combined to provide the consensus which was needed to support the regulatory reform process.

The Process

The revision and updating of Beaumont's zoning ordinance took place over a two-year period from 1979 to 1981 and involved six public hearings, 38 workshops, three public forums, and numerous subcommittee meetings.

The local development community was an active, although sometimes reluctant, participant in the process. After initially supporting the reform process, the local builders' association at one point attempted to stop the process, and even formed a political action committee for the purpose of increasing their influence with local elected officials.

The opposition of many local developers to changing the ordinance was based on the following factors:

1. Distrust of the local planning staff
2. Misunderstanding of the flexibility and negotiation concept in zoning
3. Opposition from developers who had drafted the 1955 ordinance
4. Opposition to any type of zoning
5. Reluctance to trust the judgment of the elected officials who would be making the final decision
6. Belief that the members of the planning commission were not familiar with local development practices and problems
7. Satisfaction with the current regulations and
8. General fear of change.

Despite opposition from the development community, the planning commission and city council continued their efforts to revise the ordinance. Both bodies remained convinced that the final product would ultimately have the acceptance and support of the development community.

The new draft ordinance, which had been prepared by the city planning staff, was continuously revised as a result of input from the various hearings and workshops. The spirit of cooperation and compromise which local planners, the planning commission, and the city council exhibited during the review process was reflected in the ordinance that was finally adopted. Today there is almost unanimous agreement that the new zoning ordinance will be a positive stimulus to economic development.

Perhaps the area of greatest disappointment in the reform process was the lack of general public interest and participation. Despite newspaper coverage and numerous public hearings, workshops and forums, and even written notification to every property-owner in the city, actual participation was obtained only from special interest groups and a handful of residents. The issues which were raised during the revision process were controversial and substantive, yet general public interest was almost nonexistent. Under these circumstances, the planning staff and the planning commission had to be aggressive in providing leadership for the regulatory changes needed to protect the welfare of the general public.

The Product

The following is a generalized description of the significant changes which were made in the ordinance in the interest of stimulating economic growth and development.

Ordinance simplification. As mentioned earlier, the original ordinance had often been a serious impediment to development. In general, confusing complexity in any zoning ordinance can produce regulatory duplication, hinder citizen participation in the decision making process, discourage innovations, lead to uncoordinated decisions, and delay development. Everybody is hurt by the inefficiency resulting from regulatory complexity—the consumer, the developer, the governmental decision-maker, environmental interest groups, and the general public.

Unlike its predecessor, the new ordinance is logically organized and indexed, and charts and tables were substituted for written narrative in order to reduce the length of the regulations and assist in developing an understanding of the ordinance.

For example, written regulations controlling minimum lot area, width, depth, yard, and height regulations were combined into a simplified chart and placed in a special section of the ordinance. In addition, diagrams and graphic illustrations were included in the appendix of the ordinance to help clarify the meaning of individual regulatory provisions and the specialized definitions in the ordinance.

Additionally, separate lists of permitted uses for each district were combined into a single chart based on the coding system in the U.S. Department of Commerce's *Standard Industrial Classification (SIC) Manual*. Reference to the SIC manual made it possible to reduce the length of the zoning ordinance while also making it more comprehensive and less subject to misinterpretation.

The regulations governing cluster housing were reduced from eight pages to three pages and most of the minimum design standards were eliminated. In addition, the specific use permit requirement was removed and cluster housing was listed as a permitted use in any residential zoning district, with maximum density being determined by a function of the underlying zoning district classification.

The unnecessary profusion of zoning district classifications was corrected by combining two single-family districts into one district and by combining the three existing commercial districts into a single unified commercial district.

Too many districts with trivial distinctions had over-complicated the original ordinance and created the need for frequent zone changes. At the same time, additional zoning districts were created for district developments such as the central business district, the port district, and office parks.

Cumulative zoning provisions were removed from many of the zoning districts. This was done to reduce potential opposition to the excessively large lists of permitted uses in the higher zoning districts and to protect prime industrial land from residential development.

In addition, the list of permitted uses was revised and based on functional relationships in order to be consistent with the stated purpose and intent of each district. Provisions for specific use permits were added so that compatibility requirements could be imposed upon those uses which were functionally related to other uses in the district but which were not always compatible.

Flexibility and innovation. The city planning staff and many local developers believed the existing zoning ordinance was unnecessarily rigid, antiquated in its reliance on traditional development practices, and lacked the framework needed for innovation and experimentation. To correct this situation, regulations which limited each lot to only one main building were removed and provisions for planned unit development (PUD), the zero lot line concept, performance standards, incentive zoning, and shopping center districts were added to the ordinance.

Development opportunities in most of the existing zoning districts were expanded by adding new, more intense uses to the list of permitted uses based on a specific use permit approval process. This provision was added because the opposition to many rezoning requests was often based on the expanded list of uses which a higher district would permit and not on specific objections to the actual proposed use of the property.

Landscaping bonus. Because of increased interest and desire to improve the physical appearance of the community, optional landscaping regulations were placed in the ordinance to encourage expanded landscaping while also compensating for additional development costs. In return for requiring a 10-foot landscaped strip in front yards, the minimum front yard setback was reduced from 25 feet to 15 feet.

While a 10-foot landscaped buffer strip was required between commercial, industrial, or multi-family developments and single-family districts, the new ordinance includes a substantial density bonus based on the lineal footage of the buffer strip that could amount to a 25 percent increase in density for multi-family development. Also, the new ordinance permits the area devoted to landscaping of off-street parking areas to be deducted from the total minimum off-street parking area requirements.

Regulatory reductions. All of the regulations in the pre-existing zoning ordinance were closely reviewed to ensure that they were not in excess of the minimum level of regulation necessary to protect the welfare of the general public. The following changes to the ordinance were made as a result of such review:

1. Off-street parking requirements for shopping centers were reduced by 25 percent
2. All remaining off-street parking space and design standards were lowered by various amounts and provisions were made for 25 percent of the parking spaces to be reduced to accommodate compact cars
3. Off-street parking requirements were eliminated in the central business district
4. Minimum lot area requirements in single-family residential districts were reduced between 20 and 55 percent
5. The minimum rear yard in multi-family and commercial districts was lowered from 25 feet to 10 percent of the lot depth for existing lots of record
6. Minimum residential front yard setbacks on cul-de-sacs were reduced to 15 feet
7. Powers of the board of adjustment to grant variances and exceptions were expanded and
8. The application procedure for a specific use permit was simplified and the amount and cost of required supporting information was reduced.

Cutting Regulatory Delay

Regulatory reform saves both time and money. When the development process is delayed, it can result in additional development costs which ultimately must be paid by the consumer, can lead to the abandonment of current proposed projects which are no longer economically feasible, and can seriously discourage future developments from locating in the community.

In the past, the city was able to process all rezoning applications in a maximum time of four to five weeks. In order to reduce rezoning processing time, the city is considering instituting special joint planning commission and city council public hearings and having the city council vote on the zoning request on the day immediately following the hearing at a regular council meeting.

This will result in reducing maximum rezoning processing time to three to four weeks.

The planning commission recently formed a "Joint City Development Committee" to increase the impact of the local development community on the regulatory reform process. The committee has been charged with the following duties and responsibilities:

1. Provide guidance in streamlining all zoning and permitting processes
2. Analyze and provide recommendations on all proposed land use regulations
3. Provide special training programs on private sector development to the planning commission
4. Investigate and provide solutions to problems individual developers have encountered and
5. Provide guidance on the use of public resources to encourage private development.

Conclusion

Regulatory reform is a necessary and vital component of Beaumont's economic development strategy. In the pro-development environment which exists in Texas, constant updating of all regulations is necessary to ensure that a community not only remains competitive with other development markets but also permits and encourages economical and innovative development practices that benefit the ultimate consumer.

Not all of the changes which were made in the city's zoning ordinance resulted in reduced development costs. Some changes, in fact, will increase development costs: examples include the establishment of setbacks in commercial and industrial zoning districts, height regulations in residential zones, 10-foot buffer strips, noise performance standards, and off-street loading regulations.

But these additional development expenses were modest in impact, and were considered necessary to maintain minimum residential protection levels.

Most of the changes which increased developmental costs were made in direct response to growing public opposition to zoning changes, and were undertaken with the goal of gaining future public acceptance of a more aggressive rezoning policy.

The competitive nature of economic development no longer allows the luxury of allowing regulations to go unreviewed for any great length of time. Regulatory reform must be accepted as an integral and active part of any local economic development program.

Chapter 33

Salvaging Neighborhood Shopping Centers

LAWRENCE HALL
ROBERT H. LURCOTT
KAREN LAFRANCE
MICHAEL A. DOBBINS

New Haven: Private Money First

The premise of New Haven's commercial revitalization program is simple: Public investment is tied to private performance. The city makes public improvements only in those areas where merchants are ready to commit themselves to major revitalization efforts. In other words, the city helps those who help themselves.

It works this way. Merchants in a neighborhood express interest in being designated a neighborhood commercial revitalization district. A merchant's association is formed, and over half of the merchants or property owners in the district agree, in writing, to renovate their buildings. The extent of renovation required depends on individual circumstances; however, the commitment must be specific in terms of the work being done and the costs. The association then identifies development goals and objectives and establishes a design review committee, composed of merchants, property owners, and city staff, to approve rehabilitation designs.

After designation, each owner is eligible for up to $15,000 in city matching grants. The Office of Economic Development helps with loan packaging and technical assistance.

When half of the buildings have been renovated, the district becomes eligible for public improvements and the city's "self-help grants," available to support such activities as advertising campaigns, festivals, and market studies. (The city puts up $1 for every $2 expended by the neighborhood

Reprinted with permission from *Planning,* Vol. 49, No. 3, March, 1983. Published by the American Planning Association, 1313 E. 60th St., Chicago, IL 60637.

group.) The two-year time limit on the self-help grants is an incentive to quick action.

The city negotiates the public improvements—street trees, sidewalks, parking lots, and so on—with the design review committee.

Since June 1980 when the first city grants were issued, some $500,000 in rehabilitation grants and $1 million in public improvements have leveraged about $5 million in private investment in two commercial areas.

One of those areas is Lower Whalley Avenue, the region's traditional auto row. By the mid-1970s, the number of dealerships had dwindled to five—down from twelve in 1960. Dealers who left cited as their reasons obsolete facilities and fear of crime. Other businesses followed, although there are still a substantial number of muffler, auto glass, and body shops. In 1977, a Whalley Avenue Association was formed and a director hired.

In 1979, Biagio DiLieto, campaigning for his first term as New Haven's mayor from an office on Whalley Avenue, made the condition of the street an issue. After his election, he called for a revitalization program, emphasizing the need for cooperation among merchants, property owners, and the city.

The results so far have been encouraging: the $1 million renovation of a vacant auto dealership into Storer Cable Television's regional headquarters; the renovation of three auto dealerships and several related businesses; the construction of two new fast food franchises; and several new businesses. Now that a majority of the storefronts have been renovated, the city is installing new sidewalks, bus stops, and grass planter strips along the curbs.

The impressive strength of the private sector resurgence on Whalley Avenue has offset some of the early problems, including inadequate front-end planning and a lack of design criteria. The design shortcomings have given a few of the early renovations an uneven quality. And confusion about district boundaries created uncertainty among merchants about who was eligible for facade grants. The city has developed stricter guidelines for other districts.

The Whalley Avenue Association has an ambitious agenda for 1983. It plans to publish a parking locator map, put up street banners, and promote special sales events. The association has also prepared a proposal for a special services district—a vehicle for imposing a surtax on area businesses to fund the activities of the association.

New Haven's program has been just as effective in a very different type of area, Upper State Street, a turn-of-the-century neighborhood whose population includes longtime Polish and Italian residents, black and Hispanic newcomers, Yale students and staff, and downtown workers attracted by the reasonable rents and convenient location. A few years ago, Upper State Street was deteriorating, and many of its merchants had fled to the suburbs.

Today, the neighborhood has a new, more positive image of itself, in part because of the efforts of the Upper State Street Association, which includes property owners and merchants, longtime residents and young professionals (particularly architects). The group originally lacked political sophistication, but it has attracted support because of its vitality.

Renovation has transformed the neighborhood. Several new businesses have opened — a pastry shop, two new restaurants, and two clothing stores. There will be some $500,000 in new townhouse development with potential ground-floor office space on a city-owned site and gut rehab of several residential-commercial buildings. The city is currently building a parking lot, replacing crumbling sidewalks and curbs, and adding a strip of concrete pavers, street trees, and benches along the curb.

The Upper State Street program has affected the entire community. Planning for the area has emphasized the integration of housing and commercial activity, and the participation on the design review committee of architects who live in the neighborhood has resulted in high-quality renovations.

The next step for Upper State Street is to work on creating a Main Street atmosphere through promotions, festivals, and other people-drawing activities. Also, the Upper State Street Association intends to file an application for national historic district status. If it's approved, local property owners will be able to take advantage of federal tax credits.

Pittsburgh: Market Studies

It has been nearly 10 years since the Pittsburgh planning department first took on some of the city's most decayed neighborhood commercial districts. In that time, we have learned much that can be applied elsewhere. The city's approach in the early 1970s was a physical one. It offered relatively low-interest loans for facade renovation, provided new parking lots, and made various street improvements.

Clearly, that hasn't been enough. In the last several years, the city has changed the course of its commercial revitalization program, expanding some aspects and modifying others. Changes grew out of market studies in two business districts — East Liberty and Hazelwood; suggestions from the National Development Council (the nonprofit group associated with economic development guru John Sower); an evaluation of the city's Neighborhood Commercial Loan Program; and heightened public demand for assistance.

The planning department has added a staff position for a neighborhood commercial revitalization coordinator. In addition, the city's capital budget now includes funds for market studies and for assisting small businesses with promotion and coordination. An interagency committee, chaired by a mayoral assistant and including the heads of the planning department and urban redevelopment authority, was set up as a clearinghouse for city assistance. The planning department is responsible for market evaluation and community liaison, and the urban redevelopment authority administers the commercial loan program.

The city has funded market studies in nine areas. Shoppers, merchants, and residents in all of them voiced similar complaints about "unappealing stores" and "dirty conditions." However, the areas differed in significant ways and required different approaches to revitalization, as these examples show.

East Liberty, an early focus of attention, has, in effect, become the city's commercial revitalization laboratory. This East End neighborhood includes a 450,000–square–foot shopping district, which underwent extensive urban renewal in the 1960s. Part of the area was closed to traffic. By the late 1970s, merchants were expressing dissatisfaction with traffic patterns and parking, the image of the district as a high crime area had worsened, and sales were declining.

The market study, completed in 1978, concluded that East Liberty no longer served its traditional regional market. Rather, it had become a convenience center for the surrounding neighborhood. The study noted that shop owners were generally older and unwilling to change merchandising practices to capture a younger, fashion-conscious (although not very affluent) market.

The consultants suggested that the mall be reopened to auto traffic, the police presence increased, and merchandising practices updated. The city has spent nearly $600,000 in community development funds to reopen the mall and to support merchandising and promotion programs.

The city's attempt to fund activities other than physical improvements was the most promising aspect of the new program. At the planning department's request, the East Liberty Chamber of Commerce set up a development corporation, East Liberty Development, Inc. (ELDI), to receive community development funds for promotion. Last year, ELDI became a full-fledged development entity with its own staff and financial support from major banks and corporations, social service agencies, and neighborhood churches. The city is committed to contributing $50,000 in community development funds over the next two years to help ELDI rehabilitate vacant buildings and to improve East Liberty's image through a public relations campaign.

In the second year, ELDI and the city will consider setting up a special tax assessment district to raise administrative and promotional funds in the future.

In the much smaller (90,000 square feet) Second Avenue business district in the Hazelwood neighborhood, two blocks were cleared in the early 1970s for a retail mini-mall. The neighborhood's population continued to decline, however, and its image worsened. In the late 1970s, part of the mini-mall site was used for subsidized housing for the elderly.

In 1979, a planning department market analysis showed that the area could support only a modest number of convenience shops and some auto supply stores. The $266,700 left over from a state renewal project allocation could not solve all the district's problems. Local merchants and the city agreed on a limited program of public improvements, including new sidewalks and brick ramps for the handicapped. Plans are under way now to paint the facades and boarded-up windows of vacant buildings.

A market study of the 12-block-long Penn Avenue business district in the Bloomfield-Garfield neighborhood was the key to putting that area's program on a realistic basis. In response to a community organization's request for funds, the city asked for an evaluation by an outside consultant to determine how much revitalization could reasonably be expected. The consultant said the market area could no longer support a large business district (189,000 square feet retail and 100,000 square feet light industrial and commercial, with a vacancy rate of almost 20 percent) and recommended consolidation.

The city has since paid for a "district coordinator," who is concentrating on a three-block area near the community organization's storefront office. In a year and a half, the coordinator has had modest success in encouraging facade rehab, starting up small businesses, and negotiating the purchase of vacant buildings for rehab.

In the small (80,000 square feet), troubled, commercial core of Homewood, a large, predominantly black neighborhood, the market study led to a change in emphasis in a state-funded renewal project. Once again, consolidation was recommended and is actually being implemented. The anchors for the consolidation are a new fast food outlet and a new community college branch. A community planner assigned to the neighborhood has organized a community development corporation, which will undertake security and promotion programs.

A market study also can help show that a business district no longer needs city assistance. That was the case with Western Avenue, three blocks (131,000 square feet) of mixed retail and residential uses in the newly gentrified Allegheny West neighborhood. This district contains both boutiques and convenience stores, the latter important to lower income residents of adjacent neighborhoods. The study concluded that more boutiques were likely to locate in the district without city assistance and without displacing convenience stores.

On East Ohio Street (141,000 square feet), an outside consultant recommended a promotion and store recruitment campaign to build on the district's current market strength as a collection of specialty stores.

Building on what it has learned, Pittsburgh has made several changes in its commercial district programs:

1. The city's Neighborhood Commerical Loan Program has been redirected from building rehabilitation to storefront facade rehabilitation targeted to commercially zoned properties in designated commercial districts. To complement this loan program, the urban development authority is putting in place a new, tax-exempt, long-term rehabilitation financing program.

   Separate funding support continues for market studies, business development, and staff support for business organizations in designated areas.

2. A major effort is being made to ensure long-term participation by businesses in commercial districts. Public improvements will now be undertaken only

in those areas where a business organization agrees to a maintenance code enforcement program.
3. The city is encouraging business districts to make use of special tax assessments (in areas where a substantial majority of property owners agree) to fund promotional efforts and pay for administrative staff.

Birmingham: Design Is the Key

Five years ago, the commercial district of the North Birmingham neighborhood was in terrible shape, with many vacancies, severe physical deterioration, and sagging morale. Today, things are far different — the result of positive intervention by the city, local merchants, and investors. What happened in North Birmingham illustrates in a dramatic way the effectiveness of the planning process — and especially of a dogged commitment by both public and private partners to see a program through.

Birmingham has a tradition of strong neighborhoods (all organized into an elaborate participatory structure and all receiving a set allocation of the city's revenue sharing funds); and both mayor Richard Arrington, Jr., and his predecessor, David Vann, have viewed neighborhood development as a central part of their programs. In 1976, Mayor Vann set up 12 economic revitalization committees, composed of neighborhood business leaders, property owners, and officers of neighborhood associations.

North Birmingham was one of the first neighborhoods to receive attention. About two miles north of the downtown and ringed by heavy industry, this mile-square, working class neighborhood had shifted from 90 percent white in 1970 to 90 percent black by 1978. Its commercial center once served a broad community of about two-and-a-half square miles as well as the rural mining areas north of the city line.

Before World War II, the entire north rim of Birmingham was like a series of mill towns, each with its own shopping area. After the war, the suburbs captured the population growth, the new shopping malls — and the customers. Shop vacancies in North Birmingham increased steadily. The economic revitalization committee, which began meeting in 1976, provided a forum in which neighborhood merchants could discuss the problems and the options available. In short, a planning process was launched.

The lessons learned from that experience (summarized in the accompanying boxes on pages 292–293) have provided the basis for increasingly efficient and effective programs in other Birmingham neighborhoods.

One of the first steps was to invite the American Institute of Architects to send in a Rural/Urban Design Assistance Team for an intense, multidisciplinary examination of North Birmingham and two other neighborhood commercial centers. The R/UDAT team showed in graphic form how North

Birmingham could look. That, in turn, sparked the imagination of some of the neighborhood merchants.

In June 1977, the city commissioned two consultants, National Urban Development Services, Inc., of Washington (now Urban Development Services) and Kidd, Wheeler, and Plosser of Birmingham (now Kidd, Plosser, and Sprague) to conduct a detailed planning study.

The study produced these findings:

1. That the North Birmingham business district could no longer sustain the amount of commercial space it could during its heyday as a regional center; consolidation from approximately 15 blocks to about 6 would provide the best chance of retaining existing businesses and avoiding scattered vacancies.
2. That a substantial increase in readily accessible parking was needed.
3. That some of the seriously deteriorated storefronts would have to be removed and the rest substantially rehabilitated.
4. That major, new, private investment in the area was essential.
5. That the merchants, property owners, and neighborhood residents would have to assume more of a leadership role in the revitalization effort.

A plan based on these principles was approved by the city and the neighborhood merchants in early 1979.

The plan focused on several core blocks on which the redevelopment efforts should be concentrated. Certain old buildings were identified for rehabilitation. Other sites were identified for redevelopment. A landscaped "parking mall" was proposed to establish a link between the main traffic-carrying street (26th Street) and the shopping street (27th Street). New landscaping was proposed for 27th Street. The plan also proposed that several commercial properties outside the new core commercial area be converted to housing.

What We Learned

In New Haven

- Front-end planning is crucial to link neighborhood residential and commercial needs in a common strategy and to resolve boundary issues.
- Creating a design committee allows merchants to exercise aesthetic control and shifts responsibility away from the city. It is essential, however, that the city provide competent technical assistance to the committee.
- Program deadlines (like our two-year limit on facade improvements) motivate the private sector.
- Instead of attempting to dictate market decisions, a commercial revitalization program should attempt to create a climate of confidence in which the market can reestablish itself.
- Long-term success depends on a permanent organization and a continuing source of revenue for promotion and maintenance.

In Pittsburgh
- Study the market carefully, evaluate the commercial district's economic future, and make a realistic assessment of its potential. A market study can ferret out specific opportunities that the private market may have missed. For, despite the middle-class shift to the suburbs, city households are still a substantial source of shopping dollars. A market study can be particularly useful in deciding which areas may not have a significant future as retailing centers. In such areas, the appropriate treatment may not be "commercial revitalization" as we generally view it.
- The community and the city must agree on the objectives of the revitalization effort and the nature of the city's assistance. That means that there must be an effective community organization. Ideally, retailers should participate, especially in the market study phase.
- Private reinvestment must encompass more than facade and public space improvements. Our evaluation showed that even districts whose merchants were heavily involved in the city's facade rehab program continued to suffer from market and image problems. Since commercial districts are in competition with modern shopping malls, merchants must know their market as intimately as mall managers know theirs. They must invest in their businesses, modernize their retailing practices and collectively upgrade their promotion and marketing efforts.
- Target pubic assistance where it will have the most impact, and tailor it to the needs of specific districts.

In Birmingham
- The success of a program depends on the inclusion of all sides in the planning process—merchants, property owners, investors, neighborhood leaders, and city staff.
- A mandatory rehabilitation program will produce physical changes and encourage investment. In North Birmingham, $25,000 of city rebate money leveraged $135,000 in private investment.
- UDAGs should be structured as simply as possible. Avoid multiparty agreements where each party's participation is contingent on all the others'.
- As a program proves its effectiveness, it becomes easier to extend it to other areas and to get the private sector to chip in.

New construction was to include housing, expansion of an existing medical clinic, and a new, 25,000–square foot supermarket. As called for in the contract, the consultants became involved in the first steps of implementation, including early negotiations for the city's first Urban Development Action Grant. The UDAG application brought three private sector partners together: a hospital, a supermarket firm, and a developer of Section 8 housing for the elderly. The city's role was to assemble the land and relocate existing businesses and residents and (as described below) to work with storeowners on a facade improvement program. Kidd, Wheeler, and Plosser was commissioned to prepare contract documents for the recommended public improvements.

The UDAG partnership proved to be unstable. By the time construction started, two of the original partners had been replaced and the third had significantly altered its plans. All the changes required amendments in the application and caused delays and rearrangement of financing agreements.

But despite the problems, the city's decision to inject itself into neighborhood business revitalization appears to be justified. The investment of public dollars (the $947,878 UDAG, $1,418,257 in CDBG funds, $147,851 in revenue sharing, and $697,826 in city bonds) leveraged a $9 million private investment—yielding 125 new housing units, the clinic, the supermarket, 60 new jobs, and 30 rehabilitated storefronts. The program did what it promised. It made more goods and services available to the community, added jobs, and built links between neighborhood and business leaders. The city's interest was to improve the tax base, which it did. The increased tax take is estimated at $120,000 a year.

An unusual aspect of Birmingham's program is its mandatory storefront rehabilitation, coupled with a rebate to property owners and merchants who comply. So far, $25,000 in city rebate money has leveraged $135,000 worth of private improvements, covering 32 storefronts. Each rebate was approved by the design review committee established by the city council as part of the 1979 ordinance.

The mandatory rehabilitation program was modeled after a program that began in Baltimore in 1970. Since Birmingham adopted its version in 1979, a dozen or so cities have followed suit.

As the commercial revitalization program has been extended to other neighborhoods, the initial skepticism and resistance has gradually given way to hope and even a modest backlog in demand on the city for implementation. In one area, neighborhood merchants are even pushing to make the mandatory storefront rehab requirement applicable to a larger area than originally proposed.

This change in attitude has enabled the city to establish a few modest threshold requirements and to expect a higher leverage rate. The program has also shown a kind of countercyclical success—proving effective at a time when the New Federalism has scaled down the availability of public funds. Hard times seem to produce recognition of the reality that cooperation and unity of purpose are in the best interest of everyone involved.

VI : The Future

Chapter 34

Alternatives to Shaping Tomorrow's Cities

Marcia D. Lowe

Only one in 10 people lived in cities when this century began; more than half will by the century's end. Today, the vast bulk of urban population growth occurs in developing countries. According to the United Nations, the populations of Third World cities are now doubling every 10 to 15 years, overwhelming governments' attempts to provide clean water, sewerage, adequate transport, and other basic services.

Cities in industrial countries are gaining people much more slowly, yet even as their growth rates slow or core populations decline, these urban areas continue to spread outward. In industrial and developing countries alike, chaotic, uncontrolled urban growth draws on ever more land, water, and energy from surrounding regions to meet people's needs.

The way cities physically evolve—and the way their development is planned—has profound impacts on human and planetary well-being. Their further growth can either recognize the limits of the natural environment, or it can destroy the resources on which current and future societies depend; it can meet people's needs equitably, or it can enrich some while impoverishing or endangering others. The world needs an urban-planning ethic that is sensitive to these environmental and human dimensions.

Urban Planning Around the Globe

Virtually all cities share some land-related concerns, such as congestion and pollution from motor vehicles, a lack of affordable housing, and the cancerous growth of blighted districts. Of course, prescriptions for better urban planning are not the same for all parts of the world: Many land-use issues in

Reprinted with permission from *The Futurist,* Vol. 26, No. 4, July/August, 1992. Published by the World Future Society, Bethesda, Maryland.

industrial countries seem mainly concerned with the quality of urban life, while those in Third World cities are often questions of life and death. But all cities, whether surrounded by affluent suburbs or makeshift shantytowns, now need to plan land use far more carefully than in the past—before the developing world's urban crises turn into catastrophes and the industrial world's problems become issues of survival.

Western Europe has a long tradition of actively controlling land use so that the small amount of available space serves the public's interest more than that of private developers. Paris, a city for nearly 2,000 years, has planned and regulated land use since the Middle Ages. Many of England's urban areas, still fulfilling a farsighted decree by Queen Elizabeth I in 1580, are ringed by green belts intended to protect farmland and prevent sprawl. But in postwar decades, the automobile has had a profound effect on Europe's compact character, fueling suburbanization.

Among industrial regions, North America and Australia have the weakest planning traditions. Governments on these continents have done relatively little to guide development beyond separating industrial areas from those zoned for commerce and housing. Many have enforced low-density zoning in an effort to curb urban expansion—a move that, ironically, achieves just the opposite. Zoning codes that restrict residential density, usually by requiring each house to occupy its own large lot, have forced development to consume even greater tracts of open space. And to accommodate new, outlying communities, roads have been extended farther outward, attracting even more spread-out growth.

Even older U.S. cities are becoming more dispersed now than in the pre-automobile era. Growth in the New York metropolitan region has turned to sprawl; while population has grown only 5 percent in the past 25 years, the developed areas have increased by 61 percent—consuming nearly a quarter of the region's open space, forests, and farmland. Many people move out to the suburbs and exurbs seeking open space and bonds with nature that come only in a rural setting. Yet, most of these residents continue to maintain an urban lifestyle—commuting to jobs in the city and demanding urban amenities from a suburban shopping mall near their home.

Developing countries have the loosest controls over how cities develop. The Third World is burdened by several enormous, rapidly growing cities—including São Paulo, Shanghai, and Mexico City—whose sheer size and instability create problems on an entirely different scale. These giant cities, racked with pollution and rimmed by shantytowns, have become increasingly characteristic of the developing world.

Although skilled land-use planning is badly needed in these megacities, its effectiveness is limited due to various obstacles: For instance, most of the physical growth takes place in illegal, unplanned squatter settlements, rendering useless even existing mechanisms for guiding land use. These illegal communities hold 30 percent to 60 percent of the population of many Third World cities. The unhealthy conditions in these settlements can only be addressed fully through extensive economic and social reforms that attack the root causes of poverty — not just in cities but also in the rural areas that urban migrants abandon in search of economic opportunities.

A city's land use defines its transport system more than any traffic planner or engineer can. The pattern of urban development dictates whether people can walk or cycle to work or whether they need to travel dozens of kilometers; it determines whether a new bus or rail line can attract enough riders. In short, a city's transport system functions better if things are closer to home. By failing to see land-use planning as a transportation strategy, many of the world's cities have allowed the automobile to shape them. Few could foresee that this orientation would plague cities with traffic jams, deadly accidents, noise, and smog, while marginalizing people who do not own cars.

To achieve efficiency in transport, urban areas around the globe need to adopt new land-use controls and revise existing ones. But it is important not to confuse planning future growth with attempting to slow or stop it. People in many metropolitan areas, particularly in the United States, have reacted to worsening congestion and loss of open space by starting slow-growth and no-growth movements. But it is impossible to halt further development; by prohibiting growth in their own jurisdictions, communities merely shift it to neighboring areas, where controls may be looser and more conducive to further sprawl.

More important, future development presents an invaluable opportunity to remedy past errors. If cities do not want to be frozen in their current auto-dependent patterns, they need to turn new growth to their advantage by filling in underused space to make the urban area more compact.

Several improvements in the way cities handle land use can reconcile communities' growth and transportation concerns. Antiquated zoning laws, in particular, need updating. In most industrial countries, planners have continued to segregate homes from jobs, shops, and other centers of activity long after the end of the heavy industrial period, when protecting public health required keeping slaughterhouses and smokestacks out of residential areas.

Even though most of today's commercial and industrial sites no longer pose health threats, zoning in much of the industrial world still separates different activities. In the United States, the concept of incompatible land uses is absurdly magnified; vast tracts of housing are largely abandoned in daytime, while monolithic commercial districts stand empty at night. Many neighborhoods are little more than throughways for car drivers en route to somewhere else. In some new communities on the fringes of Los Angeles, a third of commuters travel more than 80 kilometers (50 miles) daily each way.

Unfortunately, most developing countries have imported these compartmentalized zoning laws. Among the most serious repercussions are excessive distances between homes and jobs; for example, many office workers in São Paulo now spend two to three hours commuting each way. Although poorly regulated and heavily polluting industries still predominate in the Third World — making it necessary to separate factories from homes — zoning codes often segregate other, mutually dependent land uses. Throughout Asia, Latin America, and Africa, zoning that isolates activities unduly burdens public transport by creating distances too long for a walk or bicycle ride. As a result, many vital services are well out of reach for the vast majority.

Increasing Density and Diversity

A more rational approach to zoning in both the developing and industrial worlds would be to integrate homes not only with workplaces but with other amenities, so that they are easily accessible by walking, cycling, or public transport. Such reforms ideally would not hamper developers or impose uniformity, but instead would lift restrictions that inhibit mixed use and create unnaturally one-dimensional districts.

It is not too late for well-established cities to improve their landuse patterns. Dispersed areas can be made more compact by filling in underused space. Even in cities where most areas are overcrowded, a surprising amount of land in other parts is vacant or underused. For example, only about half of the urbanized land in Bogotá is actually developed, suggesting that it could be used much more effectively for homes, commercial developments, and parks.

One way to increase density in residential areas is to allow homeowners to rent out small apartments within their houses. The size of the average household in industrial countries is shrinking steadily, and many homes can now accommodate an extra unit in a converted basement, garage, or attic, or even an added story. According to a 1985 estimate, 12–18 million U.S. homes have surplus space that may be suitable for apartments. Local governments in Canada and Europe encourage this as a way to provide needed housing and make better use of space. Most U.S. communities, in contrast, prohibit apartments in houses in single-family zones. In recent years, however, housing-short communities in California, New Jersey, and Massachusetts have changed regulations to promote this arrangement.

Many large cities are finding that the most transport-efficient land-use pattern combines a dense, well-mixed downtown with several outlying, compact centers of activity — all linked by an extensive public transport system. This way, people can walk, cycle, and take short public transport trips within a given area and can reach other areas via express bus or rapid light rail. In a strategy to ease dependence on the automobile, planners in Canadian cities such as Toronto and Vancouver have achieved such a many-centered layout.

Each includes a number of high-density, diverse centers focused around public transport links.

Fortunately for the world's polluted, traffic-clogged cities, there are some outstanding models for adopting land use as a transport strategy. These cities owe their success not only to carefully guided growth but also to systematic, coordinated investments in public transport, cycling, and walking. Portland, Oregon, for example, is a rapidly growing city of roughly 500,000 people within a metropolitan area of 1.3 million. Instead of giving in to ever greater automobile dependence and sprawl, Portland has encircled itself with an Urban Growth Boundary, an invisible line similar to England's green belts, beyond which new development is not allowed. Reinforced by zoning reforms, the Urban Growth Boundary allows Portland to grow quickly but compactly.

In roughly two decades, Portland has successfully fended off sprawl and claimed valuable city space back from the automobile. The city has increased its housing density by encouraging a blend of multi- and single-family homes in pleasant, compact patterns. Its vibrant downtown boasts such green spaces as Tom McCall Waterfront Park, once an expressway, and Pioneer Courthouse Square, formerly a parking lot. City officials welcome new office construction but restrict the amount of accompanying parking. Since the early 1970s, the volume of cars entering Portland's downtown has remained the same even though the number of jobs there has increased by 50 percent.

Room Enough for All

Nearly every urban area has two faces—one well-housed and connected to a variety of services and amenities, and the other, ill-housed and excluded from many such opportunities.

Often, the disadvantaged are geographically isolated. Millions of poor people live in the developing world's squatter settlements, where governments ignore their existence; others are shut out of the industrial world's communities by a lack of affordable housing or appropriate jobs. Concentrated in segregated pockets, poor city dwellers everywhere are burdened with a disproportionate share of urban hazards—ranging from toxic waste dumps to highspeed traffic—because they lack the political power to keep such threats out of their neighborhoods. Geographic isolation reinforces deprivation by excluding poor people from the services that could improve their lives; it separates entire groups from economic and educational opportunities to help themselves out of poverty.

Municipalities can enhance the supply of affordable housing by adopting controls that promote a mixture of housing types. Again using Portland, Oregon, as an example, 54 percent of all recent residential development there consists of apartments, duplexes, and other affordable housing, compared with the 30 percent maximum allowed by previous zoning. This zoning policy has helped keep Portland housing prices reasonable, unlike those in other fast-growing cities. Measured in relation to household income, Portland's housing is two to three times as affordable as in other West Coast cities, such as Seattle, San Jose, San Francisco, and Los Angeles.

Humane Cities

For a strictly human invention, a city can be a harsh place for people. To walk along many urban streets is to brave a gauntlet of noise, smog, and the danger of being struck by a motor vehicle. If poorly planned, city landscapes may offer few glimpses of nature and little relief from relentless concrete and asphalt. Although nearly every city has its own lively districts filled with character and local color, large expanses are devoid of such urban charms. Neighborhoods often have no inviting places for friends to meet or children to play. Veering far from the model of the Greek *polis,* many cities fail to create vibrant public spaces or to include people in the decisions that will shape their own communities.

Making urban areas more humane includes planning the use of street space. In cities all over the world, automobile traffic needs to be held in check. Many European cities have redesigned roads in order to "calm" traffic. Typically this entails reduced speed limits and strategically placed trees, bushes, flower-beds, or play areas along or in the roadway — gentle inducements that make drivers proceed slowly and yield the right-of-way to pedestrians, cyclists, and children at play.

Many cities are linking stretches of verdant space along rivers, canals, or old rail lines into continuous paths for cycling, horseback riding, jogging, and walking. For urbanites, these "greenways" bring fresh air and nature closer to home. In the United States, where greenways in Washington, D.C., Seattle, and other cities have become major routes for bicycle commuters, an estimated 500 new greenway projects are currently in process. The city of Leicester, England, is planning to convert an abandoned rail line into the Great Central Way, a car-free route that will bisect the entire city from north to south.

Greenery further softens a city's rough edges. Devoting more urban space to trees and other plants can provide habitat for a surprising diversity of birds and other wildlife, giving city dwellers a needed bond with nature. Growing numbers of cities are conserving their remaining wild spaces and creating nature reserves in built-up areas. For example, the Nature Conservancy Council, a central U.K. government agency, now supports city reserve projects in more than 60 urban areas. A share of the funding is specifically aimed at greening inner cities and public housing projects, which typically lack natural amenities.

Better planning and design can create city spaces that are friendly and safe enough for people to gather and enjoy themselves. Yet, in their attempts to attract people to a given area, planners and designers often repeat familiar mistakes. Urban social critic William Whyte has noted how cities can avoid these pitfalls. To accommodate more people in a congested street, for instance, it is more effective to expand the pedestrian space, not the room given large vehicles carrying one person each. Relegating street vendors to a single area makes less sense than allowing them to space themselves in small, frequent clusters. A park or courtyard is much safer if it is not walled off but rather made visible from the street. Spikes placed on ledges to ward off "undesirables" provide less public security than do comfortable surfaces that invite plenty of people to linger in the same space.

One of the most important planning tools for a humane city is a planning process that involves the public. Neighborhood organizations can provide an effective liaison with the city administration and planning council. In several U.S. cities, including Atlanta, Cincinnati, and Washington, D.C., such groups play a legal role in zoning and other land-use decisions. Baltimore gives funding and technical assistance to its neighborhood groups to facilitate their participation in the urban-planning process.

A Groundwork for Urban Land-Use Policy

By all accounts, the growth of cities is an undeniable fact of the future. At current rates of expansion, the world's population will double in 40 years, the urban population will double in 22, and the Third World urban population in 15 — with momentous consequences for both human life and the environment.

Yet, the industrial countries' experience demonstrates that even cities with declining populations often commit the transgressions of growth. Lacking prudent land-use planning, they continue to expand into surrounding regions, squandering natural resources on which future generations depend. In rich and poor countries alike, there is an urgent need to ensure that cities do not further destroy the natural environment and so undermine the human prospect.

That cities will grow does not mean they must inevitably expand into surrounding forests or farmlands. Many have so much underused space that they could develop for decades to come without bulldozing another square meter of undisturbed land. Industrial countries have tremendous scope for making urban growth more compact by establishing green belts and growth boundaries and by requiring further development to occur only within those lines. In the developing world, great potential for filling in underused space lies in the redistribution of urban landownership, which — particularly in Latin America and Asia — is often extremely skewed. In greater Bombay, for example,

2,000 hectares of vacant land now owned by a single family could house most of the city's squatters, slum residents, and sidewalk dwellers.

With land-use planning that confines development within existing boundaries, cities can protect both their own future and that of rural areas far beyond their visible reach. Compact growth can conserve energy and protect water resources while arresting destructive sprawl. And unlike attempts to slow or stop growth, carefully guided development can make cities better able to meet people's needs. Prohibiting further development can shut out many groups of people—and by restricting the supply of housing, it tends to inflate the price of homes. More-compact growth, in contrast, can help create diverse communities and promote smaller, more-affordable housing.

To achieve these goals for cities everywhere, three conditions must be met. First, the general public and decision makers need better access to information about the characteristics of a community's population and the probable consequences of various planning decisions. Second, cities and surrounding areas need a greater degree of regional cooperation to prevent land use in one jurisdiction from producing problems in others. Third, urban areas in virtually all countries need stronger support from their national governments, giving them greater budgetary power to plan their own long-term development strategies.

To make wise land-use decisions, cities need more-generous national funding for infrastructure, education, and social services. At the same time, it is important that such investments not be made at the expense of rural areas or secondary cities. Particularly in the Third World, strong rural-development strategies—to create off-farm employment, for example—offer people a vital alternative to migrating to already-overburdened cities. In many developing countries, where the consolidation of population, power, and wealth in capitals and other megacities is extreme, national funding support is crucial for helping secondary urban areas attract some of the urban development now concentrating in the big cities.

The world's urban problems help shape people's existence within and outside cities and can deeply alter the lives of future generations. Land-use planning is not sufficient to address these problems, but it is undeniably necessary. There is much to learn from the enduring model of the ancient *polis* and from the resolve of Athenians who more than two millennia ago undertook this oath: "We will strive for the ideals and sacred things of the city, both alone and with many. . . . We will transmit this city not only not less, but greater, better, and more beautiful than it was transmitted to us."

Chapter 35

An Industry Approach
to Sustainable Development

E. S. WOOLARD, JR.

When the history of environmentalism in the last quarter of this century is written, sustainable development may well prove to be the major conceptual advance in environmental thinking to have taken place during that period. The concept of sustainable development was introduced to a broad audience in 1987 by the World Commission on Environment and Development report *Our Common Future,* which stressed that environmental and economic issues are interrelated and that environmental issues do not respect political boundaries. It emphasized that the problems of poverty and underdevelopment cannot be solved unless we have a new era of economic growth in which developing countries play a strong role and reap substantial benefits.

The report also pointed out that the traditional model of industrial development, in which wealth was created without regard for the environmental consequences of production, had led to increasingly severe environmental disruptions around the world. The commission therefore argued for an alternative approach—sustainable development—which it defined as meeting the basic needs of all the world's people today without compromising the ability of future generations to meet their needs. There can be no doubt that industrial growth and development must continue, particularly in developing countries. But it must continue within the bounds of environmental limits.

Industry, as society's producer, has a special role to play in creating sustainable development, and some of us in the industrial community are working on ways to make sustainability a characteristic of industrial programs. In April 1991, I participated in the second World Industry Conference on Environmental Management in Rotterdam. The 700 or so industrialists at that meeting endorsed a document that we call the Business Charter for Sustainable Development. More than 200 companies have already expressed written support

Reprinted with permission from *Issues in Science and Technology,* Vol. 8, No. 3, Spring, 1992, pp.29–33. Copyright 1992, by the National Academy of Sciences, Washington, D.C.

for it at the CEO or senior management level. In addition, several dozen prominent organizations, including the World Resources Institute, the United Nations Environment Programme, and the U.S. Environmental Protection Agency, have also expressed written support. It will become part of the international business community's contribution to the UN Conference on the Environment and Development this June in Brazil.

The charter includes 16 principles of environmental management designed to assist businesses around the world in acquiring the features of sustainable development (see boxes on page 307 and 308). But as with any such document, the real challenge will be to convert these principles into industrial practices. We should begin to show measurable progress immediately and during each year of this decade, so that we can enter the next century already firmly on the sustainable development track. To meet that challenge, industry should establish an action agenda in four areas for the 1990s:

Education and open dialogue. This effort should begin with people in industry and extend to the public in communities where industrial companies operate. There remain industrialists who take issue with sustainable development, saying that we're either giving in to the environmentalists or inviting government regulation and central planning. In my opinion, accepting the idea of sustainable development does not mean we're giving in to anyone. Rather, it means that we are working out a set of principles that will help industry live up to society's expectations around the world.

Moreover, far from encouraging government regulation, sustainable development practices should help minimize the need for regulation by demonstrating industry's willingness to take responsibility for the impact of its activities. From what I've seen in my career, the best way to invite regulation by governments is to remain idle in the face of a major social issue that directly involves industrial products or operations.

And sustainable development is not about central planning. As more information is released from Eastern European countries, we can see that central planning has been a disaster for the environment. The only way people in developing countries will have a chance to improve their health and longevity, their standard of living, and the welfare of their children will be through industrial development. But for such development to be effective and sustainable, it will have to be in the form of appropriate local solutions to local problems—which means market economics and entrepreneurial activity. Those are the opposite of central planning.

As we work to improve the awareness and acceptance of sustainable development principles by industry, we also have to communicate a similar understanding to the public. Again, the manner in which we communicate our principles and agenda to the public will vary from industry to industry and country to country. But some approaches may have the potential for broad application.

Business Charter for Sustainable Development
Principles for Environmental Management

From the introduction:

. . .the International Chamber of Commerce hereby calls upon enterprises and their associations to use the following principles as a basis for pursuing such improvement and to express publicly their support for them. Individual programs developed to implement these principles will reflect the wide diversity among enterprises in size and function.

The objective is that the widest range of enterprises commit themselves to improving their environmental performance in accordance with these principles, to having in place management practices to effect such improvement, to measuring their progress, and to reporting this progress as appropriate internally and externally.

1. Corporate priority: To recognize environmental management as among the highest corporate priorities and as a key determinant to sustainable development; to establish policies, programs, and practices for conducting operations in an environmentally sound manner.

2. Integrated management: To integrate these policies, programs, and practices fully into each business as an essential element of management in all its functions.

3. Process of improvement: To continue to improve corporate policies, programs, and environmental performance, taking into account technological developments, scientific understanding, consumer needs, and community expectations, with legal regulations as a starting point; and to apply the same environmental criteria internationally.

4. Employee education: To educate, train, and motivate employees to conduct their activities in an environmentally responsible manner.

5. Prior assessment: To assess environmental impacts before starting a new activity or project and before decommissioning a facility or leaving a site.

6. Products and services: To develop and provide products or services that have no undue environmental impact and are safe in their intended use, that are efficient in their consumption of energy and natural resources, and that can be recycled, reused, or disposed of safely.

7. Customer advice: To advise, and where relevant educate, customers, distributors, and the public in the safe use, transportation, storage, and disposal of products provided; and to apply similar considerations to the provision of services.

8. Facilities and operations: To develop, design, and operate facilities and conduct activities taking into consideration the efficient use of energy and materials, the sustainable use of renewable resources, the minimization of adverse environmental impact and waste generation, and the safe and responsible disposal of residual wastes.

9. Research: To conduct or support research on the environmental impacts of raw materials, products, processes, emissions, and wastes associated with the enterprise and on the means of minimizing such adverse impacts.

10. Precautionary approach: To modify the manufacture, marketing, or use of products or services or the conduct of activities, consistent with scientific and technical understanding, to prevent serious or irreversible environmental degradation.

11. **Contractors and suppliers:** To promote the adoption of these principles by contractors acting on behalf of the enterprise, encouraging and, where appropriate, requiring improvements in their practices to make them consistent with those of the enterprise; and to encourage the wider adoption of these principles by suppliers.

12. **Emergency preparedness:** To develop and maintain, where significant hazards exist, emergency preparedness plans in conjunction with the emergency services, relevant authorities, and the local community, recognizing potential transboundary impacts.

13. **Transfer of technology:** To contribute to the transfer of environmentally sound technology and management methods throughout the industrial and public sectors.

14. **Contributing to the common effort:** To contribute to the development of public policy and to business, governmental, and intergovernmental programs and educational initiatives that will enhance environmental awareness and protection.

15. **Openness to concerns:** To foster openness and dialogue with employees and the public, anticipating and responding to their concerns about the potential hazards and impacts of operations, products, wastes, or services, including those of transboundary or global significance.

16. **Compliance and reporting:** To measure environmental performance; to conduct regular environmental audits and assessments of compliance with company requirements, legal requirements, and these principles; and periodically to provide appropriate information to the board of directors, shareholders, employees, the authorities, and the public.

For example, the chemical industries in Canada, the United States, Europe, and Australia have adopted a program called Responsible Care, which entails a set of principles and Codes of Management Practices. The codes include specific guidelines in areas such as community awareness, emergency response, process safety, and pollution prevention. Every member company of the Chemical Manufacturers Association (CMA) must sign on to the codes and report back to the association on its progress. As long as a company is making good-faith progress in implementing the codes, other CMA companies provide assistance. Companies failing to implement the codes can be disassociated from CMA and denied the many benefits that come with membership.

Implementation of these codes can establish a continuing dialogue with representatives of the local community. We can build on those contacts to establish emergency preparedness procedures, recycling programs, and other projects.

Waste minimization and pollution prevention. In many nations, public concern about industry and the environment remains intensely focused on the generation and disposal of industrial and consumer wastes and on the environmental and public health effects of industrial emissions. Without question, getting control of waste and emissions is a vital part of any sustainable development scenario. One of the industry leaders in this regard has been the 3M Company, which in 1975 began an ambitious program to prevent pollution and eliminate the costs associated with "end-of-the-pipe" pollution controls. Employees were encouraged to contribute ideas on product reformulation, process modification, equipment design, and resource recovery. From 1975 to 1990, 3M estimates that the program saved the company $537 million by dramatically reducing all forms of waste and thus eliminating the cost of handling that waste.

Many companies now realize that they must make public commitments to reducing wastes and emissions by setting goals and then publicly measuring their progress toward those goals. In 1989, Du Pont, for example, committed to 11 specific targets as a basis for our approach to corporate environmentalism. Among these commitments was our pledge to reduce by 35 percent during this decade the total hazardous waste generated at our sites around the world. We also said that we will cut toxic air emissions by 60 percent by 1993. We will reduce emissions of airborne carcinogens by 90 percent by 2000, with continued reductions thereafter, always heading in the direction of zero emissions. We also included goals specific to our energy business, such as a decision to build only double-hulled tankers and to install double-walled tanks at all newly constructed and renovated gasoline outlets. Since 1990, we have published environmental summaries in our annual reports that show how we are progressing toward our goals, and we will continue to do so annually.

Another important consideration in waste minimization is to be concerned about the waste we don't see as well as the waste we do. The waste we don't see is the large quantity of nonrenewable energy resources that are used inefficiently. Energy companies and industry in general should be in the forefront of developing efficient, high-value uses of our hydrocarbon resources.

This may require a reversal in the way we traditionally think about business development. Some U.S. utility companies now have aggressive programs to help residential consumers use less of their product. State regulators can make it possible for utilities to profit from such measures.

Product stewardship. We have entered an era in which industrial corporations will have to accept responsibility for the environmental impact of their materials and products from inception in the laboratory to ulimate disposition after their useful life is over.

A classic case in point is that of chlorofluorocarbons (CFCs). Few expect the ultimate consumers of CFCs — refrigerator owners and air-conditioner users, for example — to take responsibility for the impact of these products on the earth's atmosphere. Throughout the debate over these products, responsibility has been directed to the manufacturers of CFCs and to companies that use these products in large industrial quantities. Many manufacturers of CFCs participated in the discussions that led up to the Montreal Protocol (the international agreement to reduce CFC use), have helped formulate the reduction plan, and are actively involved in the development of substitutes. If nothing else, the CFC issue was a shot across the bow, a clear indication that manufacturers will be responsible for the longterm impact of the products we produce and sell.

Similarly, concern over what to do about postconsumer plastic waste has been laid at the doorsteps of the industries that manufacture plastic resins and fabricate plastic packaging and plastic products. At Du Pont, because we are one of the world's largest producers of polymer resins, we have made a public commitment to take increasing responsibility for the plastics portion of the global solid-waste stream. We currently operate two plastics recycling plants.

Proctor and Gamble is another company that is initiating product stewardship programs, particularly with regard to the packaging of its products. P&G's approach is to seek ways to reduce solid waste throughout the product life cycle, including packaging redesign, product concentration, optimization of raw material use, and use of recycled materials.

Innovative product design and marketing. I know that for many North American companies, a traditional approach to trade was to create a product for the North American market and then look for opportunities to sell the product in other parts of the world. We will probably always have examples of this kind of marketing. But in a sustainable world economy, we can expect a new approach. Increasingly, we will have to let local needs determine the products we offer, instead of taking existing products and trying to fit them to local needs. And these needs will be defined in the context of environmental impact and resource availability, not just utility.

A simple example of this is the polyethylene pouch container, a technology developed by our Canadian subsidiary to package milk. The pouches are convenient, tamper-resistant, and, compared to competing packaging systems, reduce solid waste by up to 70 percent. As an outgrowth of this technology, we developed a similar technology to dispense cooking oil in India. Cooking oil has traditionally been sold in that country by dispensing it from a central supply, typically a 55-gallon drum, into open containers provided by the consumer. The system raises questions about contamination, adulteration, and waste from spillage.

What might seem the logical alternative, Western bottling systems, would represent a significant incremental cost to many Indian consumers. So we developed low-cost polyethylene pouches that could each hold 250 milliliters of oil, the measure for cooking a typical meal. The ployethylene film itself dissolves at cooking temperatures, is edible, and does not end up as a waste product. Consumers could buy only the amount they need and be assured of its quality. We are currently seeking to interest local firms in commercializing this technology, which we believe is an excellent example of a product that responds to local needs and lifestyles, has low environmental impact, and contributes to the standard of living in a developing nation.

If we can establish a firm base for education, waste minimization, product stewardship, and innovative product design, then we can tackle more difficult challenges. The current generation of industry leaders has the ability to see further into the future with regard to the environmental impact of our operations than any previous generation. We cannot place ourselves in the position of requiring society to choose between a strong, healthy industry and a clean and safe environment. I believe that we can have both. To do so, we have to begin by acknowledging environmental protection as a real, legitimate, and permanent factor in the planning and conduct of everything we do. If industrial growth and development cause continued environmental deterioration, then the future for industry will be an endless series of restrictions and lost opportunities. If, however, we lead industry into a new era of environmental concern and sustainable production, we can continue to reward investors, create jobs, and improve living standards in societies around the world.

Chapter 36

Downtowns in the
Year 2040

JOHN FONDERSMITH

What will America's "downtowns" be like in the year 2000? The answer to that question is not too difficult, since many public and private projects that are in the planning stage will be completed sometime in the 1990s. Almost all cities have downtown plans extending to the year 2000 or beyond. But a longer-term look of 40 to 50 years requires us to think about the state of the downtowns of major American cities in about the year 2040.

We are talking about the downtowns of approximately 60 to 80 major American cities that have a significant scale of activities concentrated in that center. Many smaller cities also have impressive downtown revitalization programs, but the scale and the competition with new outlying centers may have different results.

Many of these downtowns went through a great period of growth during the first three decades of this century. They began to feel the enormous impact of the automobile. After more-gradual change during the Depression and World War II periods, decay accelerated in downtowns during the 1950s. The period of rapid suburban expansion began. By the late 1960s, most downtowns reached their low points. Then a series of new ideas led to a major revival of almost all downtown areas of major American cities. Interestingly, the forces shaping the recent revival have not been primarily technological in nature. Instead, they have been basically simple ideas.

Downtown Office Employment

Office development has been the real "driver" of downtown development over the past 30 years and will continue to be the single most important factor

Reprinted with permission from *The Futurist,* Vol. 22, No. 2, March/April, 1988. Published by the World Future Society, Bethesda, Maryland.

in the future, even though retail and cultural activities may receive more attention. In the 1950s and 1960s, some pundits were forecasting the withering away of downtown office employment, with workers decentralized to workplaces in their homes and outlying sites.

There has been, of course, major office development in the suburbs, but downtowns have also seen an office boom. A 1984 survey of 33 large U.S. downtowns by the Urban Investment and Development Company found that approximately 58 million square feet of office space was built in the 1950s, 132 million square feet in the 1960s, 196 million square feet in the 1970s, and 218 million square feet completed or under construction from 1980 to 1984. That boom continued for several more years, though some cities are having a slow period while demand catches up with supply.

The past decades have seen the redesign of the office workplace, major changes in office routines and technology, and changes in the office work force. Change will be even more dramatic in the future. Continued advances in telecommunications and a shorter workweek will likely mean that employees will work in the downtown office several days a week and work from home or other locations on other days. Office areas will increasingly provide day-care centers, gyms, and training centers. In the ongoing effort to attract office construction, cities will stress the amenities of downtown and will improve transportation access.

The skylines of American cities have been transformed in the last 30 years, primarily by office towers. While technological advances will theoretically allow taller and taller buildings, economic and social considerations will limit the number of super skyscrapers. More attention will be given to the "ground floor" of downtown areas.

After several decades of bland metal and glass boxes, today's tall office buildings are again assuming more ornamental and sculptural forms. San Francisco has pioneered urban-design requirements to achieve less boxy forms for new buildings, and other cities are following this lead. We are likely to see more-coordinated efforts to design dramatic skylines, including new uses of light at night to create dramatic effects.

Of course, by the early twenty-first century, many skyscrapers of the mid-twentieth century will have outlived their economic life. Those that cannot be economically renovated will have to come down in large-scale demolition actions.

Downtown Is Fun

A number of approaches have been taken to attract more people downtown—to work, to learn, to shop, to play.

The "festival marketplace." The "big idea" of recent years has been the "festival marketplace." Of course, cities have always had markets and some specialized retail areas. The concept of recycling old buildings into a complex of shops and restaurants on a major scale was first done in the mid–1960s in Ghirardelli Square and the Cannery in San Francisco. However, it was James Rouse who fully conceptualized and implemented the festival-marketplace concept with the development of Faneuil Hall Marketplace in Boston in 1976.

Other festival-marketplaces and retail complexes already developed include Harborplace in Baltimore, the South Street Seaport in New York City, the Union Station project in St. Louis, the Waterside in Norfolk, Portside in Toledo, the 6th Street Marketplace in Richmond, and the Old Post Office in Washington, D.C. Almost every large city now has or is developing a marketplace.

While hugely successful as retail centers, the festival marketplaces have had a much more important role in creating new civic gathering places and in dramatically changing the image of American cities. A 1981 *Time* magazine cover story on James Rouse declared, "Cities Are Fun!"—a statement almost unthinkable in the atmosphere of the 1960s. The nurturing of this new spirit of fun and vitality at the core of cities has been a major factor in the resurgence of the American downtown in the past decade.

The success of the festival marketplace has spurred new interest in downtown retailing, which had been dormant or declining in most cities since the 1960s. Today, major retail complexes have been completed or are under construction in many cities, including development of new department stores. In many cases, the retail complexes connect existing stores. The Rouse Company has also been a pioneer in this movement, with the Gallery in Philadelphia, Grand Avenue Concourse in Milwaukee, the Shops in Washington, and the New Gallery at Harborplace in Baltimore.

In many developments, the festival marketplace and the major retail complex have come together. Horton Plaza in San Diego, a colorful collection of new and old buildings with new department stores, shops, and restaurants, represents a new generation of downtown retail development.

Major new retail complexes will be developed in downtowns over the next 40 to 50 years, and existing retail centers will be renovated and restructured. The challenge facing city planners and developers is to devise the new mix of activities to attract the customers of the future. This new mix will combine retailing with the educational, cultural, and entertainment assets of downtowns.

Historic preservation and urban design. Preservation of historic buildings has been another "big idea" and a major force in the development of downtowns over the past two decades. This is quite a contrast to the science-fiction visions of all new downtowns outlined in the 1939 World's Fair and in writings and drawings of that period. Historic preservation has helped provide a new alternative vision of the future downtown. Thousands of buildings of all types have been recycled in one form or another in downtown areas across the country. Historic districts have been established in downtowns and adjacent areas.

Although preservation vs. development conflicts continue in many cities, the role of recycled older buildings is increasingly recognized as a plus factor for downtowns compared with outlying suburban commercial centers. These buildings and historic areas provide a sense of place and history that new outlying centers cannot match.

Historic preservation will probably become relatively less important in the years ahead. By the year 2000, almost all nineteenth and early twentieth century buildings will have been recycled, sometimes more than once, or will have been demolished. Of course, as time passes, our idea of what is "historic" will evolve also. In a few years, some surviving bland 1950s buildings may even have a new appeal.

We are now in a period of "post-modern" architecture, in which architects and their clients are rediscovering ornament, color, and urban-design values. The public is much more ready to accept replacement of old buildings of no particular merit if the new buildings are of quality design. The present concern with old buildings and areas will continue to evolve into a broader concern with the quality of the overall urban environment.

Open spaces. The past 25 years have been a great period for development of new parks, plazas, and open spaces in American downtowns. Every major downtown has constructed numerous open spaces, often including pools, fountains, and outdoor sculpture. A number of great city avenues have also been rebuilt, including Pennsylvania Avenue in Washington, D.C., and Market Street in San Francisco. The success of these efforts will spur additional large-scale streetscape efforts in the future.

One of the most dramatic changes in the future will be trees. Trees and more trees! Cities will undertake major downtown forestry programs, with thousands of new trees planted along streets and in parks. A permanent urban-forestry corps will maintain them. Not only will such a program yield aesthetic dividends, but the trees will also provide shade and help cool urban temperatures.

Waterfront development. Many major cities are located on rivers, lakes, or bays. Although these waterways are generally less important for industrial and shipping purposes than they once were, they are increasingly important as urban amenities. Water has a special fascination for people, making water resources attractive focal points for new development. In most American cities, the waterfront is adjacent to or near downtowns, and almost every city with a waterfront resource has undertaken some kind of waterfront-enhancement program. Baltimore's Inner Harbor, with Harborplace, a magnificent aquarium, and growing mixed-use development of adjacent areas, is one of the nation's most impressive waterfronts. Battery Park City in New York City is a magnificent new development stretching along the Hudson River. And San Antonio's unique Paseo del Rio (Riverwalk) has become the focus of that city's downtown.

Some cities blocked their waterfronts with elevated highways and inappropriate development in the 1950s and 1960s. Today, cities such as San Francisco, Boston, and Hartford have plans to eliminate or relocate early expressways in order to reconnect downtown to the waterfront. By the year 2000, virtually all waterfront cities will have reclaimed much of their downtown waterfronts for public access and mixed-use development, and such development will continue into the twenty-first century.

Cultural centers. In the future, cities will seek to develop and expand a range of cultural and entertainment facilities in downtowns to provide learning experiences that are fun. Arts, education, and entertainment activities will be increasingly important in the downtown of the future, and these activities will be increasingly intertwined.

Cities have intensified efforts over the past 20 years to retain or build new cultural facilities downtown. Major performing arts centers have been built in Los Angeles, Houston, Denver, St. Paul, and a number of other major cities. Classic old music halls and movie palaces have been renovated for performing arts in many cities, including Pittsburgh, Cleveland, Richmond, Cincinnati, and Milwaukee.

Today, there is a new wave of "arts districts" under development. Perhaps the most extensive such district is being created in Dallas. A new art museum opened in 1985, and construction began in 1986 for a new symphony hall. This all-new arts district is to include restaurants, shops, and small theaters, as well as new office development. Washington, D.C., has outlined a Downtown Arts District and is developing local arts activities between the National Portrait Gallery/National Museum of American Art at Gallery Place and the National Gallery of Art and Smithsonian museums on the Mall. Boston is developing an arts district between Boston Common and the "Downtown Crossing" retail area, utilizing existing theaters and new development.

Downtown revitalization in many cities includes community colleges and universities. But "education" is increasingly seen in a wider context, in attractions that combine education and entertainment. Children's museums and science museums are especially popular. Elaborate planetariums and IMAX theaters attract visitors for fun and learning. Both Boston and Baltimore have built exciting downtown aquariums that are research centers and major visitor attractions. A recent *New York Times* article indicated that at least 22 cities were planning to expand or build new aquariums. Future museums will include elaborate simulation centers that will allow visitors to participate in a number of imaginary but very realistic experiences.

Visiting Downtown

All cities today make a special effort to attract visitors for a variety of purposes (e.g., business, conventions, and tourism). Visitors mean increased tax revenues, jobs, and business development. The past two decades have seen a wave of hotel construction. New hotels have been a major factor in the image of revitalized downtowns.

Another trend has been the renovation of classic old hotels that date back to the early twentieth and late nineteenth centuries. The beautifully renovated Willard Inter-Continental Hotel in Washington, D.C. (built 1901, closed 1968, reopened 1986), is the latest of many grand old downtown hotels to be rescued from oblivion.

Many visitors of downtown will just be looking for a room for the night, but the need for more moderately priced hotels is increasingly difficult to meet because of high land costs in some cities. In the future, cities will undertake special programs to encourage low-cost accommodations. Many hotels are now offering special low weekend rates. As metropolitan areas grow larger, the "special weekend" in the downtown hotel will become more of an attraction for many suburban residents. And increased nationwide hostel programs will provide travel accommodations for young people who want to see American cities.

City travel has been spurred by a substantial increase in conventions, trade shows, and meetings. To encourage such business, every major city has developed new, or expanded existing, convention and meeting centers over the past two decades. The promise of visitor business will mean continuing programs to increase the size and sophistication of convention facilities and to develop new visitor attractions in downtowns.

Surprisingly, with all the emphasis on attracting new visitors, American cities do an awful job at providing background information about the city. Visitors and city residents alike are lucky to find a few brochures and a flashy but simplistic slide show. Over the next 20 years, cities will increasingly develop innovative orientation and city-history centers. New video techniques will enable the history of the city, and its projected future, to be shown in realistic detail.

Downtown Living

In the rush to revitalize American downtowns over the past three decades, residential development has received much discussion but limited action. In most cities, the residential population in downtown and adjacent areas has declined. Some adjacent areas in a number of cities have been improved through the "gentrification" process, though sometimes with displacement problems. Some cities have managed to improve or retain center-city neighborhoods, such as Rittenhouse Square and Society Hill in Philadelphia, Beacon Hill in Boston, and Dupont Circle and Capitol Hill in Washington.

Adjacent residential areas are crucial to a lively, animated downtown. It is not that in-town populations alone provide the labor market for downtown. Customers and employees must be attracted from a wide area. But downtown residents provide the essential difference in the downtown life—a sense of community. If the downtown and adjacent residential populations are large enough, the walking-to-work and transit-use patterns of these populations can result in significant transportation and environmental advantages.

The development of downtown housing is one of the most important items on the agenda of cities today. A number of cities, led by San Francisco, are developing various forms of "linkage," which essentially means requiring some direct or indirect support of housing in return for approval of office development.

These trends will strengthen in the coming decades. By the early twenty-first century, most American cities will have significantly increased the downtown and near-downtown residential population. The increased population will also require neighborhood retail services, recreation facilities, improved security, and even new schools.

Transportation to Downtown

Fast and effective metropolitan transportation is critical for the continued vitality of downtowns. Providing access becomes more complex as metropolitan areas spread outward in all directions. The usual image of futuristic city travel is of a rapid rail system, rushing commuters to downtown stations. However, only 10 American cities have some form of "heavy" rail transit system. Los Angeles has begun construction of a rail system. A number of other cities, including Dallas, Houston, and Denver, are considering building major new rail systems.

Over the next 40 years, the existing major rail systems will be improved and extended. Major new rail systems of futuristic design will probably be built in another 5 to 10 cities, assuming a renewed national commitment to using transit for shaping urban growth.

A number of American cities have turned to light-rail systems, using modern, updated versions of the streetcar. These new systems usually include reserved rights-of-way. New light-rail systems have been built in Buffalo, Portland, Sacramento, and San Diego and are being considered in a number of other cities. The few cities that have retained some type of early streetcar systems are making improvements. Pittsburgh is an example. Over the next 50 years, specialized light-rail systems will proliferate, probably being used in close to half of the major American cities.

However, the most popular public transit is and will continue to be by bus. Improvements in bus design have not been matched by advances in busway development. Although many cities have some form of bus lanes, including some special express-bus lanes on freeways, no city has yet constructed a complete system of modern busways where buses can travel on their own reserved lanes in congested areas. The most extensive new busway in North America has recently opened in Ottawa.

Major progress has been made in the city centers, where a number of cities have constructed transit malls to bring buses on exclusive lanes into the center of the city. Portland and Denver are especially noteworthy. Over the next 50 years, bus design will continue to improve, and more cities will develop improved systems of busways to rush commuters to the downtown area.

Major access to most downtowns will continue to be by automobile, so highways and parking improvements will continue to be important. Most American downtowns are defined by a full or partial freeway ring, almost all built in the past 30 years. In many instances, freeway design was insensitive, creating a wall effect and cutting linkages to adjacent areas. Many cities will redesign and rebuild these surrounding freeways over the next 50 years. In some cases, new boulevards around downtown will be emphasized, such as the new Martin Luther King Boulevard in Baltimore.

New parking garages on the edge of downtown and underground will continue to be built as part of new mixed-use complexes. Cities will continue to try to group parking facilities so that automobiles can move from the surrounding freeways into parking facilities.

The increased use of computers in automobiles will lead to systems that will allow automobiles to be guided by remote control on "electronic highways." Whether the benefits of such systems prove cost-effective on a large scale remains to be seen. But freeways and urban arteries will increasingly be "smart highways," with access and movement controlled by traffic lights and gates tied to central computers. Drivers approaching downtown will receive information on traffic flow and parking availability on digital display screens in each car. Coordinated traffic and parking management and enforcement programs will become even more important.

One of the most dramatic "low-tech" transportation innovations in recent years has been the growing use of van pools, and that trend will continue.

Movement in Downtowns

Within downtown, walking will continue to be the most important mode of transportation. Over the past 30 years, American cities have developed a whole series of new pedestrian-movement systems. These include second-level walkways, most prevalent in Minneapolis, St. Paul, and Cincinnati, and

underground walkways, as in Houston, Oklahoma City, Chicago, and Philadelphia. Many cities have extensive ground-level pedestrian areas, although no
city has gone to the all-pedestrian center envisioned in the 1956 Fort Worth
Plan. Many cities have a combination of underground, surface, and second-
level pedestrian links. In the next 50 years, downtowns will work to increase
the ease of pedestrian movement and the attractiveness of the pedestrian environment.

Buses and rail-transit systems also provide movement within downtown
areas. Ironically, the most popular new movement system in downtown in recent years has been the trolley — actually, minibuses designed to look like late-
nineteenth-century streetcars. Such "trolleys" are now operating in some form
in almost all major downtowns. In the future, such trolleys and other mini-
vehicles will be formed into coordinated systems of movement in the downtown core and adjacent areas.

Transit planners have long envisioned the use of "personal rapid transit"
(PRT) — small vehicles operating under remote control on their own separate
guideways. Such systems have been described as "horizontal elevators" or "people movers." In the late 1970s, some PRT enthusiasts envisioned large-scale
PRT systems extending throughout metropolitan areas. So far, such systems
have been used primarily on a small scale in amusement parks, airports, and
some suburban office complexes. The first true urban people mover opened in
Miami in April 1986 — a 1.9-mile loop through downtown. Named the Metro-
mover, the system connects with the Metrorail system. A 2.9-mile people-
mover system opened in Detroit in July 1987.

Over the next 50 years, people-mover systems will be built in a number
of American downtowns, forming a partial or full loop around the downtown
and providing access to nearby activity centers, such as medical complexes.
However, the limitations of the concept seem to preclude the large-scale use
of people movers that was predicted just a few years ago. "Low-tech" uses of
existing transportation systems, such as taxicabs, rental cars, and bicycles, will
become more important in future transportation planning.

All these movement systems within downtowns — light rail, people
movers, and buses — will increasingly be designed for entertainment and
educational purposes as well as for movement.

Building Better Downtowns

Downtown improvement does not happen by accident. It takes planning,
vision, coordination and cooperation, and millions of dollars of public and
private investment. Many mayors have made downtown revitalization a key
part of their programs. In Washington, D.C., Mayor Marion Barry, Jr., has
made creation of a "Living Downtown" a high priority. In Baltimore, former

Mayor William Donald Schaefer achieved a national reputation as a result of the success of the Inner Harbor project and related new development. Most major cities have created some type of public-private partnership organization to guide downtown revitalization.

The mechanics of downtown revitalization are increasingly institutionalized through organizations such as the Urban Land Institute, the International Downtown Association, the American Planning Association, the National Trust for Historic Preservation, and the American Institute of Architects. Through publications, conferences, and site visits, new innovations in downtown development spread rapidly.

Downtowns are not islands unto themselves. They cannot long prosper if the surrounding areas and the larger society have serious economic and social problems that are not resolved. Problems of unemployment, the homeless, the underclass, crime, and drugs must be attacked on a larger scale.

In design, use, and management, America's major downtowns are becoming "theme centers" that provide special functions for city and suburban residents and out-of-town visitors. Though office employment and retail will remain the major functions of downtown, it seems clear that the role as a city symbol, as a gathering place, and as a special attraction is what sets downtown apart from outlying areas.

Each downtown should strive to develop its own design, urbanity, and special character, building on the historic physical design and special concepts for the regional base. Nothing could be more of a mistake than to create downtowns across the country that look the same.

The real "cities of the future" already exist. Even as metropolitan areas expand, the downtown areas of America's great cities are evolving and taking on new functions. The resurgence of America's major downtowns is an important national event, providing focal points and symbols for the activities of major metropolitan areas in the twenty-first century.

Chapter 37

How Business Is Reshaping America

CHRISTOPHER B. LEINBERGER
CHARLES LOCKWOOD

Since the end of the Second World War urban planners and academi-cians have warned Americans that suburban sprawl is an evil to be fought with every ounce of our national energy. They have condemned cars as the cause of city-killing growth. They have idealized mass transit. Yet, other than business and political interests in city downtowns, few have paid attention to their cries. We Americans have allowed sprawl to happen. In fact, we have reveled in our low-density suburban housing, our automobiles, and our decentralized living.

Now it appears that the much-reviled postwar suburban sprawl, with its sea of split-level houses surrounding retail businesses and apartment com-plexes strung randomly along its highways, was merely a transitional phase be-tween the traditional compact pre-war city and today's metropolitan area. Our cities are becoming groups of interdependent "urban villages," which are business, retail, housing, and entertainment focal points amid a low-density cityscape. Each urban village has its core—a kind of new downtown—where the buildings are tallest, the daytime population largest, and the traffic conges-tion most severe. And each urban village has its outlying districts, which may stretch as far as ten miles from the core.

Urban villages represent a dramatic restructuring of America's cities and suburbs—one that is already affecting how millions of Americans live and work. Almost every city is swept up in the urban-village phenomenon—not only fast-growing Sunbelt cities like Atlanta and Phoenix but also slow-growing older ones like St. Louis and Kansas City, and archetypal cities like New York and Baltimore.

Reprinted with permission from *The Atlantic*, Vol. 258, No. 4, October, 1986. Published by *The Atlantic Monthly Co.*, Boston, Massachusetts.

The Urban Villages of Los Angeles

Los Angeles is perhaps the most evolved example of the urban-village phenomenon. Although downtown Los Angeles has recently experienced an unprecedented boom in office-building, the metropolitan area has simultaneously given rise to sixteen smaller urban-village cores, among them Century City, Cost Mesa/Irvine/Newport Beach, Encino, Glendale, the Airport, Warner Center, Ontario, Pasadena, Universal City/Burbank, and Westwood.

One of the easiest ways to gauge the growth of Los Angeles's urban villages is to look at the downtown's market share of the metropolitan region's office space over the past decades. (Office space is used as a standard measure of changing patterns of urban development in this chapter, because the office is the "factory of the future." In parts of some metropolitan areas 40 to 60 percent of the people hired for newly created jobs go to work in office buildings—not only white-collar workers but also support staff like janitors and food-service workers and security guards.) Since 1960 downtown Los Angeles's share of the metropolitan office market has declined from 60 to 34 percent, as expansion has shifted to the faster-growing urban-village cores in the suburbs.

The Costa Mesa/Irvine/Newport Beach complex, in Orange County, provides a good example of how the urban-village phenomenon is reshaping greater Los Angeles. Until the early 1960s a series of small towns in a county whose total population was 868,000, the complex today is California's third largest downtown, as measured by office and business-park space. The first phase in the creation of the urban village's core was the construction of a regional shopping mall, as it has been in many other locations. In this case there were two—South Coast Plaza, in Costa Mesa, and Fashion Island, in Newport Beach, both of which opened in the early 1970s. Next developers completed modest two-story office buildings nearby for local professional firms, and light industrial facilities for aerospace and high-tech outfits.

In 1980 the population of Orange County reached 1,932,708, and jobs there numbered 1,670,100. The boom transformed the emerging Costa Mesa/Irvine/Newport Beach subcenter. Office space there now totals 21.1 million square feet—well behind downtown Los Angeles's 36.6 million square feet, but gaining fast on downtown San Francisco's 26.8 million. Both the architecture and the tenants of the new high-rises are often the equal of those of office buildings in Los Angeles and San Francisco. The urban village's new hotels include a Westin, a Meridien, and a Four Seasons. South Coast Plaza has more sales than any other shopping center in the country. It is projected that once an addition is completed later this year, the plaza's annual retail sales will surpass those for both downtown San Francisco and the "Golden Triangle" of Beverly Hills. South Coast Plaza has most of the exclusive shops found in those locations.

Many of Los Angeles's established urban villages are gaining their own identities. Los Angeles's aerospace industry is increasingly concentrated at the Airport and in Torrance. The entertainment industry, which has traditionally been located in Hollywood, is now moving over the Hollywood Hills to Universal City/Burbank. Los Angeles's insurance companies, traditionally found in the mid-Wilshire Boulevard district two miles west of downtown, have recently selected Pasadena as an insurance subcenter, because it is closer than the mid-Wilshire location to neighborhoods from which they can expect to attract clerical workers and is also close to an executive-housing neighborhood.

The insurance and financial industries are transforming Pasadena, a city of 128,500 residents eight miles northeast of downtown Los Angeles, into an urban-village core. Perhaps the best-known city of its size in America because of the annual Tournament of Roses Parade and Rose Bowl, Pasadena's history and image have long been conservative and "old money." However, by 1970 downtown Pasadena was marred by empty storefronts, fading turn-of-the-century resort hotels, and half-empty parking lots. Low-income, primarily black and Latino northwest Pasadena was troubled by crime, gangs, drugs, and welfare dependency.

In the early 1970s the I-210 freeway was completed, connecting the city to the rest of the San Gabriel Valley and eventually resulting in a spurt of office-building. Pasadena became a back-office employment center for insurance and banking offices that wanted to hire middle-class Angelenos living in the rapidly growing San Gabriel Valley suburbs. Since 1980 twenty-eight mid- and high-rise office buildings have gone up.

Because of all this office construction, the character of downtown Pasadena has changed radically. A shopping mall several blocks from City Hall, which opened in 1980, is among the most successful in southern California. Entire blocks of handsome 1920s and 1930s two-story commercial buildings have been restored, and restaurants, espresso bars, and shops are now moving into ground-floor retail space that had gone begging for many years.

On the edge of downtown, within walking distance of the new offices and shops, badly run-down single-family housing has been replaced by new condominiums and townhouses. Thousands of houses in nearby residential neighborhoods have been renovated as young families have discovered the city's turn-of-the-century architecture and tree-shaded streets.

Change has not come easily to Pasadena. Not all of the city is being renovated; residents of the still decaying northwest section fear that new construction will squeeze them out of the neighborhood. And the many new jobs have created traffic problems. Today about 60,000 people commute to work in Pasadena, whereas approximately 25,000 leave the city for jobs elsewhere.

Pasadena residents worry about the long-range impact of the downtown construction on the overall community. Why has Pasadena attracted back-office operations instead of professional and corporate tenants, which would be more in keeping with the city's lingering blue-blood image? Does Pasadena want more high-rise office towers of any kind? How will the growing traffic affect downtown Pasadena and the nearby reviving neighborhoods?

Why Suburbs Are Becoming Urban Villages

This debate over growth is being repeated in neighborhood associations and city councils across the nation, in such widely dispersed locations as Walnut Creek, California; Princeton, New Jersey; Schaumburg, Illinois; and Bethesda, Maryland. In fact, attempts to control growth and traffic congestion are among the hottest issues in local politics today. And the reason is that the urban-village phenomenon is reshaping our cities. However, most people do not see the larger picture; they simply see the consequences. The phenomenon has occurred simultaneously in all kinds of cities across the nation, mostly for five reasons. Four of these have helped to create or further the postwar pattern of sprawl. When the fifth reason comes into play, it is easier to see why our metropolitan regions are coalescing into these sub-centers.

One reason for the growth of urban villages is that the nation's economy is shifting from a manufacturing to a service and knowledge base. The number of industrial jobs has declined from one-third of all jobs in 1920 to one-sixth today. The figure may drop to less than one-tenth by the year 2000, with service and knowledge employment making up the difference, much as agricultural employment fell and industrial employment rose during the transition to an industrial economy in the late nineteenth and early twentieth centuries. From 1973 to 1985, while five million blue-collar industrial jobs were lost, the service and knowledge fields—which are as diverse as computer programming, the professions, retail sales, and fast food—accounted for all of the nation's employment growth (from 82 million to 110 million jobs). The Bureau of Labor Statistics reports that the number of service and knowledge jobs can be expected to grow by nine million in the next ten years. The shift to a service and knowledge economy has greatly accelerated the restructuring of our metropolitan areas by creating a need for much more office space. In eight years, from the beginning of 1978 through 1985, 1.1 billion square feet of office space was constructed in the United States—the equivalent of 220 World Trade Center towers.

People are willing to live near the office now, whereas they were reluctant to live near factories that were dirty, noisy, and visually unattractive. Traditionally the poor and the working class have lived near factory districts. Across the nation office buildings and high-tech business parks have appeared in middle-class and even exclusive suburbs, such as the horse country around Valley Forge, outside Philadelphia; Bellevue, near Seattle; and the Buckhead district, in the north Atlanta suburbs. In Newport Beach, California, south of Los Angeles, a new subdivision of homes costing from $300,000 to $2 million abuts a Ford aerospace facility doing research and small-component-part assembly for military contracts.

A second reason for the emergence of urban villages has been changes in transportation patterns. Business shipments have shifted from rail to truck and Americans have decided that they prefer automobile commuting to mass transit. With fixed-rail transportation, all shipments must go from central terminal to central terminal before delivery. With trucks, shipments can travel from door to door. Similarly, with automobiles, people can go from door to door whenever they choose, without having to pass through central stations and terminals at fixed times. By 1960, the first year that the U.S. Bureau of the Census kept track, 69.5 percent of all commuting trips were made by car. By 1980 the figure had increased to 86 percent.

A third reason has been recent telecommunications advances, notably the dramatic drop in long-distance telephone costs. More and more day-to-day work is being done over the telephone. Not only cheaper long-distance telephone rates but also overnight mail, telecopiers, Zap-Mail, and computer modems allow communication without physical proximity.

Fourth, it is cheaper for businesses to operate in urban villages than in cities. Suburban office, industrial, and retail rents are far lower than downtown rents are. Although construction costs are approximately the same in the two areas, land outside cities costs less—$10 to $50 per square foot in suburban office locations versus $50 to $1,000 per square foot downtown. The cost of building parking spaces is also lower in the suburbs, where most parking is located in above-ground structures or surface lots, both of which are much cheaper to construct than a downtown office tower's subterranean garage. The difference in land and parking-garage costs shows up in office rents—$15 to $24 per square foot per year for prestige high-rise suburban space versus $18 to $42 for comparable downtown space in most American metropolitan areas.

These factors might only have encouraged more suburban sprawl if another factor had not come into play: most Americans like cities and the concentration of services that they provide. A critical mass of employment and housing is necessary to support desirable everyday services such as a good selection of shops, restaurants, and hotels. But this critical mass is achieved at well below the size of the prewar downtowns. For instance, it takes about 250,000 people within a three-to-five mile radius to support a modest regional mall and about 20,000 middle-class people within an equal area to keep a good restaurant in business. And it requires roughly 2.5 million square feet of offices (about fifty typical three-story suburban office buildings) to support a 250-room hotel.

Since people do not want to drive very far for these services, particularly office workers looking for lunch or business travelers needing a hotel, a degree of concentration much greater than that of a low-density suburb is necessary. Only so many potential locations have the necessary highway access and visibility to permit this concentration, a fact that has led to the focusing of postwar suburban sprawl into urban-village cores. When prime urban-village cores become congested, developers and employers hopscotch to outlying locations where land is cheaper and commuting is easier.

Thus our metropolitan areas have expanded tremendously. In the past twenty-five years, for example, metropolitan New York's sphere of direct influence has tripled in size. The metropolitan area extends as far north as New Haven, Connecticut, and into once-rural Dutchess, Ulster, and Sullivan counties, in New York State. On Long Island the metropolitan area now encompasses Yaphank and Brookhaven, in the middle of Suffolk County, and fades away just miles from the Hamptons. Metropolitan New York has swept southward past Princeton and into Ocean County, New Jersey, and Bucks County, Pennsylvania. In several years New York's suburban growth will collide with that of slower-growing metropolitan Philadelphia.

Los Angeles has always had an enormous metropolitan area; it was knit together before the Second World War by the world's largest trolley system. By 1960 metropolitan Los Angeles's sphere of influence stretched to Santa Monica in the west, Pasadena in the east, Long Beach in the south, and the San Fernando Valley in the north. Now metropolitan Los Angeles extends westward into Ventura County, east to San Bernardino and Riverside, and south across most of Orange County to span an area many times the metropolitan area's size twenty-five years ago. Other cities—among them greater San Francisco, Phoenix, Dallas, Houston, Boston, Chicago, Atlanta, and Washington, D.C.—are also expanding quickly.

As outlying urban-village cores become more urban, with their high-rise office buildings and hotels, increasingly sophisticated shopping, and high-density housing, the center cities are becoming more suburban. This emerging trend extends beyond the fast-food restaurants on downtown business streets and festive retailing complexes like South Street Seaport, in Lower Manhattan, and Harborplace, in Baltimore. Suburban-style shopping centers—where you buy children's clothes and household appliances, not just clever T-shirts and scented soaps—have recently opened in several American cities, and are doing quite well. Large, privately financed apartment and condominium projects have been built in cities without a downtown residential tradition, including San Diego, Detroit, Atlanta, and Los Angeles.

How Urban Villages Affect Cities

Few cities have been transformed by the urban-village phenomenon as rapidly as Atlanta, whose metropolitan region has a population of 2.2 million, having gained 90,000 residents last year and 78,000 the previous year. In 1980 downtown Atlanta was the metropolitan region's unchallenged center for all kinds of office employment. Although urban-village cores were emerging around shopping malls at the intersections of major highways, office space was limited. And neither in the appearance of the buildings nor in the quality of tenants were the fledgling urban-village cores any match for the downtown high-rises. Most of the buildings were two-story wood-frame structures, and many of their tenants were banks and insurance companies renting inexpensive space for back-office operations.

By 1985 — just five years later — this pecking order had changed completely. Downtown Atlanta had gained 4.3 million square feet of new office space, but Perimeter Center, at the I-285/Georgia 400 intersection, due north of downtown, had gained 7.6 million, and Cumberland/Galleria, at the I-285/I-75 intersection, northeast of downtown, 10.6 million. Many of the new buildings were gleaming, architecturally distinguished high-rises of the kind that once had been built only downtown. If present trends continue, the amounts of office space in both the Perimeter Center and the Cumberland/Galleria urban-village cores will easily surpass the amount in downtown Atlanta by 1990.

Downtown Atlanta, like downtown Los Angeles, is losing its metropolitan hegemony and becoming just another one of the region's urban-village cores. The urban villages around it, like those around downtown Los Angeles, are gaining distinct identities. Government, professional services, finance, wholesale trade, and the convention business are still in downtown Atlanta. However, as prestigious high-rises have been completed at Perimeter Center and Cumberland/Galleria, those areas have lost many of their price-conscious back-office banking and insurance tenants and have become instead favorite Atlanta locations for corporate headquarters and business services. Nearly every major accounting firm and many downtown law firms have offices in Perimeter Center and Cumberland/Galleria, the better to serve their clients. The regional corporate headquarters of Northern Telecom and HBO are in Perimeter Center.

Despite their importance as business locations, Perimeter Center and Cumberland/Galleria do not boast that traditional downtown symbol, a soaring skyline of office buildings. The high-rises in these two urban-village cores are not clustered. Instead they are widely separated by parking lots and heavily landscaped open space. In keeping with the non-urban mood, the developers have even neglected to add sidewalks connecting the buildings, and most people use their cars instead of walking. From the top floor of a seventeen-story high-rise in Perimeter Center the view is mostly trees and lawns, not other office buildings. Like many (though not all) urban-village cores, these relatively low-density north Atlanta developments visually blend into the suburban landscape. Yet the explosive rise in the number of office workers and their cars at Perimeter Center and Cumberland/Galleria has affected once-peaceful residential neighborhoods, including the Spring Mill area, near Perimeter Center.

One surprising result of Perimeter Center's boom has also been seen in suburban Dallas, Chicago, and Washington, D.C., and may be a trend. Residents of middle-class subdivisions near high-rise office clusters are banding together in corporations, getting their neighborhoods re-zoned for offices, and selling large "assembled" land parcels to real-estate developers, who either raze the houses or move them to new sites and build high-rises on the land. The suburban homeowners see the chance to leave an increasingly congested neighborhood where house prices are not keeping pace with those in comparable but quieter subdivisions nearby. Often they can sell their lots for twice what the homes on them are worth.

One such group formed three years ago in Spring Mill, a subdivision abutted on three sides by the high-rise office complexes of Perimeter Center. Randy Campbell, a former Spring Mill resident, recalls seeing a notice in a neighborhood newsletter in July of 1983 asking residents if they wanted to sell their property to office developers. "If you were interested," Campbell says, "you tore off a strip of paper on the bottom of one page, filled in your name, and sent it to the head of the neighborhood association. All but three or four of the 117 homeowners mailed in that piece of paper, so we got together in the community room of the Perimeter Mall. The average Spring Mill house sold for $70,000 to $75,000 then, but we learned that the half-acre lots were worth three times that figure to office-building developers. We didn't know how to go about the re-zoning or sale. So all the neighbors appointed a committee of five men and four women — small-business owners, several attorneys, a clergyman, an accountant, and a stockbroker. That was me."

For the next few months the committee met almost every night, learning about real-estate development and discussing strategy. By the end of the summer Alston & Bird, Georgia's largest law firm, had agreed to represent the homeowners on a contingency basis, and the firm drafted an option agreement to create Kingsborough–Spring Mill, Inc., a nonprofit corporation. By signing this option agreement a homeowner gave Kingsborough–Spring Mill's three-person board of directors power of attorney to accept a minimum of $225,000 in cash for his home, net after any expenses. It was understood that no deal would be final until the county commissioners changed Spring Mill's zoning from single-family homes to high-rise offices and multi-family units.

The night that Alston & Bird presented the agreement, in October of 1983, eighty homeowners signed it, and by January of 1984 the figure had risen to 114 of the 117. "Once the neighborhood was 'tied up,'" Campbell says, "we looked for a buyer. They weren't knocking the doors down, because we wanted top dollar and all cash. As we explored various deals, all the neighbors wanted to know what was happening. So we prepared a newsletter almost daily, ran it off on our office copying machines, and stuffed it into everyone's mailboxes during our lunch hours."

In October of 1984 the board of directors located a buyer. "Albritton Development wanted to redevelop the twenty-seven parcel Lake Hearn Place subdivision adjacent to Spring Mill," Campbell says. "But the Dekalb County commissioners rejected the re-zoning, reportedly because the project was too small, too piecemeal. So we made a deal with Albritton, which combined Lake Hearn's twenty-seven lots, the hundred and fourteen lots that we represented, and the three other Spring Mill owners that didn't join the neighborhood corporation. That made eighty-two acres — hardly piecemeal."

In June of 1985, however, the Delkalb County commissioners denied the re-zoning request for the site. Six months later Kingsborough–Spring Mill, Inc., the Lake Hearn Place homeowners, and Albritton Development sued the county commissioners. By last June the case had ended up in the Georgia Supreme Court, which ruled six to one in favor of the homeowners.

Baltimore is another kind of city being reshaped by the urban-village trend. Despite all the good news about Harborplace and the renovation of nineteenth-century row houses, the Baltimore metropolitan area is essentially stagnant. The population of the metropolitan area, as defined by the City of Baltimore and Baltimore County, declined from 1.53 million in 1970 to 1.44 million in 1980, and it is projected to drop to 1.40 million in 1990. Employment is growing only modestly — from 771,300 jobs in 1980 to 782,400 in 1985 and to 813,400 estimated for 1990. The Baltimore metropolitan area hardly seems like the place for a surge in construction. Yet there has been a boom in the outlying districts of Towson, Owings Mills, White Marsh, and perhaps most notably Hunt Valley.

Hunt Valley, twenty miles north of downtown Baltimore, was farmland until recently. Now it has a prestigious high-rise office and hotel core, which is surrounded by surface parking and low-rise industrial and office space. The low-rise industrial and office complexes came first, when well-to-do Baltimore businessmen decided to move their plants and offices closer to their homes in the north and northwest sections of the metropolitan area. After Hunt Valley was established as an employment center that offered low rents, the major landowner — McCormick Properties, owned by the family that owns the Mc-Cormick spice company — upgraded Hunt Valley by building high-quality mid- and high-rise office space and a Marriott Hotel. The PHH Group, West-inghouse, Burroughs, and Allstate Insurance promptly moved in. Now Hunt Valley is Baltimore County's top corporate address.

Even New York City has fallen under the sway of decentralizing urban-village development — which is surprising, considering that New York is the classic example of the traditional pre–Second World War city and that Manhattan has never been more prosperous nor its skyline more crowded with construction cranes. But although Manhattan gained 23.5 million square feet of office space from 1982 to 1985, during this short time its share of the metropolitan area's more than half a billion square feet of office space fell from 67 percent to 60 percent. This year, too, 7.6 million square feet is scheduled to be completed in Manhattan, bringing its total to 317.6 million—and 16.1 million square feet of office space is scheduled to be added to suburbs within a sixty-mile radius of Times Square, bringing the suburban total to 216.1 million.

In the past the typical new office building in New York's suburbs was part of the campus-like headquarters of a major corporation in Westchester County or southwestern Connecticut. Today, though, the exodus of corporate headquarters from Manhattan—to the suburbs or other parts of the country—has slowed. Now the typical new building is built on speculation, in an urban-village core such as Stamford or Danbury in Connecticut, the Route 110 corridor on Long Island, or Morristown or Princeton in New Jersey. One kind of tenant is a corporation's back-office operations or an entire division that can be separated from the Manhattan headquarters at considerable savings in rent, taxes, and business services but linked to the main office by computers and telecommunications.

As more and more jobs move to the suburbs (most of the metropolitan region's employment growth in the next decade is expected to take place not in New York City but in northern New Jersey), housing construction is booming in outlying towns. At Brookhaven, in Long Island's Suffolk County, 4,000 homes were built last year and another 8,000 are planned. At Dover, New York, a Dutchess County town of 7,200 residents northeast of Poughkeepsie, developers have filed proposals with the planning board for 1,200 new condominium units. The transformation is likely to be even more rapid at Chester, New York, fifty-five miles northwest of New York City. The population is 7,000, and the town board has received proposals for 3,000 new condominiums and homes.

In attractive communities near the urban-village cores the prices of existing homes are rising fast, owing to the sudden demand from employees of relocated companies. That is one reason that metropolitan New York City experienced a 24.6 percent increase in the price of housing between the first quarter of 1984 and the same period in 1985. In Stamford, for example, a typical three-bedroom house now sells for at least $250,000.

The Princeton, New Jersey, area illustrates the impact of the urban-village trend on metropolitan New York. Seemingly overnight a metropolis-sized urban-village core has emerged several miles east of this tree-shaded college town on U.S. Route 1. It is estimated that by the mid–1990s the Princeton corridor will have 12 to 15 million square feet of office space—surpassing the amount currently in downtown Milwaukee, downtown Newark, or southwest Connecticut's I-95 corridor between Greenwich and Stamford. Two luxury hotels have opened in greater Princeton; a Marriott and a Radisson are planned. The number of housing units is expected to double, with over 25,000 scheduled for completion by 1990. If current growth projections prove to be accurate, greater Princeton will become New Jersey's largest city in ten years.

Housing for All Urban-Village Workers

None of the far-reaching social, economic, and political issues raised by urban villages has a broader and deeper impact than housing. Urban-village cores generally arise at the outskirts of cities and grow in a limited number of directions. Nearly all of Atlanta's urban villages, for example, are in the northern suburbs, leaving the southern part of the city largely unaffected. Dallas is growing mostly toward the north and northwest. St. Louis, not exactly a booming metropolitan area, is heading west and northwest. The vast majority of America's urban villages, in fact, have one thing in common: they are growing in white, upper–middle class areas. Executives and business owners usually make the decisions about office locations and industrial sites. Most of them are white and upper–middle class, and they usually decide to bring their offices or industrial plants nearer their homes.

This arrangement is time- and energy-efficient for executives and business owners but not necessarily for clerical, light-assembly, and service employees, nor for the employees of the stores, restaurants, and gas stations near offices and plants. These workers cannot afford the executive-priced single-family houses, townhouses, and condominiums near most urban-village cores. They face a long — and often expensive — car or bus commute to the suburban or city home they can afford to live in.

The scenes in the parking lots of north Atlanta's Perimeter Center at 5:00 show the results of this geographical mismatch. Executives and professionals get into their Cadillacs and BMWs for the relatively easy drive home or a visit to one of the nearby "formula" restaurants for a drink. At the same time, many black employees are walking through the parking lots — Perimeter Center has few sidewalks — on their way to the bus stops, which are little more than a pole with a bus sign on top, planted on a flat, grassy spot that usually turns into mud when it rains. Atlanta's working-class black sections are south of downtown, fifteen to twenty miles from Perimeter Center, but the roads and bus lines to them don't follow a straight line. With one or maybe two transfers, many bus passengers endure a one-to-two-hour ride twice a day.

Suburban fast-food restaurants, hotels, department stores, car washes, and cleaning services are already experiencing a shortage of low-paid service employees. In some fast-growing suburbs businesses are offering bounties for new employees, raising the starting pay from the $3.35 minimum wage to $4.00 or more, and offering raises after several weeks rather than a year. One solution to the shortage is to bring affordable housing closer to the employment in the suburban urban-village cores.

This idea is one of the most polarizing issues in local politics today. Most suburbs have raised the drawbridge against housing for the poor and the working class, as epitomized by new guarded and gated "secure" communities. Affluent families do not want low-income housing in their one-acre-lot neighborhoods.

Nor do they need to allow it. Our urban villages now encompass areas the size of many pre–Second World War cities. They have more than enough land for all kinds of housing — and socio-economic groups — if zoning boards permit affordable housing.

The key to truly affordable, non-subsidized suburban housing is allowing higher density, primarily in the form of rental apartments, so that fixed land costs are spread over more units. Building suburban apartments in smaller than average sizes, to reduce rents, should be permitted. Empire West, a Tucson developer, has built smaller than average apartments in the Southwest. Situated in 250-to-500-unit projects, the apartments range from 320 square-foot studios (equivalent to a 14-by-23 foot space), to 615 square-foot two-bedrooms (a 20-by-30 foot space), to 615 square-foot two-bedrooms (a 20-by-30 foot space). All apartments have complete kitchens, bathrooms, and closets, and are outfitted with scaled-down furniture.

These complexes usually offer the lowest rents in their local markets — typically from $225 to $400, at least $25 to $50 a month below rents for the cheapest conventional apartments. These rents fit the budgets of clerical employees, security guards, and maintenance workers who make less than $15,000 a year. Yet the complexes still offer "luxury" features like swimming pools, tennis courts, volleyball courts, and social events.

Of course, upper–middle class suburbanites fight almost any kind of high-density housing. But attached housing complexes don't have to be built in affluent neighborhoods. They have been successful near commercial districts, where they create a buffer between a single-family-home neighborhood and an office-and-retail district. Another logical place for apartments is next to an urban village's commercial core. It seems likely that the vast surface parking lots of regional shopping malls will eventually be redeveloped as high-density housing and commercial buildings, with the cars going into above-ground or even underground structures. When these apartment and condominium developments are built near the shopping centers that form the focal point of so many urban villages, the members of more age groups and economic classes will be able to live near where they work and shop.

New Transportation Problems

In most metropolitan areas the suburban rush hour now rivals downtown traffic, and in some surpasses it. The 1980 census reported that 27 million Americans commuted from one suburb to another, whereas only half that number traveled from suburbs to downtown cities. The imbalance has increased sharply since 1980, owing to the boom in suburban employment. Today's suburban highways are so overcrowded that once-easy five- and six-mile commutes take forty-five minutes of stop-and-go driving in locations as widely

dispersed as north Dallas; Contra Costa County, east of San Francisco; and
northern Virginia, near Washington, D.C. And the emergence of urban villages at the edges of the metropolitan areas—like Chesterfield, twenty-two
miles west of downtown St. Louis—have brought bumper-to-bumper traffic to
two-lane country roads that still run past farms and cow pastures.

Living up to its image, Los Angeles has the most heavily traveled freeways
in the nation. The three busiest points on them are now near urban villages—
miles from downtown Los Angeles and its four-level interchange, which once
held the city's traffic record but has now fallen to fifth place. To reach their
record-setting traffic levels, these Los Angeles freeways—like the slow-moving
highways outside other cities—do not have a morning rush hour in one direction and an evening rush hour in the other. Commuter traffic now comes to
a standstill at morning and early evening in both directions, and slowdowns
occur frequently throughout the day.

Unfortunately, some city planners examining metropolitan-area congestion do not acknowledge the traffic near urban villages and repeat time-worn
clichés about automobiles destroying cities. Others recommend the expansion
of highways and mass-transit systems, but continue to think only of access to
downtown, just as transportation needs soar in the suburbs. Still others
recognize the rise of urban-village cores in the suburbs but propose transportation plans that are years behind the demand.

Planners and governments are working under a serious handicap in
alleviating suburban traffic problems. Most urban-village cores are being
created by private developers in a series of unrelated, uncoordinated decisions.
To make matters worse, the process of formulating a transportation plan, gaining its approval, finding the funds, and completing the project is so time-
consuming that traffic problems are bound to become painfully obvious before
any action is taken.

How can government alleviate suburban traffic congestion near urban-
village cores? The answer is not the construction of subways or elevated trains.
Fixed-rail projects (unlike light-rail construction—for example, trolleys) justify
their enormous capital expenditure and high operating costs "only when you
have both trip originations and destinations highly clustered," according to
Peter Muller, a professor of geography at the University of Miami and one of
the earliest observers of the urban-village phenomenon. "We are building
1920s-style mass-transit systems for our 1990s metropolitan areas," he says.

One example of the gap between urban image and reality is Walnut Creek,
California, near San Francisco, which has experienced considerable office and
light-industrial development in the past decade. Although most of the new
buildings are near the *BART* (Bay Area Rapid Transit) mass-transit station connecting the town to San Francisco, Walnut Creek now has such severe traffic
congestion that last year it enacted an office-construction moratorium. Muller
suggests that mass transit failed to help the town avoid traffic problems because

the vast majority of the local workers commute by car regardless of a mass-transit option. "A great many of the people who ride the new fixed-rail mass-transit systems in cities like San Francisco, Atlanta, or Miami used to ride buses," he says.

Nonetheless, fixed-rail transit remains a gleam in many a downtown businessman's or politician's eye. Some proponents may imagine that it takes a subway for a city to be a city, and some may have in mind that the federal government has paid up to 90 percent of the bill in the past (though it will not in the future, if the policies of the present Administration remain in place). Even Los Angeles—the capital of California's "car kingdom"—wants to build an 18-to-20-mile "metrorail" subway system, at a cost of $3 billion. According to an official of the Southern California Rapid Transit District, the metrorail system "may come close to breaking even on an operating basis, but there is no way that it will pay for the construction of the system." Of course, this statement is based on predictions of operating cost and ridership. The reality of Atlanta's new *MARTA* fixed-rail system is that the fare box brings in only 35 to 40 percent of the annual operating budget, which would more than double if a reasonable amortization of the capital cost were included. Moreover, the proposed Los Angeles subway route serves downtown and only two of the sixteen other urban-village cores in the metropolitan region.

Even buses do not fully meet the needs of the emerging urban-village cores, because serving all the possible permutations between where people live and work would require too many routes to be economically feasible. In the new urban-village cores office and industrial buildings are not closely packed together, as they are in midtown Manhattan or Chicago's Loop; they are widely separated by parking lots and landscaped areas.

This lack of density means that only a few people will find it convenient to walk to any given bus or subway station, and that office workers must have a car during the day if they want to visit a client or go out to lunch. And where internal transit programs using buses and mini-vans have been tried, such as Tysons Corner, Virginia, and south of the Los Angeles International Airport, they have quickly failed for lack of patronage. In fact, even an official of the federal Urban Mass Transportation Administration asserts that conventional fixed-route transit systems will never carry more than a small percentage of non-downtown commuters. The official thinks that the only kind of mass transit with any chance of significantly decreasing commuter traffic is ride-sharing, and particularly car-pooling.

That leaves us with our automobiles. The new office complexes provide more room for cars than for the workers who drive them. The typical building allots approximately 200 square feet of space for each employee. The usual planning assumption is that one out of five workers uses a car pool or public transportation, and so a building will require four parking spaces for every 1,000 square feet of office space. Each parking space requires approximately

325 square feet for the space itself, ramps (if a garage, rather than a lot, is planned), and aisles. That means the developer must set aside 1,300 square feet of parking for every 1,000 square feet of office space.

Two years ago some of the nation's leading urban planners gathered in Scottsdale, Arizona, and searched for solutions to suburban traffic congestion. The planners expressed considerable disagreement, presented a myriad of solutions but little data to support the ideas, and were greatly concerned about finding the money to pay for any transportation improvements. The planners did for the most part agree on an approach to the problem: government working together with developers. This is already happening. In north Atlanta's fast-growing Buckhead urban-village core, for instance, developers paid $1 million toward a new $5.2 million bridge over a highway interchange. And in Montgomery County, Maryland, developers will pay half of the $109 million needed for road improvements around Germantown, an emerging urban-village core. Many developers favor this new spirit of public-private cooperation, because they realize that the alternative could be government-ordered construction slowdowns or moratoriums.

Planning for Urban Villages

Local governments can resist developers, but they can't resist them indefinitely or protect their communities from the bad effects of rapid growth. They are decentralized nineteenth-century entities trying to deal with far-reaching twenty-first–century issues. Greater Los Angeles, for instance, consists of well over a hundred cities and five counties. Metropolitan Atlanta has forty-six cities and seven counties. How can so many governmental jurisdictions possibly coordinate their actions to handle the amorphous growth of urban-village cores, which, like multinational corporations, know no loyalty to any single governmental body?

Real-estate developers most often deal directly with local governments. In this high-stakes game the developers hold many of the cards, because they can play one jurisdiction off another. Many local governments, in their desire to expand their tax bases, generate employment, and welcome "progress," try to entice developers with liberal zoning, temporary tax abatements, and improvements to such things as roads and sewers at little or no cost.

Contrary to what their residents often think, well-to-do communities cannot totally control growth on their own, unless they are geographically isolated, like Santa Barbara, California. When a town is part of a metropolitan area, its fate is inextricably tied up with the region's, no matter how wealthy its residents or how stringent its growth regulations.

Even Beverly Hills finds itself relatively powerless to resist the relentless development pressures from Los Angeles, which almost completely surrounds the 5.7-square-mile city. Several years ago Four Seasons Hotels wanted to build a high-rise hotel on Wilshire Boulevard near Rodeo Drive, in the heart of the city's commercial Golden Triangle. The issues of building density and hotel-generated traffic congestion became so controversial that the city council refused to vote on the Four Seasons project and instead placed a hotel-development ordinance on the ballot. Last year Beverly Hills voters overwhelmingly defeated the ordinance, thereby eliminating the possibility that another major hotel will open in the city. That didn't stop Four Seasons. Earlier this year the company started construction on a 287-room, 15-story hotel on Doheny Drive and Burton Way, literally across the street from the Beverly Hills city line. Beverly Hills lost the new hotel's sales and occupancy tax revenues but will still be affected by the traffic.

What can local government do about growth pressures? Probably the best solution is the creation of strong, effective, multi-city and multi-county agencies, and perhaps even entire government structures, that correspond to the actual economic and psychological boundaries of a metropolitan area and its urban villages. Such broad-based government has already been pioneered by Indianapolis (Mario County) and Miami (Dade County). This governmental reorganization is not easy, because it can involve jealously competing towns, townships, cities, and counties—not to mention states, as are involved in greater New York, Philadelphia, Washington, D.C., St. Louis, and Kansas City. But much as the number of school districts nationwide has shrunk from 100,000 in 1940 to 15,000 now, the number of planning, jurisdictions can be brought down.

One possible first step toward the creation of more-effective local governments is metropolitan-wide zoning and planning boards that have real clout in granting zoning changes and allocating improvements to the region's physical facilities. Some metropolitan areas are already moving in this direction. In 1979 Phoenix—the nation's ninth largest city, according to the most recent census—took the revolutionary course of adopting the urban-village concept in its planning process. In 1985 the city finished its General Plan to guide the municipality's growth, and this established nine urban villages. "Each [urban village] would become relatively self-sufficient in providing living, working and recreational opportunities for residents," the General Plan said. The city also encouraged the "concentration of shopping, employment and services located in the village core."

Phoenix is using zoning approvals and planned allocations of money for physical improvements to try to match employment with housing. The city has clearly specified goals. In 1980 only two of the now defined urban villages had more than half as many jobs as people, indicating that they had moved beyond being bedroom communities. Phoenix hopes that by the year 2000 five urban villages will have more than half as many jobs as people, with the remaining four urban villages having between one-fourth and half as many, clearly showing that jobs and people have moved closer together.

Elsewhere, developers, employers, and local governments have created transportation-management associations (TMAs) to find solutions to transportation problems. What are perceived locally as transportation crises have brought TMAs into existence in Baltimore's airport area; Warner Center, in Los Angeles's San Fernando Valley; north Dallas; and Tysons Corner, Virginia. According to Kenneth Orski, the president of Urban Mobility Corporation, which is a TMA proponent based in Washington, D.C., TMAs "fill a vacuum in suburban areas."

Besides organizing ride-sharing and van pools, promoting staggered work hours, and lobbying for government-funded capital improvements, some TMAs are expanding their role into child care, private police, and other services for their geographic areas. It is imaginable that TMAs, born of the traffic-congestion crisis, could mature into an echelon of government well suited to the realities of our emerging urban villages.

Considering what has happened so far, is the urban-village trend a good or a bad thing for our cities and our citizens? To a certain extent the question is irrelevant, because the trend is already so advanced that it is irreversible. But it is hard to imagine the ideal urban village as being anything but very good. The opportunity for all kinds of Americans to live, work, shop, and play in the same geographic area—while retaining easy access to other urban-village cores with specialized features that their own district lacks—seems almost too good to be true.

As the nation's cities reshape themselves along the urban-villages model, we must ask ourselves, "What are the design features, housing policies, transportation solutions, and governmental structures that will make our cities and the lives of their residents more productive and satisfying?" Unfortunately, the questions and opinions vastly outnumber the solutions and directions. A great deal of study, experimentation, and planning needs to be done—and done quickly—to help cities that are being rebuilt almost from scratch.

About the Contributors

Affiliations are as of the time the articles were written.

Patricia Adell, director of program development, Philadelphia Industrial Development Corporation, Philadelphia, Pennsylvania.

Tom Arrandale, correspondent, *Governing* magazine, Congressional Quarterly, Inc., Washington, D.C.

Rita J. Bamberger, research associate, Public Finance Center, The Urban Institute, Washington, D.C.

James J. Bellus, director, Department of Planning and Economic Development, City of St. Paul, Minnesota.

Renee Berger, consultant, Partnerships Data Net, Washington, D.C.

J. Thomas Black, staff vice president for research, Urban Land Institute, Washington, D.C.

William A. Blazar, independent consultant, Minneapolis, Minnesota.

Lewis Bolan, director of investment advisory services, Real Estate Research Corporation, Chicago, Illinois.

Barbara Bonnell, director of information, Charles Center–Inner Harbor Management, Baltimore, Maryland.

Deborah L. Brett, vice president and project manager, Real Estate Research Corporation, Chicago, Illinois.

J. Paul Brownridge, city treasurer, City of Los Angeles, California.

James Carras, president, Carras Associates, Boston, Massachusetts.

Barbara A. Coe, principal, Coe Consultants, Oakland, California.

Michael A. Dobbins, architect, Department of Community Development, City of Birmingham, Alabama.

Thomas P. Doud, major loan officer, Real Estate Lending Division, Occidental/Nebraska Federal Savings Bank, Lincoln, Nebraska.

Kenneth P. Fain, managing editor, *Lenders Community Investment Report,* Washington, D.C.

Cheryl A. Farr, assistant director, Office of Information Services, International City/County Management Association, Washington, D.C.

John Fondersmith, chief, Downtown Section, Office of Planning, City of Washington, D.C., Washington, D.C.

Glenda Glover, assistant professor, Department of Accounting, School of Business, Howard University, Washington, D.C., and President, National Center for Enterprise Zone Research, Washington, D.C.

Al Gobar, principal, Alfred Gobar Associates, Placentia, California.

Timothy W. Gubala, director of economic development, Roanoke County, Roanoke, Virginia.

Lawrence Hall, neighborhood assistance coordinator, Office of Housing and Neighborhood Development, City of New Haven, Connecticut.

Ed Henning, principal revitalization planner, Edward Henning & Associates, Whittier, California.

William Hoffer, freelance writer, Laurel, Maryland.

Lawrence O. Houstoun, Jr., principal, The Atlantic Group, Cranbury, N.J.

Libby Howland, managing editor, Urban Land Institute, Washington, D.C.

Gunnar Isberg, president, Isberg and Associates Planning and Development Services, Northfield, Minnesota.

Roger L. Kemp, career city manager, having served in California, Connecticut, and New Jersey, and author/consultant on local government productivity.

Ruth Knack, managing editor, *Planning* magazine, American Planning Association, Chicago, Illinois.

M. Leanne Lachman, president, Real Estate Research Corporation, Chicago, Illinois.

Karen LaFrance, senior planner, Planning Department, City of Pittsburgh, Pennsylvania.

Christopher B. Leinberger, managing partner, Robert Charles Lesser & Co., Beverly Hills, California.

Charles Lockwood, president, Charles Lockwood & Associates, Santa Monica, California.

Marcia D. Lowe, senior researcher, Worldwatch Institute, Washington, D.C.

Robert H. Lurcott, director of planning, City of Pittsburgh, Pennsylvania.

Bruce W. McClendon, director of planning and growth management, City of Fort Worth, Texas.

Virginia M. Mayer, senior staff associate, National League of Cities, Washington, D.C.

Delores Palma, president, Hyett Palma, Inc., Washington, D.C.

Robert B. Pender, partner, Law Offices of Nixon, Hargrave, Devans & Doyle, Washington, D.C.

George E. Peterson, director, Public Finance Center, The Urban Institute, Washington, D.C.

Thomas Ressler, freelance writer, Athens, Ohio.

Kjell Rodne, chief administrative officer, City of Duluth, Minnesota.

David H. Roeder, editor, *Chicago Enterprise* magazine, Chicago, Illinois.

Stuart L. Rogel, managing editor, Urban Land Institute, Washington, D.C.

Lawrence D. Rose, city manager, City of Mercer Island, Washington.

Herbert J. Rubin, professor of sociology, Northern Illinois University, DeKalb, Illinois.

Marina Sampanes, senior associate, Carras Associates, Boston, Massachusetts.

Frank C. Shaw, associate, Law Offices of Nixon, Hargrave, Devans & Doyle, Washington, D.C.

Julie Sinclair, staff writer, *Alabama Municipal Journal,* Alabama League of Municipalities, Montgomery, Alabama.

Richard Starr, vice president, Real Estate Research Corporation, Chicago, Illinois.

Jan Stokley, staff attorney and director, Local Government Research Project, National Economic Development & Law Center, Oakland, California.

Philip R. Thompson, research associate, The Urban Center, Cleveland State University, Cleveland, Ohio.

Wilbur R. Thompson, Albert A. Levin chair of urban studies and public service, Levin College of Urban Affairs, Cleveland State University, Cleveland, Ohio.

Virginia L. Wolf, economic development specialist, Midwest Research Institute, Kansas City, Missouri.

E. S. Woolard, Jr., chairman, Du Pont Co., Inc., Wilmington, Delaware.

Index